KT-432-866

FOOTBALL THE COMPLETE FACTS STATS AND RECORDS

THIS IS A CARLTON BOOK

This edition published in 1998 for
Parragon Books
Units 13–17 Avonbridge Industrial Estate
Atlantic Road
Avonmouth, Bristol BS11 9QD

Copyright © Carlton Books Limited 1998

All rights reserved. No part of this publication may be reproduced, stored in a retrieval system, or transmitted in any form or by any means, electronic, mechanical, photocopying, recording or otherwise, without the prior permission of the publishers.

ISBN 0 75252 437 2

Printed and bound in Great Britain

FOOTBALL THE COMPLETE FACTS STATS AND RECORDS

Keir Radnedge

Contents

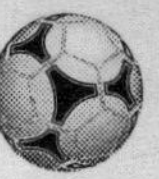

The Great Countries

FIFA, the world governing body of association football, boasts more than 200 members. They are grouped into six regional confederations representing Europe (UEFA), South America (CONMEBOL), Central and North America (CONCACAF) as well as Africa, Asia and Oceania.

Such is football's worldwide democracy that each country has one vote in FIFA's two-yearly congress – the same power belonging to both England and Ethiopia, Brazil and Botswana. International football is thus organised as a pyramid with the individual countries representating a third level of power – and with the clubs beneath them in the structure. Modern association football owed its creation to the English but it spread rapidly throughout the world thanks to British sailors, engineers and bankers but also thanks to students who travelled to England to study and took home with them a new-found love of what is now the world's greatest game. In each country, football developed along the same lines. Enthusiastic amateurs spread the word among their friends, they formed clubs and those clubs formed associations or federations and then knock-out cup competitions and league championships. As early as 1904 FIFA, the international federation of association football, was set up in Paris by delegates from Belgium, Denmark, Framce Holland, Spain, Sweden and Switzerland. FIFA was happy, in its early years, to accept the Olympic Games as a de facto world championship. After the first world war however, it became clear to FIFA's French president, Jules Rimet, that the advance of professionalism demanded a world championship of its own. Thus the World Cup was born.

Argentina

Asociacion del Futbol Argentino

Founded:

1893

FIFA:

1912

World Cup:

1978, 1986

South American Championship:

1910, 1921, 1925, 1927, 1929, 1937, 1941, 1945, 1946, 1947, 1955, 1957, 1991, 1993

Football was brought to Argentina by the British in the 1860s, and although, at first, it was exclusive to the British residents in Buenos Aires, by the turn of the century numerous clubs had been formed.

The Argentine Football Association was founded in 1891 by an Englishman, Alexander Hutton, and a league was formed the same year.

The national side also made an early start, and in 1901 a representative side played neighbouring Uruguay, in the first international match to be staged outside Great Britain. The seeds were sown for a rivalry which has grown into one of the most enduring and intense derby matches in the world. Professionalism was adopted in 1931, and River Plate and Boca Juniors soon emerged as dominant forces in the new professional league.

Championship Winners

The 1950s saw the birth of an exceptional side that won the South American Championship twice during the 1950s and then made an unsuccessful bid to host the 1958 World Cup. Little progress was made in the 1960s and 1970s, and Argentina had to wait until 1978 for her first success in the World Cup.

On home soil, and with a side containing only one overseas-based player, the prolific goalscorer Mario Kempes, Argentina deservedly won the tournament beating Holland 3–1 in a final best remembered for the noise and passion that filled the River Plate Stadium in Buenos Aires. They did so again in Mexico in 1986, when the side was led by Diego Maradona – who ranks as one of the greatest players the world has ever seen. In fact, Argentina featured in the final of three of the four World Cups from 1978 to 1990, they won the first two South American Championships of the 1990s, and they continue to produce extremely gifted footballers. The captain of the 1978 World Cup winning team, Daniel Passarella, became national coach in 1995 and guided his team straight to the 1998 World Cup Finals in France. The national team finished top of their tough nine-team group which included Colombia, Chile and Ecuador.

Austria

Österreichischer Fussball-Bund

Founded:

1904

FIFA:

1905

Vienna arguably was the focal point of continental European football in the first half of the twentieth century, a situation which lasted until the 1960s. Britons living in Vienna provided Austrian football's early impetus and, as long ago as 1902, Austria trounced Hungary 5–0 at the Prater in what has become the world's second oldest regular international fixture after England vs. Scotland.

The inter-war period was Austria's most successful era, when the "Wunderteam" – led by Matthias Sindelar ("The Man of Paper") – swept all before them. In 30 matches from spring 1931 to summer 1934, the "Wunderteam" scored 101 goals, and the 1934 World Cup seemed to be at their mercy. But a defeat in the semi-final by the hosts Italy, on a quagmire of a pitch in Milan, ended their hopes. Austria's chances in the 1938 event were destroyed by the German occupation, and from 1938 "Austrian" football ceased to exist.

Regular Qualifiers

A new side came together in the 1950s, led by Ernst Ocwirck and Gerhard Hanappi, which looked set for World Cup success in 1954. But the Germans again spoiled the plan, winning the semi-final, 6–1. A poor showing in 1958 in Sweden was followed by an inexorable decline, and despite qualifying for the 1978, 1982, 1990 and 1998 World Cup finals, Austria have continued to slide to the lower end of the middle-ranked nations in Europe.

For the national team, the lowest point was reached on September 12, 1991 when the minnows of the Faroe Islands – playing their first ever competitive match – won 1–0 in a European Championship qualifier. It was a humiliating result for Austria, a once great footballing nation, and a sign of how their football had suffered since the halcyon days of the 1930s.

But the country took stock and began the job of re-building both the pride and structure of the sport within Austria. They qualified for France and the 1998 World Cup, looking stronger than they had for a long time. They lost just one game on the way to the finals and conceded only four goals in a final group that included tough-to-beat Scotland and the original group favourites Sweden.

At long last it looks like Austrian football could be making a long-awaited comeback to the world stage.

Brazil

Confederacao Brasileira de Futebol

Founded:
1914
FIFA:
1923
World Cup:
1958, 1962, 1970, 1994
South American Championship:
1919, 1922, 1949, 1989

Brazilian football has a romantic air about it that sets it apart from other nations. Between 1958 and 1970 they won the World Cup three times, with a team packed full of star players, including arguably the greatest footballer in history – Pele. Brazil remains the only country to have played in every World Cup finals tournament since 1930 and the only nation to have won the cup four times.

Brazilian football developed at the end of the nineteenth century, prompted by migrant British workers, and leagues were established in Rio de Janeiro and São Paulo by the turn of the century. The vast size of Brazil meant that a national league was impractical and until the 1970s these leagues dominated domestic football. The "classic" Rio derbies between Flamengo, Fluminense, Botafogo and Vasco da Gama regularly attracted massive crowds to the 200,000-capacity Maracana Stadium.

The national team was a little slower out of the blocks, and their first real international was not played until 1914 with a visit to Buenos Aires. In 1916 Brazil entered the South American Championship but, perversely, this event has not been a rewarding one for the Brazilians, who have won it only four times – three of them on home soil.

The World Cup, however, is another matter. The first attempt on the trophy was made in 1930, when they went out in the first round. The 1934 campaign was equally bad, despite the presence of such fine players as Leonidas da Silva and Artur Friedenreich. In 1938, however, they showed the first signs of what was to come by reaching the semi-finals, where they lost to Italy.

Two Golden Decades

The golden age of Brazilian football was between 1950 and 1970, and it is the sides of this era that stick in the memory. In 1950 they were runners-up as Uruguay pipped them 2–1 for the title in the deciding match. Although they lost on that occasion, the final demonstrated just how popular the game was becoming in Brazil. The final was played at the Maracana Stadium in Rio de Janeiro and a record 200,000 fans crammed in to watch the contest.

Moving forward to 1954, with Nilton and Djalma Santos established at the back and Didi running the midfield, they reached the quarter-finals in Switzerland, where they lost to Hungary's "Magical Magyars".

In 1958 Brazil finally won the honour the nation's fans craved. With a forward line consisting of Garrincha, Vava, Zagalo and the 17-year-old Pele, they stormed to victory in Sweden, beating the hosts 5–2 in the final. In Chile in 1962, an almost identical team – minus the injured Pele – triumphed again, beating Czechoslovakia 3–1 in the final in Santiago.

In 1966, in England, the side was being rebuilt and Brazil fell in the first round. But the newcomers Tostao, Gerson and Jairzinho were present in Mexico four years later when Brazil clinched a hat-trick of World Cups, earning them the right to keep the Jules Rimet Trophy in perpetuity.

The 1970 side has been described as the best ever seen, and with some justification. The defence, marshalled by Carlos Alberto, was not all that strong, but this did not matter as the Brazilian approach at this time was all-out attack – and simply to score more goals than they conceded. This was football with a flourish and the global TV audience loved it. In attack, Pele was back to his best and he was superbly assisted by Jairzinho, Rivelinho and Tostao.

After 1970, it was 24 years before the national side again scaled such heights by winning the 1994 World Cup – albeit thanks to a penalty shoot-out after a disappointing 0–0 draw with that other great World Cup side Italy.

Even though Brazil experienced a decline in playing standards in the years between their third and fourth World Cup triumphs, they certainly didn't disgrace themselves: fourth place in 1974, third place in 1978 and the quarter-final stage in 1986 is hardly the mark of a poor team. Arguably their best showing along the way, however, was in the 1982 World Cup, when a side containing Zico, Socrates, Junior and Falcao should have gone further than the second round in Spain, but were beaten in a thrilling match by eventual winners Italy.

International Domination

Ironically, in the 1994 qualifying matches, Brazil lost to Bolivia, their first defeat ever in a World Cup qualifier, and ultimately scrambled through in an unconvincing and uncharacteristic fashion. At club level, Brazilian football is in a parlous state, with too many meaningless and time-consuming competitions, games against mismatched opponents and continual rows between the various regional governing bodies.

The legacy of those glorious Pele years continues to weigh heavily, for any Brazil side, regardless of its capabilities, is expected to play what Pele himself once called "the beautiful game".

Chile

Federacion de Futbol de Chile

Founded:

1895

FIFA:

1912

Until Colo Colo's Libertadores Cup triumph in 1991, no Chilean side had ever won a major honour, and Chile have often been seen as the "nearly-men" of South American football. Colo Colo, Chilean nickname for a wildcat, were founded by five angry members of the old Magallanes FC. Even though Chilean football is generally held to lag far behind that of traditional giants Brazil, Argentina and Uruguay, Colo Colo have an enviable reputation throughout the continent. The club's vision has always stretched beyond the Andes. Such a tradition was laid down by David Orellano. He was a founder member of Colo Colo and one of the five Magallanes rebels who disagreed over the choice of a new club captain. The choice of the five fell upon Orellano and, within two years of Colo Colo's foundation, they had sent a team off to tour Spain.

Never Quite Made It

Chile qualified for five of the 11 post-war World Cups, but have only once progressed beyond the first round, in 1962, when they reached the semi-finals on home soil before losing to eventual winners Brazil. However, despite their sterling performances during that World Cup, what lingers most in the memory is the disgraceful group match with Italy that was more like a boxing match than a game of football. At one stage, police, officials and photographers wrestled on the pitch with players as order dissolved in a melée of bodies.

Their best performances in the South American Championship came in 1979 and 1987, when they were runners-up. Chile, like many of its neighbours, is continually drained of its best players by European clubs, and it is unlikely that the Chileans will ever be able to improve on their third place in the 1962 World Cup. The country continues, however, to turn up outstanding players and the strikeforce of Ivan Zamorano and new hero Marcello Salas – both players rated near the £10 million-pound mark – proved lethal in the 1998 World Cup qualifiers – scoring 23 of Chile's 32 goals. Chile scraped through to World Cup qualification by coming fourth in the tough South American qualifying group. They had the same points total as Peru, but their far greater goal difference secured their passage to France and the World Cup. Along the way they managed to draw with Argentina, thrash Venezuela 6–0 and beat Colombia 4–1.

Czech Republic

Cesko Moravsky Fotbalovy Svaz

Founded:
1993

FIFA:
1994

European Championship:
1976

Olympics:
1980 *(as Czechoslovakia)*

When the 1994 World Cup ended and Czechoslovakia ceased to exist as a football nation, the Czech Republic and Slovakia went their separate ways, each setting up a new association, league and national team. From the time Czechoslovakia came into existence in 1918, the Czechs were at the forefront of European football. They were runners-up in both the 1920 and 1964 Olympic Games, before finally winning the tournament in 1980, in Moscow. They were finalists at the 1934 World Cup with a side containing Antonin Puc, Frantisek Planicka, the finest pre-war goalkeeper, and Oldrich Nejedly.

The Communist take-over after the war led to the usual reorganization of the domestic game, which hindered rather than helped as clubs like Sparta and Slavia Prague had been doing very well as professional sides. The army team Dukla Prague rose to prominence and provided the basis of the 1960s Czech side which was among the best in the world. Josef Masopust, Czechoslovakia's most famous player, led the side to third place in the inaugural European Championship in 1960, and to the 1962 World Cup Final, which was lost 3–1 to Brazil.

Europe's Best

Czechoslovakia's biggest success came at the 1976 European Championship when, with stars such as goalkeeper Ivo Viktor, defender Anton Ondrus, Antonin Panenka, in midfield, and Zdenek Nehoda, in attack, they beat West Germany on penalties in the final after the Germans had equalized in the last minute of normal time.

The political split in 1994 affected Slovakia more than the Czech Republic, who qualified for Euro 96 and proved to be the most spirited of dark horses – beating Italy, Portugal and France and drawing with Russia en route to the final where they lost 2–1 to Germany by a "Golden Goal" scored in extra time. As a follow-up, the team were expected to qualify for France '98, but failed to do so. They eventually came third in a tough qualifying group which saw Spain and Yugoslavia qualify ahead of them, despite leaking only six goals in their last ten group games.

England

The Football Association

Founded:
1863
FIFA:
1905–1920, 1924–1928, 1946
World Cup:
1966
Olympics:
1908, 1912 *(as Great Britain)*

England, as every schoolboy enthusiast knows, gave soccer to the world. Developed on the playing fields of England's great public schools in the middle of the nineteenth century, the game was first codified and organized in the 1860s, when the Football Association was formed – hence the name Association Football, and the nickname "soccer", to distinguish it from Rugby Football. The FA Cup was introduced in 1871, both the first and now the oldest surviving tournament in the world, and was fundamental in the development of the game – pitting the established amateur sides of the south against the burgeoning professional outfits of the north.

Early Internationals

A year later, the very first international match was played, between England and Scotland in Glasgow, and in 1888 the Football League was formed – to organize what was, by now, a largely professional game based mostly in the industrial north.

As the century closed, the British Championship, played between England, Scotland, Wales and Ireland, was the zenith of world football. Before the First World War, England and Scotland were well above the rest of the world and, as Great Britain, comfortably won Olympic gold in 1908 and 1912.

The FA joined FIFA in 1905, always took a disdainful attitude towards it, and withdrew in 1920, horrified at the prospect of having to play with wartime adversaries, and again in 1928 over the definition of the word amateur. It is doubtful whether they would have bothered to compete in the prewar World Cups anyway, such was the English view of their own superiority.

That view was unchanged even by the humiliating 1–0 defeat by the United States in the 1950 World Cup which was dismissed as a fluke, even though England had a side containing such greats as Tom Finney and Billy Wright. However, in 1953, Hungary's "Magic Magyars" came to Wembley, led by the legendary Ferenc Puskas and finally destroyed English arrogance once and for all.

It was not merely the 6–3 scoreline, or the fact that this was England's first defeat by a non-British side at home, which

changed attitudes: it was the manner of the defeat. The Hungarians were far superior technically and tactically. Further defeats at the 1954, 1958 and 1962 World Cup finals confirmed this and forced England to face the facts of the modern game, which had left them behind in the immediate post-war years.

The challenges presented by the new order were spectacularly answered in 1966, however, when England's "wingless wonders" won the World Cup on home soil, beating West Germany 4–2 in the Wembley final. Alf Ramsey, the stolid manager who led Ipswich to the Championship in 1962 during their first season in Division One, moulded his side around the outstanding talents of goalkeeper Gordon Banks, captain Bobby Moore, and the Charlton brothers Bobby and Jack. He created a system which worked with the players at his disposal, and instilled a team spirit and an understanding which no subsequent England side has matched.

European Club Victory

The 1966 success was the springboard from which English clubs launched an unprecedented assault on the three European competitions, winning trophy after trophy between 1964 and 1985. Conversely, as the clubs prospered the national side suffered. A defeat by West Germany in the quarter-final of the 1970 World Cup in Mexico marked the beginning of the end of the Ramsey era, and failure to qualify for the 1974 and 1978 finals, despite an abundance of talented players, confirmed England's slump.

Following dismal performances at the 1988 and 1992 European Championship finals and, worse, the failure to qualify for the 1994 World Cup Finals, the structure of the English game came under scrutiny. Changes forced by the appalling loss of life at Bradford (1985) and Hillsborough (1989) led to a modernization of stadia, These moves, assisted by the influx of cash from a lucrative Sky TV contract, have drawn the crowds back to the game and, at the same time, seen an improvement in the fortunes of the national side.

Things began looking up in the mid-nineties, as British clubs began to have more of an impact abroad. Arsenal won the 1994 European Cup-Winners Cup and Manchester United reached the semi-final of the Champions Cup in 1997.

The national side at last got its act together under the stewardship of Terry Venables during the 1996 European Championship. After destroying Holland 4–1 in their last group match, they saw off the Spanish before losing to their perennial foes, the Germans, in a nail-biting semi-final penalty shoot-out. Shortly after, Glenn Hoddle became coach and steered the side to the 1998 World Cup Finals.

France

Fédération Française de Football

Founded:
1918

FIFA:
1904

European Championship:
1984

Olympics:
1984

The French were prime movers behind the creation of FIFA, UEFA, the World Cup, the European Championship and the European club cups, yet the 1984 European Championship victory and Olympic title are all they have to show for their wide-ranging skills in innovation and organization.

The FFF, formed in 1918, brought order to a chaotic domestic club scene in the aftermath of the Great War. Professionalism was accepted in 1932 and a league was set up.

In the 1950s, Stade de Reims emerged as the best club side France had produced. They twice reached the European Cup Final, but lost both times.

The Platini Era

In the late 1970s, Michel Platini arrived and transformed France into the most attractive side Europe had seen since the 1950s. Platini, a midfielder with immense skill, vision and grace, had a glorious club career with Juventus in Italy, and inspired France to reach the final stages of three World Cups (1978, 1982 and 1986). They put up their best World Cup performance in 1982 in Spain, when they were 3–1 up in the semi-final against West Germany in extra time… only to lose on penalties amid great controversy after a horrendous foul on striker Battiston by German goalkeeper Schumacher just outside the penalty area went unpunished.

Platini's finest hours came in 1984, on French soil, when his nine goals in five games earned France the European Championship and confirmed him as the greatest player in French history.

International club success proved elusive until May 1993, when Marseille beat Milan to win the Champions Cup. Marseille was engulfed by a match-fixing scandal which prevented them defending the Cup and brought suspensions and legal action against players and officials, including president Bernard Tapie.

Paris Saint-Germain reached European club semi-finals four straight seasons in the 1990s, and won the 1996 Cup-winners' Cup, while Bordeaux reached the 1996 UEFA Cup Final. France will be among the favourites for a first-ever World Cup triumph when they host the finals in 1998.

Germany

Deutscher Fussball-Bund

Founded:
1900

FIFA:
1904–1946, 1950

World Cup:
1954, 1974, 1990

European Championship:
1972, 1980, 1996

Olympics:
1976 *(East Germany)*

Since the Second World War, Germany have enjoyed a record of success unparalleled in the history of the game.

Yet Germany's pre-war record was poor, with third place at the 1934 World Cup the peak of their achievement. The war brought division and in 1948 East Germany formed its own association, league and national side as a member of the Eastern Bloc. But while the East floundered, the West flourished. Banished from FIFA in 1946, they were readmitted in 1950 as West Germany… and won the World Cup just over four years later.

From that initial breakthrough, the Germans pressed on and reached even greater heights of achievement in the following years. In the World Cup, they were semi-finalists in 1958, losing to Sweden, quarter-finalists in 1962 and then runners-up to England in 1966.

Ongoing Successes

The 1970s seemed to belong to Bayern Munich and West Germany. Bayern won a hat-trick of European Cups in 1974, 1975 and 1976, and provided the nucleus of the national side, including Franz Beckenbauer, which won the European Championship in 1972, the World Cup in 1974 and, after finishing second in 1976, the European Championship again in 1980.

And the success story continues to grow. The 1970s sides were replaced by new stars of the world game: Karl-Heinz Rummenigge, Lothar Matthäus, Rudi Völler, Jürgen Klinsmann, Thomas Hässler and Matthias Sammer (voted European Footballer of the Year in 1996).

Following the World Cup success and German reunification in 1990, they have gone from strength to strength by securing victory in the 1996 European Championship – defeating England again on penalties in the semi-final – with a 2–1 "golden goal" defeat of the Czech Republic and then qualifying easily for the World Cup Finals in France in 1998.

Borussia Dortmund won the 1997 UEFA Champions Cup while Schalke 04 surprised Europe by defeating AC Milan on penalties in the final of the UEFA Cup.

Holland

Koninklijke Nederland Voetbalbond (KNVB)

Founded:
1889
FIFA:
1904
European Championship:
1988

The Dutch were early devotees of football, partly owing to the country's close proximity to Britain, and were among the continent's leading amateur sides in the early 1900s. Indeed, they reached the semi-finals of four consecutive Olympic Games from 1908 to 1924… but lost them all. Third place in 1908 and 1912 was their best. The 1920s marked a move away from amateurism in other countries, and Dutch football entered a steep decline which lasted until the 1960s.

In 1957, a national league was created and professionalism was introduced in an attempt to staunch the flow of Dutch players going abroad. The main beneficiaries of the reorganization were Ajax of Amsterdam, Feyenoord of Rotterdam and PSV Eindhoven – the "big three" who have dominated Dutch football ever since. The big breakthrough came in 1970, when Feyenoord won the European Cup. It was the beginning of a golden era for Dutch football, in which Ajax won a hat-trick of European Cups (1971, 1972, 1973), Feyenoord and PSV both won the UEFA Cup, and Holland reached two consecutive World Cup finals.

Total Football

The generation of Dutch players which emerged in the 1970s was among the finest the modern world game has seen. Coach Rinus Michels was the architect of success with his "total football" system, which involved moulding highly skilled players, such as Johan Cruyff and Johan Neeskens, into a team unit, with the emphasis on interchangeability and with every player totally comfortable in possession. But despite a plethora of talented players, they lost the 1974 and 1978 World Cup Finals.

As the "total football" side broke up, the Dutch slipped into decline, failing to qualify for the 1982 and 1986 World Cup finals. But a revival was soon to follow, spearheaded by a new generation of players at Ajax and PSV. Ruud Gullit, Frank Rijkaard, Marco Van Basten and Ronald Koeman, once again under Rinus Michels' guidance, triumphed in the 1988 European Championship – Holland's only major success.

Observers from all over the world converged on Amsterdam to study Ajax's youth system which also provided Holland with their national team backbone at the 1996 European Championship finals.

Hungary

Magyar Labdarugo Szovetseg

Founded:

1901

FIFA:

1906

Olympics:

1952, 1964, 1968

Just as Austria will always be renowned for the "Wunderteam" of the 1930s, so Hungary will be for the "Magic Magyars" side of the 1950s. This side was the finest the world had ever seen and had lost only one international in five years before, heartbreakingly, they failed in the 1954 World Cup Final. The forward line of Zoltan Czibor, Jozsef Toth, Nandor Hidegkuti, Sandor Kocsis and Ferenc Puskas – the greatest player of his era and still regarded as one of the best ever. The "Galloping Major", as Puskas was known, terrorized opposition defences the world over and scored 173 goals in this spell. In 1953, they became the first non-British side to beat England at home, winning 6–3, and shattering the aura of arrogance and invincibility that had enveloped the English for too long.

Chasing Success

Yet this was not the first outstanding side Hungary had produced. Hungarian clubs, notably MTK Budapest, who won 10 consecutive titles (1914–25), dominated European football in the inter-war period, winning five Mitropa Cups in the 1930s. The national side reached the World Cup Final in 1938, where they were comfortably beaten 4–2 by the hosts Italy. The 1930s side contained such fine players as Gyorgy Sarosi and Gyula Zsengeller.

The Hungarian uprising of 1958 broke up the "Magic Magyars" side, but by the 1960s another had emerged. The new stars were Florian Albert and Ferenc Bene, who led Hungary to the 1962 and 1966 World Cup quarter-finals and Olympic gold in 1964 and 1968. The 1970s marked the beginning of an insipid decline for the national side, despite some notable successes for the clubs, particularly Ujpest who won nine titles in 11 years. Failure to qualify for the 1970, 1974, 1990 and 1994 World Cup finals was matched by poor performances at the 1978, 1982, and 1986 tournaments, especially in Mexico in 1986 when they lost 6–0 to the Soviet Union.

The lowest point came, however, in a World Cup qualifier in June 1992 when Hungary lost 2–1 to unfancied Iceland... in Budapest of all places!

Hungary seemingly came close to qualification for France '98 when they earned a play-off place against Yugoslavia. Unfortunately they were beaten 12–1 on aggregate, including a humiliating 7–1 loss at home.

Italy

Federazione Italiana Giuoco Calcio

Founded:

1898

FIFA:

1903

World Cup:

1934, 1938, 1982

European Championship:

1968

Olympics:

1936

The first 30 years of Italian football were chaotic and complicated, with various regional leagues and the industrial cities of the north – Milan and Turin – competing for power. But the Association settled in Rome, in 1929, and a national league was formed in 1930.

Under legendary coach Vittorio Pozzo, Italy lost only seven games during the decade, winning the World Cup in 1934 when they beat Czechoslovakia 2–1 after extra-time.

Four years later, on home soil and in front of fascist dictator Mussolini, Italy triumphed once more as they defeated Hungary 4–2 in a gripping final. In between these two successes, they also claimed the 1936 Olympic title to confirm their superiority.

After the war Torino were the dominant side, winning four consecutive titles, and providing virtually all of the national team. But, returning from Lisbon, their plane crashed into the Superga Hill outside Turin killing all on board. Hardly surprisingly, this led to a decline for both Torino and Italy during the 1950s.

Foreign Influence

Many blamed the failure on the large number of foreign imports in the Italian game, which grew considerably in the 1950s. Consequently, the importation of foreigners was banned in 1964. This hampered the clubs, but allowed a new generation of Italian players to develop.

The 1970s, though, witnessed the rise of *catenaccio* – defensive, sterile football, reflecting the attitude that not losing was more important than winning. For the clubs it was a lean time in Europe, but the national side did better, reaching the 1970 World Cup Final. The import ban was lifted in the early 1980s, and it was to be a decade of great successes for the clubs, who made full use of their foreign quota. Juventus, with French midfield genius Michel Platini, dominated the first half of the decade, while the national side, skippered by 40-year-old Dino Zoff, swept to victory at the 1982 World Cup in Spain.

Serie A is now an exciting league with many strong teams. The national side failed both to win the 1990 World Cup, in Italy, and to qualify for the 1992 European Championship. But a rebuilding programme halted the slide and Italy reached the 1994 World Cup Final.

Mexico

Federacion Mexicana de Futbol Asociacion

Founded:
1927
FIFA:
1929
CONCACAF Championship:
1963, 1971, 1977, 1993

Mexico utterly dominate their Central American region, but this has hindered rather than helped their game. With no decent local opposition for the national side or the clubs, Mexico have enjoyed their greatest moments in the World Cup against opposition teams who can provide them with sterner tests than they are otherwise used to.

The federation was formed in 1927, and a trip to the Amsterdam Olympics a year later ended after just one match. Two years later they entered the World Cup and have qualified for 10 of the 15 finals tournaments, a statistic most other countries would be proud to have. It is also a record which includes the 1990 finals in Italy, which they were barred from by FIFA for breaches of age regulations in a youth tournament.

Mexico's best World Cups were in 1970 and 1986, when they were hosts. They reached the quarter-finals of both and in 1986 were unlucky to lose on penalties to the eventual finalists West Germany.

The Cartwheeling King

Star of the 1986 World Cup side was Hugo Sanchez, an agile forward who led Spanish giants Real Madrid to many honours in the 1980s. Famous for his exuberant, cartwheeling celebrations when he scores, Sanchez is Mexico's greatest player since Antonio Carbajal, the goalkeeper who created a unique record by playing in all five World Cup finals tournaments from 1950 to 1966. Mexico won the CONCACAF Championship four times, but were shocked in 1991 when the United States beat them in the semi-finals, though Mexico regained the upper hand in 1993 with a convincing display. Many believe Mexico would benefit from joining the South Americans, and in 1993 they, and the USA, were invited to take part in the South American Championship.

Mexico embarrassed their hosts by reaching the final, losing narrowly to Argentina. Mexico then qualified for the 1994 World Cup finals with comparative ease, only to lose to Bulgaria in a second round penalty shoot-out. They then made their way swiftly to the next World Cup finals, France '98. They were nearly overtaken by the United States but managed to hold out to top their group of six from which three qualified for the tournament.

Russia

Russian Football Federation

Founded:

1922 *(as Soviet Union)*

FIFA:

1922 *(as Soviet Union)*

European Championship:

1960 *(as Soviet Union)*

Olympics:

1956, 1988 *(as Soviet Union)*

Russia's footballing history is inextricably entwined with that of the former Soviet Union, and it is under the banner of the latter that her greatest achievements have occurred down the years.

The Communists reorganized the structure of football methodically from top to bottom, with the emphasis on teamwork rather than individual flair. Moscow, then the Soviet capital, became the main football centre with five great workers' clubs: Dynamo (electrical trades), Spartak (producers' co-operatives), Torpedo (car manufacturers), Lokomitive (railways) and CSKA (the army).

In the 1950s the national side began to venture out to take on the rest of the world. They won a poorly-attended 1956 Olympic Games and then reached the quarter-finals of the 1958 World Cup at their first attempt. In 1960 they entered and won the first European Championship. This, however, remains the only major triumph that either the Soviet Union or Russia has ever had.

No Russian Success

The Soviet sides of 1986 and 1988 were arguably the best since the 1960s, but were composed of mainly Kiev Dynamo players. Indeed, it is a curious fact that despite Russia's dominance of Soviet football, the only Soviet sides to win European club competitions were not Russian. Kiev, in the Ukraine, won the Cup-winners' Cup in 1975 and again in 1986, and Tbilisi Dynamo, from Georgia, won the same tournament in 1981.

In September 1991, the Soviet Union began to disintegrate. The three Baltic states achieved independence and went their own way, quickly followed by the other 12 republics. The Soviets had qualified for the 1992 European Championship finals and took part under a "flag of convenience" name, the Commonwealth of Independent States – a television commentator's worst nightmare!

Russia picked up where the Soviet Union left off, entered the 1994 World Cup qualifying competition and qualified, with what proved misleading ease, from a very poor group. In the finals, Oleg Salenko scored a record five goals in a game against Cameroon, but they lost the other two games.

They came close to qualifying for France '98, but lost out to Italy in a two-legged play-off game played in poor conditions.

Romania

Federatia Romana de Fotbal

Founded:

1908

FIFA:

1930

Romania embraced football before most of her Balkan neighbours, mainly owing to the influence of the country's sovereign, King Carol, who was a soccer fanatic. He instigated the formation of a federation in 1908 and, having returned to power in 1930 after an abdication, he was determined that Romania should enter the first World Cup.

Romania duly made the long trip to South America and Uruguay, but were beaten by the hosts in the first round. They also entered the 1934 and 1938 tournaments, but could not progress beyond the first round, despite the presence of Iuliu Bodola, their top scorer to this day.

Bucharest Dominate

The Communists took over in 1944 and, as usual, reorganized the domestic game. Two of the clubs created in Bucharest, Steaua, the army team, and Dinamo, the police team, have dominated Romanian soccer ever since. After the war, the national side enjoyed a brief upsurge with qualification for the 1970 World Cup Finals, and a quarter-final finish in the 1976 European Championship. But, despite Anghel Iordanescu, one of the true greats of Romanian football, it was not until 1984 that they qualified for the finals of a major tournament again, the European Championship in France. But their inexperience was cruelly exposed as they failed to register a win in their three group matches.

In the 1980s, under the direct influence of the brutal and ruthless Ceaucescu regime, Steaua and Dinamo dominated even more. In 1986 Steaua became the first team from behind the Iron Curtain to win the European Cup, beating the mighty Barcelona in a penalty shoot-out after the match had finished 0–0. Not surprisingly, as they formed the nucleus of the national side, Romania now entered the most successful era in their history.

Despite the midfield inspiration of Gheorghe Hagi, they did not enjoy the best of luck at the World Cups of either 1990 or 1994. Both times Romania were eliminated after a penalty shoot-out. They fell to the Republic of Ireland in the second round in Italy, and four years later it was the turn of the Swedes to shatter Romanian dreams in a similar fashion.

It says everything about their underlying quality that Romania dropped only three points in 10 games in qualifying for the 1996 European Championship finals.

Scotland

Scottish Football Association

Founded:

1873

FIFA:

1910–20, 1924–28, 1946

Scotland boasts a proud footballing heritage and, for such a small country in terms of population, it has been a remarkable story. Founded way back in 1873, the Scottish FA still retains a permanent seat on the international board.

Scotland was also the venue for the world's first international match when, on November 30, 1872, Scotland and England drew 0–0. The Scotland vs. England rivalry has continued ever since, sharpened by the fact that many of England's most successful club sides have been managed by Scots: Bill Shankly at Liverpool, Matt Busby at Manchester United, Alex Ferguson also at Manchester United and George Graham at Arsenal. Add to this list the plethora of Scots who have plied their trade in the English league – Denis Law, Hughie Gallacher and Kenny Dalglish to name but three – and it's easy to see why the two countries love to beat each other whenever they meet.

This continual draining of manpower would have withered many countries. But the Scottish League survives, thanks mainly to the two great Glasgow clubs, Celtic and Rangers. These two, representing the Catholic (Celtic) and Protestant (Rangers) halves of Scottish society, have dominated the domestic scene unlike any other country in Europe. Scottish club football was at its peak in the 1960s, with Celtic winning the European Cup in 1967 – the first British side to do so – and reaching the final again in 1970. Rangers won the 1972 European Cup-winners' Cup.

Always At The Finals

At the same time, the national side made steady progress. Having entered the World Cup for the first time in 1950, they then qualified for the finals in 1970, 1974, 1978, 1982, 1986 and 1990. The 1974 and 1978 finals, although not very successful in terms of results, caused no end of joy to Scottish fans because England failed to qualify for either.

In 1992 the Scots reached the European Championship finals for the first time, after seven attempts, and gave a good account of themselves in a tough group containing both Germany and Holland.

They qualified again in 1996, but herein lies their problem. They seem capable of reaching finals, but unable to survive the first round. They came agonizingly close to the second round in 1996, but lost out on goal difference to the Dutch.

Spain

Real Federacion Española de Futbol

Founded:

1913

FIFA:

1904

European Championship:

1964

Olympics:

1992

Football first got a foothold in the Basque country of Northern Spain, through migrant British workers, in the 1890s. Spain's oldest club, Athletic Bilbao, still retain their English title. The game spread rapidly and was soon popular in Madrid, Barcelona and Valencia. The various regional organizations were brought together in 1913, when the Real Federacion Española de Futbol was formed.

Club Success

The Civil War and the Second World War halted internationals for almost a decade. But the domestic league grew stronger as the rivalry between Real Madrid, the "Royal" club, and Barcelona, the Catalan people's club, intensified. Real Madrid won the first five European Cups (1956–60), heralding the 1960s as a decade of huge success at club and national level. Barcelona won the Fairs Cup in 1959, 1960 and again in 1966; Valencia won it in 1962 and 1963, Real Zaragoza in 1964. Meanwhile Atletico Madrid won the European Cup-winners' Cup in 1962, and Real Madrid won the European Cup again in 1966.

The national side qualified for the 1962 and 1966 World Cup finals and won the European Championship in 1964. It was not until 1979 that European success returned, when Barcelona won the European Cup-winners' Cup. Spain hosted the 1982 World Cup, but failed miserably. They qualified again in 1986 and 1990 but could do no better than the quarter-finals in Mexico. But the clubs continued to do well. Real won two UEFA Cups in the 1980s, while Barcelona won the European Cup-winners' Cup in 1982 and 1989 and completed a hat-trick of European trophies by winning the European Cup in 1992 – seven years after losing a final to Steaua Bucharest.

When the national side failed to qualify for the 1992 European Championship finals, the question was raised again of whether Spanish clubs' liking for foreign imports was damaging the national side's chances.

However, the Under-23s success at the 1992 Barcelona Olympics and the continued successes of Barcelona and Real, domestically and in Europe, are reasons for hope. Several of the young Olympic victors were integrated into the full national side, which reached the quarter-finals of both the 1994 World Cup and the 1996 European Championship.

Sweden

Svensk Fotbollforblundet

Founded:
1904
FIFA:
1904
Olympics:
1948

Sweden have, since the 1920s, been Scandinavia's top national side and have a deserved reputation for producing quality players. An Association was formed in 1904 and joined FIFA the same year.

Gothenburg was, and still is, the centre of Swedish domestic football and the National League, instituted in 1925, has been dominated by Gothenburg's clubs, Orgryte, IFK and GAIS, along with AIK and Djurgardens of Stockholm. Sweden's national side made their debut in 1908 and entered the first four Olympic tournaments – with mixed success. Sweden were at their best in the late 1940s when they boasted one of the most famous forward lines in history. Gunnar Gren, Gunnar Nordahl and Nils Liedholm – the "Gre-No-Li" trio – sparked Sweden to Olympic gold in 1948 and were promptly signed up by Milan, where they enjoyed great success. Swedes were regularly bought by European clubs but were then barred from the national side by the strictly-amateur rules of the association. Despite this handicap, Sweden finished third in the 1950 World Cup, with Nacka Skoglund the new star of his country.

The import ban was lifted in time for the 1958 World Cup Finals, which Sweden hosted, and with all their players available they reached the final. A decline followed in the 1960s, but Sweden qualified for all three World Cup finals in the 1970s, with Bjorn Nordqvist clocking up a record 115 appearances between 1963 and 1978.

UEFA Cup Triumph

The clubs too began to make an impact, and Malmo reached the European Cup Final in 1979 where they lost to English side Nottingham Forest. IFK Gothenburg enjoyed the greatest success, though, winning the UEFA Cup in 1982 and 1987 – a feat made all the more remarkable as the team consisted of part-timers, because Sweden has not yet introduced full professionalism. Until it does, its top stars will continue to find football employment in other countries.

Sweden's first appearance in the European Championship finals came in 1992, by virtue of being hosts, but they were beaten in the semi-finals by Germany. They followed up by finishing third in the 1994 World Cup and toppling Denmark as Scandinavia's best.

Uruguay

Asociacion Uruguaya de Futbol

Founded:
1900
FIFA:
1923
World Cup:
1930, 1950
South American Championship:
1916, 1917, 1920, 1923, 1924, 1926, 1935, 1942, 1956, 1959, 1967, 1983, 1987, 1995
Olympics:
1924, 1928

Before the Second World War, Uruguay were undoubtedly the best team in the world, effectively winning three World Championships. Today, Montevideo dominates the domestic scene and, as it is located just across the River Plate estuary from Buenos Aires, the two cities can rightly claim to be the centre of South American football. Montevideo's two great clubs, Peñarol and Nacional, have dominated Uruguayan football, winning more than 80 championships between them.

The national side dominated world football in the first half of this century, but has faded since the 1950s. Early successes in the South American Championship were followed by victories in the 1924 and 1928 Olympics. Two years later, as the host nation, Uruguay swept to victory in the first World Cup finals defeating South American neighbours Argentina 4–2 in the final.

The side of the 1920s and 1930s contained many of Uruguay's all-time greats: skipper Jose Nasazzi, the midfield "Iron Curtain" of Jose Andrade, Lorenzo Fernandez and Alvarez Gestido, and outstanding forwards Hector Castro, Pedro Cea and Hector Scarone.

World Cup Glory

In 1950 Uruguay pulled off one of the biggest World Cup finals shocks in history, coming from a goal down to beat Brazil 2–1 in the deciding match in front of 200,000 seething Brazilian fans.

In Switzerland in 1954, the defence of their crown ended with a 4–2 semi-final defeat by favourites Hungary in one of the best World Cup games ever.

Since then, Uruguay have enjoyed regular success in the South American Championship, but in the World Cup they have failed to match their feats of the 1930s and 1950s.

With so many foreign-based players, Uruguay developed a schizophrenic approach to the World Cup and South American Championship, often entering wildly different teams for tournaments staged less than a year apart. This unpredictability was shown in 1995, when Uruguay won the Copa America, beating 1994 World Cup winners Brazil after a penalty shoot-out in the final.

The Great Clubs

Professionalism swept through British football in the 1880s and western Europe in the late 1920s. The big clubs of Spain, Italy, France and Portugal were importing star foreigners by the turn of the 1930s, and it was not until the mid-1950s that Belgium, Holland and then Germany caught up with full-time professionalism.

When it did, the balance of the European game changed again. The great traditions of football have thus been kept alive, week in, week out, by the clubs. From Ajax in Holland to Vasco da Gama in Brazil, from Barcelona in Spain to Liverpool in England, they provide the first call of loyalty of the public. People who may never have attended a match in years still look out for the result of "their" club each week.

Evidence of the depths of loyalty which certain clubs can inspire is widely available – from the way Real Madrid's fans came up with the money to build the Estadio Bernabéu in the 1940s to the proud boast of Portugal's Benfica of its 122,000 members. Every club has its tales of the great days and the great victories. Some, like Manchester United, have been touched by tragedy. Others, like Marseille, with scandal. The greatest, clearly, are those who have repeatedly proved their power and strength by winning the continental cup competitions in Europe and South America. Soon, if FIFA has its way, their claims to pre-eminence will be tested by the leading clubs of Africa, Asia, Latin and North America and Oceania in a world club championship. Such a tournament, featuring the world's eight top clubs, could be launched as early as the summer of 1999 – as long as the game's rulers can adjust the international fixture calendars appropriately.

Ajax Amsterdam

Holland

Founded:
1900

Stadium:
Arena (50,000)

Colours:
Red and white broad stripes/white

League:
26

Cup:
12

World Club Cup:
1972, 1995

European Champions Cup:
1971, 1972, 1973, 1995

European Cup-winners Cup:
1987

UEFA Cup:
1992

Super Cup:
1972, 1973, 1995

Ajax, on beating Torino in the 1992 UEFA Cup Final, became only the second team after Italy's Juventus to have won all three European trophies and a full house of all seven titles on offer to clubs. The achievement was popular, bearing in mind the entertainment and style the club had consistently provided. The first hints of glory to come were evident in 1966–67 when, under former Dutch international Rinus Michels, Ajax thrashed Liverpool 5–1 in a European Cup tie. Two years later, they became the first Dutch side to reach the European Cup Final, losing 4–1 to Milan. In 1971, Ajax were back, beating Panathinaikos 2–0 at Wembley. In the next two finals, they beat Inter 2–0, then Juventus 1–0, Johan Cruyff their inspiration.

Total Skill

Ajax's trademark was the "total football" system, taking advantage of a generation of skilled all-rounders whose versatility and footballing intelligence allowed bewildering changes of position. It was "The Whirl", as envisaged early in the 1950s by that football prophet, Willi Meisl. After the sale of Cruyff to Barcelona in 1973, Ajax fell away and it took his return, a decade later, as technical director, to propel them back to the peaks of the European game. Under Cruyff, the new generation took the Cup-winners Cup in 1987 – his pupil Marco Van Basten scoring the goal which beat Lokomotiv Leipzig in Athens. Cruyff's successor, Louis Van Gaal, secured the UEFA Cup five years later. Despite continuing to sell their best players, Ajax's 1994–95 squad was statistically their best ever, winning the League title without losing a game and the European Cup for the fourth time. Injuries foiled their bid for a fifth triumph the following season when Ajax lost on penalties to Juventus in Rome.

Anderlecht

Brussels, Belgium

Founded:
1908

Stadium:
Constant Vanden Stock/Parc Astrid (28,063)

Colours:
White with mauve/white

League:
23

Cup:
7

European Cup-winners Cup:
1976, 1978

UEFA Cup:
1983

Super Cup:
1976, 1978

Anderlecht's international debut was not a happy one: they crashed 10–0 and 12–0 on aggregate to Manchester United in an early European Cup. Since then, however, the Royal Sporting Club have earned respect far and wide for their domestic domination and an international outlook which has brought success in both the European Cup-winners Cup and the UEFA Cup. Much credit reflects on the coaching work of Englishman Bill Gormlie, a former Blackburn goalkeeper, who helped lay the foundations for success in the late 1940s and early 1950s. Equally important was the financial power of the millionaire brewer, Constant Vanden Stock. Before his takeover Anderlecht relied mainly on homegrown talent like Paul Van Himst, the greatest Belgian footballer of all time.

International Selection

As Anderlecht's prestige grew, they were able to compete in the international transfer market. A significant coaching influence, in the early 1960s, was Frenchman Pierre Sinibaldi, who perfected a tactical formation which relied on a flat back four, the offside trap and possession football in midfield. It worked well against all opposition except British clubs, whose more direct style constantly caught the defenders on the turn. Thus, the first time Anderlecht reached a European final – the Fairs Cup in 1970 – they were beaten by Arsenal. European success, in the Cup-winners Cup in 1976 and 1978, had to await the more pragmatic coaching approach of Dutchman Wiel Corver and Belgian Raymond Goethals. Later, with Van Himst back as coach, Anderlecht won the UEFA Cup and in Enzo Scifo produced the finest Belgian player since Van Himst himself. The club's reputation nosedived in the late 1990s, however, when a match-fixing scandal surfaced concerning Anderlecht's UEFA Cup campaigns a decade earlier – most notably their semi-final victory over Nottingham Forest in 1984.

Arsenal

London, England

Founded:
1886
Stadium:
Highbury (38,500)
Colours:
Red/white
League:
10
Cup:
6
European Cup-winners Cup:
1994
Fairs Cup:
1970

Arsenal, today a North London club, had their origins south of the Thames, at the Woolwich Arsenal. The club turned professional in 1891 and entered the Football League a year later, reaching the First Division in 1904 and the FA Cup semi-finals in 1906. After the First World War, they moved to Highbury, and appointed the legendary Herbert Chapman as manager in 1925.

Chapman had a flair for publicity, an innovative approach to tactics and a talent for motivation. He spent heavily but wisely on the likes of Charlie Buchan and Alex James, introduced the stopper centre-half and created the all-conquering outfit which won the League five times in the 1930s and the FA Cup twice. Arsenal won the League twice more and the FA Cup once in the eight years after the war. A 17-year hiatus followed before the Gunners ended their longest trophy drought by winning the Fairs Cup in 1970.

Highbury Heroes

Suddenly, the jinx was broken. A year later manager Bertie Mee was celebrating a historic League and Cup double. His team mixed the volatile flair of Charlie George, determined leadership of Frank McLintock, rugged tackling of Peter Storey and creative class of George Graham. Graham later returned as manager, masterminding a string of successes in the League, League Cup, FA Cup and Cup-winners Cup, but his reign ended abruptly in 1995 amid controversy over transfer "bungs". Another Scotsman, Bruce Rioch, was hired for about a year, but he turned out to be only a stop-gap manager, filling in for a bigger name signing.

French coach Arsène Wenger, previously at Monaco and Grampus 8 in Japan, was hired in 1996 and rapidly transformed one of the most English of Premiership squads into a cosmopolitan mixture with the presence of Dutchmen Dennis Bergkamp and Marc Overmars and Frenchmen Patrick Vieira, Emmanuel Petit, Gilles Grimandi, Nicolas Anelka and Remi Garde.

Aston Villa

Birmingham, England

Founded:

1874

Stadium:

Villa Park (39,339)

Colours:

Claret with blue sleeves/white

League:

7

Cup:

7

League Cup:

5

European Champions Cup:

1982

Aston Villa were one of the founders of the Football League back in the early days of organized football in the late 19th century. Those were also the club's greatest days since they won five of their championships and two of their FA Cups – including the double in 1896–97.

Honours have been gained in a rather more sporadic manner since then, though Villa did set the First Division scoring record with 128 goals in the 1930–31 season when they finished runners-up behind Herbert Chapman's Arsenal. Villa made history – for a brief time – when they won the FA Cup for a seventh time amid controversy in 1957. Villa beat Manchester United 2–1 at Wembley though United played much of the match with 10 men after goalkeeper Ray Wood was badly injured by a challenge from Villa's top-scoring outside left, Peter MacParland.

Villa's Greatest Achievements

At one stage in the succeeding decades, Villa suffered the indignity of relegation to the Third Division but regained their pride under the management of former wing-half Vic Crowe. Ron Saunders then took over and built the team which won the League in 1981 and his assistant and successor Tony Barton guided Villa to their greatest achievement when they beat Bayern Munich in Rotterdam to win the European Cup the following year. South African-born Peter Withe scored the decisive goal from close range in the Feyenoord stadium.

Villa used the income from their European runs to redevelop their home into one of the finest grounds in the Premier League while the team, simultaneously, underlined their competitive reputation with two League Cup successes in three seasons in the mid-1990s.

And in 1997–98, the club showed signs of making an impact on the European scene once more, reaching the last eight of the UEFA Cup.

Atlético Madrid

Spain

Founded:
1903

Stadium:
Vicente Calderón/Manzanares (62,000)

Colours:
Red and white stripes/blue

League:
9

Cup:
9

World Club Cup:
1974

European Cup-winners Cup:
1962

Atlético Madrid have always existed in the shadow of neighbours Real, but they still rank among the Big Three of Spanish football and boast a proud record at international level. Not that life has always been easy. In the late 1930s, after the Spanish Civil War, it took a merger with the Air Force club to keep Atlético in business; in 1959, they just failed to reach the European Cup Final when Real beat them in a semi-final play-off; in the early 1960s they had to share Real's Estadio Bernabéu, because Atlético's Metropolitano had been sold to developers before the club's new stadium could be completed. European glory did come to Atlético in the shape of the Cup-winners Cup in 1962 and was a well-deserved prize for players such as inside-left Joaquín Peiro and his wing partner Enrique Collar. But it was not until the early 1970s that Atlético put together a comparable team, thanks to the purchases of Argentines Ruben Hugo Ayala and Ramon Heredia. In 1974, Atlético secured that elusive place in the European Cup Final. But, after taking the lead against Bayern Munich in extra time, Atlético conceded a last-kick equalizer.

One Team in Madrid

Consolation for their 4–0 defeat in the replay came with the opportunity to substitute for reluctant Bayern in the World Club Cup against Independiente of Argentina. By the time the tie came around, Atlético had appointed as coach Luis Aragones, the midfielder who had scored their goal in the European Cup Final against Bayern. Atletico duly beat Independiente 1–0 and were, for a year at least, on top of the world. In the late 1980s, the club was taken over by the extrovert builder Jesus Gíl. He pumped millions of pounds into the club but generated more bad publicity than good, hiring and firing coaches at a breathtaking rate. It all came together in dramatic fashion when Atlético won the league and cup double in 1996.

Barcelona

Spain

Founded:
1899
Stadium:
Nou Camp(115,000)
Colours:
Blue and red stripes/blue
League:
14
Cup:
23
European Champions Cup:
1992
European Cup-winners Cup:
1979, 1982, 1989, 1997
Fairs Cup:
1958, 1960, 1966
Super Cup:
1992

Barcelona finally ended a duel with destiny when, in 1992, they beat Sampdoria 1–0 at Wembley to win the European Cup. It was a case of third time lucky, for the greatest prize in the European club game had twice eluded them at the final hurdle. Barcelona had been the first winners of the Inter-Cities Fairs Cup and had won the Cup-winners Cup three times. But their European Cup campaigns seemed to have been jinxed. First, in 1961, when Barcelona had apparently achieved the hard part by eliminating title-holders and bitter rivals Real Madrid, they lost to Benfica in the final, in Berne. Barcelona hit the woodwork three times, yet lost 3–2 against the run of play. Great players such as Luis Suarez, Ladislav Kubala, Sandor Kocsis and Zoltan Czibor had everything on their side except luck. History repeated itself in even more galling circumstances in 1986. Barcelona, coached by Terry Venables and gambling on the fitness of long-time injured Steve Archibald, faced Steaua Bucharest in Seville but lost on penalties after a goalless draw.

Second Generation

It took the return of 1970s inspiration Johan Cruyff, this time as coach, to steer a new generation of international stars – including Ronald Koeman, Hristo Stoichkov and Michael Laudrup – to victory long overdue for one of the world's biggest clubs. Barcelona's 1994 League title was their fourth in a row, the last three achieved in the closing moments of the final day, twice at the expense of Real Madrid.

Failure to win a trophy in 1995 or 1996, however, resulted in Cruyff's dismissal after eight years in charge. He was replaced by Bobby Robson whose recapture of the Cup-winners Cup and Spanish Cup could not save him from a move "upstairs" and replacement as coach by another Dutchman, Louis Van Gaal.

Bayern Munich

Germany

Founded:
1900

Stadium:
Olimpiastadion (69,261)

Colours:
All red

League:
14

Cup:
8

World Club Cup:
1976

European Champions Cup:
1974, 1975, 1976

European Cup-winners Cup:
1967

UEFA Cup:
1996

Bayern are Germany's most glamorous club, even though high tax rates mean they have never been able to retain players tempted by the rich pickings of Italy. In the 1980s, Bayern became almost an Italian nursery as they lost Karl-Heinz Rummenigge, Andreas Brehme and Lothar Matthäus to Inter and Stefan Reuter and Jurgen Kohler to Juventus. All this transfer activity underlines the fact that the Bayern success story is relatively recent.

Top Line-up

The identities of the men who secured all the glittering titles read like a *Who's Who* of the world game: Franz Beckenbauer, Gerd Müller, Sepp Maier, Paul Breitner, Rummenigge and Matthäus. The German championship was originally organized in regional leagues, with the winners playing off at the end of each season for the title: only once in the pre-war years did Bayern win all the way through. That was in 1932, when they defeated Eintracht Frankfurt 2–0. Not until 1957, and a 1–0 win over Fortuna Düsseldorf in the cup final, did Bayern have anything more to celebrate. Their record was so mediocre they were not included in the inaugural Bundesliga in 1963–64. But, a year later, Bayern won promotion; in 1966 they won the cup, and in 1967 secured the European Cup-winners Cup. That was the team led by Beckenbauer as an attacking sweeper, with Maier in goal and Müller up front. All three starred in Bayern's European Cup hat-trick in the mid-1970s. In the 1980s, Bayern were twice European Cup runners-up, but it was not until Beckenbauer returned – as vice-president, coach, then president – that they triumphed again. Their 1996 UEFA Cup success made Bayern the fourth club to win all three European trophies.

Benfica

Lisbon, Portugal

Founded:
1904
Stadium:
Estádio do Benfica/Da Luz
(92,385)
Colours:
Red/white
League:
29
Cup:
26
European Champions Cup:
1961, 1962

Benfica are a national institution with their huge stadium – with a 130,000 capacity before recent security constraints – and 122,000 membership. Living up to the standards of history is what Benfica believe they owe Cosme Damiao who, on February 28, 1904, organized the first recorded local game of *futebol* on a patch of Lisbon wasteland. The next day he formed his "team" into a club named Sport Lisboa and, two years later, was instrumental in arranging a merger with neighbours Sport Clube de Benfica.

In the early years, it was cycling which brought the club its first prizes. Following the launch of a Portuguese championship in the late 1920s, Benfica lorded it over Portuguese sport. In due course, Benfica set their sights on international glory and, in 1950, won the Latin Cup – a forerunner of the European Cup. English manager Ted Smith laid the foundations of a team which would dominate not only Portugal but then Europe.

Taking on All-comers

In 1954, Benfica followed the example being set in Spain and built a vast new stadium. An exiled Hungarian named Bela Guttman became coach, and his team filled the new stadium as Benfica broke Real Madrid's grip on the European Cup, sweeping to success in 1961 and 1962.

First they beat Barcelona, amid intense drama, by 3–2 in Berne, then Real Madrid 5–3 in Amsterdam. On both occasions Benfica were captained by their veteran centre-forward, José Aguas. They also introduced one of the most famous Portuguese footballers of all time in Eusebio (*see* page 104), greatest of the many fine players Benfica had discovered in the Portuguese colonies of Mozambique and Angola.

Benfica's boast of using only Portuguese (including colonial) players was scrapped in the mid-1970s, when the African colonies were cast adrift. Now they hunt Brazilians, Slavs and Danes with the rest – rewarded with nothing like the success of their earlier triumphs.

Boca Juniors

Buenos Aires, Argentina

Founded:
1905
Stadium:
Bombonera (58,740)
Colours:
Blue with yellow hoop/blue
League:
19
World Club Cup:
1977
South American Club Cup:
1977, 1978
South American Supercup:
1989
Inter-American Cup:
1989

Boca are one of the two great clubs in the Argentine capital of Buenos Aires, along with rivals River Plate. They were founded by an Irishman named Patrick MacCarthy and a group of newly-arrived Italian immigrants. They joined the League in 1913 and were immediately caught up in a domestic football "war" which saw two championships being organized for most of the 1920s and early 1930s.

Boca stood astride the two eras. They won the final Argentine amateur championship in 1930 and the first unified professional one the following year. Two more titles followed in the next four years, thanks to some fine players, including the great Brazilian defender Domingos da Guia. In the 1940s and 1950s, Boca slipped into River Plate's shadow, re-emerging in 1963 when a team fired by the goals of José Sanfilippo reached the final of the South American Club Cup.

World Club Champions

Winning the title, however, would have to wait until the late 1970s. Then they reached the final three years in a row – beating Brazil's Cruzeiro in 1977 and Deportivo Cali of Colombia in 1978 before losing to Olimpia of Paraguay the following year.

Boca's rugged style, under Juan Carlos Lorenzo, proved controversial. Not one of the club's players figured in the squad which won the 1978 World Cup Final against Holland on home soil. But Boca had already secured their own world crown, defeating West Germany's Borussia Mönchengladbach in the World Club Cup in 1977. Boca rebuilt their team around Diego Maradona in 1981, but had added few prizes to their trophy room when he rejoined them in 1995 – and none during his controversial two-year stay peppered with "retirements."

Borussia Dortmund

Germany

Founded:
1909

Stadium:
Westfalenstadion (42,800)

Colours:
Yellow/black

League:
5

Cup:
2

World Club Cup:
1997

European Champions Cup:
1997

Cup-winners Cup:
1966

Borussia Dortmund hold a particular place in history as the first German club to have won a European trophy. That was in 1966, when they beat Liverpool 2–1 after extra time in the final of the Cup-winners Cup at Hampden Park, Glasgow. Pride in that achievement extended almost to superstition when the members of that team were flown by Dortmund to the away leg of their 1993 UEFA Cup semi-final against French club Auxerre. The lucky charms paid off again, with Dortmund losing 2-0 but winning the penalty shoot-out 6–5. The magic failed temporarily when they lost the final against Juventus but they had their revenge four years later – beating Juventus 3–1 in the Champions League Final, in Munich.

Serious Success

The foundations had been in preparation for several years. Evidence was available when Dortmund finished runners-up in 1992 then in January 1993, when they paid £3 million to bring home outstanding sweeper Matthias Sammer from Inter. Sammer, a former East German international, had been sold to Inter only the previous summer by Stuttgart. But he failed to adapt to football, life and the language in Italy and Dortmund's enterprise in bringing him home was rewarded with European and world club titles. Sammer himself was voted 1996 European Footballer of the Year. Dortmund's home, the Westfalenstadion, is one of the few modern German stadia which was created specifically for football. There is no athletics track surrounding the pitch and every survey among players finds Dortmund voted one of their favourite venues. Dortmund previously played in the 30,000-capacity Rote Erde stadium, part of a larger complex and which now sits in the shadow of the Westfalenstadion and is used for athletics and training. The new stadium was built for the 1974 World Cup Finals.

Celtic

Glasgow, Scotland

Founded:
1888

Stadium:
Celtic Park (51,709)

Colours:
Green and white hoops/white

League:
35

Cup:
30

European Champions Cup:
1967

Celtic and rivals Rangers are Scottish football's greatest clubs, but it was Celtic who first extended that hunger for success into Europe when, in 1967, they became the first British club to win the European Cup. It was a measure of the way they swept all before them that season that they won every domestic competition as well: the League, the Cup and League Cup.

No other team in Europe had, until then, ended the season with a 100 per cent record in four major competitions. In winning the European Cup, Celtic refuted accusations – mostly from England – that their Scottish honours owed more to a lack of solid opposition than their own abilities. Celtic's 1967 team was shrewdly put together by manager Jock Stein, a former Celtic player. As well as new Scottish stars, he included veterans such as goalkeeper Ronnie Simpson and scheming inside-left Bertie Auld. In the Lisbon final, they beat former holders Inter 2–1 with goals from full-back Gemmell and centre-forward Chalmers.

On Top of Europe

Sadly, Celtic's golden touch did not survive long. A few months later they were beaten by Kiev Dynamo at the start of their European Cup defence, and were then dragged down to defeat and fisticuffs in the infamous World Club Cup battle with Racing of Argentina.

In 1970, Celtic returned to the European Cup Final, only to lose to Feyenoord in Milan; and, two years later, they lost only on penalties after two goalless draws in the semi-finals against Inter. More trouble lay ahead as Celtic proved unable to match Rangers' commercial and playing achievements in the late 1980s and slipped to the brink of bankruptcy before turning the corner after a boardroom revolution.

The subsequent appointment as manager of Wim Jansen, a Dutch World Cup hero of the 1970s, brought the promise of better days ahead as Celtic desperately sought to end the domestic dominance of Rangers, who had triumphed in the Championship for nine successive seasons between 1989–97, thus equalling Celtic's record.

Feyenoord

Rotterdam, Holland

Founded:
1908

Stadium:
De Kuyp (52,000)

Colours:
Red and white halves/black

League:
13

Cup:
10

World Club Cup:
1970

European Champions Cup:
1970

UEFA Cup:
1974

Feyenoord were founded by mining entrepreneur C. R. J. Kieboom. Their star player in the successful pre-war years was left-half Puck Van Heel, who appeared in the final tournaments of the 1934 and 1938 World Cups and set what was for many years a Dutch record of 64 international appearances. The post-war period was bleak until after the introduction of professionalism in the late 1950s. Then, Feyenoord entered their most glorious domestic era, winning the League six times in 13 years. Indeed, their 1965 and 1969 titles were half of League and Cup doubles. Stars included goalkeeper Eddie Pieters-Graafland, a then record £20,000 signing from Ajax, half-backs Reinier Kreyermaat, Hans Kraay and Jan Klaasens and, above all, outside-left Coen Moulijn. He was still a key figure when they won the European Cup in 1970, along with Swedish striker Ove Kindvall and burly midfield general Wim Van Hanegem. Feyenoord's coach, for their extra time victory over Celtic in Milan, was Ernst Happel, the former Austrian international. Feyenoord – and not Ajax – were thus the first Dutch club to taste European success, and went on to beat Estudiantes de La Plata of Argentina in the World Club Cup Final.

Ups and Downs

In 1974 Feyenoord added the UEFA Cup to their trophy room. But they gradually lost their grip on the Dutch game. Key players were sold to balance the books, among them Ruud Gullit, who Feyenoord discovered at Haarlem. He was sold to PSV Eindhoven and later moved to Milan and Chelsea. Not until the arrival as general manager of Wim Jansen, a former Feyenoord favourite who starred with Holland at the 1974 World Cup, did Feyenoord regain the title in 1993. They appeared in the UEFA Champions League in 1997–98 but that was courtesy of a rule change to admit runners-up from Europe's top footballing leagues.

Flamengo

Rio de Janeiro, Brazil

Founded:
1895 as sailing club;
1911 as football club
Stadium:
Gavea (20,000) and
Maracana (130,000)
Colours:
Black and red hoops/white
Rio state league:
22
Brazil championship (incl. Torneo Rio-São Paulo):
5
World Club Cup:
1981
South American Club Cup:
1981

Flamengo are the most popular club in Brazil, having been formed by dissident members of the Fluminense club but under the umbrella of the Flamengo sailing club – which now boasts more than 70,000 members. They first competed in the Rio league in 1912, winning the title two years later. In 1915, they regained the crown without losing a game. A string of great names have graced the red-and-black hoops over the years, among them defenders Domingos Da Guia and centre-forward Leonidas da Silva. Known as the "Black Diamond", Leonidas played for Flamengo from 1936 to 1942, inspiring two state championship triumphs and earning a worldwide reputation through his brilliance in the 1938 World Cup finals.

On Top of the World

Flamengo ran up a Rio state hat-trick in the mid-1950s with their team nicknamed the "Steamroller", but had to wait until 1981 for their greatest success. Then, riding high on the goals of a new hero, Zico – the so-called "White Pele" – they won the South American and World Club Cups. The former campaign was one of the most hostile in memory. Flamengo won a first round play-off against Atletico Mineiro after their rival Brazilians had five players sent off, provoking referee José Roberto Wright to abandon the game. In the final, Flamengo beat Cobreloa of Chile in a play-off, in Uruguay, which saw the expulsion of five players. Fears about the outcome of Flamengo's world showdown against Liverpool proved unfounded. Zico was in a class of his own, creating all of Flamengo's goals in a 3–0 win. The players dedicated the success to the memory of Claudio Coutinho, a former coach who had died in a skin-diving accident. In the mid-1990s, Flamengo sought to revive the glory days by twice bringing World Cup-winning striker Romario home from Spain – first from Barcelona and then from Valencia.

Fluminense

Rio de Janeiro, Brazil

Founded:

1902

Stadium:

Laranjeira (20,000) and Maracana (130,000)

Colours:

Red, green and white stripes/white

Rio state league:

27

Brazil championship (incl. Torneo Rio-São Paulo):

4

Fluminense have yet to win an international trophy, but that does not alter their status as one of South America's great clubs. "Flu" were founded in 1902 by an Englishman named Arthur Cox, and many of their first players were British residents.

The club's wealth and upper-class clientele resulted in the nickname "Po de Arroz" ("Face Powder", after the fashion of the time at the turn of the century). Today, the club's fans wear white powder on their faces as a sign of loyalty.

In 1905, "Flu" were founder members of the Rio de Janeiro league and of the Brazilian confederation; they won the first four Rio (Carioca) championships in 1906–09; and, in 1932, they became the first Brazilian club to go professional.

Superteam

By this time the "Flu-Fla" derby (against Flamengo) had been flourishing for 20 years, the first meeting between the clubs having taken place in 1912. In 1963, their clash drew an official crowd of 177,656 to the Maracana stadium in Rio, which remains a world record for a club game.

By 1930, Flu's stadium was the home of the national team and the club had launched a weekly newspaper, among other schemes. A few years later and Flu were ruling the roost with five Rio titles between 1936 and 1941. Star players were forwards Romeu, Carreiro and Tim – who coached Peru at the 1978 World Cup Finals.

In the early 1950s, Fluminense's star was the World Cup winning midfield general Didi. In the late 1960s and early 1970s the key player was another World Cup winner, Brazil's 1970 captain and right-back, Carlos Alberto Torres. In the 1980s, the mantle of inspiration-in-chief passed to the Paraguayan Romerito (Julio César Romero).

Fluminense collected a hat-trick of Rio titles in 1983, 1984 and 1985 with Romero their guiding light. He was rewarded by being nominated South American Footballer of the Year in 1985 and later starred at the 1986 World Cup Finals in Mexico.

Independiente

Avellaneda, Argentina

Founded:
1904
Stadium:
Cordero (55,000)
Colours:
Red/blue
League:
11
World Club Cup:
1973, 1984
South American Club Cup:
1964, 1965, 1972, 1973, 1974, 1975, 1984
Inter-American Cup:
1973, 1974, 1976

Independiente are perhaps the least familiar of international club football's great achievers, outside Argentina at least. This is because, despite two lengthy periods of command in South American club football, they won the world title only twice in five attempts, and that at a time when the competition's image was tarnished.

Also, Independiente have always relied on team football rather than individual inspiration. One outstanding player who made his name with the club, however, was Raimundo Orsi. He was the left-winger who played for Argentina in the 1928 Olympics, signed for Juventus then scored Italy's vital equalizer on their way to victory over Czechoslovakia in the 1934 World Cup Final.

Later, the Independiente fans had the great Paraguayan centre-forward, Arsenio Erico, to idolize. Erico had been the boyhood hero of Alfredo Di Stefano and, in 1937, set an Argentine First Division goalscoring record of 37 in a season.

Red Devils

Independiente did not regain prominence until the early 1960s, when coach Manuel Giudice imported an Italian-style *catenaccio* defence which secured the South American Club Cup in 1964 and 1965. Independiente were the first Argentine team to win the continent's top club prize. But in the World Club Cup Final they fell both years to the high priests of *catenaccio*, Inter of Italy.

In the 1970s, Independiente's Red Devils won the South American Club Cup four times in a row and collected the World Club Cup. It was an odd victory: European champions Hamburg declined to compete, so runners-up Juventus took their place – on condition that the final was a one-off match in Italy. Independiente not only agreed, they won it with a single goal from midfield general Ricardo Bochini.

In the late 1990s, Independiente sought to battle back out of a spell in the doldrums by signing Cesar Luis Menotti, Argentina's chain-smoking World Cup-winning coach of 1978.

Internazionale

Milan, Italy

Founded:
1908

Stadium:
Meazza (85,443)

Colours:
Blue and black stripes/black

League:
13

Cup:
3

World Club Cup:
1964, 1965

European Champions Cup:
1964, 1965

UEFA Cup:
1991, 1994

Internazionale, known as Inter, were founded out of an argument within the Milan club in the early years of the century. Some 45 members, led by Giovanni Paramithiotti, broke away in protest at the authoritarian way the powerful Camperio brothers were running the club. In the 1930s, fascist laws forced Internazionale into a name change to rid the club of the foreign associations of their title. So they took the name of the city of Milan's patron saint and became Ambrosiana. Under this name they led the way in continental club competition – being one of the leading lights in the pre-war Mitropa Cup.

European World-beaters

After the war, the club reverted to the Inter name and pioneered a tactical revolution. First manager Alfredo Foni, who had been a World Cup-winning full-back before the war, won the League twice by withdrawing outside-right Gino Armani into midfield; then Helenio Herrera conquered Italy, Europe and the world with *catenaccio*. Keeper Giuliano Sarti, sweeper Armando Picchi and man-marking backs Tarcisio Burgnich, Aristide Guarneri and Giacinto Facchetti were the foundation on which Spanish general Luis Suarez built the counter-attacking raids carried out by Brazilian Jair da Costa and Italian Sandro Mazzola.

Inter won the European and World Club Cups in 1964 and 1965 – beating Real Madrid and Benfica in Europe, and Argentina's Independiente twice for the world crown. But in 1966, Real Madrid toppled Inter in the European Cup semi-finals, Celtic repeated the trick a year later in a memorable Lisbon final, and Herrera was lured to Roma. Only when West German Lothar Matthäus drove them to the 1989 League title, followed by success in the 1991 UEFA Cup, were Inter a force again.

Inter spent the following years in Milan's shadow, but returned to the limelight by paying £19.5 million in 1997 for Brazilian Ronaldo.

Juventus

Turin, Italy

Founded:
1897
Stadium:
Delle Alpi (71,012)
Colours:
Black and white stripes/white
League:
24
Cup:
10
World Club Cup:
1985, 1996
European Champions Cup:
1985, 1996
European Cup-Winners Cup:
1984
UEFA Cup:
1977, 1990, 1993
Super Cup:
1984, 1996

Juventus were founded by a group of Italian students who decided to adopt red as the colour for their shirts. In 1903, however, when the club was six years old, one of the committee members was so impressed on a trip to England by Notts County's black-and-white stripes that he bought a set of shirts to take home to Turin. In the 1930s Juventus laid the foundations for their legend, winning the Italian league championship five times in a row. Simultaneously they also reached the semi-finals of the Mitropa Cup on four occasions and supplied Italy's World Cup-winning teams with five players in 1934 and three in 1938. Goalkeeper Gianpiero Combi, from Juventus, was Italy's victorious captain in 1934, just as another Juventus goalkeeper, Dino Zoff (*see* page 162), would be in 1982.

Black and White

After the war, the Zebras (after the colours of their shirts) scoured the world for talent to match their import-led rivals. In 1971 they lost the Fairs Cup Final to Leeds on the away goals rule, but in 1977 they beat Bilbao in the UEFA Cup Final on the same regulation.

In 1982 no fewer than six Juventus players featured in Italy's World Cup winning line-up, and Cabrini, Tardelli, Scirea, Gentile and Paolo Rossi helped Juve win the 1984 European Cup-Winners Cup and the 1985 European Cup. Seeking new magic in the 1990s, Juventus paid huge fees for Roberto Baggio and Gianluca Vialli. Both shared in the 1995 league and cup double triumph but Baggio then left for Milan on the eve of a season which saw Vialli captain Juventus to victory in the European Champions Cup Final over Ajax in Rome. They were runaway favourites to retain the Cup the next year but surprisingly slipshod work in defence saw them lose to Borussia Dortmund in the final.

Kiev Dynamo

Ukraine

Founded:
1927

Stadium:
Republic (100,100)

Colours:
White/blue

League:
4 Ukraine, 13 Soviet

Cup:
2 Ukraine, 9 Soviet

European Cup-winners Cup:
1975, 1986

Super Cup:
1975

Kiev were founder members of the Soviet top division, yet had to wait until 1961 before they became the first club outside Moscow to land the title. They achieved the league and cup double five years later and went on to a record-equalling hat-trick of league titles. Midfielders Iosif Sabo and Viktor Serebryanikov were key men, as too were forwards Valeri Porkuyan and Anatoli Bishovets. Porkuyan starred at the 1966 World Cup finals in England, and Bishovets four years later in Mexico.

Soviets in Europe

In 1975 Kiev became the first Soviet team to win a European trophy when they beat Ferencváros of Hungary 3–0 in the Cup-Winners Cup. Later that year, they clinched the league title for the seventh time in 14 seasons. It was then the Soviet federation grew too demanding, saddling the Ukraine club en bloc with all the national team fixtures and, when the Olympic qualifying team began to falter, with their schedule too. It all proved too much. But that did not deter Kiev coach Valeri Lobanovsky from going back to square one and painstakingly developing another formidable team around record goal-scorer Oleg Blokhin.

In 1985, the renewed Kiev stormed to another league and cup double. A year later, Kiev charmed their way to the European Cup-Winners Cup, defeating Atlético Madrid 3–0 in the final.

Kiev were the richest and most powerful club in Ukraine on the collapse of the Soviet Union, but failed to carry that influence into Europe and were expelled from the 1995–96 Champions League after officials were accused of trying to bribe a referee.

A three-year ban was later quashed by UEFA and Kiev took their chance, restoring veteran coach Valeri Lobanovsky as team manager and bringing through talented new youngsters, headed by striker Andrei Shevchenko.

Liverpool

England

Founded:
1892
Stadium:
Anfield (41,000)
Colours:
All red
League:
18
FA Cup:
5
League Cup:
4
European Champions Cup:
1977, 1978, 1981, 1984
UEFA Cup:
1973, 1976
Super Cup:
1977

Liverpool: a name which says so much in pop music, in sport – specifically, in soccer. The Beatles may have split up and become part of the memorabilia of a major industrial centre, but the football club goes on, purveyor of dreams for the thousands who fill the seats and the millions on Merseyside who achieved international acclaim through their team.

For years, the proud boast of English football's hierarchy had been that such was the depth of talent, no one club could ever dominate the championship in the manner of Juventus in Italy, Real Madrid in Spain or Benfica in Portugal. Then, along came Bill Shankly. He was appointed manager of shabby, run-down, half-forgotten Liverpool in December, 1959. In two-and-a-half years he won promotion; the purchases of left-half Billy Stevenson and outside-left Peter Thompson, for a total of just £60,000, secured the Championship in 1964; and a year later they won the FA Cup. The next 20 years brought success on the greatest scale.

England's Most Successful Club

The secret was continuity. Shankly was succeeded by two of his former assistant coaches, Bob Paisley and Joe Fagan. A new player would be bought young and cheap, consigned to the reserves for a year to learn "the Liverpool way", then slotted in to replace one of the fading heroes.

Thus the generation of Emlyn Hughes, Ian St John, Roger Hunt and Ron Yeats gave way to the likes of Kevin Keegan and John Toshack, followed in turn by Alan Hansen, Kenny Dalglish and Graeme Souness, the last two of whom later took the manager's hotseat. Under Dalglish, Liverpool became only the third English club to achieve the League and Cup double this century in 1986 – a fine achievement tarnished by the disasters at Heysel in 1985 and Hillsborough four years later.

Manchester United

England

Founded:
1878

Stadium:
Old Trafford (55,000)

Colours:
Red/white

League:
11

FA Cup:
9

League Cup:
1

European Champions Cup:
1968

European Cup-Winners Cup:
1991

Super Cup:
1991

Manchester United were appropriate leaders of English re-entry into Europe in 1990, after the five-year Heysel disaster ban, since they had been the first English club to play in Europe in the mid-1950s when they reached the semi-finals of the European Cup in 1957 and 1958. On the latter occasion they lost to Milan with a somewhat makeshift side in the wake of the Munich air disaster in which eight players, including skipper Roger Byrne and the inspirational Duncan Edwards, died.

Rebuilding Complete

It took United 10 years to recover, in international terms. Thus it was in May 1968 that Busby's European quest was rewarded as United defeated Benfica 4–1 in extra time at Wembley. Bobby Charlton, a Munich survivor along with defender Bill Foulkes and Busby, scored twice to secure the club's most emotional triumph. Busby had been a Scotland international wing-half with Manchester City in the 1930s and took over United when war damage to Old Trafford meant playing home games at Maine Road.

Within three years, his side had beaten Blackpool in the 1948 FA Cup Final and created an entertaining, attacking style. In the 1960s, United boasted crowd-pullers such as Scotland's Denis Law and Northern Ireland's George Best. Later came England's long-serving skipper Bryan Robson, still there in 1993 when United, under Alex Ferguson, took the title for the first time in 26 years.

Robson left in 1994, when United became the fourth team this century to complete the double. They became the first club to repeat the feat in 1996, thanks to French genius Eric Cantona, wing wizard Ryan Giggs, Danish keeper Peter Schmeichel – and, above all, Ferguson's deft management.

Marseille

France

Founded:
1898

Stadium:
Vélodrome (46,000)

Colours:
All white

League:
9 (1993 title revoked)

Cup:
10

European Champions Cup:
1993

No French club had ever won the European Cup before Marseille; and no one will ever forget what happened when they did. Millionaire entrepreneur Bernard Tapie, the club's high-profile president, had invested millions of pounds in pursuit of European glory. Unfortunately, some of the money had been used to try to fix matches along the road – if not in Europe, then in the French championship.

Barely had Marseille finished celebrating their Cup-winning 1–0 victory over Milan, in Munich, in May 1993, than it emerged midfielder Jean-Jacques Eydelie had passed cash to three players from Valenciennes to "go easy" on Marseille in a League fixture a week earlier. Marseille were duly banned from their European defence in 1993–94, the French federation revoked their League title and they were subsequently penalised with enforced relegation. Bankruptcy, inevitably, followed but now they are once more challenging for the French title, led from the front by the enigmatic Italian striker Fabrizio Ravanelli.

Marseille's Rich Roots

Marseille's first championship had been celebrated back in 1929. Personalities in those days included Emmanuel Aznar (scorer of eight goals in a 20–2 league win over Avignon) and three English managers in Peter Farmer, Victor Gibson and Charlie Bell. After the war, Marseille collected the championship in 1948, but heavy expenditure on big-name foreigners such as Yugoslavia's Josip Skoblar, Swede Roger Magnusson and Brazil's Jairzinho and Paulo César drew only sporadic rewards, and Marseille had slipped into the Second Division by the time ambitious businessman-turned-politician Tapie took over the helm in 1985.

Marseille immediately gained promotion and then, thanks to the attacking genius of Jean-Pierre Papin and Chris Waddle, swept to four League titles in succession. They also suffered a penalty shoot-out defeat by Red Star Belgrade of Yugoslavia in one of the most disappointing European Cup finals of all time, in 1991.

AC Milan

Italy

Founded:
1899

Stadium:
Meazza (85,443)

Colours:
Red and black stripes/white

League:
15

Cup:
4

World Club Cup:
1969, 1989, 1990

European Champions Cup:
1963, 1969, 1989, 1990, 1994

European Cup-Winners Cup:
1968, 1973

Super Cup:
1989, 1990

AC Milan's domination of the European club game in the late 1980s and the early 1990s was achieved on a unique stage which would appear to represent the pattern of the future for a sport increasingly controlled by the intertwined commercial interests and demands of big business and television. In Milan's case, all these strands were in the hands of a puppet-master supreme in media magnate and then Prime Minister of Italy, Silvio Berlusconi. He had saved them from bankruptcy in 1986 by investing £20 million and turning Milan into a key player in his commercial empire. Milan had been one of the founders of the Italian championship back in 1898, but until the Second World War tended to be in the shadow of Inter.

Foreigners Help Out

After the war, Milan achieved spectacular success largely thanks to the Swedish inside-forward trio of Gunnar Gren, Gunnar Nordahl and Nils Liedholm. They also paid a then world record fee of £72,000 for Uruguay's Juan Schiaffino. They were dangerous rivals to Real Madrid in the new European Cup – losing narrowly to them in the 1956 semi-finals and only in extra time in the 1958 final. That was the year Milan's scouts first saw the teenage "Golden Boy" Gianni Rivera, whose inside-forward play and partnership with José Altafini inspired Milan to the 1963 European Cup triumph over Benfica. Rivera was Milan's figurehead as they won the European Cup again in 1969 and the Cup-Winners' Cup in 1968 and 1973.

But even his charisma could not save the club from the scandals and financial disasters inflicted by a string of presidents. That was where Berlusconi came in, providing the cash and the men – Dutchmen Ruud Gullit and Marco Van Basten, Liberian George Weah and Yugoslavia's Dejan Savicevic – and turned Milan into a millionaires' club.

Millonarios

Bogotá, Colombia

Founded:
1938

Stadium:
El Campin – Estadio Distrital Nemesio Camacho (57,000)

Colours:
Blue/white

League:
13

Millonarios remain a legendary name, if only because of the manner in which they led Colombia's fledgeling professional clubs into the El Dorado rebellion which lured star players from all over the world in the late 1940s and the early 1950s.

Many famous names in the game made their reputations there. The then club president, Alfonso Senior, later became president of the Colombian federation and a highly-respected FIFA delegate while star player Alfredo Di Stefano used Millonarios as a springboard to European greatness with Real Madrid.

Blue Ballet

Taking massive advantage of an Argentine players' strike, Millonarios led the flight from FIFA and the chase for great players – not only Di Stefano but the acrobatic goalkeeper Julio Cozzi, attacking centre-half Nestor Rossi and attacking general Adolfo Pedernera. Nicknamed the "Blue Ballet", they dominated the pirate league and, when an amnesty was negotiated with FIFA, made lucrative "farewell" tours in Europe.

Credit for the club's name goes to a journalist, Camacho Montayo. The club had been founded as an amateur side, Deportivo Municipal, in 1938. But as they pushed for a professional league, so Montayo wrote: "The Municipalistas have become the Millonarios." The name stuck. Millonarios remain a leading club but, despite appearing frequently in the South American Club Cup, the glory days have never been repeated in this corner of the Colombian capital.

Moscow Dynamo

Russia

Founded:
1923

Stadium:
Dynamo (51,000)

Colours:
White/blue

League:
11 Soviet

Cup:
6 Soviet

Dynamo are probably the most famous of all Russian clubs, having been the first Soviet side to venture out beyond the Iron Curtain in the 1940s and 1950s. Also, they were fortunate enough to possess, in goalkeeper Lev Yashin, one of the greatest personalities in the modern game – a show-stopper wherever he went.

East to West

Dynamo's origins go back to the beginning of soccer in Russia, introduced by the Charnock brothers at their cotton mills towards the end of the last century. The team won successive Moscow championships under the name Morozovsti and, following the Russian Revolution, were taken over first by the electrical trades union and then by the police. Thus the 1923 date marks the formal setting-up of Moscow Dynamo rather than the foundation of the original club.

Immediately after the end of the Second World War, Dynamo became a legend as a result of a four-match British tour in the winter of 1945. They drew 3–3 with Chelsea and 2–2 with Rangers, thrashed Cardiff 10–1 and beat a reinforced Arsenal 4–3 in thick fog. Inside-forward Constantin Beskov later became national manager, but it was goalkeeper Alexei "Tiger" Khomich whose reputation lasted long after he had retired to become a sports press photographer.

He was succeeded in the team by an even greater goalkeeper in Yashin, who was to become the first Soviet player to be nominated as European Footballer of the Year. Given Dynamo's leadership, it was appropriate that, in 1972, they became the first Soviet side to reach a European final. But their 3–2 defeat by Rangers in Barcelona also stands as the high point of their modern achievement. Back home, Dynamo were pushed back down the ranks by regular title winners and neighbours Moscow Spartak, and even their status as second club in the city has in recent seasons come under threat from Lokomotiv, Torpedo and CSKA.

Moscow Spartak

Russia

Founded:
1922

Stadium:
Olympic-Lenin/Luzhniki
(102,000)

Colours:
Red and white/white

League:
5 Russia; 12 Soviet

Cup:
10 Soviet

Spartak, champions of Russia for both the first two seasons after the collapse of the Soviet Union, face an enormous challenge in the years ahead. They were a power in the land under the old system, but those were the days when players were not allowed to move abroad. Now Spartak must maintain their domestic command and compete effectively in Europe in an "open" transfer society.

That will be all the more challenging because Spartak had, for years, represented the official Communist Party line. They play their home matches in what was previously known as the Lenin stadium in the Luzhniki suburb, and their former heroes included such officially-approved characters as the 1950s top scorer Nikita Simonian (a club record-holder with 133 goals) and left-half Igor Netto (another club record-holder with 367 appearances). Spartak's best season in European competitions was 1990–91, when they beat the Italians of Napoli and Spanish giants Real Madrid to reach the semi-finals of the European Cup, before falling 5–1 on aggregate to Marseille.

In With The New

For years, the club had been ruled by the most respected members of the managerial old guard in veteran administrator Nikolai Starostin and former national coach Constantin Beskov. Starostin, a Spartak player in the club's formative days, stayed on after the political upheaval, but Beskov handed over the coaching mantle to his former pupil and international full back, Oleg Romantsev.

Despite the loss of sweeper Vasili Kulkov and midfielders Igor Shalimov and Alexander Mostovoi, Romantsev kept Spartak on top of the table. The latest generation of heroes included left-back and skipper Viktor Onopko, versatile Igor Lediakhov and the young forward Mikhail Beschastnikh. Not only did Spartak mop up the 1992, 1993, 1994, 1996 and 1997 Russian League titles, they also won – in both 1993 and 1994 – the pre-season Commonwealth of Independent States Cup, contested by the champions of all the former Soviet states.

Nacional

Montevideo, Uruguay

Founded:
1899

Stadium:
Parque Central (20,000) and Centenario (73,609)

Colours:
White/blue

League:
36

World Club Cup:
1971, 1980, 1988

South American Club Cup:
1971, 1980, 1988

South American Recopa:
1988

Inter-American Cup:
1971

Nacional and Peñarol are the two great clubs of Uruguay and bitter rivals on the domestic and international stages. Nacional were formed from a merger of the Montevideo Football Club and the Uruguay Athletic Club, and in 1903 were chosen to line up as Uruguay's national team against Argentina in Buenos Aires. Nacional won 3–2 and have enjoyed the limelight ever since.

Peñarol won the first South American Club Cup in 1960, but Nacional soon set about catching up: runners-up three times in the 1960s, they first won the cup by defeating Estudiantes de La Plata in 1971. That led Nacional to the World Club Cup, where they beat Panathinaikos of Greece (European title-holders Ajax having refused to compete). The two decisive goals in Montevideo were scored by Nacional's former Argentine World Cup spearhead, Luis Artime. It was nine years before Nacional regained those crowns. They had a new centre-forward in Waldemar Victorino, who scored the only goal in the 1980 South American Club Cup triumph over Internacional of Brazil, and the lone strike which decided the world final against Nottingham Forest in Tokyo. By the time Nacional regained the crown in 1988, Victorino had left for Italy, just as so many Uruguayan stars before and since.

The Old Days

Back in the 1930s, Nacional sold centre-half Michele Andreolo to Italy, with which he won the 1938 World Cup. But Nacional quickly replaced him and, from 1939 to 1943, achieved what is nostalgically recalled as their Quinquenio de Oro: their golden five years. Nacional won the League in each of those seasons with a forward line built around the prolific Argentine marksman Atilio Garcia, who ended his career with 464 goals in 435 games. Under Scottish manager William Reasdale, Nacional also celebrated an 8–0 thrashing of the old enemy, Peñarol.

Peñarol

Montevideo, Uruguay

Founded:
1891
Stadium:
Las Acacias (15,000) and Centenario (73,609)
Colours:
Black and yellow stripes/black
League:
44
World Club Cup:
1961, 1966, 1982
South American Club Cup:
1960, 1961, 1966, 1982, 1987
Inter-American Cup:
1969

Peñarol were the first club to win the World Club Cup three times, but their success is no modern phenomenon. Peñarol have been the pre-eminent power in Uruguayan football since its earliest days, providing a host of outstanding players for Uruguay's 1930 and 1950 World Cup-winning teams.

Their own international awakening came in 1960, when Peñarol won the inaugural South American Club Cup (the Copa Libertadores). They were thrashed by the all-conquering Real Madrid in the World Club Cup, but made amends the following year with a victory over Benfica, the first team to break Real Madrid's domination of European club football. It was no less than the talents of players such as William Martinez, centre-half Nestor Goncalves and striker Alberto Spencer deserved.

World Club Champions

Peñarol regained the world club crown in 1966, at the expense of Real Madrid, and again in 1982 when they beat Aston Villa in Tokyo. By now, Peñarol had unearthed another superstar in centre-forward Fernando Morena. He was the latest in a long line of great players, which included the nucleus of the Uruguayan national team who shocked Brazil by winning the 1950 World Cup.

Goalkeeper Roque Maspoli – later World Club Cup-winning coach in 1966 – captain and centre-half Obdulio Varela, right-winger Alcide Ghiggia, centre-forward Oscar Miguez, right-half Rodriguez Andrade and inside-right Juan Schiaffino all came from Peñarol with Schiaffino going on to become one of the game's all-time greats.

Peñarol had been founded as the Central Uruguayan Railway Cricket Club in 1891, and changed their name in 1913 as the British influence waned. The railways sidings and offices were near the Italian Pignarolo district – named after the landowner Pedro Pignarolo – and so the Spanish style of the name was adopted for the club.

FC Porto

Oporto, Portugal

Founded:
1893

Stadium:
Das Antas (76,000)

Colours:
Blue and white stripes/white

League:
16

Cup:
11

World Club Cup:
1987

European Champions Cup:
1987

Super Cup:
1987

Porto were always considered to be number three in the Portuguese football hierarchy until their thrilling European Cup victory over Bayern Munich in Vienna, in 1987. Events then and since have ensured that, while their trophy count may not yet match those of Benfica and Sporting, Porto are clearly seen as an alternative centre of power in the domestic game.

Porto beat Bayern with the Polish goalkeeper Mlynarczyk, Brazilians Celso and Juary, and Algerian winger Rabah Madjer supporting Portugal's own wonderboy, Paulo Futre. But that was entirely appropriate since, in the early 1930s, Porto had been pioneers in the international transfer market.

Importers of Talent

They began by bringing in two Yugoslavs, and that ambition was reflected in Porto's initial championship successes in 1938 and 1939. In those days, Porto's home was the old, rundown Campo da Constituçião. Now, as befits a club with European Cup winning pedigree, home is the impressive 76,000-capacity Estádio das Antas.

Not only have Porto won the Champions Cup; they also finished runners-up to Juventus in the European Cup-Winners Cup in 1984. The creative force behind the club's progress in the 1980s was the late José Maria Pedroto. He led Porto to the cup in 1977 and league title in 1978 and 1979.

His work would be carried on by his pupil, former national team centre-forward Artur Jorge, who coached Porto to their 1987 European title and later took over the national side. Subsequently, under Brazilian Carlos Alberto da Silva, duly succeeded by Bobby Robson, Porto enhanced their standing as members of the European establishment when they reached the semi-finals of the Champions League in 1994 and the quarter-finals in 1997. Robson left Porto in 1996 after building a team which won a hat-trick of league titles.

PSV

Eindhoven, Holland

Founded:
1913
Stadium:
Philips (30,000)
Colours:
Red and white stripes/white
League:
14
Cup:
7
European Champions Cup:
1988
UEFA Cup:
1978

PSV equalled the achievements of Celtic (in 1967) and Ajax Amsterdam (in 1972) when they defeated Benfica in a penalty shoot-out to win the 1988 European Cup. Only those other two clubs had previously secured the treble of European Cup and domestic league and cup all in the same season. Remarkably, PSV achieved all they did despite having sold their finest player, Ruud Gullit, to Milan at the start of the season for a world record £5.7 million. The money was, however, invested wisely to secure the best players from Holland, Denmark and Belgium.

Such success was the reward for a long wait since PSV had been one of the invited entrants in the inaugural European Cup in 1955–56, when they crashed 1–0, 1–6 to Rapid Vienna in the first round. Surprisingly, considering PSV's position as the sports club of the giant Philips electronics corporation, they were long outshone by Ajax and Feyenoord. For years the Philips company took comparatively little interest in PSV, even though an estimated 40,000 of the 200,000 urban population of Eindhoven work directly or indirectly for the company. Only in the past decade have Philips become seriously involved with club policy and finance.

Advertising Deals

PSV had won the 1976 UEFA Cup without much fanfare. But 10 years later, realizing the potential to be reaped from soccer sponsorship, the company came up with the funds, and were duly rewarded two years later with the European Cup. In 1992, taking the process a stage further, the club changed its name in order to promote itself outside Holland as Philips SV (while domestic sponsorship regulations required it to stick with the PSV abbreviation in Holland).

Eindhoven finally broke Ajax's stranglehold on the Dutch league in 1997, falling just short of scoring 100 goals in their 34 games, but proved a huge disappointment in the following season's Champions League, going out at the group stage.

Rangers

Glasgow, Scotland

Founded:
1873

Stadium:
Ibrox Park (50,471)

Colours:
Blue/white

League:
47

Cup:
27

League cup:
19

European Cup-Winners Cup:
1972

Rangers are one half of the "Old Firm" – their rivalry with Celtic having dominated Scottish football for a century. Yet Rangers have never extended that power into Europe, their only prize from virtual non-stop international competition being the 1972 Cup-winners' Cup Final win over Moscow Dynamo. Not that Rangers' history is short on proud moments. One particularly glorious era was the 1920s, when Rangers' heroes included the legendary "Wee Blue Devil", Alan Morton.

Poor in Europe

In the 1960s, Rangers sustained some heavy European defeats at the hands of Eintracht Frankfurt, Tottenham and Real Madrid.

The start of the 1970s was a time of mixed emotions: 1971 brought the Ibrox disaster, when 66 fans died in a stairway crush at the end of a game against Celtic, which led to the introduction of the Safety of Sports Grounds Act in 1975. Then, a year later, Rangers' European Cup-winners' Cup triumph was immediately followed by a European ban because of the way their celebrating fans ran amok in Barcelona.

The upturn began in November 1985, when Lawrence Marlboro bought control of the club. He brought in the former tough-tackling Liverpool midfielder Graeme Souness as player-manager. In 1988, David Murray bought Rangers, and Souness revolutionized their image by buying 18 English players and smashing the club's traditional Protestants-only ethic with his £1.5 million capture of Catholic and one-time Celtic favourite Mo Johnston, a move which proved deeply unpopular with certain sections of supporters.

Subsequent big-name signings such as Dane Brian Laudrup and Paul Gascoigne enabled Rangers to maintain their league title dominance for a remarkable nine seasons in a row between 1989-97 – equalling Celtic's record. Striker Ally McCoist capitalized by smashing the club record of 233 goals set 60 years earlier by the legendary Bob McPhail.

Rapid

Vienna, Austria

Founded:
1873
Stadium:
Hanappi (19,600)
Colours:
Green and white/green
League:
29
Cup:
13

Rapid were founded as the 1st Arbeiter-Fussballklub (First Workers Football Club) but, on changing their name, also set about refining the short-passing style of the "Vienna School" to such good effect that they won the championship eight times between 1912 and 1923. The success story did not end there. In 1930, Rapid became the first Austrian club to win the Mitropa Cup, defeating powerful Sparta Prague 2–0, 2–3 in the final. Several of Rapid's key players were members of the "Wunderteam", the national side who finished fourth in the 1934 World Cup under the captaincy of Rapid centre-half Pepe Smistik.

Politics and Football

Four years later, Austria was swallowed up into Greater Germany, and the Austrian league was incorporated into the Greater German championship. To the mischievous delight of their fans, and no doubt much of the rest of Europe, Rapid not only won the German Cup in 1938 (3–2 against FSV Frankfurt in the final) but also the German championship in 1941.

On a day which has entered football folklore, Rapid hit back from three goals down to defeat an outstanding Schalke side 4–3 before a 90,000 crowd in the Olympic stadium in Berlin. Their hero was centre-forward Franz "Bimbo" Binder, whose hat-trick was crowned by the winning goal when he hammered a free-kick through the defensive wall. Binder ended a great career with an astounding 1,006 goals and later became club coach.

Many of Rapid's old heroes returned as coaches, among them Karl Rappan (who developed the Swiss Bolt system), Edi Fruhwirth and Karl Decker. Great players in the post-war years included wing-half Gerhard Hanappi – an architect by profession, who laid out the designs for the club's stadium, known locally as the Wiener – the tough defender Ernst Happel and another prolific goal-scoring centre-forward in Hans Krankl. He led Rapid's attack in 1985 in the first of their two defeats in the European Cup-Winners Cup Final, but had retired long before they fell to Paris Saint-Germain in the 1996 final.

Real Madrid

Spain

Founded:
1902

Stadium:
Santiago Bernabéu (105,000)

Colours:
All white

League:
28

Cup:
17

World Club Cup:
1966

European Champions Cup:
1956, 1957, 1958, 1959, 1960, 1966

UEFA Cup:
1985, 1986

What else is there left to say about Real Madrid? Six times champions of Europe, 28 times champions of Spain – both record achievements. They have also won the World Club Cup, two UEFA Cups and 16 Spanish cups, which add up to a football honours degree for the club founded by students as Madrid FC. (The Real prefix, or Royal, was bestowed on the club by King Alfonso XIII.)

Madrid were not only among the founders of the domestic competitions: it was also their president, Carlos Padros, who attended on Spain's behalf the inaugural meeting of FIFA in Paris in 1904. In the late 1920s, Real paid a then Spanish record fee of £2,000 for Ricardo Zamora, still revered as the greatest ever Spanish goalkeeper.

Rich History

The Civil War left Madrid's Chamartín stadium in ruins. At the time, the club had no money, but boasted one of the greatest visionaries in European football. He was Santiago Bernabéu, a lawyer who had been, in turn, player, team manager and secretary, and now club president. Bernabéu launched an audacious public appeal which raised the cash to build the wonderful stadium which now bears his name. The huge crowds who attended provided the cash to build the team who dominated the first five years of the European Cup. Argentine-born striker Alfredo Di Stefano was the star of stars, though Bernabéu surrounded him with colleagues such as Hungary's Ferenc Puskas, France's Ramond Kopa and Brazil's Didi. They set high standards for all who followed. Madrid won the European Cup again in 1966 and the UEFA Cup twice in the 1980s, but later stars such as Pirri, Santillana, Juanito, Hugo Sanchez, Emilio Butragueno and the latest hero, Raúl, would complain nothing they achieved would ever be enough. The 1960 team had been, if anything, too good.

Red Star Belgrade

Yugoslavia

Founded:
1945

Stadium:
Crvena Zvezda (Red Star) (97,422)

Colours:
Red and white stripes/white

League:
20

Cup:
15

World Club Cup:
1991

European Champions Cup:
1991

This may be the most schizophrenic club in the world. In Germany they are known as Roter Stern; in France as Etoile Rouge; in Spain as Estrella Roja; in Italy as Stella Rossa; in Serbo-Croat it's Fudbalski Klub Crvena Zvezda; in English, of course, Red Star Belgrade. Under whichever name, the 1991 European and world club champions stood revered as one of the pillars of the worldwide establishment until civil strife in the former Yugoslavia led to international suspension for both country and clubs. The consequences for Red Star were almost disastrous, since millions of pounds paid in transfer fees for their star players were suddenly frozen in banks around Europe.

Mass Exodus

But Red Star are no strangers to disaster, having been the last team to play Manchester United's "Busby Babes" before the Munich air crash. Red Star fought back from 3–0 down to draw 3–3, but lost on aggregate despite the efforts of balletic goalkeeper Vladimir Beara, gypsy midfielder Dragoslav Sekularac and dynamic striker Bora Kostic (scorer of a club record 157 goals in 256 league games). All three later moved abroad, members of an on-going exodus of more than 40 players including Dragan Dzajic (to Bastia), Dragan Stojkovic (to Marseille), Robert Prosinecki (to Real Madrid) and Darko Pancev (to Inter). This explains, perhaps, why Red Star, for all their talent, boast only one victory in the European Cup (the 1991 penalty shoot-out victory over Marseille in Bari) and one runners-up spot in the UEFA Cup (beaten on away goals by Borussia Mönchengladbach in 1979).

Red Star were formally set up by students of Belgrade University after the war. They play their home matches in the so-called "Marakana", the first stadium in eastern Europe to host a mainstream European final, when Ajax beat Juventus to claim the 1973 European Cup.

River Plate

Buenos Aires, Argentina

Founded:
1901

Stadium:
Antonio Liberti/Monumental (76,000)

Colours:
White with red sash/black

League:
26

World Club Cup:
1986

South American Club Cup:
1986, 1996

Inter-American Cup:
1986

River Plate are one of the two giants of Argentine football, Boca Juniors being the other. Traditionally the club from the rich side of Buenos Aires, River were founder members of the First Division in 1908, then took a leading role in the "war" which accompanied the introduction of professional football in the 1920s. Over the years River have fielded some wonderful teams. In the 1930s, they boasted Bernabe Ferreyra; in the late 1940s, their high-scoring forward line was so feared and admired they were nicknamed "La Maquina" (The Machine). The names of Mu–oz, Moreno, Peder-nera, Labruna and Loustau mean little outside Argentina today, but there they inspire awe as do the great Real Madrid side in Europe.

The greatest players

Later, River produced more great players: Alfredo Di Stefano, who would one day turn Real Madrid into possibly the greatest team of all time; Omar Sivori, who would form a wonderful partnership with John Charles after joining Juventus; and then 1978 World Cup winners Ubaldo Fillol, Daniel Passarella, Leopoldo Luque and Mario Kempes. In 1986, they were joined in River's Hall of Fame by the likes of goalkeeper Nery Pumpido, centre-back Oscar Ruggeri and schemer Norberto Alonso, after victory in the South American Club Cup provided River with formal confirmation of their lofty status. River really should have succeeded to the crown years earlier, but were unlucky runners-up in 1966 to Peñarol of Uruguay and in 1976 to Cruzeiro of Brazil. In 1986, they made no mistake, beating America of Colombia, then adding the World Club Cup by defeating Steaua of Romania 1–0 in Tokyo. One of their stars, midfielder Americo Gallego, was later one of a triumvirate of coaches who all guided River to league championships – the others being Daniel Passarella and Ramon Angel Diaz.

Santos

São Paulo, Brazil

Founded:
1912
Stadium:
Vila Belmiro (20,000)
Colours:
All white
São Paulo state league:
15
Brazil championship (incl. Torneo Rio-São Paulo):
5
World Club Cup:
1962, 1963
South American Club Cup:
1962, 1963

The name of Santos will always be synonymous with that of Pele, who played all his mainstream career with the club and returned as a director at the end of 1993 to try to help lift his old club out of the depths of a severe financial and administrative crisis.

Santos had been founded by three members of the Americano club, who stayed home in the port of Santos when their club moved to São Paulo. Santos joined the São Paulo state championship in 1916, became only the second Brazilian club to embrace professionalism in 1933, but did not hit the headlines until the mid-1950s. Then, to organize a host of talented youngsters, they signed the 1950 World Cup veteran, Jair da Rosa Pinto, and discovered the 15-year-old Pele.

Pele's Home

To say that Santos were a one-man team, as it often appeared from the publicity, would be unfair. Santos harvested millions of pounds from whistle-stop friendly match tours around the world and reinvested heavily in surrounding Pele with fine players: World Cup winners in goalkeeper Gilmar, centre-back Mauro and wing-half Zito; an outside-left with a ferocious shot in Pepe; and the precocious young talents of right-winger Dorval, schemer Mengalvio and centre-forward Coutinho, Pele's so-called "twin" with whom he established an almost telepathic relationship on the pitch. Santos were more than a football team; they were a touring circus.

The constant tours burned out many youngsters before they had a chance to establish themselves. But not before Santos scaled the competitive heights as Pele led them to the South American Club Cup and the World Club Cup in both 1962 and 1963.

Independiente beat Santos in the 1964 South American Club Cup semi-finals, and it was all over. Santos went on touring and raking in cash, capitalizing on Pele's name for as long as possible. Pele returned, briefly, as a director in the 1990s, but without inspiring the level sort of success in the 1960s.

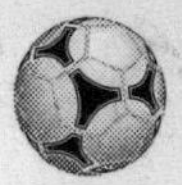

São Paulo

Brazil

Founded:
1935

Stadium:
Morumbi (150,000)

Colours:
White with a red and black hoop/white

São Paulo state league:
17

Brazil championship (incl. Torneo Rio-São Paulo):
4

World Club Cup:
1992, 1993

South American Club Cup:
1992, 1993

São Paulo's victories over Barcelona and Milan in the 1992 and 1993 World Club Cups in Tokyo left no doubt about which was the finest club side in the world – for all the European hype which had surrounded the Italian champions. Those victories also underlined the depth of talent at São Paulo, since key midfielder, Rai (younger brother of 1986 World Cup star Socrates), had gone to Paris Saint-Germain in 1993. They also enhanced the reputation of coach Tele Santana, Brazil's World Cup manager in 1982 and 1986, and one of the most eloquent and down-to-earth of football coaches.

São Paulo are, even so, comparative newcomers – founded in 1935, at a time when the likes of River Plate and Peñarol were already well-established powers in their own lands. The club was formed from a merger between CA Paulistano and AA Palmeiras. A leading light was Paulo Machado de Carvalho, who would later, as a senior administrator, contribute behind the scenes to Brazil's World Cup hat-trick.

Strong start

Within a decade of being founded, São Paulo developed into the strongest team in the country, winning the state title five times in the 1940s. They imported Argentine inside-forward Antonio Sastre, and the continuing pressure of success led to the construction of the 150,000-capacity Morumbi stadium – the world's largest club-owned sports arena.

In the 1960s, São Paulo had to take a back seat to Santos. In 1974, they reached their first South American Club Cup Final (losing to Argentina's Independiente), but it was not until the arrival of Santana, in the late 1980s, that São Paulo emerged from the doldrums. Despite the continuing sale of star players – key defender Ricardo Rocha went to Real Madrid – São Paulo secured three state league titles in four years, used the cash to strengthen their squad and were rewarded with those recent World Club titles – the first team to triumph in successive years.

Sparta Prague

Czech Republic

Founded:
1893

Stadium:
Letna (36,000)

Colours:
All red

League:
22

Cup:
9

Sparta are the most popular club in what is now the Czech Republic, as well as one of the oldest. They were founded as King's Vineyard in 1893, and took the name of Sparta, from one of the states of Ancient Greece, a year later.

They were one of Europe's great sides preceding the Second World War, winning the Mitropa Cup in the inaugural final in 1927 against Rapid Vienna. Victory over Ferençvaros of Hungary followed in 1935, and they were runners-up in 1936. Sparta's team then included the great inside-left, Oldrich Nejedly. He played a starring role in the 1934 World Cup, when Czechoslovakia finished runners-up. Again in 1962, when the Czechs next reached the World Cup Final, there were key places in the team for Sparta men such as right-winger Tomas Pospichal and schemer Andrzej Kvasnak.

All In The Name

Sparta suffered after the last war, and were forced to alter their name to Sparta Bratrstvi and then Spartak Sokolovo. But their loyal fans never called them anything but Sparta, and reality was recognized when the club's present title was adopted in 1965.

That same year they celebrated their first league title in more than a decade. Memories of the glory days of the Mitropa Cup were revived by the club's run to the European Cup-winners Cup semi-finals in 1973 and by the impressive 1983–84 UEFA Cup campaign, during which they scored notable victories over Real Madrid and Poland's Widzew Lodz.

Sparta's continuing domination of the domestic game in the early 1990s was remarkable because, immediately after the World Cup finals, they lost a string of senior internationals, such as goalkeeper Jan Stejskal, defenders Julius Bielik and Michal Bilek, midfield general Ivan Hasek and striker Tomas Skuhravy, the second-top scorer at Italia '90 with five goals. But they were unable to come to grips with Europe's best, eliminated from their group, which contained holders Borussia Dortmund in the 1997–98 Champions League.

Sporting Clube

Lisbon, Portugal

Founded:
1906

Stadium:
José Alvalade (70,000)

Colours:
Green and white hoops/white

League:
16

Cup:
16

European Cup-Winners Cup:
1964

Sporting Clube do Portugal last reached a European final back in 1964, when they won the Cup-winners Cup. Now Benfica's deadly rivals – the grounds are barely a mile apart – dream of the day when they can bring those old heroes out of retirement obscurity to celebrate a European revival. The late 1980s and early 1990s brought Sporting the worst era in their history, an empty decade following the heady 1981–82 season in which they won the league and cup double under Englishman Malcolm Allison.

In 1992 the new president, José Sousa Cintra, brought in ex-England manager Bobby Robson to try to recapture the Allison magic. Robson was given only 18 months, however, before former Portugal national coach Carlos Queiros, instead, was given the task of reviving the glories of the 1950s, when Sporting rivalled Benfica as the country's top club and took the championship seven times in eight years.

Single Trophy

En route to Sporting's sole European trophy, they beat APOEL Nicosia of Cyprus in the second round first leg by a European record 16–1. In the final against MTK Budapest, an entertaining match saw Sporting go 1–0 down, recover to lead 2–1 then go 3–2 behind before securing a 3–3 draw and a replay.

That took place in Antwerp where a single goal after 20 minutes from winger Morais, direct from a corner, was enough to win the cup. Their back four of Morais, Batista, José Carlos and Hilario starred in the Portugal team which finished third in the 1966 World Cup finals in England.

The nearest Sporting have since gone to European success was in 1990–91, when they reached the UEFA Cup semi-finals before falling 0–0, 0–2 to eventual winners Inter while in the Portuguese league, they have recently failed to make any impact on Porto, who have marched off with the title every season since the 1993-94 triumph under Bobby Robson.

Tottenham Hotspur

London, England

Founded:
1882

Stadium:
White Hart Lane (33,083)

Colours:
white/blue

League:
2

Cup:
8

Cup-winners Cup:
1963

UEFA Cup:
1972, 1984

Tottenham Hotspur are commonly considered one of the Big Five of English football but their achievements on the pitch in recent times hardly justify such status. Spurs do hold a place in British football history, however, having been the first English club in the 20th century to achieve the League and Cup double and follow up by becoming the first British club to win a European trophy. That was the European Cup-winners Cup, which Spurs won in 1963, thrashing holders Atlético Madrid 5–1 in the Feyenoord stadium in Rotterdam.

The Professionals

Spurs were founded by a group of ex-grammar school boys who called the club Hotspur. The "Tottenham" label was added some years later to avoid confusion with a Hotspur club in nearby Wood Green. Spurs adopted professionalism in 1895, moved to their present home in 1899, won the Southern League championship in 1900 and, a year later, became the only non-league team ever to have won the FA Cup since the inception of the Football League.

Remarkably, Tottenham were not voted into the League until 1908 as replacements in the old Second Division for Stoke City.

The post-war years saw Spurs in the Second Division but, under the management of Arthur Rowe, they staged a memorable revival. The so-called "push and run" team won promotion in 1950 and the club's first league title a year later. Rowe's traditions of simple, effective football were taken to new heights when one of his players, Bill Nicholson, managed the so-called "Glory, Glory" team of the early 1960s.

This was Tottenham's greatest era, inspired by the leadership example of wing-halves Danny Blanchflower and Dave Mackay. The team was enhanced by the signing in 1962 of goal-poacher supreme Jimmy Greaves – a deal which set a big-spending reputation maintained with later captures such as Martin Peters, Martin Chivers, Argentina's Osvaldo Ardiles and Ricardo Villa and German captain Jürgen Klinsmann.

Vasco Da Gama

Rio de Janeiro, Brazil

Founded:
1898 as sailing club, 1915 as football club

Stadium:
São Januario (50,000) and Maracana (130,000)

Colours:
All white with black sash

Rio state league:
17

Brazil championship (incl. Torneo Rio-São Paulo):
5

Like Flamengo, one of their long-time Rio de Janeiro rivals, Vasco grew from a sailing club – the impetus for football coming from former members of a club called Luzitania FC, who had been refused entry to the early Rio de Janeiro state championship because of their "Portuguese-only" policy. Transformed into Vasco da Gama, however, they were elected to the championship in 1915 and had progressed to the top flight by 1923. Support, both vocal and financial, has come to the club over the years from the city's Portuguese community. In spite of their original policies, Vasco quickly became noted for their inclusion of mixed-race players at a time, early in Brazilian football's development, when the game was riven by race and class divisions. Vasco led the way, too, by creating the São Januario stadium, which was the first national stadium in Brazil and hosted all major club and national team matches before the building of the Maracana in 1950.

Brazilian Skill Supply

In 1958 Vasco supplied Brazil's World Cup-winning team with centre-back Luiz Bellini, the captain, and centre-forward Vava. They earned a long-awaited consolation for events eight years earlier when no fewer than eight Vasco players had figured in the Brazilian squad which was pipped to the World Cup by Uruguay. In the 1960s and 1970s Vasco figured, as ever, among the most powerful of challengers to Fluminense and Flamengo.

Their 1997 national championship victory was remarkable in that both legs of the play-off final against Palmeiras ended in 0–0 draws. Vasco took the title thanks to a better record in tournament countback – and despite having seen star marksman Edmundo sent off no fewer than seven times during the year.

The Great Coaches

Managers and coaches are either hero or scapegoat: one thing or the other. There is no in-between. He is responsible for choosing the team to represent a club, a city or a country. As Brazil's World Cup boss Mario Zagallo once said: "In my country we have millions of national managers and every one thinks he can do the job better than me. Maybe he or she can. But I am the one whose opinion matters – for the moment."

In the early days of association football, teams were chosen by committee. Later came the secretary-manager who was the club's administrator – a role which also included picking the team. That was the system which served British football largely through to the 1930s. But it did not last as long abroad. The reason was simple. The English took association football around the world.

But the "new" countries needed to be taught the game and so the coach – the teacher, men such as the legendary Jimmy Hogan in Austria in the early decades of the 20th century – gained a greater power. He taught the game – the technique and the tactics – and therefore he assumed the right to pick the team. In England the manager remained encumbered by working the transfer market, negotiating employees' terms and a myriad of other responsibilities now largely devolved upon the shoulders of a chief executive or managing director. But in the rest of the world the division of responsibility was made much earlier. Each system produced great individuals: coaches who could teach their players new skills and systems… and then motivate them to national and then international pre-eminence.

Sir Matt Busby

Manchester United manager 1945–71

Born: May 26, 1909

Died: January 20, 1994

Busby was a Scotland wing-half who played pre-war for Liverpool for four years and Manchester City for six years. He also earned one cap for Scotland in 1933. He took over United in 1945 when air raid damage had reduced Old Trafford to near-rubble. Such was his gift for management that, within three years, he had created the first of three memorable teams. His 1948 side won the FA Cup, his Busby Babes of the mid-1950s went twice to the Champions Cup semi-finals before being wrecked by the Munich air disaster, and his third team completed the European quest with victory over Benfica in 1968. Busby's love of entertaining football inspired some of British football's greatest talents – from Johnny Carey to Duncan Edwards, from Bobby Charlton to Denis Law and George Best. He was appointed to the Manchester United board in 1971 and became club President in 1982. He will be remembered as one of the most successful managers that the English game has ever known.

Hitting the target

- Busby was a hero on both sides of Manchester – first as a player for City then as manager of United.
- Eight of the so-called "Busby Babes" were killed at Munich, and Busby himself was seriously injured in the air crash in February 1958.
- After retiring as manager, Busby remained at Old Trafford as a director of United until his death.

Josef 'Sepp' Herberger

Germany manager 1936–63

Born: March 28, 1897

Died: April 28, 1977

Herberger was the founder of a German management dynasty. As a player, he was an inside-forward who played three times for Germany between 1921 and 1925, and he became assistant national manager to Dr Otto Nerz in 1932 and then succeeded him after what was seen as a disastrous defeat by Norway at the 1936 pre-war Berlin Olympics. Herberger travelled widely to keep abreast of the world game and astutely managed his players and tactics to maximum effect, above all at the 1954 World Cup.

There he took the bold step of fielding his reserves for a first-round match against Hungary. He was unfazed by the 8–3 defeat, knowing that his fresh "first team" could still reach the later stages and go on, as they did, to beat the Hungarians in the final. The Hungarian team had previously beaten England 6–3 at Wembley and 7–1 in Budapest and were probably the hottest ever favourites to win the World Cup.

Hitting the target

- Herberger was the second of only six German national team managers in 70 years.
- He played his football in the 1920s for two clubs, Waldhof and Mannheim, who later merged to form the present Bundesliga club, Waldhof-Mannheim.
- Playing his part in Germany's football dynasty, Herberger handed over on his retirement to assistant Helmut Schön.

Helenio Herrera

Coach of Red Star Paris, Stade Francais (France), Atlético Madrid, Valladolid, Sevilla (Spain), Belenenses (Portugal), Barcelona (Spain), Internazionale and Roma (Italy); also Spanish and Italian national teams

Born: April 17, 1916

Died: November 9, 1997

Herrera was one of the world's most innovative and single-minded coaches. Born in Argentina, brought up in Morocco, Herrera was a player in France, experimented at Barcelona in the 1950s by using inside-forwards at wing-half to turn "easy" matches into goal sprees. His attacking tactics proved ineffective at Inter so Herrera developed, instead, the most ruthlessly disciplined *catenaccio*. Herrera demanded total obedience, insisting that his players place their hands on the ball and swear loyalty to each other before going out for a match. Stars who baulked at such rituals were sold, however popular or successful. This ruthless method of dealing with players obviously worked, because under Herrera, Inter won the World Club and Champions Cups twice each. Herrera's career went into decline after he moved to Roma.

Hitting the target

- Herrera started his playing career as centre-forward as a teenager in Morocco – but made the grade as a full-back in France.
- So demanding was Herrera as a coach that he was nicknamed "Slave Driver" by many of his players.
- Great players who fell out with Herrera included Hungary's Ladislav Kubala and the Italo-Argentinian Antonio Valentin Angelillo.

Hugo Meisl

Austria manager and general secretary 1906–37

Born: November 16, 1881

Died: February 17, 1937

Meisl was the errant son of a Viennese banking family who was too infatuated with football in Central Europe in the early years of the century to want to enter the business. Meisl was playing inside-forward for FK Austria when he met the English coach, Jimmy Hogan, whom he persuaded to come and work in Vienna. Later Meisl became involved with neighbours Admira and then became secretary of the Austrian federation. Simultaneously he was also national manager, and his partnership with Hogan led to the rise of the legendary Austrian "Wunderteam" of the 1920s and early 1930s. Amongst other feats, his team beat Scotland 5–0, Germany 6–0 and lost narrowly 4–3 to England at Wembley. Meisl, Vittorio Pozzo from Italy and Herbert Chapman from England were the three most dominant figures in pre-war football. Meisl is known as the 'Father of Austrian Football' and influential in the early days of FIFA, the game's administrative body.

Hitting the target

- Meisl's first involvement in football was arranging summer tours in Austria in the early 1900s by clubs such as Manchester United, Everton and Tottenham.
- FIFA Congress took place in Vienna in 1908 at Meisl's invitation to mark the 60th anniversary of Emperor Franz Josef.
- Meisl sold Austria's star goalkeeper, Rudi Hiden, to Arsenal in 1930... but he could not get a work permit.

Marinus 'Rinus' Michels

Coach of Ajax Amsterdam (Holland), Barcelona (Spain), Los Angeles Aztecs (USA), Bayer Leverkusen (Germany); also Holland national team

Born: February 9, 1928

Michels, a Dutch international centre-forward in the early 1950s, led a revolution in the late 1960s when he developed the "total football" philosophy at Ajax. Much of Michels's coaching career linked with the presence, as leader on the pitch, of Johan Cruyff. Michels went to Barcelona after winning the Champions Cup with Ajax in 1971, went back to Ajax to sign Cruyff, and the pair were partners again when Holland finished runners-up at the 1974 World Cup. "Iron Rinus" was never afraid to take tactical risks, such as when he guided Holland to European Championship success in 1988 by using Ruud Gullit as a static, right-side attacker. Nor was Michels ever afraid of stating his opinions, however blunt.

Hitting the target

- In 1969, under Michels' management, Ajax became the first Dutch team to reach the Champions Cup Final.
- Michels had two spells in charge at Barcelona, but the nearest he got to winning the Champions Cup was the semi-finals in 1975.
- In the 1980s Michels was granted a special permit to coach in the Bundesliga because of his international record – even though he did not hold the German coaching certificate.

Vittorio Pozzo

Italy Manager 1932–48

Born: March 12, 1885

Died: December 21, 1968

Pozzo was a giant figure in Italian football history. He "found" football when he came to England as a student before the First World War. His admiration for Manchester United, their centre-half Charlie Roberts and football in general led to his refusing family orders to come home until he was sent a return ticket. In 1912 Pozzo managed Italy's team at the Olympic Games in Stockholm, where he met Hugo Meisl. He later became an admirer of Herbert Chapman. At club level Pozzo was long associated with Torino and he was manager, director and psychologist of the Italian team which won the World Cup in 1934 and 1938 and the Olympic Games tournament in 1936.

Hitting the target

- Under Pozzo, Italy lost only seven matches during the 1930s.
- Legend has it that before the 1938 World Cup Final against Hungary, the players received a telegram from fascist dictator Benito Mussolini, warning them: "Win or die!"
- Of the 1938 World Cup winners, Pozzo had retained only inside forward Meazza and Ferrari from the triumphant 1934 team.

Sir Alf Ramsey

England manager 1963–74

Born: January 22, 1920

Ramsey earned a knighthood for managing England to World Cup victory over West Germany at Wembley in 1966, the peak of a double international career as both player and administrator. As a player, Ramsey was a creative and intelligent right-back with Southampton and Tottenham and an integral member of Spurs' push-and-run team which won the Second and First Division titles in successive seasons in 1950 and 1951. He joined the side in May 1949. He was a regular choice in the same position for the English national team as well. On retiring in 1955, Ramsey became manager of Ipswich and his success in taking the East Anglian club from the Third Division to the First Division title in just seven years earned his appointment in 1963 as England's first "proper" manager with sole responsibility for team selection. He was England's most successful manager – his team famously won the World Cup in 1966 and lost only 17 matches of the 113 he was in charge for. He was dismissed after the World Cup qualifying failure against Poland in 1974. He returned to management briefly with Birmingham City in the late seventies.

Hitting the target

- Ramsey was at right–back when Hungary became the first foreign side to beat England at Wembley. The Hungarians humiliated England 6–3.
- One of Ramsey's Ipswich successors, Bobby Robson, also followed him as an England manager.
- Ramsey later had a brief spell back in management – as caretaker boss of Birmingham City.

Tele Santana

Coach of Atletico Mineiro, Gremio, Flamengo, Fluminense, Palmeiras (Brazil), Al Ahly (Saudi Arabia), Sao Paulo FC (Brazil); also Brazil national team

Born: July 25, 1933

Santana was an outside-right with South American club side Fluminense in the early 1950s but never good enough to challenge Julinho or Garrincha in Brazil's World Cup teams. Instead, he reached the World Cup finals in both 1982 and 1986 as manager of Brazil. Santana's insistence on attacking football was criticised as naive after Brazil's failures in, respectively, the second round and quarter-finals. But Santana had the last laugh when he won the World Club Cup twice as boss of São Paulo in 1992 and 1993. Simultaneously, Santana was not afraid to pinpoint high levels of corruption in the Brazilian game as well as poor refereeing for the failure to regain World Cup supremacy in the 1980s and early 1990s.

Hitting the target

- Santana once played at West Ham – for Fluminense in a friendly in 1952.
- Attacking brothers Socrates and Rai both owed promotion to stardom to Santana – Socrates with Brazil, Rai with São Paulo.
- Santana became, in 1980, Brazil's first full-time manager; previous bosses had also held club jobs simultaneously.

Helmut Schön

West Germany manager 1963–78

Born: September 15, 1915

Died: February 23, 1996

Schön scored 17 goals in 16 internationals for Germany between 1937 and 1941 when he was a star inside-forward with the famous Dresden SC. After the war he played on in Berlin for a while and then stepped up to become national coach to the briefly independent federation of the Saar. In 1955 Schön was appointed number two to Sepp Herberger as manager of West Germany and succeeded him, with enormous success, in 1963. Schön took West Germany to the World Cup runners-up spot in 1966 (losing to England at Wembley), third place in 1970 (West Germany lost to Italy after taking the game to gripping extra time) and finally to victory in 1974 (Johan Cruyff's Holland were unable to win, despite being favourites with their 'Total Football' playing style). Under Schön, Germany were also European Champions in 1972 (beating the Soviet Union 3–0 in the final) and runners-up in 1976 (losing only to Czechoslovakia in a penalty shoot-out after extra time.)

Hitting the target

- Schön lost potentially the best years of his playing career during the Second World War.
- Away from football Schön was never happier than living a quiet family life – and walking his beloved dogs.
- Just as Schön took over from Herberger, so he handed over in due course to his own assistant, Jupp Derwall.

Gustav Sebes

Hungary manager 1949–56

Born: June 21, 1906

Died: January 30, 1986

Sebes was a successful player in the 1920s with Vasas and MTK Budapest, but is best-known for the creation of the "Magic Magyars" of the late 1940s and 1950s. The Communist take-over allowed the Hungarian federation to transfer Hungary's top players into the two top clubs, Honved and Red Banner (formerly MTK), and Sebes fused their talents for the national team, built around the tactic of the withdrawn centre-forward. Hungary won the 1952 Olympic title but lost the 1954 World Cup Final, against all the odds, to West Germany. Sebes resigned following the loss of many star players who fled abroad after the 1956 Revolution.

Hitting the target

- Sebes played as a wing-half in the 1920s in both Hungary and France.
- He won only one cap himself for Hungary – in a 3–2 win over Germany in Budapest in 1936.
- In the late 1950s Sebes became a vice-president of newly-formed European confederation, UEFA.
- Honved were considered to be the best club side in Europe, if not the world, in the 1940s

Bill Shankly

Manager of Carlisle, Grimsby, Workington, Huddersfield and Liverpool

Born: September 2, 1913

Died: September 29, 1981

Shankly played for Carlisle and then Preston North End in 1933. He won an FA Cup with them in 1938 and played for Scotland five times in the 1938–39 season. He returned to Carlisle in the late 1940s, after the Second World War, to begin his managerial career. After brief spells at Grimsby, Workington and Huddersfield, he took over a faded Liverpool in the Second Division in December 1959, and there was no stopping either him or the club once promotion had been achieved in 1962. Shankly's dry humour struck a chord with Anfield fans. He brought them the League, FA Cup and League championship again in successive seasons, signed some of the club's greatest servants and laid foundations for further success both on and off the pitch. "His" Liverpool also won the UEFA Cup in 1974, and the year after he was awarded an OBE. Shankly had an eye for youthful talent – which he squirrelled away in the reserves until they were ready – and for managerial expertise. Successive managers Bob Paisley and Joe Fagan came out of Shankly's fabled "boot room."

Hitting the target

- Shankly played in two FA Cup Finals himself – for Preston in 1937 and 1938, collecting a winners' medal in the latter.
- The most famous protégé from Shankly's time at Huddersfield was a great fellow Scot, Denis Law.
- Shankly was famous for one-liners such as the reputed: "Some people say football is a matter of life and death. They're wrong. It's more important than that."

Giovanni Trapattoni

Coach of Milan, Juventus, Internazionale, Bayern Munich, Cagliari and Bayern Munich

Born: March 17, 1939

Trapattoni was a wing-half in the late 1950s and early 1960s whose sure tackling and football brain earned him a reputation as the only man who could play Pele out of a game by fair means rather than foul. After winning two Champions Cups with club side Milan, Trapattoni retired to a post on the youth coaching staff. In time he became first-team caretaker before moving to Juventus with whom he became the most successful club coach of all time. Inside eight years, Trapattoni guided Juve to the World Club Cup, Champions Cup, European Cup-Winners Cup, UEFA Cup, European Super Cup, seven Italian championships and two national cups. Late in his career he took a major gamble by moving to Bayern Munich in Germany and was quickly rewarded with league title success in 1997.

Hitting the target

- Trapattoni won the European Champions Cup with Milan in 1963 and 1969.
- Trapattoni's collection of 14 major honours at Juventus is a record for an Italian manager.
- Franz Beckenbauer appointed him at Bayern Munich because "German footballers need to improve their defensive skills."

The Great Players

Football is a team game, but if that were the beginning and end of it then few people would cross the street to watch. It's the great players – the individuals with crowd-pleasing flair, style and personality – who provide the addictive allure which draws fans back, week in, week out. But all the great players down the years have been so different.

South America has produced players with a unique explosive talent – the likes of Brazil's Pele and Argentina's Diego Maradona. Europe, by contrast, has boasted players with a professional consistency of high standard such as Ferenc Puskas and Franz Beckenbauer. A majority of the greatest players have honed their skills by moving around the world – leaving their home country for the technical challenge offered abroad. Many more export players have failed than have succeeded, whether in Italy, Spain or England. But the greatest players have imposed themselves across all borders, styles and competitions.

Down the years the game has changed. As Franz Beckenbauer once said: "In the old days a player had time to stop a ball, look around, decide what to do and then do it. Nowadays the ball arrives just a split second ahead of two opponents determined to stop you playing." But Beckenbauer, like all the superstars, believes that great ability will always triumph. Thus the great players of yesteryear would be great today, given all the advantages of the modern game's physical conditioning. Just as well for the World Cup, however, that they have been spread out down the years.

Osvaldo Ardiles

1952 Born on August 3 in Cordoba.

1969 Turned professional with Huracan of Buenos Aires.

1978 Key midfielder in Argentina's World Cup-winning side who beat Holland 3–1 in a passionate final under the management of Cesar Luis Menotti. Then transferred, sensationally, to Tottenham Hotspur (*see* page 70) for £300,000 in July of that year – along with Argentina team-mate Ricardo Villa.

1981 Ardiles achieved career ambition of winning the FA Cup, as Tottenham beat Manchester City 3–2 in a replay after the original match had ended all-square at 1–1.

1982 Ardiles returned to South America as a dispute over the Falkland Islands between Britain and Argentina escalated into full-scale war. By doing so he was denied the opportunity to win a second consecutive FA Cup winners' medal as Spurs beat QPR.

1982 Ardiles played in his second World Cup but Argentina failed to make the semi-finals. After a short and unhappy spell in France, he returned to Tottenham in December.

1983 A broken shin in only his fourth game back ruled him out for 10 months.

1984 Won the UEFA Cup with Tottenham in a thrilling penalty shoot-out victory over Belgian club Anderlecht.

1987 Made up for the disappointment of 1982 by appearing in the 1987 FA Cup Final against Coventry City. For the first time in their history, Tottenham lost in an FA Cup Final.

1988 Following Terry Venables' arrival as manager at White Hart Lane, Ardiles was loaned to Blackburn in March before joining QPR on a free transfer in the summer.

1989 Became manager of Swindon Town.

1991 Took over the manager's chair at Newcastle United.

1993 Returned to Tottenham as manager under the chairmanship of Alan Sugar in succession to Terry Venables.

1994 Sacked as Tottenham manager and went to work in Mexico.

Roberto Baggio

1967 Born on February 18 in Caldogno.

1983 Made his league debut with local club Vicenza in the Italian third division aged only 15.

1985 Transferred to Fiorentina.

1988 Makes his international debut for Italy.

1989 In his fifth and final season at the club, Baggio scored 17 goals in 32 league games and led Fiorentina to the semi-finals of the UEFA Cup where they lost to Juventus.

1990 Was sold by Fiorentina, despite three days of fans' protests on the streets of Florence that needed the intervention of riot police, to Juventus for a world record £8 million. Helped justify his fee with a marvellous solo goal against Czechoslovakia in the World Cup finals in 1990.

1991 In a match against Fiorentina, Baggio was substituted after he refused to take a penalty against his old club. He left the pitch wearing a Fiorentina scarf.

1993 Won the UEFA Cup with Juventus, topped a century of Italian league goals and was voted FIFA World Footballer of the Year and European Footballer of the Year.

1994 Played a starring role as Italy progressed to their first World Cup Final appearance since 1982. He scored the 88th minute equalizer that saved Italy from humiliation against Nigeria in the Second Phase, then scored the winner from the penalty spot. In an absorbing semi-final with Bulgaria, Baggio scores another brace to take them through to the final and a clash with Brazil. The match fails to live up to expectations and, for the first time in World Cup history, the final is decided by a penalty shoot-out. Baggio misses the decisive kick and Brazil are crowned champions.

1995 Won the Italian league with Juventus – then transferred to Milan after failing to agree terms for a new contract.

1996 Won the Italian league with Milan, only the third player in Italian history to win the championship with different clubs in successive seasons.

1997 Failed to impress with Milan and transferred to Bologna.

Gordon Banks

1937 Born on December 20 in Sheffield.

1955 Turned professional with Chesterfield.

1959 Transferred to Leicester City.

1961 FA Cup runner-up against Tottenham's double-winning side.

1963 Experienced an unhappy afternoon in his second FA Cup appearance as Manchester United beat Leicester 3–1. Banks is held responsible for two of the United goals.

1963 Made his England debut against Scotland in rather inauspicious circumstances as the Scots win 2–1 at Wembley, their first victory in London for 12 years.

1964 A winner at last with Leicester as they beat Banks' future club Stoke City 4–3 on aggregate in the League Cup Final.

1966 Member of the England team which won the World Cup beating West Germany 4–2 in a thrilling final. In the semi-final against Portugal, the great Eusebio scored from the penalty spot to bring to an end Banks' record of seven consecutive clean sheets.

1967 Sold to Stoke City for a British goalkeeping record fee of £65,000.

1970 Illness caused Banks to miss, crucially, England's 3–2 World Cup quarter-final defeat by West Germany in Leon, Mexico. His absence encouraged the Germans who fought back from 2–0 down to win through to the semi-final. In a group match against Brazil, Banks made what many still believe to be the greatest save the world has ever seen. A Pele header was destined for the bottom corner, but as the great man wheeled away to celebrate, Banks somehow manged to turn it round the corner.

1970 Awarded the MBE for services to football.

1972 Won the prestigious Footballer of the Year award and the League Cup with Stoke.

1972 Won his 73rd and last cap in the 1–0 defeat of Scotland. Despite his advanced age of 34, Banks had just signed a new six-year contract with Stoke when he was involved in a serious car accident and lost the sight of one eye. Although his international career was over he did continue to play in the short-lived North American Soccer League.

Francesco 'Franco' Baresi

1960 Born on May 8 in Taravagliato.

1974 Along with his elder brother Giuseppe, Baresi attended trials with Internazionale in Milan. Big brother is accepted, but Baresi junior was rejected as being too frail. A week later he joined AC Milan.

1977 Turned professional with Milan, to whom he stayed loyal for the rest of his career. Was then an attacking midfielder but was soon switched to sweeper with considerable success.

1978 Made his league debut still aged only 18.

1979 Installed as first-choice sweeper and played a large part in helping AC win the Italian Championship.

1980 Personal and team fortunes took a dive when Baresi suffered from a blood disorder and Milan were relegated to the Second Division following a betting scandal.

1982 Member of Italy's World Cup-winning squad in Spain, though he did not play in any of their matches in the finals. Made his national team debut in a 0–0 draw against Romania in Florence.

1988 Won the Italian league with Milan – the first of his five national championships.

1989 Won the European Champions Cup and the World Club title, the start of Milan's nine international club honours in the Sacchi–Capello era.

1990 Steered Milan to their second consecutive "double" – a Champions Cup triumph against Benfica and a 3–0 thrashing of Olimpia in the World Club Championship.

1990 Cornerstone of the Italian national side who beat England 2–1 in the Third Place Play-off at the World Cup finals in Italy.

1994 Suspension ruled him out of Milan's magnificent Champions Cup Final victory against Barcelona.

1994 World Cup runner-up as sweeper in the Italian side beaten on penalties by Brazil.

1997 Retired after 20 years with the one club.

Franz Beckenbauer

1945 Born on September 11 in Munich.

1955 Began playing for the schoolboy team, FC 1906 Munich.

1959 Joined Bayern Munich youth section.

1962 Gave up a job as a trainee insurance salesman to sign full-time with Bayern.

1964 Made his Bayern debut in a 4–0 win away to St Pauli in Hamburg.

1965 Made his national team debut in a 2–1 World Cup qualifying win in Sweden.

1966 Starred in midfield, on the losing side, for West Germany in the 4–2 World Cup Final defeat by England at Wembley.

1967 Captained Bayern Munich (*see* page 38), from sweeper, to victory over Rangers in the European Cup-Winners' Cup Final.

1970 Took part in his second World Cup tournament, and scored the goal that sparked the German revival against England in the quarter-final. They lost to Italy in the semis.

1972 Captained West Germany to European Championship victory over the Soviet Union in Brussels. Won the European Footballer of the Year award.

1974 Captained Bayern Munich to victory in the European Cup Final and then West Germany to victory in the World Cup Final against Holland.

1976 Collected his second European Footballer of the Year award.

1976 Completed a record 103 appearances for West Germany before transferring to the New York Cosmos in the North American Soccer League. During his time in the USA, Beckenbauer won the NASL Soccer Bowl in 1977, 1978 and 1980.

1984 Appointed national manager of West Germany in succession to Jupp Derwall.

1986 Guided an average side to the World Cup Final, where they lost 3–2 to Argentina.

1990 Became the first man to captain and then manage a World Cup-winning team when West Germany beat Argentina 1–0 in Rome.

1993 After a short spell as coach of Olympique Marseille, returned to Bayern as executive vice-president.

1994 Took over as coach and guided Bayern to the league title.

Dennis Bergkamp

1969 Born on May 10 in Amsterdam. He was named after his father's favourite footballer, Scotland star Denis Law. His name had two 'Ns' because the registrar said 'Denis' was too much like the girl's name 'Denise'.

1984 Hailed by the Dutch media as a star of the future after outstanding displays in the Ajax youth squad.

1986 Promoted to the Ajax first team at 17 and praised as either a "new Cruyff" or a "new Van Basten."

1987 Appeared as substitute as Ajax beat Lokomotiv Leipzig 1–0 in Athens to win the European Cup-Winners Cup under the management of Cruyff.

1992 Leading role as Ajax won the UEFA Cup, defeating Torino of Italy on the away goals rule in the final. Then starred for Holland at the European Championship finals in Sweden, despite the semi-final upset by Denmark.

1993 Transferred to Internazionale of Italy who beat off competition from Barcelona and Juventus. In 103 matches for Ajax he had scored 103 goals.

1994 Found a new role with Holland at the World Cup finals in the United States, playing behind the main striker – turned on a match-winning performance against the Irish Republic.

1995 Could not adjust to life or lifestyle in Italy. Having scored only 11 goals in 52 matches he was sold by Inter to English giants Arsenal (*see* page 34) for a club record £7.5 million in the summer.

1996–97 Helped Arsenal to third in the English Premiership with a total of 12 goals.

1997 Scored a hat-trick against Wales in a World Cup Qualifier – Holland qualified at the top of their group. Bergkamp closed in on the Dutch all-time national scoring record held by 1970s star Johan Neeskens.

1997 Started the 1997–98 season in outstanding form for Arsenal and became the first player ever to win the top three goals in the BBC's *Match of the Day* 'Goal of the Month' competition.

George Best

1946 Born on May 22 in Northern Ireland.

1961 Joined Manchester United as an amateur, aged 15.

1963 Signed as a professional for Manchester United (*see* page 51) on his 17th birthday and made his Football League debut in a 1–0 win over West Bromwich Albion at Old Trafford in September.

1964 Made his debut for Northern Ireland in a 3–2 win over Wales at Swansea.

1965 Won his first league championship.

1966 Scored two majestic goals in what was perhaps the greatest match of his career, a 5–1 win away to Benfica in the Champions Cup quarter-finals. After his display, the Portuguese nicknamed him "El Beatle", a tribute to British soccer's first superstar.

1967 Scored twice in Manchester United's 4–1 victory over Benfica in the European Champions Cup Final at Wembley.

1968 Voted domestic Footballer of the Year and then European Footballer of the Year.

1970 Suspended for four weeks and fined £100 for bringing the game into disrepute after knocking the ball out of referee Jack Taylor's hands following the Manchester City vs. United League Cup semi-final… then marked his first game after suspension by scoring six times in United's 8–2 win over Northampton Town in the FA Cup fifth round.

1972 Announced he was quitting the game a week after he'd failed to show for a Northern Ireland match. He flew off to Spain for a holiday.

1974 Made his last appearance for United in a 3–0 defeat by Queens Park Rangers after a succession of retirements and comebacks.

1976 Scored within 71 seconds of his debut for Fulham. A month later he became one of the first players to be shown a red card – a recent introduction into the English league – for using foul language.

1978 Won the last of his 37 international caps against Holland. After his spell at Fulham, Best moved to Hibernian in Scotland and finished his career with the Tampa Bay Rowdies in the ill-fated NASL.

Danny Blanchflower

1926 Born on February 10 in Belfast.

1945 Joined Irish side Glentoran who were managed at the time by former Spurs player Frank Grice. He played once for Swindon Town during the war years.

1949 Transferred to English football with Barnsley for £6,500, later moving on to Aston Villa in 1951.

1949 Made his international debut against Scotland in October.

1954 Transferred to Tottenham Hotspur (*see* page 70) for £30,000.

1955 Played for Great Britain in a match against a Europe XI.

1957 Captained Northern Ireland to their shock, first-ever victory over England at Wembley.

1958 Blanchflower's year started disastrously when brother Jackie was badly injured in Manchester United's Munich air crash. Despite the absence of his brother from the team, Danny led Northern Ireland to the quarter-finals of the World Cup.

1958 Won the coveted Footballer of the Year award.

1961 Inspirational captain and right-half of Tottenham Hotspur's League and FA Cup double-winning side – the first club to achieve the double in the 20th century. Won his second Footballer of the Year award.

1962 Captained Spurs to victory in the 3–1 FA Cup win against Burnley.

1963 Captain of Tottenham as they became the first British side to win a European club trophy, beating Atlético Madrid 5–1 in the Cup-Winners Cup Final in Rotterdam.

1963 Won the last of his 63 Northern Irish caps against Poland.

1964 Troubled by a knee injury, Blanchflower retired from playing in June.

1965 Adapted to life after Spurs by becoming a successful and much-respected football journalist.

1978 Became manager of Chelsea in December but left the following year.

1993 Died in London in December aged 67.

Billy Bremner

1942 Born on December 9 in Stirling.

1960 Made his debut for Leeds United as a right-winger aged only 17. One of his team-mates was Don Revie, a man nearly twice his age and who would later become Bremner's manager at Leeds.

1965 Won the first of his 54 caps for Scotland in a 0–0 draw with Spain at Hampden Park.

1965 Scored Leeds' only goal as they went down 2–1 to Liverpool in the FA Cup Final.

1967 Tasted defeat again as Leeds lost 2–0 on aggregate to Dinamo Zagreb in the final of the Inter-Cities Fairs Cup.

1968 After 50 years of famine, Leeds won two trophies within six months. Arsenal were beaten 1–0 in the League Cup and then Ferençvaros were defeated by the same scoreline in the Inter-Cities Fairs Cup.

1969 Bremner scored six league goals as he helped Leeds win their first ever Championship.

1970 Won the Footballer of the Year award which compensated for defeat against Chelsea in the FA Cup Final.

1972 Leeds defeated holders Arsenal 1–0 in the FA Cup Final.

1974 Bremner collected his second Championship medal in a season in which he scored nine league goals.

1974 Played in all three of Scotland's matches at the World Cup finals in West Germany.

1975 Unlucky to be refused a "goal" for a controversial offside as Leeds lost 2–0 to Bayern Munich in the European Champions Cup Final in Paris.

1976 Played in his last league match for Leeds before he joined nearby Hull City. Bremner had scored 90 goals in 587 league appearances for Leeds.

1985 Returned to Leeds as manager but found the club in disarray.

1988 Despite having reached the semi-final of the 1987 FA Cup, Bremner was sacked early in the 1988–89 season.

1997 Leeds, Scotland and soccer fans around the world mourn Bremner's untimely death.

Eric Cantona

1966 Born on May 24 in Paris.

1983 Made his French league debut for Auxerre.

1987 Played his first match for France against West Germany.

1988 Achieved his first major transfer, joining Marseille for £2 million from Auxerre.

1990 Helped Montpellier win the French Cup.

1990 Banned from the national team for a year for insulting manager Henri Michel.

1991 Ended a further odyssey via Bordeaux, Montpellier and Nimes by quitting the game after a shouting match with a disciplinary panel.

1992 Tempted by the offer of a trial with Sheffield Wednesday, Cantona arrived in England but found himself bought by Leeds United for £900,000.

1992 A cult figure with his new club and won the league title with Leeds.

1992 Cantona became the target for Manchester United (*see* page 51) and Leeds were shocked when he was transferred for £1.2 million at the end of 1992.

1993 Cantona was instrumental as Utd won the Championship for the first time since 1967 and the era of Matt Busby and Bobby Charlton.

1994 Again Cantona was the man running the show as United became only the fourth club this century to win the League and Cup "double".

1995 An astonishing attack on a hooligan fan at Crystal Palace stunned the football world and cost him a seven-month ban from football and a community service sentence from the courts.

1996 Voted Footballer of the Year and then, as captain, sealed United's second and historic "double" when he scored the winning goal in the FA Cup Final against Liverpool. Despite his weekly displays in England, his past behaviour in France led to his omission from their Euro 96 squad.

1997 Manchester United won the league again, but despite having scored 11 goals Cantona stunned the world when he announced his retirement during the close season aged only 31 to pursue a career as an actor.

Bobby Charlton

1937 Born October 11 in Ashington, County Durham.

1954 Signed as a professional for Manchester United, one of the most exciting of the so-called "Busby Babes".

1957 Played in the FA Cup Final at 19 but was on the losing side against Aston Villa.

1958 A year of tragedy and triumph for Charlton. In February he was lucky to escape with his life from the wreckage of Manchester United's plane which had crashed in thick snow at Munich airport. Eight of the "Babes" were killed and manager Busby (*see* page 74) was in hospital for months. He recovered with such speed that he played in United's 2–0 defeat against Bolton in the FA Cup Final a few months later. The same year he won the first of 106 England caps when he played against Scotland in a 4–0 victory.

1963 Played in his third FA Cup Final, and was at last on the winning side as United beat Leicester City 3–1.

1965 Won the Championship with United, a feat they repeated in 1967.

1966 Took a starring role for England in the World Cup triumph – including scoring their magnificent first goal in the finals, against Mexico. Won both the European Footballer of the Year and English Footballer of the Year awards.

1968 Scored two goals as captain in inspiring United to victory over Benfica at Wembley in the European Champions Cup Final. Charlton and Bill Foulkes were the only two of the 1968 team who had survived the Munich air disaster. Signed an eight-year contract with Manchester United that was the longest-ever in English football.

1970 Won his 106th and last cap for England in the 3–2 defeat by West Germany in the World Cup quarter-finals in Leon. His record of 49 goals for England has yet to be beaten.

1972 Retired as a player at United, having scored 198 goals for them in 606 league appearances. He became briefly player-manager at Preston North End before subsequently returning to Old Trafford as a director.

1994 Received a knighthood.

Johan Cruyff

1947 Born on April 25 in Amsterdam.

1959 Enrolled by his mother in the Ajax youth section.

1963 Signed his first Ajax (*see* page 32) contract at 16 on the recommendation of English coach Vic Buckingham, then marked his debut with a goal.

1966 Made his debut for Holland in a 2–2 draw against Hungary and scored a last-minute equalizer in the first of his 48 internationals.

1969 Made his first European Cup final appearance with Ajax, but Milan won 4–1 in Madrid.

1971 Won the first of three successive European Cups, helping Ajax defeat Panathinaikos of Greece at Wembley. He was also voted European Footballer of the Year.

1973 Sold by Ajax to Barcelona for a then world record transfer fee of £922,000.

1974 Captained and inspired Holland to reach the 1974 World Cup Final in Munich, where they lost 2–1 to hosts West Germany. The thrilling Dutch style of play, labelled "Total Football" won Cruyff and his team-mates countless admirers. Won the European Footballer of the Year award for the third time, the first player to achieve such a distinction.

1978 Retired from the national team before the World Cup finals in Argentina, and left Barcelona to play in America with Los Angeles Aztecs and Washington Diplomats.

1981 Returned to Europe to play for minor club Levante in Spain, then to Holland with Ajax and, finally, Feyenoord.

1984 Went back to Ajax, this time as technical director.

1987 Guided Ajax to victory in the European Cup-Winners Cup as a parting gift before being appointed coach to Barcelona.

1992 Managed Barcelona to their long awaited victory in the European Cup Final, where they beat Sampdoria 1–0 at Wembley.

1996 Left Barcelona after a record nine years in charge including four consecutive league championships.

Kenny Dalglish

1951 Born on March 4 in Glasgow.

1967 Joined Celtic just as the senior team were winning the European Champions Cup against Internazionale in Lisbon.

1971 Made the first of his record 102 appearances for Scotland as a substitute against Belgium.

1977 Joined Liverpool (*see* page 50) for £400,000 as replacement for Hamburg-bound Kevin Keegan after winning eight League titles, six cups and four League Cups while with Celtic, and scoring 112 league goals.

1978 Scored Liverpool's winner against Club Brugge in the European Champions Cup Final at Wembley.

1985 Was appointed player-manager of Liverpool, in succession to Joe Fagan, on the eve of the tragic Champions Cup Final against Juventus in Brussels when 39 died after crowd trouble.

1986 Made history as the only player-manager ever to have won the League and FA Cup double.

1987 Made his last appearance for Scotland in a 0–0 draw with Luxembourg. With 30 goals he equalled Denis Law's record.

1989 Manager of Liverpool on the club's disastrous day, when 89 fans died in a crush before the FA Cup semi-final against Nottingham Forest at Hillsborough, Sheffield.

1989 Made his last league appearance for Liverpool having scored 118 goals, thus becoming the only player to have scored 100 league goals in both England and Scotland.

1990 Resigned as manager of Liverpool in the middle of an FA Cup sequence against Everton, largely as a result of the stress of helping Liverpool, both football club and city, cope with the aftermath of Hillsborough.

1991 Returned to football as manager of Blackburn Rovers.

1995 Thanks to the millions of owner Jack Walker, Dalglish's big-spending style took Blackburn to victory in the Premiership – then moved up to an uncertain role as director of football.

1996 Quit Blackburn before the start of the season.

1997 Returned to management as successor to Kevin Keegan at ambitious, big-spending Newcastle United.

Billy 'Dixie' Dean

1907 Born on January 22 in Lancashire.

1924 Signed professional for Tranmere Rovers and broke his skull early on in his career.

1925 Joined Everton where he remained until 1938.

1927 Began his international career as England centre-forward against Scotland with a dream sequence by scoring 2, 3, 2, 2 and 3 goals in successive games. Two of the goals came in the 2–1 win against Scotland at Hampden Park, England's first success in Glasgow since 1904.

1928 Completed his record season in which he scored 60 League goals for Everton in only 39 league matches, finishing with two, four and three to overhaul George Camsell's 59 for Middlesbrough. He also scored 22 goals in other competitions to bring his total for the season to 82. Perhaps not surprisingly, Everton were crowned English champions.

1932 Won another Championship medal with Everton.

1933 Played his last game for England against Northern Ireland – having scored 18 goals in 16 appearances – as well as 47 in 18 other representative matches.

1933 For the first time numbered shirts were worn in an FA Cup Final and Dean scored one of Everton's three goals as Manchester City are beaten 3–0.

1936 Passed Derby County's Steve Bloomer's pre-war record of 352 goals and finished the season with 375.

1938 Transferred to Notts County but played only a handful of games before he moved to Ireland and Sligo Rovers. Helped Rovers to the final of the Irish Cup.

1939 Retired from football having scored 379 English league goals in 437 matches, including 34 hat-tricks.

1964 Retired from his job as a licensee in Chester.

1980 Fittingly, Dean died at Goodison Park after collapsing while watching Everton play Liverpool.

Alfredo Di Stefano

1926 Born Alfredo Stefano Di Stefano Lauhle on July 4 in Barracas, Argentina.

1940 Hinted at things to come by scoring a hat-trick in 20 minutes for his first youth team, Los Cardales.

1942 Left Los Cardales after a row with the coach, to join his father's old club, River Plate.

1943 Made his debut for River Plate, playing as a right-winger, aged 17, against Buenos Aires rivals San Lorenzo.

1944 Transferred on loan to Huracan, for whom he scored the winner in a league game against River Plate.

1946 Returned to River Plate (*see* page 65) to succeed the great Adolfo Pedernera at centre-forward in an attack nicknamed La Maquina (the Machine).

1947 Already an international, won the South American Championship with Argentina.

1949 Lured away, during the famous Argentine players' strike, to play in a pirate league outside of FIFA's jurisdiction in Colombia for Millonarios of Bogota.

1953 Moved to Spain where he joined Real Madrid.

1956 Inspired Madrid to the first of five successive European Cup victories and topped the Spanish League scoring tables for five of the six seasons between 1954–59, with a record 49 goals in 58 European Cup matches.

1956 Won the first of his 31 caps for Spain (*see* page 27), for whom he scored 23 goals. Also won seven caps for Argentina and three for Colombia.

1960 Scored a hat-trick in Real's legendary 7–3 victory over Eintracht Frankfurt in the European Cup final at Hampden Park, Glasgow.

1963 Kidnapped – and later released unharmed – while on tour with Real in Venezuela.

1964 Left Madrid for one last season as a player with Español of Barcelona, before becoming coach for Elche.

1968 Returned to Argentina to coach and revived the fortunes of Boca Juniors.

1970 Took up a coaching position with Valencia in Spain and took them to their first league title in 24 years.

Duncan Edwards

1936 Born on October 1 in Dudley.

1950 Made his England representative debut, playing for the under-14s against Ireland at Oldham.

1952 Signed for Manchester United (*see* page 51).

1953 Made his league debut at 16 years 185 days in a 4–1 home defeat by Cardiff City but is soon labelled one of the "Busby's Babes" in recognition of manager Matt Busby's young side.

1955 Became England's youngest international this century when he made his senior debut in a 7–2 win over Scotland aged only 18 years and 183 days – the first of 18 full internationals in which he scored six goals. Edwards also played for England Youth, England Under-23, England B and the Football League.

1956 Played a large part in helping Manchester United win the Championship title. Established himself as one of the world's best players with a supreme display in Berlin as England trounce West Germany 3–1. Edwards scored the first goal and earned the nickname "Boom-Boom" for the power of his shooting.

1957 FA Cup Final runner-up with Manchester United against Aston Villa, but won his second Championship title. The club made their first venture into European football, reaching the semi-final of the European Cup before losing to eventual winners Real Madrid.

1958 Scored United's first goal away at Arsenal in what is considered one of the greatest ever matches in the English league. United lead 3–0 at half-time, but Arsenal rallied and drew level. United came back and scored two more goals, Arsenal got a fourth but lost 5–4.

1958 Travelled to Belgrade for the European Cup quarter-final with Red Star. United drew 3–3 to secure their place in the semi-final. On the return flight, the plane stopped to re-fuel at Munich. As it attempted to take off in heavy snow it crashed killing eight of the side. Edwards was critically injured and died in hospital two weeks later.

Eusebio

1942 Born Eusebio Da Silva Ferreira on January 25 in Lourenco Marques, Mozambique.

1952 Joined the youth teams of Sporting (Lourenzo Marques), a nursery team for the Portuguese giants of the same name.

1961 Sporting tried to bring Eusebio to Lisbon, but he was "kidnapped" on arrival by Benfica. In the autumn, with barely a dozen league games to his name, he made his debut for Portugal against England at Wembley and played so well he was already being talked of as a new star.

1961 Between 1961 and 1973, Eusebio won the Portuguese League seven times and he was the top scorer in the league in seven of these years; also won the Portuguese Cup five times.

1962 Scored two thundering goals as Benfica beat Real Madrid 5–3 in a classic European Cup Final in Amsterdam. He was also a runner-up three times with Benfica in this competition in 1963, 1965 and 1968.

1963 Scored a cracking consolation goal for Benfica against AC Milan in a 2–1 European Cup Final defeat at Wembley.

1965 Voted European Footballer of the Year.

1966 Crowned top scorer with nine goals as Portugal finished third in the World Cup finals in England, where he was nicknamed the "new Pele" and the "Black Panther." In all, he scored 38 goals in 46 internationals.

1974 Having scored 316 league goals in 294 matches he left Benfica and travelled to North America to take part in the new NASL. Started with Boston Minutemen, then moved to Toronto Metros and finished with Las Vegas Quicksilver.

1977 Returned to Benfica as coach.

1992 A statue in his honour was unveiled at the entrance to Benfica's Estadio da Luz (*see* page 192) in Lisbon and a film about his life was released entitled *Sua Majestade o Rei* – His Majesty the King.

Giacinto Facchetti

1942 Born on July 18 in Treviglio.

1956 Joined youth system of local club CS Trevigliese where he started out as a centre-forward.

1960 Signed professional for Internazionale, his only senior club, where master coach Helenio Herrera (*see* page 76) converted him to full back.

1961 Made his league debut in a 2–0 away win over Roma.

1963 Won the first of four league championships with Inter and made his Italy debut in a 1–0 win over Turkey in Istanbul.

1964 Won the European Champions Cup with Inter against Real Madrid in Vienna and then the World Club Cup against Independiente of Argentina – in a play-off in, ironically, Madrid.

1965 Won both European and World club cups for a second successive year.

1966 Scored 10 goals in 1965–66 season, a record for a full-back in Serie A. Became captain of the national side in his 25th international.

1968 Became a European champion at national team level when Italy defeated Yugoslavia after a replay in the European Nations Final in Rome.

1970 World Cup runner-up as captain of Italy against Brazil in Mexico City.

1971 Converted from left-back to sweeper. His 59 goals in 476 games for Inter were a record for an Italian full-back.

1971 Became the most capped Italian player of all time when he passed Umberto Caligaris's previous record of 59 appearances in September of this year.

1972 Surprisingly dropped by Italy, but returned to play in the 1974 World Cup finals in West Germany.

1977 Played his last international for Italy in a 2–0 defeat by England at Wembley in a World Cup qualifier – but Italy still qualified for the finals. Injury prevented Facchetti playing in the finals in Argentina – or adding to his then record total of 94 caps.

Tom Finney

1922 Born on April 5 in Preston.

1938 Signed for Preston North End his local, and only, senior club.

1941 Played for Preston in the 1941 wartime FA Cup Final.

1942 Served in North Africa with the British Eighth Army.

1946 Eight years after signing for Preston he made his first league appearance for them.

1946 One month later he played for England against Scotland – although caps weren't awarded for the match.

1947 Won the first of his 76 caps against Wales in a career notable for ongoing controversy over whether he, or Stanley Matthews, was the better right-winger. He won 40 caps at outside-right, 33 at outside-left and three as a centre-forward.

1950 Played in England's first World Cup finals but it ended in disaster when they lost to the USA 1–0.

1954 Came closest to a major club honour when Preston lost 3–2 to West Bromwich Albion in the FA Cup Final. Voted English Footballer of the Year.

1954 Second World Cup finals appearance as England reached the quarter-final stage.

1957 Won the Footballer of the Year award for a second time.

1958 A key veteran member of the England team which reached the 1958 World Cup finals – his third finals – but were eliminated in a first-round play-off by the Soviet Union with Finney missing through injury.

1959 Played his last international for England against the Soviet Union, 13 years after first appearing for his country, and his English record of 30 international goals stood until broken by Bobby Charlton

1960 Played last of his 433 league matches for Preston, for whom he scored 187 goals.

1975 Elected president of Preston North End.

1998 Awarded a knighthood in the New Year Honours List. Still with Preston – as club president.

Just Fontaine

1933 Born on August 18 in Marrekech.

1953 Brought up in Morocco, he turned professional in France with Nice.

1954 Helped Nice to win the French Cup.

1956 Won French league honours with Nice before being transferred to Reims as replacement for Real Madrid-bound centre-forward Raymond Kopa. Made his debut for France.

1958 Won the French league and cup with Reims.

1958 Injury to Reims team-mate René Bliard opened the door for Fontaine to lead the French attack at the World Cup finals in Sweden despite having played only once more since his debut in 1956. He scored 13 goals during the finals, a record which still stands, including a hat-trick in France's opening game against Paraguay and four in the 6–3 win over West Germany to secure third place for his country. A semi-final defeat by eventual winners Brazil had ended France's hopes of winning the cup.

1960 Broke a leg in March of this year in a league game. The break proved so bad that it was feared he may never play again.

1961 Suffered an extraordinary stroke of ill-luck when, on one of his first games back from his broken leg, he broke the same for a second time.

1962 Forced to retire after failing to recover fully from his double leg fracture. French football was plunged into despair at the announcement. Fontaine's record of twice being top league scorer and totalling 27 goals in 20 internationals was testimony to his greatness as a striker.

1963 Became the first president of the French Professional Footballers' Union.

1967 Appointed director of the French national team but didn't hold the position for long.

Paul Gascoigne

1967 Born on May 27 in Gateshead.

1983 Joined Newcastle United as an apprentice.

1985 Made his first team debut for Newcastle a month before he turned professional.

1987 Made his debut for England Under-21s.

1988 Transferred to Tottenham for £2 million in July and made his full England debut a month later when he came on as a sub against Denmark. Also voted Young Player of the Year.

1990 Suddenly achieved international superstar status with his displays at the World Cup finals, culminating in his tearful exit from the semi-final against West Germany.

1990 Won the BBC's Sports Personality of the Year.

1991 Won an FA Cup-winner's medal even though he was on a stretcher at the time, having incurred a career-threatening cruciate ligament injury early in the game with a rash challenge on Nottingham Forest defender Gary Charles.

1992 Sold to Lazio for a reduced fee of £5.5 million, a year later than planned because of his knee injury that cut his price. Made his first appearance for England for over a year.

1995 Returned to British football with Rangers (*see* page 61) after playing only 42 league games in his three seasons with Lazio – missing a significant chunk because of a leg fracture suffered in training.

1996 Won his first-ever league championship medal in his first season with Rangers and was voted Footballer of the Year in Scotland.

1996 Embroiled in trouble with the English media for drunken antics on a short tour to the Far East, "Gazza" responded in stunning fashion when he scored a magnificent goal against Scotland in the European Championships and helped England to the semi-finals.

1997 Won a second Championship medal with Rangers and played a large part in steering England to the 1998 World Cup finals.

Jimmy Greaves

1940 Born on February 20 in London.

1957 Made his first-team debut with Chelsea and reached a century of goals within 133 appearances.

1959 Scored on his debut for England against Peru.

1961 Joined Milan for £80,000 in June after scoring a remarkable 124 goals in 157 league games for Chelsea including a club record 41 in the 1960–61 season. Never adjusted to the lifestyle or discipline of Italian football though he scored nine goals in the first 10 games of what was ultimately a league championship-winning season. Sold back to English football in December with Tottenham Hotspur – though manager Bill Nicholson insisted on paying £99,999 so Greaves would not be saddled with the label of the first £100,000 footballer!

1962 Won the FA Cup with Tottenham (*see* page 70).

1963 Scored twice for Tottenham in the 5–1 win over Atlético Madrid which made them the first British club to lift a European trophy, the Cup-winners Cup. Also scored what was then a Tottenham club record 37 league goals in the 1962–63 season.

1966 Hit the lowest point of his career when he was injured in the first round of the World Cup finals against France and failed to regain his place from Geoff Hurst for the Final.

1967 His last club triumph – winning the FA Cup with Tottenham. In the first all-London final, Spurs beat Chelsea 2–1 and Greaves and captain Dave Mackay are the only two survivors from the 1962 triumph.

1967 Won the last of his 57 caps against Austria. Scored a total of 44 goals for England.

1970 Transferred to West Ham United as part of the £200,000 deal which took Martin Peters to Tottenham.

1971 Retired at "only" 31 after totalling 357 league goals. Now a much-loved and popular television soccer analyst.

John Greig

1942 Born on September 11 in Edinburgh.

1960 Moved from junior club Whitburn to Rangers – his only senior club whom he continued serving in managerial and administrative capacities long after his retirement.

1962 Established himself as Rangers right-half though it was subsequently in the centre of defence that he made most of his record 496 league appearances for the club.

1964 Won the first of his 44 caps for Scotland in a 1–0 defeat of England at Hampden Park. Voted Scottish Player of the Year.

1966 Voted Scottish Footballer of the Year for a second time.

1967 Senior member of the Rangers side beaten after extra time by Bayern Munich in the European Cup-winners Cup Final in Nuremberg. To compound matters for Greig and the Rangers team, Celtic succeed where they failed and became the first British side to win the European Cup.

1971 Endured the horror of witnessing 66 people crushed to death during the New Year's Day Old Firm clash at Ibrox.

1972 Won that elusive European medal and became the only Rangers skipper to lift a European trophy when Rangers defeated Moscow Dynamo 4–3 in the Final of the Cup-winners Cup in Barcelona's Nou Camp stadium.

1976 Five years after his last cap, Greig is recalled by Scotland for one more appearance against Denmark. It was his last international.

1977 Awarded the MBE.

1978 Stopped playing and became manager of Rangers. In 16 years as a player, Greig had made a record 496 league appearances for the club. His managerial career started in blazing fashion, winning both cups and enjoying a good run in Europe.

1983 Resigned as manager of the club, despite winning four trophies in five seasons, ending an association with Rangers that had begun in 1958.

Ruud Gullit

1962 Born on September 1 in Surinam.

1978 Discovered by Welsh coach Barry Hughes who signed him for Haarlem.

1980 Joined Feyenoord, playing sweeper, but subsequently converted to forward after moving to PSV Eindhoven.

1981 Won the first of his 65 caps in 1981 on the day of his 19th birthday in a 2–1 defeat by Switzerland.

1985 Moved to PSV Eindhoven.

1987 Sold to Milan for a world record £5.5 million and helped inspire their first league championship victory in nine years. Won his first World Footballer of the Year award and also voted European Player of the Year.

1988 A few weeks after winning the Italian league, Gullit captained Holland (*see* page 23) to European Championship glory in Munich – scoring the first of their two goals in the Final victory over the Soviet Union.

1989 Scored two goals in Milan's 4–0 thrashing of Steaua Bucharest in the European Champions Cup Final in Barcelona's Nou Camp. Voted World Footballer of the Year for the second time.

1990 Came back from a serious knee injury to win a second Champions Cup-Winners medal as Milan beat Benfica 1–0 in Vienna.

1993 Joined Sampdoria and made his last appearance for Holland.

1995 Left Italy, after restless and unsatisfactory spells with Sampdoria, Milan again and then Sampdoria again, to start a new career in England with Chelsea under the managership of Glenn Hoddle.

1996 Appointed player-manager of Chelsea after Hoddle's departure to become manager of England.

1997 Became the first continental coach to land an English prize as Chelsea beat Middlesbrough 2–0 to win the FA Cup.

Gheorghe Hagi

1965 Born on February 5 in Constanta.

1980 Played first-team football for local club FC Constanta as well as making his debut for Romania's youth team.

1982 He was by now an established league player, at 17, with Sportul Studentesc of Bucharest.

1983 Made his debut for the Romanian senior team against Norway aged 18.

1984 Was a member of Romania's team at the European Championship finals in France, but the team failed to spark and they return home having failed to win any of their three pool matches.

1985 Hailed as the league leading marksman after scoring 20 goals in the 1984–85 season from his position as an attacking midfielder. By this time he had already developed a reputation for his skill with free kicks and penalties.

1986 Became top league scorer again, this time with 31 goals after scoring six in one match, and was "stolen" by Steaua Bucharest without a transfer fee – an escapade approved by the ruling Ceaucescu family, who were Steaua supporters and directors.

1990 Starred for Romania as they reached the second round of the World Cup finals before losing to the Republic of Ireland in a penalty shoot-out. Was later transferred to Spain with Real Madrid.

1992 Fell out with Madrid's other star players and was sold to Italian club Brescia, who already had two other Romanian players and a Romanian coach in Mircea Lucescu.

1994 Hailed as one of the great stars at the World Cup finals where Romania were eliminated once again after a penalty shoot-out, this time against Sweden, in the quarter-finals. On returning to Europe, Hagi was transferred back to Spanish football, with Barcelona.

1996 Failed to impress Johan Cruyff and was sold off yet again, this time to top Turkish club Galatasaray. Played in a disappointing European Championship campaign for Romania.

Helmut Haller

1939 Born on July 21 in Augsburg.

1957 Turned semi-professional with local club BC Augsburg.

1958 Made his senior national team debut at inside-right for West Germany in a 1–1 draw with Denmark in Copenhagen – the Germans' first match since their 6–3 defeat by France in the World Cup third place match. Haller was injured, however, and had to be substituted by Hans Cieslarczyk.

1961 Transferred to Italian club Bologna.

1963 Haller's attacking partnership with Danish striker Harald Nielsen inspired Bologna to their first league championship in more than 20 years – after they beat Inter 1–0 in a title play-off in Rome after both clubs finished level on points.

1966 Was one of the most influential players at the World Cup finals – even before he pounced on a mistake by Ray Wilson to shoot West Germany into a 1–0 lead against England in the Final at Wembley. Unfortunately for Haller, England came back to win 4–2.

1968 Left Bologna after six seasons to join Juventus with whom he won two league championships – in 1972 and 1973.

1970 Played his 33rd and last international for West Germany in the struggling 2–1 win over Morocco in Leon at the World Cup finals. He was dropped immediately after the match and therefore had to watch from the sidelines as West Germany avenged their 1966 World Cup Final defeat to England by knocking the holders out in a gripping quarter-final encounter. The Germans go out 4–3 in the semi-finals to the Italians, but claim third place after beating Uruguay in the decider.

1973 Haller comes close to a European club medal, when he appeared as a substitute in Juventus' 1–0 Champions Cup Final defeat by Ajax in Belgrade.

Johnny Haynes

1934 Born on October 17 in London.

1950 Joined Fulham as a schoolboy.

1952 Turned professional with his only English club, Fulham, after playing for England at youth and schools levels.

1955 Won the first of 56 caps against Northern Ireland and, in the process, became the first English player to be capped at all five international levels – Schoolboy, Youth, Under-23, 'B' and Full.

1960 Appointed captain of England in succession to Ronnie Clayton.

1961 Became English football's first £100-a-week footballer after the abolition of the maximum wage. Key man in midfield for England after manager Walter Winterbottom switched to the 4–2–4 system with Haynes partnered in the engine room by Bobby Robson. In successive games, England won 5–2, 9–0, 4–2, 5–1, 9–3 and 8–0. The 9–3 result was a thrashing of Scotland at Wembley in 1961, perhaps the best performance of Haynes' England era.

1962 Captained England in the World Cup in Chile. After a win, a draw and a defeat in the pool matches, his appearance against Brazil in the 3–1 quarter-final defeat turned out to be his last because of injuries suffered in a serious car crash that August which sidelined him for a year. He captained his country on 22 occasions during his 56 caps and scored 18 goals.

1963 Haynes decided to stay with Fulham despite a record-breaking bid from Tottenham Hotspur, then the strongest team in England.

1969 Retired from English football still with Fulham and after scoring 145 goals in 594 league games.

1970 Ended his playing career in South Africa, winning a championship medal with Durban City.

Geoff Hurst

1941 Born on December 8 in Lancashire.

1959 Signed for West Ham, as a wing-half or inside-forward but was converted into a striker by manager Ron Greenwood and scored 180 goals in 409 league starts – ultimate reward for his decision to pursue football instead of a cricket career.

1964 Scored a strangely premonitory in-off-the-crossbar goal as West Ham beat Preston 3–2 in the FA Cup Final.

1965 Led West Ham's attack in their 2–0 win over TSV 1860 Munich in the European Cup-winners Cup Final.

1966 Made his senior debut for England against Scotland having previously played for his country at youth and under-23 level. Considered a reserve in the squad for the World Cup finals but was brought in for the quarter-final against Argentina after Jimmy Greaves was injured playing against France. Hurst scored the winner against Argentina, set up one of Bobby Charlton's goals in the semi-final victory over Portugal… and then scored the historic hat-trick in the 4–2 victory over West Germany in the Final.

1970 Played in the World Cup Finals in Mexico and this time lost out to the Germans as England lost 3–2 in the quarter-finals.

1972 Transferred from West Ham to Stoke City after 13 seasons with the London club. In that time he scored 180 goals in 410 league matches. Played his last match for England against West Germany. He scored 24 goals in 49 appearances.

1975 Moved on from Stoke to West Bromwich Albion. After retiring he tried his hand at management in the League with Chelsea but, after his dismissal after 18 months, went out of football and into the insurance business.

1996 Was one of the "front men" for the 1996 European Championship promotional campaign and then for the bid to bring the 2006 World Cup finals to England.

Jairzinho

1944 Born on December 25 in Rio de Janeiro, full name Jair Ventura Filho.

1959 Moved from his home town to sign professional with Botafogo at 15 and play outside-right as deputy to the great Garrincha.

1963 Won a gold medal at the 1963 Pan American Games.

1964 First capped by Brazil.

1966 Played in the same squad as Garrincha, his hero, at the World Cup finals in England, but played just three games.

1970 Made history by scoring in every game in every round of the World Cup finals on Brazil's way to their ultimate 4–1 victory over Italy in the Final. Jairzinho scored seven goals, including two in Brazil's opening win over Czechoslovakia and one in the climactic defeat of Italy.

1971 Broke a leg and spent several months on the sidelines.

1972 Transferred to Europe to play for Marseille but returned home within a year after disciplinary problems.

1974 Played in his third World Cup, but this year it was the turn of Holland to play the beautiful football and they knocked Brazil out in the second round. Retired shortly afterwards having scored a total of 37 goals in 87 appearances for Brazil.

1976 Re-emerged as a veteran hero with Cruzeiro of Belo Horizonte in their run to the final of the South American Club Cup, the Copa Libertadores. In the final Cruzeiro beat River Plate 4–1 in the first leg but lost 2–1 away in the return. Jairzinho missed the play-off, which Cruzeiro won 3–2 in Santiago, because of injury. He was back for the World Club Cup final but Cruzeiro lost 0–2, 0–0 against European champions Bayern Munich of West Germany.

1991 Jairzinho re-emerged into the international headlines after discovering a talented youngster named Ronaldo. Subsequently Jairzinho was appointed coach to his old club Cruzeiro.

Pat Jennings

1945 Born on June 12 in County Down, Northern Ireland.

1961 Made his debut in goal for his Northern Irish home-town team, Newry.

1963 Moved to England with Watford, for whom he played 48 matches.

1964 Transferred to Tottenham Hotspur as goalkeeping successor to double-winning Scotland keeper Bill Brown. Won his first Northern Irish cap against Wales.

1967 FA Cup-winner with Tottenham Hotspur then scored a goal with a goal kick during the Charity Shield against Manchester United.

1971 Won the first of three cup medals in consecutive years. This year it was the League Cup, followed by the UEFA Cup in 1972 and ending with another League Cup triumph in 1973.

1973 Voted Footballer of the Year.

1977 Surprisingly released by Spurs after playing 472 league matches in 12 years and snapped up by North London neighbours Arsenal for a paltry £40,000 – with whom he extended his career by a further seven years and 237 league games.

1979 FA Cup-winner this time with Arsenal having finished on the losing side the previous season – and before picking up a further loser's medal in 1980.

1982 Played in Northern Ireland's World Cup campaign as they top their group, which includes a controversial 1–0 defeat of hosts Spain. They eventually lose 4–1 to France in the second round.

1985 Earned a reputed £100,000 from his testimonial game between Spurs and Arsenal. Having not played a senior club match for nearly a year, Jennings performed heroically as his saves booked Northern Ireland a place in the 1986 World Cup.

1986 Bowed out of football in a big way by winning his 119th cap on his 41st birthday – in the World Cup finals against Brazil in Guadalajara, Mexico.

1993 Returned to football as goalkeeping coach with Tottenham.

Jimmy Johnstone

1944 Born on September 30 in Glasgow.

1964 Made his Scotland debut against Wales – the first of his 23 caps. He would almost certainly have won more caps but for an aversion to flying which he overcame, to some extent, only later in his career. He scored four goals for his country.

1965 Career really took off at Celtic after the managerial takeover by Jock Stein which started with Scottish Cup success. Went on to win 16 medals altogether with the club – one European Cup, eight league, three Scottish Cup, four League Cup.

1966 Won his first league championship with Celtic.

1967 One of the heroes of Celtic's 2–1 comeback victory over Internazionale in the European Champions Cup Final in Lisbon when Johnstone became one of the few right-wingers to give Giacinto Facchetti a tough time of it. This was the end of the season in which Celtic achieved a unique quartet of trophies – also winning the Scottish league, the League Cup and the Scottish FA Cup.

1970 A night of unbridled passion and raw emotion as the kings of Scottish football, Celtic, faced their English counterparts, Leeds United, in the semi-final of the European Cup. In front of 134,000 fans at Hampden Park, Johnstone reigned supreme as he tormented the Leeds defence. Celtic won 2–1 (3–1 on aggregate), but lost 2–1 to Feyenoord in the final.

1972 Celtic reached their eight consecutive League Cup Final, against lowly Partick Thistle, but were stunned 4–1 in an amazing match. To compound Johnstone's misery he was taken off injured.

1974 Celtic won the league championship for the ninth consecutive season; they also won the Scottish Cup.

1975 Won the last of his 23 caps in the 1–1 draw with Spain in the European Championship qualifier.

Kevin Keegan

1951 Born on February 14 in Yorkshire.

1968 Turned professional with Scunthorpe United.

1971 Cost Liverpool a bargain £35,000 when he signed from Scunthorpe as an orthodox outside-right. Proved an overnight success at Anfield, later as a free-ranging attacking raider.

1973 Won the first of his three league championships with Liverpool, the others coming in 1976 and 1977. Made his debut for England against Wales in a 3–0 victory.

1976 Won the UEFA Cup against Club Brugge.

1977 Inspired Liverpool to their first European Champions Cup victory, a 3–1 win over Borussia Mönchengladbach in the Olympic stadium in Rome. Immediately after the final he transferred to Hamburg for £440,000.

1979 Won the German championship with Hamburg.

1980 Collected a European Champions Cup runner-up medal after Hamburg lose 1–0 to Nottingham Forest in the Bernabéu stadium in Madrid.

1980 Returned to England with Southampton.

1982 Keegan's only World Cup opportunity is sadly wasted because of a back injury which prevented him appearing until just a substitute's second-half appearance in England's last match, a 0–0 draw against Spain in the second round. It turned out to be the last of his 63 caps.

1982 Moved to Newcastle for two seasons and proved a huge hit with the fans.

1984 Announced his retirement from the game.

1992 Returned to Newcastle, this time as manager, in February and guided them to promotion.

1997 Quit as Newcastle manager shortly before the club's flotation on the stock market. At the end of the year he was appointed Director of Football at Fulham with the aim of guiding the club back to the top flight.

Mario Kempes

1952 Born on July 15 in Bellville.

1967 Turned professional with home-town club Instituto de Cordoba.

1970 Transferred to Rosario Central.

1974 Made his senior national team debut for Argentina and was hailed as one of the outstanding young players on view at the World Cup finals in West Germany, where Argentina reached the second round before losing to Holland 4–1 and South American rivals Brazil.

1976 Sold by Rosario Central to Valencia of Spain where he developed into such a devastating hammer of opposing defences that he was the only foreign-based player recalled to join the hosts' World Cup squad under Cesar Luis Menotti in 1978.

1978 Voted Player of the Tournament in recognition of top-scoring with six goals as Argentina won the World Cup for the first time. Kempes had scored the first goal of the final after 38 minutes, but the Dutch equalized eight minutes from normal time and the match went into extra-time. Again it was Kempes who broke the deadlock and it was his deft one-two with Bertoni that made the scoreline 3–1 and ensured the World Cup went to Argentina for the first time. Kempes was rewarded for his magnificent efforts with the much coveted South American Player of the Year award.

1980 Won his one and only European club trophy when Valencia defeated English club Arsenal on penalties to win the European Cup-Winners' Cup in the Heysel stadium in Brussels.

1981 Left Spain to return to Argentina where he joined River Plate.

1982 Recalled by Argentina for the 1982 World Cup finals in Spain but this time could not work the same magic, failing to co-ordinate effectively with the new Argentinian hero Diego Maradona, and Argentina drifted out in the seond round. When he retired shortly afterwards, Kempes had scored 20 goals in 43 internationals.

Jürgen Klinsmann

1964 Born on July 30 in Boblingen.

1972 Started with TB Gingen before moving to SC Geislingen and then Stuttgart Kickers, also making his debut for the German national youth team.

1984 Joined VfB Stuttgart and was, in his first season, the club's second-highest scorer with 15 goals. Made his debut for Germany at under-21 level.

1986 Became only the 11th player in Bundesliga history to score five goals in a match.

1987 Made his full international debut in a 1–1 draw with Brazil.

1988 Was the Bundesliga's top scorer with 19 goals. Made a big international impression during the European Championship finals in West Germany. Also a member of the bronze-medal winning team at the Seoul Olympic Games. Voted German Footballer of the Year.

1989 Helped Stuttgart reach the UEFA Cup final in which they lost to Napoli. Then made his first move abroad, to Italy and Internazionale.

1990 Makes a fine start in Serie A, scoring 13 times in his first season. Then enjoyed his greatest triumph as West Germany won the World Cup.

1992 Member of the German team surprisingly beaten in the European Championship Final by Denmark. Left Inter to play for Monaco.

1994 Enjoyed a major personal success at the World Cup finals even though Germany lost in the quarter-finals – then transferred, surprisingly, to Tottenham Hotspur.

1995 Overcame a reputation for theatrics to be voted Footballer of the Year. Also captains the German national team for first time against Spain before leaving Tottenham to join Bayern Munich.

1996 Returning to England to captain Germany to victory in the European Championship as well as scoring a one-season record 15 goals in Bayern Munich's UEFA Cup triumph.

1997 Won his long-awaited league championship medal in Germany with Bayern – then returned to Italy with Sampdoria… before returning to England with Tottenham to help them in a relegation fight.

1998 Breaks his jaw in an FA Cup match that Tottenham lose.

Michael Laudrup

1964 Born on June 15 in Copenhagen.

1978 Joined youth section at Brondby.

1981 Made league debut aged 17 for KB Copenhagen before moving back to Brondby.

1982 Brilliant as a new kid on the block with Brondbyernes and was duly voted Footballer of the Year. Made his national team debut against Norway on his 18th birthday.

1984 Transferred by Brondby, where his father was youth coach, to Juventus – despite rival bids from the likes of Liverpool, Ajax and Anderlecht. Juventus loaned Laudrup out to Lazio.

1985 Recalled by Juventus as replacement for Zbigniew Boniek and helped them win the World Club Cup. Voted Denmark's Footballer of the Year for a second time.

1986 Starred at the World Cup finals in Mexico, above all inspiring Denmark's 6–1 thrashing of Uruguay in the Neza stadium in Mexico City.

1989 Grew tired of the disciplines of Italian football and transferred to Barcelona – winning the league championship with them for four successive years from 1991 to 1994.

1992 Missed Denmark's shock European Championship win after falling out with coach Richard Moller Nielsen over team selection and tactics.

1994 Omitted from Barcelona's team that played in the European Champions Cup Final. Transferred to Barcelona's great rivals, Real Madrid and returns to the Danish national team after making his peace with Moller Nielsen.

1995 Demonstrated his winning class by leading Real Madrid to their first league championship in five years.

1996 Captained Denmark at the finals of the European Championship and then moved on yet again, this time to Vissel Kobe in Japan – which was expected to mean the end of his national team career.

1997 Insisted on continuing to play for Denmark and returned to Europe to pick up his top-level club career with Ajax Amsterdam (*see* page 32).

Denis Law

1940 Born on February 22 in Aberdeen, Scotland, in the same week as another goalscorer supreme, Jimmy Greaves.

1955 Joined Huddersfield Town as a teenager, later coming under the guidance of a fellow Scot, manager Bill Shankly.

1959 Made his international debut for Scotland against Wales aged 18, the first of 55 caps and 30 goals – a Scottish international record until equalled by Kenny Dalglish.

1960 Sold to Manchester City for a British record £55,000.

1961 Sold to Italian club Torino for £100,000, then a world record, and including a £10,000 signing-on fee, but never settled in Italy despite achieving considerable popularity. Later that year he returned to Manchester, joining Matt Busby's United and raising the world record transfer fee to £115,000.

1963 Scored the first goal in helping Manchester United beat Leicester City 3–1 to win the FA Cup, and scored for the Rest of the World against England on the same Wembley pitch.

1964 Chosen as European Footballer of the Year.

1965 Helped United to win the League Championship.

1967 Another Championship winners' medal, despite recurring injuries.

1968 Missed United's European Cup triumph against Benfica through knee trouble.

1973 Returned to Manchester City.

1974 Played his 452nd and last league game, scoring the City winner that condemned bitter derby rivals United to the Second Division. He scored more than 250 club goals during his league career.

1974 Played in his 55th and last international against Zaire in the 1974 World Cup Finals, his only appearance in the competition.

Tommy Lawton

1919 Born on October 6 in Bolton, England.

1935 Joined Burnley as an amateur after scoring 570 goals in three seasons as a schooboy.

1936 Made his senior debut four days after his 17th birthday against Tottenham, and became the youngest player in the Football League to score a hat-trick.

1937 Bought by Everton as a replacement for the great Dixie Dean for £6,500, a record for a teenager.

1938 First Division top scorer with 28 goals.

1939 Top again with 34 as Everton won the Championship, and at least one in all his first six internationals. A penalty on his debut, against Wales, made him England's youngest-ever scorer, at 19 years and 17 days.

1946 Resumed career after 24 goals in 23 wartime internationals. Sold to Chelsea.

1947 Scored 28 First Division goals, a club best.

1948 Joined Notts County, then in Division Three South, for £20,000 (a 25 per cent increase on the previous record). Won his last four caps with Notts, and ended his England career against Denmark with a 0–0 draw having scored 22 goals in 23 full internationals.

1950 Shot Notts County to promotion with 31 goals.

1951 Became player-manager of Brentford.

1953 Reverted to player only, in order to have a final fling with Arsenal.

1955 Retired after 390 League games, 231 goals and not a single booking.

1956 Player-manager of non-league Kettering.

1958 A brief spell back at Notts County, as manager.

1972 Testimonial match at Everton raised £6,300.

1997 Died from pneumonia, aged 77.

Gary Lineker

1960 Born on November 30 in Leicester, England.

1977 Signed for Leicester City.

1979 January 1 marked the first of his career total of 430 Football League games.

1980 Helped City to promotion from Division Two.

1984 First of his 80 caps, as a substitute away to Scotland.

1985 First of his 48 England goals, against Eire at Wembley. Sold to Everton for £1.1 million.

1986 Footballer of the Year but a losing FA Cup Finalist despite scoring the first goal against Liverpool. Then scored six in the World Cup finals, the highest ever by a British player, and was sold to Barcelona for £2.75 million.

1987 Scored all four for Barcelona against Real Madrid.

1988 Helped his club to win the Spanish Cup.

1989 In the Barcelona team which won the Cup-winners Cup, beating Sampdoria in the final. Sold to Tottenham for £1.2 million.

1990 Top First Division scorer for the third time with a third club – Leicester, Everton and now Spurs. Another four goals in Italia 90, making him one of only nine players to reach double figures in World Cup finals. Unable to prevent England losing to West Germany in a semi-final penalty shoot-out.

1991 Missed an FA Cup Final penalty (saved by Forest's Crossley) and had a goal disallowed, but finished a winner, 2–1.

1992 Lineker, without a goal in five games, was controversially taken off by coach Graham Taylor during the sixth, thus ending his career one short of Bobby Charlton's England scoring record. Voted Footballer of the Year for the second time.

1994 Went to Nagoya Grampus Eight in a "missionary" move to Japan that was badly hampered by a persistent toe injury.

1996 Retired from soccer and became a media figure.

Ally McCoist

1962 Born on September 24 in Glasgow.

1978 Left local minor football for Perth, and joined St Johnstone.

1979 Made senior debut and in his first season he played nine games plus six as substitute, all without scoring.

1981 Remarkable improvement led to his transfer to Sunderland for £300,000, but he struggled again.

1983 After 56 appearances and only eight goals, the first of them against Forest's Peter Shilton, he gladly returned to Scotland, to join Rangers (*see* page 61) (despite coming from a largely pro-Celtic family), and scored in the first minute of his debut – against Celtic! – and helped them to an incredible list of trophies. Possibly the best £180,000 they ever spent.

1986 Won his first Scotland cap against Holland.

1992 Voted Scotland Player of the Year and won Europe's "Golden Boot" award for leading goalscorer with 34 goals.

1993 League Cup and Championship secured. Broke a leg in a World Cup qualifier against Portugal and missed another Scottish Cup Final victory.

1994 League Cup, Championship.

1995 Championship.

1996 After a 28-month absence from the national team, McCoist marked his return with a winner against Greece.

1996 Scorer of Scotland's only goal in Euro 96. Broke Scotland's post-war scoring record, 264, and won an eighth Championship, but missed another Scottish Cup through injury.

1997 Part of a Rangers team that equalled Celtic's record of winning nine Scottish Championship titles in a row.

1998 Began the year with 58 caps and 19 goals.

Billy McNeill

1940 Born March 2, Blantyre, Scotland.

1957 Signed professional forms for Celtic on his 17th birthday, although he had gone to a rugby-playing school in Hereford.

1959 Made the first of more than 500 senior appearances for his club, as a splendid central defender and skipper.

1961 Won his first cap – in the infamous 9–3 defeat by England – but survived the repercussions and made at least one appearance for his country for 11 successive seasons, gaining 29 caps in all.

1965 Voted Scotland's Footballer of the Year, and helped Celtic to win the Scottish Cup after an 11-year gap.

1966 League Cup, Championship.

1967 Captained Celtic to victory in every competition they entered – Scottish Cup, League Cup, Championship, and also the European Cup where Celtic became the first British side to win the competition after a torrid 2–1 victory against Inter Milan.

1968 League Cup, Championship.

1969 European Cup runner-up, Scottish Cup, League Cup, Championship.

1972 Made his last appearance for Scotland – like his debut it was against England, and although the Scots lost, it was only 1–0, an improvement on his debut result!

1974 Scottish Cup, Championship – his ninth in a row. In those nine years he appeared in 282 League games out of a possible 306, more than any other Celtic player.

1975 Retired after winning both domestic cups yet again. His final total: European Cup 1, Championship 9, Scottish Cup 7, League Cup 6, plus numerous second places.

1983 Became manager of Manchester City.

1986 Left City and became manager of Aston Villa.

1987 Villa were relegated and McNeill was sacked after only eight months in the job. He also had two spells as manager of his old club.

Sepp Maier

1944 Born on February 28 in Haar.

1960 Started making a name for himself as a teenage goalkeeper with regional league TSV Haar. Impressed Bayern officials even though he was the goalkeeper on the wrong end of Haar's 8–1 defeat in a junior league match!

1964 Turned professional with Bayern Munich.

1966 Made his debut for West Germany in a 4–0 win over the Republic of Ireland in Dublin on the eve of the World Cup finals – for which he was the Germans' third-choice keeper. That was the first of his 95 caps.

1967 Helped Bayern win the European Cup-winners Cup in extra-time against Rangers in Nuremberg.

1972 Collected another continental title, winning the European Championship with West Germany.

1973 Won his first league championship with Bayern, despite being an object of fun for his trademark long, baggy shorts.

1974 Reached the pinnacle of his career – winning the European Champions Cup on the first of three occasions with Bayern and then the World Cup with West Germany in his home stadium in Munich against Holland. Maier was thus the first goalkeeper ever beaten by a penalty (from Johan Neeskens) in a World Cup Final.

1975 Invested much of his earnings in a centre specialising in what he called his "real favourite sport" – tennis. Voted Footballer of the Year.

1976 Became a double world champion when Bayern defeated Cruzeiro of Brazil to win the World Club Cup. Suffered one of only a few career setbacks when West Germany lost a penalty shoot-out to Czechoslovakia in the European Championship Final in Belgrade.

1977 Voted Footballer of the Year twice in succession – in both 1977 and 1978. Forced by injury to retire having played 473 league matches, including a record run of 422 consecutive games. Maier won the European Cup three times with Bayern as well as the World Club Cup against Atletico Mineiro of Brazil in 1976.

Paolo Maldini

1968 Born on June 26 in Milan.

1982 Joined Milan's youth system under the coaching direction of his father, Cesare Maldini, a former Milan captain, Italian international – and future national team manager.

1985 Made his Milan league debut in January in a 1–1 draw away to Udinese, at the age of 16 – sensational in Italian football.

1988 Won the first of five league championships with Milan under the managerial guidance of one of his greatest fans, Arrigo Sacchi – who would later appoint Maldini as national team captain. Also made his senior national team debut for Italy in a 1–1 draw against Yugoslavia in Split.

1989 Won the first of three European Champions Cups (the other were in 1990 and 1994) in a 4–0 win over Steaua Bucharest in Barcelona.

1990 Member of the Italian side which beat England 2–1 to finish third at the World Cup staged on Italian soil, having lost to Argentina in the semi-final stage.

1994 One of the heroes of Milan's outstanding 4–0 thrashing of Spanish giants Barcelona in the European Champions Cup Final in Athens – a particularly notable performance because Maldini had to play in the centre of defence due to the absence through suspension of regular skipper and Italian clubmate Franco Baresi. Was then one of the heroes of Italy's run to the World Cup Final where his duel with Brazil's raiding full-back Cafu was one of the highlights of the match (which Italy, of course, lost on penalties). Was then unanimously voted World Player of the Year by the London magazine, *World Soccer*.

1996 Captained Italy during their disappointing European Championship performance in England.

1997 Helped Italy beat Russia in the World Cup qualifiers play-off to secure their place in the 1998 Finals.

Diego Maradona

1960 Born on October 30 in Lanus, Buenos Aires.

1976 Made his league debut at 15 for Argentinos Juniors.

1977 Made his international debut at 16 for Argentina (*see* page 10) in a friendly against Hungary.

1978 Fell out with national coach Cesar Menotti after he was overlooked for the Argentine squad which won the World Cup in front of their home crowd.

1980 Sold to Boca Juniors for £1 million, a record for a teenager.

1982 Sold to Barcelona for another world record £3 million, then out of the game for four months after a reckless tackle by Bilbao's notorious defender Andoni Goicochea.

1984 Sold to Napoli for a third world record, now £5 million.

1986 Inspired Argentina to victory at the World Cup finals in Mexico: was unanimous choice as Player of the Tournament, but made himself the most umpopular man in England with his "Hand of God" goal against England in the quarter-final.

1987 Led Napoli to their first-ever Italian league title plus victory in the Italian cup.

1988 Won his only European prize as Napoli beat Stuttgart in the UEFA Cup Final.

1990 Despite a collection of injuries, Maradona led Argentina back to the World Cup Final, where they were defeated 1–0 by West Germany.

1991 Failed a dope test and was banned for 15 months.

1992 Made a disappointing comeback with Sevilla in Spain.

1993 Sacked by Sevilla, Maradona began a second comeback in Argentina with Newells Old Boys.

1994 Banned again, for 15 months, after a positive drugs test during the World Cup.

1995 Returned briefly to playing with Boca Juniors after coaching stints with Deportivo Mandiyu and Racing Avellaneda.

1996 Retired again.

1997 Tried another brief comeback with Boca.

Lothar Matthäus

1961 Born on March 21 in Erlangen.

1977 Left school and studied interior design and decorating before deciding on a life in football.

1978 Turned professional with Borussia Mönchengladbach.

1980 Was a substitute for the West German side who won the 1980 European Championship – making his national team debut against Holland – the first of a national record 122 caps. Scored for Monchengladbach in their UEFA Cup Final defeat.

1984 Joined Bayern Munich for a then domestic record of £650,000.

1986 Established himself in the national side after scoring a magnificent winner against Morocco in the World Cup second round on the way to defeat by Argentina in the Final – where his task, despite a broken wrist, was to mark Diego Maradona.

1988 Moved to Italy with Internazionale for £2.4 million.

1990 Matthaus's career reached its zenith when he was not only West Germany's World Cup-winning captain in Rome, but was also voted Player of the Tournament by the world's media. Duly voted World, European and German Footballer of the Year.

1991 Won the UEFA Cup with Inter Milan and scored a penalty.

1992 Missed the European Championship finals – in which Germany lost to Denmark in the Final – because of a serious knee injury. Subsequently returned from Internazionale to Bayern Munich.

1993 Restored to the German side.

1996 Led Bayern from both midfield and sweeper roles to victory in the UEFA Cup.

1996 Missed the European Championships because of injury and didn't add to his tally of 122 international caps.

1997 German league champion with Bayern for the third time.

Stanley Matthews

1915 Born on February 1 in Hanley, Stoke-on-Trent.

1932 Turned professional with local club Stoke City and played his first league game for them aged only 17.

1933 Won Division Two honours with Stoke, something he repeated 30 years later.

1935 Made his debut for England in a 4–0 win over Wales in Cardiff.

1946 Sold to Blackpool for £11,500.

1948 Played a key role in one of England's greatest victories, by 4–0 over Italy in Turin, and was voted Footballer of the Year, the first time the award was made.

1953 Sealed his place among football's legends by inspiring Blackpool's FA Cup Final comeback against Bolton which came to be known as the "Matthews Final". 3–2 down with only minutes remaining, it seemed that Matthews was destined never to win the major domestic English honour, but he inspired his side as Blackpool scored twice in the last three minutes to snatch a 4–3 victory.

1955 One of his many summer exhibition tours took him to Mozambique, where among the ball boys mesmerized at a match in Lourenzo Marques was Eusebio.

1956 Won the inaugural European Footballer of the Year award.

1957 Played the last of 84 games for England aged 41 (including wartime internationals) in a 4–1 World Cup qualifying victory over Denmark in Copenhagen. He won a total of 54 official caps and scored 11 goals.

1961 Returned to Stoke for a mere £2,800 and, despite his 46 years, inspired their successful campaign to get back into the First Division.

1963 Won the Player of the Year award for the second time.

1965 After becoming the oldest player to play in the First Division (a record that seems destined to remain unbroken), when he played for Stoke against Fulham aged 50 years and five days, he retired from the game a short while later, after a star-spangled Farewell Match at Stoke's Victoria Ground featuring the likes of Di Stefano, Puskas and Yashin. Was knighted for his services to soccer the same year.

Joe Mercer

1914 Born August 14, Ellesmere Port.

1932 Signed for Everton as a 16 year-old.

1939 Won First Division Championship. Also made his debut for England against Scotland. Won four more caps that season but didn't play again after the war.

1946 Returned to Everton after serving as a physical training instructor during World War Two and played 25 non-cap internationals for England. Troubled by a knee injury, and transferred to Arsenal, where a career that appeared to be over got better as the years passed.

1948 An inspirational skipper as Arsenal won the Championship.

1950 In tandem with manager Tom Whittaker, Mercer led Arsenal to a 2–0 FA Cup victory over Liverpool. Voted Footballer of the Year.

1952 Perhaps his finest performance, as injury-battered Gunners held Newcastle until a late, lone goal denied them victory

1953 His third Championship.

1954 Career ended by a broken leg in his 40th year.

1955 Became manager of Sheffield United.

1958 Took over at Aston Villa, helping them to promotion and the League Cup.

1964 Retired through ill-health but later joined Manchester City as manager, with Malcolm Allison as coach. In 1967 they won promotion to Division One and the following year won the Championship.

1969 Won FA Cup, thus completing the Double Double of both Cup and League as both player and manager.

1970 Won Cup-winners Cup.

1972 Retired again.

1974 Had a seven-match spell as England's caretaker manager – won three, drew three, lost one.

1990 Died on his beloved Merseyside, on his 76th birthday.

Roger Milla

1952 Born on May 20 in Yaoundé, real name Roger Albert Miller.

1967 Began making a teenage name for himself for Leopard of Douala then transferred to Tonnerre Yaoundé.

1976 Voted African Footballer of the Year for the first time. Moved to French football with Valenciennes.

1980 Won his first European club prize by helping Monaco triumph in the French cup. Was then transferred to the Corsican club, Bastia.

1981 Proved a lucky mascot by winning the French cup again, this time with Bastia. Later moved on to Saint-Etienne and Montpellier.

1982 First appeared at the World Cup finals, leading Cameroon's attack in Spain. They were eliminated in the first round on goal difference in a group which included Poland, Peru and Italy – the prospective champions with whom Cameroon finished level on points!

1984 Won the African Nations Cup with Cameroon, beating Nigeria 3–1 in the Final.

1986 Runner-up in the African Nations Cup, Cameroon having lost on penalties in the Final against hosts Egypt in Cairo.

1990 One of the stars of the World Cup finals, after being persuaded out of retirement to return to the national team. Milla scored both Cameroon's goals in their 2–1 win over Romania in the first round then the extra-time winner against Colombia in the second round after a blunder by South American keeper Rene Higuita. Delighted crowds with his celebratory dances around the corner flags. Duly voted African Footballer of the Year again, the first player to win the award twice.

1994 Persuaded out of retirement once again for the World Cup and became, at the age of 42, the oldest player ever to appear in the finals at USA'94. Also then became the oldest to score a goal in the finals when he struck Cameroon's consolation in their 6–1 thrashing by Russia.

Bobby Moore

1941 Born April 12, Barking, England.

1958 Signed for his local team, West Ham, and went on to make 642 appearances in competitive matches – the club record.

1962 After playing for England Youth (winning a record 18 caps) and Under-23s, he won the first of his 108 international caps.

1964 Captained West Ham when they beat Preston North End in the last minute to take the FA Cup. Voted Footballer of the Year.

1965 Led the Hammers to another victory in a Wembley final, 2–0 against Munich 1860 in the European Cup–Winners' Cup.

1966 Moore's – and England's finest hour and a half – as he leads his country to World Cup glory on home soil. In a pulsating final, Moore receives the cup from the Queen after England win 4–2. Another appearance at Wembley, this time for West Ham, ended in a defeat against West Bromwich in the two-leg League Cup Final.

1970 Defeat by Germany in the World Cup quarter-final in Mexico, with Moore as calm as ever despite having being under arrest in Colombia, falsely accused of stealing a bracelet.

1973 His last cap (and his 90th as captain).

1974 Transferred to Fulham.

1975 Final Wembley appearance as Fulham are beaten 2–0 by West Ham in the FA Cup Final.

1977 Retired after 150 games for Fulham, giving him a career total of exactly 900 for two clubs and his country. Later played briefly in the USA.

1984 Began a two-year spell as Southend manager.

1993 Died aged 53 in London after a courageous fight against Cancer. Footballing stars from all around the world attended his funeral.

Stan Mortensen

1921 Born May 26 in South Shields.

1940 oined the RAF as a wireless operator on the outbreak of World War Two and the only survivor when his bomber plane crashed.

1943 Having scored dozens of wartime goals he was an England reserve against Wales at Wembley, then played for the Welsh because they did not have a substitute of their own.

1947 Scored four against Portugal in Lisbon on his full international debut for England.

1948 Scored Blackpool's second goal in the FA Cup Final, but they lost 4–2 to Manchester United.

1950 Has the dubious honour of representing England in their first ever World Cup Finals. Tipped as pre-match favourites, England are dumped out of the tournament when they lost 1–0 to the USA.

1951 Another Final, another defeat, this time 2–0 by Newcastle. Morty, ever the sportsman, shook Milburn's hand after his second goal.

1953 A FA Cup winners' medal at last, and he became the first man to score a hat-trick in a Wembley final. Despite Mortensen's goals which win Blackpool the cup 4–3 against Bolton, the final is rather unfairly called the "Matthews Final" in tribute to Mortensen's teammate Stanley Matthews. Later that year he scored his 23rd and last goal in his 25th international, the infamous 6–3 defeat by Hungary.

1955 Left Blackpool after 197 League goals, all in the top division, and 30 in the Cup. Joined Hull.

1957 Moved to Southport, later playing non-league with Bath and Lancaster.

1967 Began a two-year spell as Blackpool manager.

1989 Made a Freeman of Blackpool, where he had been prominent in civic affairs, and had auctioned his medals to help his old club through a tough spell.

1991 Died just before his 70th birthday. More than 700 people attended his funeral.

Alan Morton

1893 Born April 24 in Airdrie, Scotland.

1913 Joined Queens Park, playing as an amateur against professional opponents in Scotland's top division. He was naturally right-footed, but operated at outside-left and earned fame as "The Wee Blue Devil", a nickname given to him by an admiring English journalist.

1920 Capped twice at full international level, first against Wales in a 1–1 draw at Cardiff and then in a 3–0 thrashing of Northen Ireland. He then turned professional for Rangers. He was the first signing made by Will Struth, who was to manage the club for 34 years.

1921 Won the first of his Championship titles with Rangers.

1928 Although Morton stood a mere 5ft 4ins, was a mining engineer by profession and trained only in the evenings, his career lasted 20 years. The highlight was the 1928 5–1 win over England by the team who became known as the Wembley Wizards. Three of Scotland's goals in the win were as a direct result of Morton's inch-perfect crosses.

1928 One of the great days in Rangers' history as Celtic are thrashed 4–0 in the final of the Scottish FA Cup. A crowd of 118,000 was present to see this fifth 'Old Firm' Cup Final.

1932 Won the last of his 31 caps aged 39 in a 3–1 win against France. Won his second FA Cup winners' medal as Partick Thistle are beaten.

1933 Retired from playing after 495 games for Rangers, all in the first team, and 115 goals. During his time at Ibrox the club had won the Championship nine times and the Cup three times, and they achieved further glories during the next 30 years ,which he spent as one of their directors until he stepped down in 1968.

1971 Died peacefully in Glasgow at the age of 78.

Gerd Müller

1945 Born on November 3 in Zinsen, Bavaria.

1964 Joined Bayern from TSV Nordlingen at the insistence of president Wilhelm Neudecker. Coach Tschik Cajkovski was not impressed, saying: "I can't put that little elephant in among my string of thoroughbreds." But once he had done so, Bayern never looked back. He went on to score well over 600 goals, including a record 365 in the Bundesliga.

1966 Müller shot Bayern to his first major trophy, the West German cup, with a 4–2 victory over Meideriecher SV. Made his senior national team debut in a 2–0 win over Turkey in Ankara. Went on to score an astonishing 68 goals in 62 internationals for West Germany.

1967 Won the European Cup-winners Cup with an extra-time victory over Rangers in Nuremberg. Was voted Footballer of the Year for the first time – collecting the award again in 1969. Was joint league top scorer with 28 goals, also collecting this accolade in 1960, in 1970, in 1972, in 1973, in 1974 (jointly) and in 1978.

1969 Won the first of his five league championships with Bayern.

1970 A sensation at the World Cup finals in Mexico, being top scorer with 10 goals including two in the remarkable semi-final defeat by Italy. His goals earned him selection as European Footballer of the Year.

1974 Retired from the national team after scoring his most famous goal – the one with which West Germany beat Holland in the 1974 World Cup Final in his home club stadium in Munich. That same year Muller also helped Bayern Munich win the first of three successive European Champions Cups – scoring twice in the 4–0 replay win over Atletico Madrid.

1976 Became a double world champion as Bayern defeated Cruzeiro of Brazil to land the World Club Cup. Later emigrated to the United States where he played for Fort Lauderdale in the North American Soccer League.

1995 Returned to Germany to take up a role on the Bayern Munich coaching staff.

Johan Neeskens

1951 Born on September 15. in Heemstede.

1968 Made his name in midfield with Haarlem – where Ruud Gullit would later begin his career, too.

1971 Helped Ajax win the first of their three European Champions Cups in a 2-0 victory over Panathinaikos at Wembley.

1972 Won the Champions Cup again, now firmly entrenched in midfield alongside Arie Haan, in a 2–0 win over Internazionale in Rotterdam.

1973 Completed the Champions Cup hat-trick with Ajax's 1–0 win over Juventus in Belgrade.

1974 Starred for Holland as the midfield enforcer of the team who reached the World Cup Final before losing 2–1 to hosts West Germany in Munich. Under coach Rinus Michels, Neeskens was one of the key components in the "Total Football" Holland were encouraged to play under their coach. The concept of "Total Football" thrilled the world and deserved better than to lose out to the more pragmatic and dour approach of the Germans. Neeskens scored the most memorable of his 17 goals in 49 internationals when he earned a place in history by converting the first-ever World Cup Final penalty within the first two minutes of the match.

1975 Followed former Ajax team-mate Johan Cruyff to Barcelona.

1978 Won his only Spanish club trophy – the cup.

1978 Appeared in his second World Cup Finals, but again emerged a loser as Holland lost 3–1 to Argentina.

1979 Key man in midfield as Barcelona won the European Cup-winners Cup – beating Fortuna Dusseldorf 4–3 after extra-time in Basle.

1981 Wound down his career in the North American Soccer League, although he later tried an ill-fated comeback in Switzerland.

Gunter Netzer

1944 Born on September 14.

1961 Joined his only senior German club, Borussia Möenchengladbach where he became the key midfield general in the side built by master-coach Hennes Weisweiler.

1965 Won the first of his 37 West German caps against Austria.

1970 Won his first domestic honour as Borussia won the league championship.

1971 Won his second championship medal with Borussia.

1972 Seen at his very best in West Germany's successful European Nations Championship campaign. Having ousted Wolfgang Overath in midfield, Netzer forged an inspired creative partnership with Franz Beckenbauer which reached a peak when West Germany defeated the Soviet Union 3–0 in the Final in Brussels. On the way to the final, West Germany beat England in the quarter-final and the Belgians 2–1 in the semi-final.

1973 Was a West German cup-winner with Borussia and was voted Footballer of the Year for the second successive time.

1974 Lost his place in the national team to Overath as his team-mates went on to beat Holland 2–1 in the final – his only appearance in the World Cup finals being in the shock 1–0 defeat by East Germany in Hamburg in the first round. Transferred to Spain with Real Madrid.

1975 Won the first of two successive Spanish league championships with Real Madrid. Madrid also won the Spanish cup in 1975.

1977 Left Spain for one last playing season with Grasshopper in Switzerland.

1978 Retired from playing and returned to German football as general manager of Hamburg, overseeing their 1979 league title win and run to the 1980 European Champions Cup Final (where they lost 1–0 to Nottingham Forest in Netzer's old "home" Real Madrid stadium).

Wolfgang Overath

1943 Born on September 29, 1943.

1961 Turned professional – part-time at first – with Köln.

1963 Key young member of the Köln side which won the first Bundesliga championship – scoring 83 goals in 409 league games with his only club up until his retirement in 1977.

1963 Made his senior national team debut for West Germany in a 3–0 win over Turkey in Frankfurt. Overath entered the game late-on as a second-half substitute for Timo Konietzka.

1966 Now a fixture in midfield but unable to spark West Germany as they finished World Cup runners-up to England in a 4–2 thriller at Wembley.

1970 Avenged England's 1966 World Cup triumph by helping to beat them in the quarter-final and then scored the goal with which West Germany secured third place at the World Cup finals after defeating Uruguay 1–0 in the semi-final losers' play-off.

1971 Dropped from the national team in favour of Gunter Netzer after a disappointing 0–0 draw at home to Poland in Hamburg in the European Championship qualifying competition.

1974 Timing his return to form to perfection, he regained his place in the West German team from Netzer in time to help guide his country to a 2–1 World Cup victory over the Dutch in front of a delirious home crowd. By doing so, Overath thus became one of the handful of players in history to have finished winner, runner-up and placed third in the World Cup. Having achieved just about every honour in world football he retired from the national team after the World Cup Final victory over Holland, having scored 17 goals in 81 internationals.

1978 Honoured with selection for the World XI which played Brazil in Rio de Janeiro.

Pele

1940 Born on October 21 in Tres Coracoes. Universally known as Pele, but full name is Edson Arantes do Nascimento.

1950 Began playing with local club Bauru, where his father was a coach.

1956 Transferred to big-city club Santos and made his league debut at 15.

1957 Made his debut for Brazil, aged only 16, against Argentina and scored.

1958 Became the youngest-ever World Cup winner, scoring two goals in the final as Brazil beat Sweden 5–2. In the semi-final Pele had scored a hat-trick in the 5–2 demolition of France.

1962 Brazil won the World Cup for a second time but Pele missed the final win against Czechoslovakia because of injury in the first round. But he compensated for the disappointment by winning the World Club Cup with Santos.

1963 Won the World Club Championship for a second time with Santos.

1970 Inspired Brazil to complete their historic World Cup hat-trick in Mexico. Pele sparked Brazil's rampage that destroyed Italy in the final with the opening goal, Pele's fourth of the tournament. The final scoreline of 4–1 proved to the world that this Brazilian team was the best the world had ever seen.

1971 Won the last of his 111 international caps having scored 97 goals in that time (77 goals from 92 matches on a stricter international definition).

1974 Retired from the game.

1975 Ended an 18-month retirement to play for Cosmos of New York in the dramatic, short-lived North American Soccer League.

1977 Retired again after lifting Cosmos to their third NASL championship. This time it was permanent and Pele could look back on a career in which he had scored 1281 goals in 1363 matches.

1982 Presented with FIFA's Gold Medal Award for outstanding service to the worldwide game.

1994 Appointed Brazil's Minister for Sport.

Michel Platini

1955 Born on June 21 in Joeuf.

1972 Joined Nancy from AS Joeuf.

1976 First appeared on the international stage at the 1976 Olympic Games in Montreal.

1978 His first World Cup, in Argentina, where Platini gave an indication of the great things to come.

1979 Moved to St Etienne.

1982 Inspired France to fourth place at the World Cup when he was man of the match in the dramatic semi-final defeat by West Germany in Seville. After the finals Platini was sold to Juventus.

1983 The first of three seasons in which he was the Italian league's top scorer. Was also voted European Footballer of the Year and subsequently became the only player to win the accolade three years in a row.

1984 The greatest year of his career. Platini was captain and nine-goal top scorer as hosts France won the European Championship. He scored the first goal in the 2–0 victory over Spain in the Final in the Parc des Princes in Paris.

1985 Converted the penalty kick which brought Juventus their long-awaited European Champions Cup victory over Liverpool (albeit overshadowed by the Heysel tragedy).

1987 Shocked French and Italian football by retiring while still comparatively young to concentrate on commercial interests and TV work. He had scored 348 goals in 648 matches, including 41 from 72 international appearances.

1990 Persuaded back into football as national manager and guided France to the finals of the 1992 European Championship. France disappointed, and Platini left the job to become joint head of the team set up by the French federation to organize the 1998 World Cup finals.

1996 Turned down the official proposal that the new World Cup stadium in Paris should be named after him. It thus became, instead, the Stade de France.

Ferenc Puskas

1927 Born on April 2 in Budapest.

1943 Made his debut for his father's old club, Kispest.

1945 Played his first international for Hungary against Austria aged only 18. He went on to play 84 times for Hungary and scored a record 83 goals.

1948 Transferred with the entire Kispest playing staff to the new army club, Honved, and top-scored with 50 goals in the League championship. Because of his army connections he became known as the "Galloping Major".

1952 Captained Hungary to victory over Yugoslavia in the final of the Olympic Games soccer tournament in Helsinki.

1953 Earned a place in history by inspiring Hungary's historic 6–3 victory over England at Wembley.

1954 Played despite injury, amid controversy, in the World Cup Final which Hungary lost 3–2 to West Germany in Berne – their first defeat for four years.

1956 Stayed in western Europe when the Hungarian Revolution broke out while Honved were abroad to play a European Cup tie against Bilbao.

1958 Signed for Real Madrid by his old manager at Honved, Emil Oestreicher. For the Spanish club, he scored an amazing 35 goals in 39 European tie matches.

1960 Scored four goals for Madrid in their famous 7–3 demolition of Eintracht Frankfurt in the European Cup Final at Hampden Park, Glasgow.

1962 Played in the World Cup finals in Chile, this time for his adopted country of Spain.

1966 Retired and turned to coaching.

1971 Achieved his greatest success as a trainer, guiding outsiders Panathinaikos of Athens to the European Cup Final (they lost 2–0 to Ajax at Wembley).

1993 Appointed, briefly, as caretaker-manager of Hungary during the 1994 World Cup qualifiers.

Frank Rijkaard

1962 Born on September 30 in Surinam.

1979 Turned professional with Ajax under the management of Johan Cruyff.

1981 Made his senior national team debut for Holland against Switzerland despite protests from Ajax that he should not have been picked because at the age of 18 he was too young.

1987 Won the European Cup-winners Cup with Ajax, was then appointed captain after the departure for Milan of Marco Van Basten... and fell out with manager Cruyff.

1988 After hardly playing for Ajax in the first half of the 1987–88 season, Rijkaard was sold to Sporting of Lisbon in the spring – and then sold onto Milan in the summer. In between he was a key man in the centre of defence as Holland won the European Championship in West Germany in blissful style, avenging their 1974 defeat in the World Cup Final by the Germans by beating them 2–1 in the semi-final, before defeating the Soviet Union 2-0 in the final in Munich.

1989 Milan coach Arrigo Sacchi described Rijkaard as: "So good I don't know which position to use him in." In fact he played midfield for Milan as they won the Champions Cup, beating Steaua Bucharest 4-0 in the final in Barcelona, the biggest winning margin in a Final since 1974.

1990 Won a second successive Champions Cup with Milan, this time beating Benfica 1–0 in Vienna.

1990 Experiences a miserable World Cup in Italy; Holland slump and Rijkaard is sent off against Germany.

1993 Played virtually his last game for Milan in the 1–0 defeat by Marseille in the European Champions Cup Final in Munich. Afterwards Rijkaard returned to Holland with Ajax.

1995 Played his last game against Milan, helping Ajax beat them 1–0 in the Champions Cup Final in Vienna – thus joining the ranks of the handful of players who have won the competition with different clubs. Retired at the season's end.

Bryan Robson

1957 Born January 11, Chester-le-Street.

1975 Joined West Bromwich from local amateur football in the North-East, making his senior debut at 18. Despite two broken legs and numerous other injuries, he went on to become an outstanding midfielder, with a strong tackle, excellent passing ability and a spirit that adversity never quenched.

1980 The first of 90 England caps (65 as captain, and 26 goals).

1981 Joined his former manager, Ron Atkinson, at Manchester United, for £1.5 million – then the British record fee.

1982 Scored in the first minute of England's first match in the World Cup Finals (a goal often wrongly credited as being the fastest in the tournament's history).

1983 The first of three FA Cup-winning appearances as United captain (followed by 1985 and 1990).

1984 Scored a hat-trick against Turkey, becoming the first England skipper to get three in a match for 75 years.

1986 Dislocated a shoulder in a friendly before the World Cup, then did it again in the second of England's games in the tournament. The team reached the quarter-final, but lost to Argentina.

1990 Another injury kept Robson out of the later stages of the World Cup, in which his team reached the semi-final before losing to West Germany.

1991 Captained the United team to victory in the European Cup–Winners' Cup, beating Barcelona.

1993 Club captain as United ended a 25-year gap by winning the Championship, although he makes only five full appearances.

1994 Appointed player-manager of Middlesbrough,

1995 Boro promoted to the Premiership as champions of the new First Division.

1997 Boro relegated, despite Robson's huge spending on transfers. They also reached the League Cup and FA Cup Finals for the first time, and lost both.

Romario

1966 Born on January 29 1966 in Rio de Janeiro.

1983 Joined Olario Juniors.

1985 Scored four goals against Vasco da Gama and impressed so much they signed him.

1988 Finished top scorer at the Seoul Olympics with seven goals.

1989 Having scored 73 goals for Vasco da Garma in 123 matches he moved to Dutch side PSV Eindhoven.

1990 Travelled to the World Cup in Italy with the Brazilian squad but played only 65 minutes of football after criticizing selection policies. Manager Carlos Parreira was so incensed by his outbursts he later banned him from the Brazilian squad for the 1994 qualifying games.

1991 A broken leg sidelined him for much of the year.

1993 After a turbulent spell at PSV where he often fell out with team-mates and complained about the weather he was bought by Johan Cruyff, manager of Barcelona, for £3 million. He had scored 125 goals for PSV. Scored a hat-trick in his first game for his new club.

1993 Brought back into the Brazilian side that faced Uruguay in the vital match that would decide who qualified for USA 1994. Romario scored the two goals that won the match for Brazil 2–0.

1994 Showed his true colours with a masterful display during the 1994 World Cup in the USA. He scored five goals in the tournament including the 81st minute winner against Sweden in the semi-final that sent Brazil through to the final where they beat Italy.

1995 Returned to Brazil to play for Flamengo.

1997 A regular once again in the Brazilian side, Romario scored the winner against England during Le Tournoi competition in France.

Paolo Rossi

1956 Born on September 23 in Prato.

1972 Moved from Prato to the Juventus youth system but they gave him away to Como on a free transfer in 1975 after operations on both knees.

1976 Signed for Lanerossi Vicenza in Serie B and his 21 goals in 36 games shot them to promotion.

1977 Made his Serie A debut with Juventus.

1978 Emerged from the league shadows to star for Italy at the World Cup finals, scoring in the victories over France, Hungary and then, in the second round, Austria.

1979 Perugia paid a world record £3.5million to sign Paolo Rossi from relegation-bound Vicenza.

1980 Perugia were relegated and Rossi was suspended for two years after being convicted of alleged involvement in a betting-and-bribes scandal.

1981 Juventus bought Rossi from Perugia for £650,000 while he was still in the middle of his suspension.

1982 Was only three matches out of his ban when Italy took him to the World Cup finals, where he top-scored with six goals and collected a winners' medal from the Final victory over West Germany in Madrid where he opened the Italian scoring. His finest hour, however, came in the the thrilling quarter-final win over favourites Brazil where he scored a stunning hat-trick as Brazil crashed out 3–2. Voted European Footballer of the Year and also World Footballer of the Year.

1984 Helped Juventus win the Cup-Winners' Cup with a 2–1 win over Porto.

1985 Won the European Champions Cup with Juventus against Liverpool at the Heysel stadium in Brussels, a match marred by the deaths of Juventus fans caused by crowd trouble.

1986 Starred for Juventus with the World Club Cup then retired, aged 29, because of recurring knee trouble. He had scored 20 goals in 48 internationals for Italy.

Karl-Heinz Rummenigge

1955 Born on September 25 in Lippstadt.

1974 Gave up his job as a bank clerk when Bayern Munich paid Lippstadt just £4,500 for their young, blond right-winger.

1976 Rummenigge collected his only Champions Cup winners medal as Bayern defeat St-Etienne 1–0 in Glasgow. Later he also won the World Club Cup with Bayern against Cruzeiro of Brazil. Made his West German national team debut versus Wales, the first of 95 international appearances which also brought 45 goals.

1978 Shot to international stardom at the World Cup finals in Argentina, scoring twice in a 6–0 win over Mexico and once in a 3–2 defeat by Austria.

1980 Key influence in West Germany's European Championship victory – as well as providing the corner from which Horst Hrubesch headed the injury-time winner in the final against Belgium in Rome.

1981 Elected European Footballer of the Year for the second successive season.

1982 As captain of Germany he carried a leg injury throughout the World Cup finals in which he eventually finished as a runner-up to Italy. In the semi-finals, it was the introduction of substitute Rummenigge in extra time which was crucial to Germany recovering from 3-1 down to 3-3 against France – and then winning on penalties.

1984 Bayern sold Rummenigge to Internazionale of Italy a decade after he joined them for more than £2 million.

1986 Finished a World Cup runner-up again, this time in a 3–2 defeat by a Diego Maradona-inspired Argentina.

1987 Moved from Inter to Servette Geneva in Switzerland.

1989 Retired and moved into television commentating.

Ian Rush

1961 Born October 20, Flint, Wales.

1978 Joined Chester and made his debut at 17.

1980 Cost Liverpool a £300,000 fee when still only 19, but went on to repay it many times over with his splendid scoring record and general all-round usefulness. In the same year he won the first of 73 Welsh caps.

1981 Gained his first medal when he deputised for the injured Heighway in the League Cup Final replay against West Ham.

1982 Won the League Cup and the Championship.

1983 A third League Cup and a second Championship.

1984 League Cup No. 4 ,Championship No. 3, a European Cup, 48 goals in all games, and Footballer of the Year..

1986 A fourth Championship and a first FA Cup, Rush scored twice against Everton.

1987 On the losing side in the League Cup Final - the first time Liverpool had lost after a Rush goal in 140 games: won 118, drawn 21. Went to Juventus for £3.2 million, but did not settle in Italy.

1988 Rejoined Liverpool for £2.8 million.

1989 Ill for part of the season, but returned in triumph as a substitute in the FA Cup and scored twice – against Everton again.

1990 Rush's fifth Championship medal.

1992 A fifth FA Cup Final goal, against Sunderland, and a third victory.

1995 A record fifth League Cup Final win, this time as captain.

1996 His Liverpool career ended with him as the club's highest scorer in history, as well as being the top scorer in the FA Cup competition and in FA Cup finals this century, joint top for the League Cup, and top for Wales. Went to Leeds but scored only three goals in almost a full season, often being used in midfield.

1997 Another surprise transfer, this time joining old pal Kenny Dalglish at Newcastle.

Peter Schmeichel

1963 Born November 18 in Gladsaxe, Denmark.

1975 Joined local club Gladsaxe Hero.

1984 Moved to Hvidovre and also made his debut for Denmark Under-21s.

1987 Transferred to Brondby and capped for Denmark in the 5–0 win against Greece.

1988 Helped Brondby to win the Danish Championship and kept goal for his country in the Olympic qualifying tournament.

1989 Another winner in his home country, this time in the Danish Cup.

1991 Manchester United signed him in a bargain £500,000 deal and he made his debut in August in a 2–0 win over Notts County.

1992 Helped Denmark to their surprise victory in the European Championship, making vital saves against Holland in the semi-final and Denmark in the final. Denmark had only entered the tournament at the last minute after Yugoslavia were banned because of the political unrest in their country.

1993 United won the first of the new Premiership titles, and their first Championship title since 1967, and much of it was due to the acrobatics and skill of Schmeichel's goalkeeping.

1994 By this time he was perhaps the world's best goalkeeper, helping United to the Championship-and-Cup double, only the fourth club this century to achieve such a feat.

1995 A loser in the FA Cup Final to Everton, and a runners-up medal in the Premiership.

1996 A star again as United did the double for the second time in three years, an achievement unmatched in English soccer. Represented Denmark in the European Championships, but no repeat of the 1992 success. Passed 85 caps for his country.

1997 A fourth Championship in only five seasons, and a semi-final place in the European Cup. Even in his mid-thirties, Schmeichel was still in superb form as he approached 250 appearances for United.

1998 Helped Denmark qualify for the 1998 World Cup.

Uwe Seeler

1936 Born on November 5 in Hamburg.

1952 Joined his father's old club, Hamburg, at the age of 15.

1954 The West German national squad was decimated by illness so the young Seeler was called up for his international debut against France as substitute for Termath. He was only 17. His first international start was in the subsequent 3–1 defeat by England at Wembley. In all, he scored 43 goals in 72 internationals.

1958 Played in the first of his four World Cup finals as West Germany make it to the semi-finals before losing 1–0 to hosts Sweden.

1960 Won his only German league championship, with Hamburg. Was voted the first German Footballer of the Year. Collected the honour again in 1964 and 1970.

1961 Narrowly failed to reach the European Champions Cup Final when Hamburg lost in a semi-final play-off to Barcelona.

1963 Won the German cup with Hamburg.

1964 Top scorer with 30 goals in the first-ever unified Bundesliga championship.

1966 Seeler captained West Germany in their World Cup Final defeat against England at Wembley in 1966.

1968 Captained Hamburg in the final of the European Cup-Winners Cup against AC Milan.

1970 Gained a measure of revenge against England by scoring a remarkable back-headed goal when Germany won 3–2 in extra time in the dramatic 1970 quarter-final. Seeler and Pele are the only men to have scored in four World Cups. Played in his last and 21st World Cup finals match. Only Wladyslaw Zmuda of Poland has matched this incredible total.

1971 Seeler retired after playing for Hamburg throughout his career from 1952, loyally rejecting a string of offers from Italy and Spain.

1996 Returned to Hamburg as club president.

Alan Shearer

1970 Born August 13 in Newcastle.

1986 Joined Southampton from minor soccer in the North-East.

1988 Came on as a substitute in March for his Southampton debut against Chelsea. Made his full debut a few games later, against Arsenal, aged 17 years and 240 days, and scored a hat-trick – the youngest First Division player ever to do so in his first full game.

1991 Made England Under–21 debut and scored 13 goals in his 11 internationals.

1992 Made his senior international debut, and scored a brilliant goal against France, but a knee injury kept him out of the England team in the 1992 European Championships. In the same year he joined Blackburn for £3.3 million, then a British record fee, after scoring a moderate 23 goals in 118 internationals.

1993 After suffering a serious knee injury on Boxing Day 1992, Shearer is out of action for eight months. The 1993–94 season saw him net 31 goals in 40 matches.

1995 His goals help Blackburn win the Premiership title for the first time since 1914. Shearer is voted Player of the Year.

1996 Scored 31 League goals, becoming only the second player ever to pass 30 in the top division in each of three successive seasons (David Halliday did it it four seasons running for Sunderland in the 1920s). First player to reach 100 goals in the Premiership.

1996 After sensational form in the European Championships – he finished top scorer with five goals – where England reached the semi–final he was sold to Newcastle for £15 million, almost double the existing British transfer record.

1997 Scored 25 goals in 31 League games for his new club and took his England record to 16 goals in 35 appearances. In a pre-season friendly he suffered an horrific ankle injury that threatened his career.

1998 Returned to action after a lengthy spell out and immediately returned to his old ways, scoring in his first full game.

Peter Shilton

1949 Born 18 September in Leicester.

1965 Made his Football League debut for Leicester as a 16 year-old.

1969 Played in his one and only FA Cup Final, a 1–0 defeat for Leicester against Manchester City.

1971 Made his England debut against East Germany at Wembley.

1974 Joined Stoke City and spent three seasons with the club.

1977 Transferred to Nottingham Forest where he came under the command of Brian Clough at the peak of his managerial powers. With Forest he won the European Champions Cup in 1979 and 1980, the League title in 1978 and the League Cup in 1979.

1982 Played in the World Cup in Spain where he made five appearances, the first of 17 World Cup matches. England remained unbeaten throughout the tournament and in his five matches Shilton let in only one goal. Transferred from Nottingham Forest to Southampton.

1986 Played in all five of England's World Cup matches and again limited the opposition scoring opportunities; three goals in five games but England lost controversially to Argentina and Maradona's "Hand of God" in the quarter-finals.

1987 On the move again, this time to Derby County.

1990 Made his 125th and last appearance – an English record – in the third/fourth play-off match in the World Cup. In the semi-final against Germany it had taken a wicked looping deflection off one of his own players to beat him. England finished fourth, their best result for 24 years. During those 125 appearances, Shilton conceded a mere 80 goals.

1992 Became player-manager of Plymouth Argyle.

1996 After further spells with Bolton and West Ham, Shilton played in his 1000th league match on 22 December at the age of 47. In goal for Third Division Leyton Orient, Shilton kept a clean sheet as his side won 2–0 against Brighton.

Graeme Souness

1953 Born 6 May in Edinburgh.

1969 Having played for Scotland Schools, Souness joined Tottenham Hotspur as an apprentice.

1970 Turned professional but first team chances were limited and made only one appearance as a sub in the 1971 UEFA Cup.

1973 Joined Middlesbrough for £32,000.

1974 Made his Scotland debut against East Germany.

1978 Transferred to Liverpool where he made a total of 352 appearances and scored 56 goals. He won just about every major club honour available including five Football League titles, four League Cups and three European Cups.

1984 Moved to Italian club Sampdoria.

1986 Returned to Scotland in April where he was unveiled as Rangers' new player-manager. In his first full season, his new club won the Scottish League title and Cup. In the next five years he continued to win a host of trophies for Rangers including the championship title in 1988–89, 1989–90 and 1990–91 (the last being achieved shortly after his departure). The structure set in place at the club continued long after his departure and Rangers won their ninth consecutive title in 1997.

1986 Won the last of his 54 Scotland caps against West Germany in the World Cup.

1990 Caused controversy when he signed Mo Johnston, the first high-profile Catholic to join Rangers.

1991 Stunned Rangers when he quit to become manager of Liverpool.

1992 Despite having undergone extensive heart surgery only weeks before, Souness was present to see Liverpool beat Sunderland to lift the FA Cup.

1994 After continued criticism, Souness resigned as manager of the club in January.

1995 Became manager of Turkish side Galatasaray.

1996 Appointed manager of Southampton.

1997 Resigned as manager of Southampton to take up an appointment with Torino.

Hristo Stoichkov

1966 Born on August 2 in Plovdiv.

1985 Suspended by the federation after becoming involved in player mayhem during the domestic cup final between Stoichkov's CSKA Sofia and old rivals Levski.

1987 Won his first international cap against Belgium.

1989 Won the first of four consecutive Bulgarian Footballer of the Year awards.

1990 Bought by Barcelona from CSKA after winning three league titles with the club for a Bulgarian record £2 million in 1990, on the specific personal recommendation of coach Johan Cruyff. Shared the "Golden Boot" award for Europe's leading scorer with Mexico and Real Madrid star Hugo Sanchez who also scored 39 goals in the season.

1992 Helped Barcelona achieve their dream by winning the European Champions Cup. Stoichkov nearly did not play against Sampdoria at Wembley after falling out with Cruyff over a transfer offer from Napoli.The match went to extra-time but the Spanish club emerged 1–0 winners.

1993 Furious when voted only runner-up to Roberto Baggio in the European Footballer of the Year poll.

1994 Was the inspiration from an attacking midfield role of Bulgaria's best-ever fourth-place finish at the World Cup finals. They had started terribly with a shock 3–0 defeat by Nigeria but Stoichkov was in inspirational form. He finished the World Cup joint top scorer with six goals – and thus earned the European Footballer of the Year prize.

1996 Captained Bulgaria to first-round elimination at a disappointing European Championships, and then boycotted the national team after falling out with the federation over various national team issues.

1997 Made peace with new national coach Hristo Bonev in time to return to duty for what turned out to be a successful World Cup qualifying campaign.

Carlos Valderrama

1961 Born on September 2 in Santa Marta.

1977 Joined local club Santa Marta.

1987 Starred for Colombia at the Copa America finals in Argentina and was then voted South American Footballer of the Year.

1988 Moved to Europe with Montpellier.

1990 Won the French cup with Montpellier, led Colombia to the second round of the World Cup finals after a solid first round draw with eventual winners West Germany. In the next round they lost to the surprise package of the tournament the Cameroons. Then transferred to Spain with Valladolid, under the managership of Colombian boss Pacho Maturana.

1992 Returned home to Colombia and rediscovered his old form with Atletico Junior of Barranquilla and then Nacional of Medellin.

1993 Inspired Colombia to a sensational 5–0 win over Argentina in Buenos Aires in the World Cup qualifying competition and was duly voted South American Footballer of the Year for the second time.

1994 One of the few Colombian players to have done themselves justice in a disappointing – and ultimately tragic – first-round failure at the World Cup finals. Touted beforehand as one of the pre-tournament favourites, Colombia sank without trace, losing first to Romania and then the USA. In the game against the United States, centre-back Andres Escobar had inadvertently scored an own goal. Days after returning home, he was shot dead.

1997 Became the first Colombian player to reach a century of international appearances, in a World Cup qualifying match.

1998 Colombia qualified for the 1998 World Cup in France where the priority wasn't football but to honour the memory of former team-mate Escobar.

Marco Van Basten

1964 Born on October 31 in Utrecht.

1980 Signed by Ajax after being spotted during the club's annual youth talent "gala."

1983 Hit the international headlines for the first time as centre-forward with Holland at the World Youth Cup finals.

1986 Won the Golden Boot for the top league marksman in Europe thanks to his 37 goals for Ajax in the 1985–86 season.

1987 Captained Ajax to victory in the European Cup-winners Cup Final victory over Lokomotiv Leipzig when he also scored the winning goal. Then, having scored 128 league goals in Holland, he was sold for a bargain £1.5 million to Milan.

1988 Van Basten's attacking partnership with fellow Dutchman Ruud Gullit helped inspire Milan to their first league title win in nine years – and then brought Holland European Championship victory over the Soviet Union. Holland won the final 2–0 in Munich and Van Basten's goal, an exquisite volley from wide out – Holland's second – was hailed as one of the greatest in international history. Voted European Footballer of the Year.

1989 Won the European Footballer of the Year award for a second time and scored twice as Milan beat Steaua Bucharest 4–0 in the final of the European Champions Cup.

1990 Van Basten and Holland experience World Cup misery as they crash out in the second round phase losing 2-1 to West Germany.

1992 Voted World and European Footballer of the Year. Rejected medical advice to cut short his career after suffering a string of serious ankle injuries only to miss a decisive penalty in the European Championship semi-final shoot-out against Denmark after he had performed brilliantly in normal time. In 58 appearances for his country he scored 24 goals.

1993 Made a brave comeback for Milan in the European Champions Cup Final but they lost 1–0 to Marseille in Munich – and that proved to be his last game.

Billy Wright

1924 Born on February 6 in Shropshire.

1940 Signed by the legendary Major Buckley for his only club, Wolverhampton Wanderers, even though Buckley thought he was probably too small to make the grade.

1946 Made his England debut against Scotland – the first of Wright's then-record 105 caps. Of those, 51 were won at right-half, 46 at centre-half and eight at left-half. He captained England in 90 of his 105 matches.

1949 Captained Wolves to a 3–1 victory against Leicester City in the FA Cup Final.

1950 Played at wing-half and then centre-half, being a key member of the first England side to appear at the World Cup finals, in Brazil in 1950. Unfortunately, it was not a memorable experience as England lost 1–0 to the USA and crashed out. Also played in the finals in Switzerland in 1954 and in Sweden in 1958.

1952 Voted Footballer of the Year.

1954 Led Wolves to the club's first League Championship title.

1958 Collected another Championship title with Wolves.

1959 Won his 100th cap against Scotland and his third championship title with Wolves before he retired prior to the start of the following season after being omitted by Wolves manager Stan Cullis for a pre-season warm-up match. He had played in 490 league matches for the club, and a grand total of 541 peacetime appearances.

1959 Awarded the CBE for services to football. Played his 105th and last international against the USA. He missed only three of England's first 108 matches after the Second World War.

1962 Wright moved into management with Arsenal.

1966 Parted company with Arsenal and moved into television as a match analyst and executive with independent television in the Midlands.

1990 Made a director at Wolves.

1994 Died at the age of 70.

Lev Yashin

1929 Born Lev Ivanovich Yashin on October 22 in Moscow.

1946 Joined Moscow Dynamo as an ice hockey goaltender.

1951 Made his first-team debut for Moscow Dynamo. He went on to win the Russian League five times with Dynamo.

1953 Finally took over as Dynamo's first-choice keeper after "Tiger" Khomich suffered a long-term injury.

1954 Made his Soviet Union senior debut in a 3–2 win over Sweden.

1956 Goalkeeper with the Soviet side that won the Olympic Games gold medal in Melbourne.

1960 Star of the Soviet side that won the inaugural European Nations Championship, beating Yugoslavia in the final in Paris.

1962 Played in his second World Cup Finals in Chile but under-performed in the USSR's shock defeat against the hosts in the quarter-final.

1963 Became the only goalkeeper to win the European Footballer of the Year presented by Paris magazine *France Football*. Played for FIFA's World XI at Wembley in a match to mark the centenary of the Football Association.

1966 Played in his third successive World Cup finals – this time in England – helping the Soviet Union to a best-ever fourth place after losing 2–1 to West Germany in the semi-final.

1967 Won the last of his 78 caps for the USSR.

1968 Awarded the Order of Lenin by the Soviet government.

1971 Such was Yashin's fame and reputation that Pele, Eusebio, Bobby Charlton and Franz Beckenbauer were among world superstars who flew to Moscow to play in his farewell match. He was appointed manager of Dynamo the next day as a reward for services rendered.

1990 Died tragically from cancer in Moscow and was mourned throughout the world.

Zico

1953 Born on March 3 in Rio de Janeiro (as Artur Antunes Coimbra) but nicknamed Zico from an early age.

1968 Youngest of three professional football brothers, Zico was at first considered too lightweight when he signed for Flamengo. Special diets and weight training were prescribed.

1975 Scored with one of his speciality free-kicks on his Brazil debut against Uruguay. He went on to score 66 goals in 88 internationals.

1977 Won his first South American Footballer of the Year award.

1978 Went to the World Cup finals hailed as the "white Pele" but proved a flop after squabbling over tactics with coach Claudio Coutinho and Brazil had to watch rivals Argentina win the cup.

1981 Inspired Flamengo to victory over Cobreloa in the South American Club Cup final then to a memorable 3–0 win over European champions Liverpool in the World Club Cup final in Tokyo.

1981 Voted South American Footballer of the Year for the second time.

1982 Probably Zico's best personal World Cup – even though Brazil were surprisingly eliminated in the second round by a Paolo Rossi-inspired Italy. Won the South American Footballer of the Year award for the third time. Moved from Flamengo to Italian club Udinese.

1985 Transferred back to Flamengo.

1986 Plagued by injury during the World Cup Finals in Mexico, Zico never fulfilled his potential. He played in the thrilling quarter-final clash with France. One apiece after extra-time, Zico missed his spot kick in the penalty shoot-out and Brazil were eliminated.

1992 Retired from playing and appointed Brazil's Sports Minister.

1993 Returned to playing for Kashima Antler to help launch the new J-League in Japan.

Dino Zoff

1942 Born on February 28 in Mariano del Friuli.

1967 Hit the big-time on transferring to Napoli after graduating through Udinese and Mantova.

1968 Made his debut for Italy in a 2–0 win over Bulgaria in April 1968 then held the job to help Italy win the European Championship for the first time in a replay win over Yugoslavia in Rome.

1972 Hit the big-time aged 30 when he transferred to Italian giants Juventus with whom he won the UEFA Cup in 1977 as well as five Italian league titles and two Italian cup wins.

1974 Set a world record of 1,143 international minutes (12 matches) without conceding a goal – until he was beaten by Haiti's Emmanuel Sanon in Italy's first match at the World Cup finals in West Germany. The goals conceded against Poland and Argentina meant Italy were knocked out at the first hurdle.

1978 A better World Cup for Zoff and Italy as they reached the third place decider before losing 2–1 to Brazil.

1982 Emulated Juventus' pre-war keeper Gianpiero Combi by captaining Italy to World Cup victory over West Germany in Spain. The Final was the 106th cap of Zoff's career.

1983 Retired after playing a record-breaking112 internationals for Italy in a career that spanned three decades, and having made 570 First Division and 74 Second Division appearances in the Italian league.

1988 Appointed coach to Juventus.

1990 Zoff guided Juventus to success in the 1990 UEFA Cup when they beat Fiorentina 3–0 on aggregate.

1992 Left Juventus for Rome club Lazio, where he subsequently rose from coach to executive director.

Andoni Zubizarreta

1961 Born on October 23 in Bilbao.

1981 Discovered by Athletic Bilbao while playing for minor regional club Alaves in the heart of his native Basque region.

1984 Played for Spain when they lost to England in the Under–21 European Championship.

1985 Made the first of a record 100-plus international appearances for Spain after appearing as a second-half substitute for Luis Arconada in a 3–1 victory against Finland.

1985 Won the Zamora Trophy – in honour of Spain's goalkeeper in the 1930s – for the best Spanish goalkeeper.

1986 Sold by Bilbao to Barcelona for a then world record fee for a goalkeeper of £1.2 million – the first goalkeeper to be transferred for over £1 million. Played in his first World Cup Finals as Spain lost to Belgium on a penalty shoot-out in the quarter-finals.

1990 A disappointing World Cup for Spain which ended in the second round when they lost 2–1 to Yugoslavia after extra-time.

1992 Kept goal in the Barcelona side which achieved the club's long-overdue ambition of winning the European Champions Cup, in a 1–0 extra-time defeat of Sampdoria at Wembley.

1993 Overtook Jose Camacho's record of 81 international appearances for Spain in a World Cup qualifier against the Republic of Ireland in Dublin.

1994 Joined Valencia, reviving his career after being released on a free transfer by Barcelona who were seeking scapegoats after their 4–0 defeat by Milan in the Champions Cup Final. Played in his third World Cup as Spain lost to Italy in the quarter-finals.

1997 Played regularly for Spain as they qualified comfortably for the 1998 World Cup in France.

The Great Matches

The prospect of great players scoring great goals on the great occasions is the lure which fills the stadia. Often, the big match will not live up to its billing. The passes are wasted, the shots fly wide. But once every so often a game unfolds which features all the disparate elements which make soccer such great theatre. Cup finals lend themselves easily to such a status. It's sudden death for one team or the other, the outcome resting on one man's mistake or another man's flash of genius.

That's why the 1994 World Cup Final remains in the memory: not because of the quality of the football – two tired teams could produce precious little – but because of the dramatic penalty failures of Franco Baresi and Roberto Baggio in the decisive shoot-out after extra time. Thus it is no accident that the World Cup and the European Cup have produced probably a greater share of great games than other competitions. It is logical that the greatest players produce the greatest football – and they are brought into conflict in the greatest competitions. Real Madrid's 7–3 defeat of Eintracht Frankfurt in the 1960 Champions Cup Final remains popularly established as the greatest game of all. Great players such as Alfredo Di Stefano and Ferenc Puskas reached the peak of their careers. Those fans with longer memories might argue for Hungary's 4–2 defeat of Uruguay in the 1954 World Cup semi-final. Those whose football memories rest largely on the projection of the age of colour television might well opt for Italy's thrill-a-minute 4–3 victory over West Germany in the 1970 World Cup semi-finals. That was simply… great.

White Horse Cup Final 1923

April 28, 1923 Wembley, London, FA Cup Final

Bolton Wanderers 2
(Jack 3, Smith, J.R., 55)
West Ham United 0

Half Time:
1–0.
Attendance:
126,047 (officially, though many thousands more forced their way in)
Referee:
D. D. H. Asson (West Bromwich)
Bolton:
Pym, Haworth, Finney, Nuttall, Seddon, Jennings, Butler, Jack, Smith, J.R., Smith, J., Vizard.
West Ham:
Hufton, Henderson, Young, Bishop, Kay, Tresadern, Richards, Brown, Watson, Moore, Ruffell.

King George V was there, and somehow a match was laid on for him which, through good fortune and the crowd's good sense, was not the tragedy it might have turned out. Otherwise, the first event staged at the now historic Wembley Stadium might well have been the last. Such was the over-crowding that there could have been a disaster beyond even the awful proportions of Heysel or Hillsborough. Thanks to the self-discipline of the fans in a less impatient age, and to the police – led by Constable George Scorey on his legendary white horse, Billy – the Cup Final took place, starting almost an hour late. The match was not ticket-only, and nobody had anticipated such an enormous turn-out at the new stadium, built as part of the complex to house the Empire Exhibition. The ground was estimated to have a capacity of 125,000, but the combination of a fine spring day, the new arena and the appearance of a London club in the Final (even if a Second Division club) led to an estimated 250,000 trying to gain admittance – and mostly succeeding.

Many who had bought seats were unable to claim them in the crush. Some of the Bolton directors, travelling separately from the team, did not see a ball kicked, but the match went on and football entered the mass consciousness.

The first goal, by David Jack, came as an opponent was trying to climb back out of the crowd next to the touchline; and the second, by the Scot, Jack R. Smith, was thought by some observers to have rebounded from a post, but had in fact bounced back from the wall of spectators pressed against the back of the netting.

Uruguay vs. Argentina 1930

July 30, 1930
Centenario, Montevideo
World Cup Final

Uruguay 4

(Dorado 12, Cea 57, Iriarte 68, Castro 90)

Argentina 2

(Peucelle 20, Stabile 37)

Half Time:

1–2.

Attendance:

93,000

Referee:

J. Langenus (Belgium)

Uruguay:

Ballesteros, Nassazzi, Mascharoni, Andrade, Fernandez, Gestido, Dorado, Scarone, Castro, Cea, Iriarte.

Argentina:

Botasso, Della Torre, Paternoster, Evaristo, Monti, Suarez, Peucelle, Varallo, Stabile, Ferreira, Evaristo.

Few newspapers outside South America and Central Europe bothered to report the match. The Belgian referee John Langenus wore a tie and plus-fours, and several players covered their heads with handkerchiefs to keep the sun at bay. What little film survives shows a near laughable standard of goalkeeping and defensive technique. Yet this game went into history simply because it could not be repeated. The first World Cup was over, and international football now had a standard to surpass.

Soccer statesmen Guérin from France and Hirschman from Holland had mooted the idea of a World Cup and brought it to fruition, even though only 13 nations turned up, including a mere four from Europe. Uruguay, celebrating 100 years of independence, guaranteed to refund all expenses of the other competing nations, just managed to get a new stadium built in time, and fittingly reached the final. There were no seeds, just four groups, each of which sent one team to the semi-final, where Yugoslavia and the United States both lost 6–1. So the final pitted hosts against neighbours, with thousands crossing the River Plate to play their part in a deafening climax to the fledgeling tournament.

The Uruguayans took the lead, fell behind, then went ahead again at 3–2 before striker Guillermo Stabile hit the bar for the host nation. Castro, who had lost part of an arm in childhood, then headed the goal which clinched Uruguay's victory, to be greeted by a national holiday in his country… and bricks through the windows of the Uruguayan Embassy in Buenos Aires.

Germany vs. England 1938

May 14, 1938
Olympic Stadium, Berlin
Friendly International

Germany 3

(Gauchel 20, Gellesch 42, Pesser 70)

England 6

(Bastin 12, Robinson 26, 50, Broome 36, Matthews 39, Goulden 72)

Half Time:

2–4

Attendance:

103,000

Referee:

J. Langenus (Belgium)

Germany:

Jakob, Janes, Muenzenberg, Kupfer, Goldbrunner, Kitzinger, Lehner, Gellesch, Gauchel, Szepan, Pesser.

England:

Woodley, Sproston, Hapgood, Willingham, Young, Welsh, Matthews, Robinson, Broome, Goulden, Bastin.

One of England's most effective displays followed a shameful incident brought about by political pressures of the era. In an effort to placate Hitler, still furious at the way the majority of his athletes had been humbled in the same stadium at the 1936 Olympics, the England team were ordered to join the Germans in giving the Nazi salute as the German national anthem was played. The instruction came from the British Ambassador, Sir Neville Henderson, supported by Stanley Rous (later Sir Stanley), then FA secretary. The players, unwilling to make a fuss, reluctantly got on with it, then showed their feelings by beating a very good German team out of sight. Stanley Matthews said later that he and his team-mates had been inspired by hearing – despite the roars of the German fans – "a few piping voices from behind one goal shouting: Let'em have it, England." Don Welsh, one of two men making their England debut, was to say later: "You couldn't have asked for a greater team performance than this. Only when the heat got to us in the second half did we have to slow down a bit. I honestly thought we could have scored ten." Jackie Robinson, only 20, was a perfect partner for Matthews, and little Len Goulden hit a tremendous 30-yard goal to add to his all-round industry. The other debutant, Frank Broome, also scored. An unsung hero in defence was wing-half Ken Willingham, who barely allowed the German star, Fritz Szepan (nicknamed Saucepan by England's players), a kick.

Brazil vs. Uruguay 1950

July 16, 1950
Maracana, Rio de Janeiro
World Cup final pool

Brazil 1

(Friaca 47)

Uruguay 2

(Schiaffino 66, Ghiggia 79)

Half Time:

0–0

Attendance:

199,000

Referee:

G. Reader (England)

Brazil:

Barbosa, Da Costa, Juvenal, Bauer, Alvim, Bigode, Friaca, Zizinho, Ademir, Jair, Chico.

Uruguay:

Maspoli, Gonzales, Tejera, Gambetta, Varela, Andrade, Ghiggia, Perez, Miguez, Schiaffino, Moran.

Figures for the attendance vary from source to source, but this was certainly the highest at any soccer match since Wembley 1923. The first post-war World Cup, played without a knock-out final stage, provided what was in effect a final and established the tournament as the leading worldwide soccer competition. Even England were in it this time, having snubbed the three pre-war events. They failed miserably, however, struggling to beat Chile, then losing to the United States and Spain. So the Spaniards went through to the final pool, with Brazil, Uruguay and Sweden, and the fixtures worked out perfectly.

Brazil, overwhelming favourites, won their first two games, scoring 13 goals to two. Uruguay trailed both Spain and Sweden 2–1, but drew the first game and won the second. So they had to beat Brazil at the enormous newly-built Maracana, while Brazil needed only to draw. Coach Flavio Costa seemed the only Brazilian unsure of victory, but his warnings about previous encounters in which Uruguay had disturbed Brazil went unheeded.

Even after winger Friaca hit their 22nd goal in six games, Brazil kept pressing forward: Costa later protested that he had ordered men back into defence, but his words had gone either unheard or unheeded. Uruguay, remarkably calm amid the crescendo, equalized through Schiaffino. Then Ghiggia slipped through on the right and shot between Barbosa and his near, left-hand post: not a great goal, but an historic one. Uruguay's inspiration was their attacking centre-half and skipper Obdulio Varela. After listening to manager Juan Lopez's gloomy team-talk, he told his players: "Forget all that. Keep your heads and your positions – and we can win this."

Blackpool vs. Bolton 1953

May 2, 1953
Wembley, London,
FA Cup Final

Blackpool 4

(Mortensen 35, 68, 89, Perry 90)

Bolton Wanderers 3

(Lofthouse 2, Moir 41, Bell 55)

Half Time:

1–2

Attendance:

100,000

Referee:

M. Griffiths (Wales)

Blackpool:

Farm, Shimwell, Garrett, Fenton, Johnston, Robinson, Matthews, Taylor, Mortensen, Mudie, Perry.

Bolton:

Hanson, Ball, Banks, Wheeler, Barrass, Bell, Holden, Moir, Lofthouse, Hassall, Langton.

Stanley Matthews, at 38, stood football on its head. He gained a Cup-winners' medal after being on the losing side twice, he played a barely credible part in his team's rally from three down (the first of only two such recoveries in Wembley history) and he persuaded the hidebound FA to add him to their party to go to South America a few days later, after they had left him out on the grounds of his age.

Blackpool's victory now appears to have been achieved by fate as much as their footballing ability: in Coronation Year, with Everest climbed, the Ashes regained and Gordon Richards winning his first Derby, how could unfancied, homespun Bolton have won the Cup?

But they very nearly did, in a game of remarkable drama, poor goalkeeping – the first, third, fifth and sixth goals ought to have been stopped – and tactical naivety. In the last half-hour, Bolton kept both goalscorer Eric Bell – limping badly from a first-half injury and Ralph Banks, also hobbling on bravely – on their left (this was 13 years before substitutes). That was also Blackpool's right, the flank which Fenton and Taylor ensured was stuffed full of passes for the shuffling, mesmerizing genius that was Matthews.

In the incredible final moments, after the other Stanley, Mortensen, completed his hat-trick (still the only one in a Wembley FA Cup Final) with a free-kick, and Matthews had made the winner for Perry, the scoreboard momentarily showed the score as 4–4. Even today, when the talk is of cup finals, 1953 is usually No. 1.

England vs. Hungary 1953

November 25, 1953
Wembley, London
Friendly International

England 3

(Sewell 15, Mortensen 37, Ramsey 62 pen)

Hungary 6

(Hidegkuti 1, 20, 56, Puskas 22, 29, Bozsik 65)

Half Time:

2–4

Attendance:

100,000

Referee:

L. Horn (Holland)

England:

Merrick, Ramsey, Eckersley, Wright, Johnston, Dickinson, Matthews, Taylor, Mortensen, Sewell, Robb.

Hungary:

Grosics (Geller 74), Buzansky, Lantos, Bozsik, Lorant, Zakarias, Budai, Kocsis, Hidegkuti, Puskas, Czibor.

Why were England so confident? Did they not know that Hungary went to Wembley having won 25 and drawn six of their previous 32 games, and having scored in every match they had played for six seasons? Yet England, fielding two debutants in a team averaging more than 30 years of age, still looked on the match as something of a training spin, fooled by a xenophobic Press which had little or no direct knowledge of Ferenc Puskas and his colleagues. "This will be easy," said one England player as the teams walked out, "they've all got carpet slippers on."

Indeed, Hungary's footwear did look like slippers compared with England's thunderous boots, but they could smack the ball pretty hard when they needed to, as Nandor Hidegkuti did in the opening seconds, from 20 angled yards, his shot arrow-straight past goalkeeper Gil Merrick.

The Hungarians played in tight little triangles, then suddenly opened up with a raking pass of 30, 40, 50 yards or more to a sprinting colleague. They gave the impression that they could always score a goal if they really needed one – and skipper Puskas scored one marvellous individual goal which is still considered one of the greatest of all time.

The defeat, clear and unequivocal, was England's first by a continental invader. That was not in itself important, but the manner and margin of the massacre forced a furious tactical rethink in succeeding seasons. So great a rethink that it is fair to consider whether, without the shock treatment administered by Puskas and Co. England would have won the World Cup 13 years later.

Brazil vs. Hungary 1954

June 27, 1954
Wankdorf, Berne
World Cup quarter-final

Brazil 2

(D. Santos 18 pen, Julinho 65)

Hungary 4

(Hidegkuti 4, Kocsis 7, 90, Lantos 55 pen)

Half Time:

1–2

Attendance:

40,000

Referee:

A. Ellis (England)

Brazil:

Castilho, Santos, D., Santos, N., Brandaozinho, Bauer, Pinheiro, Julinho, Didi, Humberto, Indio, Maurinho.

Hungary:

Grosics, Buzansky, Lantos, Bozsik, Lorant, Zakarias, Toth, M., Kocsis, Hidegkuti, Czibor, Toth, J.

This violent clash between two outstanding teams had a cleansing effect on soccer for a short time. The appalling scenes and continuing controversy served to warn players and officials that football could go close to anarchy unless all concerned showed some respect for the traditions of the game as well as for its rules.

Hungary's part in this disgrace made a lot of people glad when they eventually lost the final, although victory in the world championship would have been a fitting reward for a team of majestic power. Some of the blame must attach to referee Ellis, who sent off three players but never had the match under control.

Hungary, 2–0 up within eight minutes, showed unseemly arrogance, and a wild tackle cost them a penalty, halving their lead. When another penalty enabled them to go two up again, after most people felt that Kocsis had committed the foul, Brazil lost their heads.

Offence followed offence on both sides of Julinho's goal, until Ellis eventually sent off Bozsik (a member of the Hungarian Parliament) and Nilton Santos for fighting, followed by Humberto for a deliberate kick. Kocsis headed a clinching goal in the last seconds, but the violence spilled over into the dressing-rooms, and Ellis needed an armed guard.

FIFA abstained from punitive action, but the Hungarian authorities threatened all sorts of sanctions if there was any repetition. In the semi-final, three days later, Hungary – with nine of their quarter-finalists in action again – played superbly, and cleanly, to beat Uruguay 4–2. The lesson had been learned.

West Germany vs. Hungary 1954

July 4, 1954
Wankdorf, Berne
World Cup Final

West Germany 3

(Morlock 10, Rahn 18, 82)

Hungary 2

(Puskas 6, Czibor 8)

Half Time:

2–2

Attendance:

60,000

Referee:

W. Ling (England)

West Germany

Turek, Posipal, Kohlmeyer, Eckel, Liebrich, Mai, Rahn, Morlock, Walter O., Wal

Hungary:

Grosics, Buzansky, Lantos, Bozsik, Lorant, Zakarias, Czibor, Kocsis, Hidegkuti, Puskas, Toth, J.

German fortitude overtook Hungarian class in a thrilling final, played with great speed and skill despite steady rain. The match was perhaps the first major indication that West Germany's well-organized methods could prove too much for technically superior opposition. Germany have been a force in virtually every World Cup since, whereas Hungary have rarely approached the heights of the Puskas era.

The game also showed the benefit of tactical awareness. German coach Sepp Herberger had fielded only six of his eventual finalists in an earlier group game, which Hungary won 8–3, gambling on doing well in the play-off against Turkey that this defeat would bring. Sure enough, the Turks were beaten 7–2, and Germany went into the quarter-finals and then on to eventual victory.

Ironically, Puskas could be held responsible for his team's defeat. He had been injured in the qualifying game against the Germans a fortnight earlier and had not played since. Although he said he was fit, and scored the first goal, he was nowhere near 100 per cent. The offside decision by linesman Mervyn Griffith that prevented what would have been his late equaliser was another decisive blow. Two early goals took Hungary's total for the tournament to 27, still the record for all finals, but two defensive errors enabled Germany to level with only 18 minutes gone. More than another hour passed before the powerful Rahn – a late addition to the squad after his international career had seemed over – shot Germany's third. Hungary had lost for the first time in 32 games, and the Germans had outsmarted the rest.

Real Madrid vs. Reims 1956

May 13, 1956
Parc des Princes, Paris
European Cup Final

Real Madrid 4

(Di Stefano 15, Rial 30, 80, Marquitos 72)

Reims 3

(Leblond 4, Templin 11, Hidalgo 63)

Half Time:

2–2

Attendance:

38,238

Referee:

A. Ellis (England)

Real Madrid:

Alonso, Atienza, Lesmes, Mu-oz, Marquitos, Zarraga, Joseito, Marsal, Di Stefano, Rial, Gento.

Reims:

Jacquet, Zimny, Giraudo, Leblond, Jonquet, Siatka, Hidalgo, Glovacki, Kopa, Bliard, Templin.

The European Champions Club Cup at last struggled into life, having been conceived and forced through a difficult birth by Gabriel Hanot, a former French international full back and by now the editor of the influential daily newspaper, *L'Equipe*. Only 16 clubs were invited to compete – not all of them national champions: Hibernian, who reached the semi-finals, had finished only fifth in Scotland the previous season.

England, still insular, did not take part, Chelsea meekly complying with a Football League ruling that a European tournament would complicate the fixture list. Attack was the order of the day, or night, in those earlier, more innocent times. The 29 games contained 127 goals (an average of 4.37 per match), with Real scoring 20 and Reims 18, while attendances averaged 31,000. The tournament was a winner, beyond any shadow of doubt.

So too were Real, inspired off the field by far-seeing president Santiago Bernabéu and on it by Alfredo Di Stefano, arriving from Argentina via a brief stop in Colombia's rebel, unrecognized league. Real's exploits over this and the next few seasons established them at the top of the Spanish and European trees, proving the wisdom of Bernabéu's expenditure on a ground capable of holding 125,000. Reims scored two early goals and under Raymond Kopa's direction – Real had already arranged to sign him immediately afterwards – looked capable of more. But Real, on a then huge bonus of £400 each, battled on to earn the first of their five successive European victories. A great team had arrived.

Brazil vs. Sweden 1958

June 29, 1958
Rasunda, Stockholm,
World Cup Final

Brazil 5

(Vava 9, 30, Pele 55, 90, Zagalo 68)

Sweden 2

(Liedholm 4, Simonsson 80)

Half Time:

2–1

Attendance:

49,737

Referee:

M. Guigue (France)

Brazil:

Gilmar, Santos, D., Santos, N., Zito, Bellini, Orlando, Garrincha, Didi, Vava, Pele, Zagalo.

Sweden:

Svensson, Bergmark, Axbom, Borjesson, Gustavsson, Parling, Hamrin, Gren, Simonsson, Liedholm, Skoglund.

Brazil's victory over the host nation in Stockholm proved to a vast audience – thanks to the spread of television – that South Americans can, after all, travel well. The team deservedly went into history as one of the greatest ever, after wonderful performances in the semi-final (5–2 against France) and the final, when they overcame an early deficit with unstoppable power.

Manager Vicente Feola had restored Didi, thought by some to be too old at 30, and preferred Vava to 19-year-old Mazzola as striker. These changes worked well, as did Feola's decision to bring back Djalma Santos in defence after Di Sordi had played all the previous games in the final stages. Santos, thought Feola, had the necessary pace to deal with brilliant Swedish left-winger Lennart Skoglund – and so it proved.

Perhaps the most crucial decision in Brazil's path to glory, however, was made by the players and their insistence that Feola find a place for Garrincha on the right wing. Feola somewhat reluctantly agreed – and Garrincha, often tantalisingly inconsistent, responded superbly. His speed left the Swedes for dead to make two goals for Vava, and Pele conjured a magical third, controlling a long cross from Mario Zagallo on one thigh, flicking the ball over his head, whirling and shooting, all in a fraction of a second.

After adding the final goal, Pele dissolved in tears of joy on the shoulders of veteran goalkeeper Gilmar. Pele, perhaps the greatest player ever, had made a worldwide mark on the sport he would later describe as "the beautiful game". At 17 he was the youngest ever winner of a competition he would still be dominating 12 years later.

Real Madrid vs. Eintracht Frankfurt 1960

May 18, 1960
Hampden Park, Glasgow
European Cup Final

Real Madrid 7

(Di Stefano 27, 30, 73, Puskas 36, 48 pen, 58, 63)

Eintracht Frankfurt 3

(Kress 18, Stein 72, 80)

Half Time:

3–1

Attendance:

127,621

Referee:

A. Mowat (Scotland)

Real Madrid:

Dominguez, Marquitos, Pachin, Vidal, Santamaria, Zarraga, Canario, Del Sol, Di Stefano, Puskas, Gento.

Eintracht Frankfurt:

Loy, Lutz, Hofer, Weilbacher, Eigenbrodt, Stinka, Kress, Lindner, Stein, Pfaff, Meier.

Real Madrid's fifth successive European Cup was achieved by their greatest performance in front of yet another great crowd. In their seven matches they scored 31 goals and were watched by 524,097 people – an average of nearly 75,000 per game. In the semi-final, Real beat Barcelona 3–1 home and away, after Barça had crushed Wolves, the English champions, 9–2 on aggregate. In the other semi-final, Eintracht performed the barely credible feat of twice scoring six goals against Rangers, but in the final they conceded hat-tricks to Di Stefano and Puskas in a wonderful performance watched by a crowd so big that only one larger attendance has been recorded in Britain since. Hardly any left early, even though the Germans were a beaten team well before the end. The fans stayed to bay a seemingly never-ending roar of tribute to one of the finest displays ever put on by any team, anywhere. The Scots were quick to appreciate their good fortune.

Real were now under their fourth coach in five years, wing-half Miguel Mu-oz from their 1956 team having taken over. His two signings, Del Sol and Pachin, augmented an already illustrious squad, with the Uruguayan Santamaria a rock in defence, Gento a rapier on the left, and – towering above all – Di Stefano and Puskas, creators and finishers of a standard rarely seen before or since. Yet not even Real could win everything. Although they went on to beat Peñarol 5–1 in the first (unofficial) club championship, they were only runners-up in their domestic league and cup.

Benfica vs. Barcelona 1961

May 31, 1961
Wankdorf, Berne
European Cup Final

Benfica 3

(Aguas 30, Ramallets 31 (o.g.), Coluna 55)

Barcelona 2

(Kocsis 20, Czibor 79)

Half Time:

2–1

Attendance:

33,000

Referee:

G. Dienst (Switzerland)

Benfica:

Costa Pereira, Mario Joao, Angelo, Neto, Germano, Cruz, José Augusto, Santana, Aguas, Coluna, Cavem.

Barcelona:

Ramallets, Foncho, Gracia, Verges, Garay, Gensana, Kubala, Kocsis, Evaristo, Suarez, Czibor.

A curious match which showed a corporate rise and some individual falls. Benfica, little known outside Portugal and rank outsiders beforehand, took the European Cup and began a parade of domestic success that brought 12 championships in the next 16 seasons, all in bunches of three: 1963–64–65, 1967–68–69, 1971–72–73 and 1975–76–77. And the Hungarian link with European Cup finals was now almost severed. Kocsis and Czibor, who both scored for Barcelona, had been on the losing side – beaten by the same score on the same ground – in the 1954 World Cup Final. They were virtually the last link with the marvellous Magyar team, though Puskas was to have the final word with a hat-trick for Real in the European Cup Final a year later. Another Hungarian, Kubala – who played for three countries – was a third key figure for Barça, but their downfall was due to a home-bred player.

Their international keeper Ramallets missed a cross and let in Aguas for Benfica's equalizer. A minute later, he fumbled a back-header by Gensana and allowed the ball to cross the line before knocking it back. Even Coluna's thunderous, long-range third might have been saved had he reacted more quickly.

Those errors sapped Barça's confidence, but they battled on, hitting the woodwork three times, four if Kubala's shot that came out after striking both posts is counted twice. Benfica, however fortunate with their goals, were a good, adventurous side and held out calmly even after conceding a late second. Kocsis and Czibor left the field in tears… the Wankdorf stadium having robbed them, as in 1954.

Celtic vs. Internazionale 1967

May 25, 1967
National Stadium, Lisbon
European Cup Final

Celtic 2

(Gemmell 73, Chalmers 85)

Internazionale 1

(Mazzola 8 pen)

Half Time:

0–1

Attendance:

45,000

Referee:

H. Tschenscher (W Germany)

Celtic:

Simpson, Craig, Gemmell, Murdoch, McNeill, Clark, Johnstone, Wallace, Chalmers, Auld, Lennox.

Internazionale:

Sarti, Burgnich, Facchetti, Bedin, Guarneri, Picchi, Domenghini, Mazzola, Cappellini, Bicicli, Corso.

Celtic, one of Scotland's big two clubs, were minnows in the mainstream of Europe, despite frequent forays. Only two of their team on this balmy night in Portugal, before a frenzied crowd of adoring travellers, had any experience of the game outside their native land. Bertie Auld spent a none-too-productive spell at Birmingham, and Ronnie Simpson had left Newcastle more than a decade earlier (and now, at 37, was Scottish Footballer of the Year). The rest were a mixture of Glasgow lads and small-fee bargains recruited by Jock Stein, a manager adept at making the whole much greater than the sum of the parts – nowadays he would have a degree in Human Resources.

Inter, European champions in 1965, returned to the final with the help of a 'deal' that would not now be allowed: after two draws with CSKA Sofia, Inter won the right to stage a vital home play-off in Bologna simply by promising the impoverished Bulgarians 75 per cent of the takings. When Inter won through by a lone goal, many neutrals turned against them: certainly Celtic had incredible support in a comparatively small crowd at Lisbon, where they won the right to be called Lions.

Inter were also hampered by the absence through injury of their Spanish playmaker, Luis Suarez, upon whom their counter-attacking tactic depended. Even though the Scots trailed for more than an hour, their faith in hard work and uncomplicated, attacking football paid off with two goals. So bargain-basement Celtic won every tournament they contested that season, while big-money Inter did not win anything. Delightful irony, but how things have changed from the late 1960s.

Manchester United vs. Benfica 1968

May 29, 1968
Wembley, London
European Cup Final

Manchester United 4

(Charlton 53, 104, Best 91, Kidd 95)

Benfica 1

(Graça 85). After extra time.

Half Time:	***Full Time:***
0–0	1–1

Attendance:

100,000

Referee:

C. Lo Bello (Italy)

Manchester United:

Stepney, Brennan, Dunne, Crerand, Foulkes, Stiles, Best, Kidd, Charlton, Sadler, Aston.

Benfica:

Henrique, Adolfo, Cruz, Graça, Humberto, Jacinto, José Augusto, Eusebio, Torres, Coluna, Simoes.

One shot, one save… so much glorious English football history might never have happened. Eusebio, the mainspring of a fine Benfica side, had a chance to win the game, moments after Graça's late equalizer of a rare Bobby Charlton headed goal had sent United reeling. A thunderous right-foot shot from 18 yards after he had been put through the middle brought an instinctive save from Alex Stepney and a rueful clap from Eusebio: did he realize, even then, that a more delicate placing could have won the cup for his own team?

In extra time, United regained their poise and power, with a glorious solo goal by George Best just a minute into the deciding half-hour being followed by two others, one from Brian Kidd, on his 19th birthday, who headed the ball in at the second attempt after the goalkeeper had parried his first header, pushing it back out to him, and the other by skipper Charlton, one of the World Cup winners on the same pitch two years earlier.

So United, the third fine team assembled by manager Matt Busby in 20 years, became the first English club to annex Europe's leading trophy. The early post-war United were too soon for Europe: the mid-1950s Busby Babes reached the semi-finals in 1957, losing to Real Madrid, and the patched-up, post-Munich side suffered an inevitable defeat against Milan in 1958.

Thus a decade passed after Munich before Busby's third great team swept to their majestic triumph. Charlton and Foulkes were Munich survivors in the team. In so doing, they gave extra heart to other English clubs who had faltered on Europe's threshold: in the next decade, nine English clubs reached various finals on the Continent.

Italy vs. West Germany 1970

June 17, 1970
Azteca, Mexico City
World Cup semi-final

Italy 4

(Boninsegna 7, Burgnich 97, Riva 103, Rivera 111)

West Germany 3

(Schnellinger 90, Müller 95, 110) aet

Half Time: 1–0 ***90 Minutes:*** 1–1

Attendance:

80,000

Referee:

A.Yamasaki (Mexico)

Italy:

Albertosi, Burgnich, Cera, Bertini, Facchetti, Rosato (Poletti), Domenghini, Mazzola (Rivera), De Sisti, Boninsegna, Riva.

West Germany:

Maier, Vogts, Beckenbauer, Schulz, Schnellinger, Grabowski, Patzke (Held), Overath, Seeler, Müller, Löhr (Libuda).

Six goals in 21 minutes made this one of the most exciting matches in the history of the World Cup or any other competition. Sadly, such are the demands of modern tournament structures, both teams ended up as losers. Three days earlier, in a thrilling quarter-final, Germany had played extra time before beating England 3–2, and coach Helmut Schön blamed defeat by Italy on the draining effects of that match. Four days later, an unchanged Italian side crashed 4–1 in the final, and although there was no mistaking Brazil's right to the Jules Rimet Trophy, equally there was no doubting the fact that the Italians, in turn, had not fully recovered from their exertions against the Germans.

Players, no matter how fit, need ample time to recuperate from two tense, testing hours in the Mexican sun. Schön, usually a master at tactical substitution, was caught out this time and forced to leave Beckenbauer on the field after he had dislocated a shoulder – bravery unquestioned but ability impaired. The gallant Beckenbauer played for an hour, including extra time, with the shoulder strapped.

Germany could not afford such luxuries. Italy led for nearly all normal time, after Boninsegna's early snap shot, but Schnellinger, playing in his fourth World Cup, equalized in injury time – only seconds from defeat. That began a remarkable scoring burst, with Germany leading 2–1, Italy going 3–2 ahead, the Germans levelling – Müller's 10th goal of the tournament – and Rivera carefully rolling in what proved to be the decider, from the restart.

Italy vs. Brazil 1982

July 5, 1982
Sarria, Barcelona
World Cup Group C

Italy 3

(Rossi 5, 25, 75)

Brazil 2

(Socrates 12, Falcao 68)

Half Time:

2–1

Attendance:

44,000

Referee:

A Klein (Israel)

Italy:

Zoff, Gentile, Collovati (Bergomi), Scirea, Cabrini, Tardelli (Marini), Antognoni, Oriali, Graziani, Conti, Rossi.

Brazil:

Waldir Peres, Leandro, Oscar, Luisinho, Junior, Toninho Cerezo, Socrates, Zico, Falcao, Serginho (Paulo Isidoro), Eder.

On the morning of April 29, 1982, Paolo Rossi returned from suspension, having been banned for three years – later reduced to two – for allegedly accepting a bribe and helping 'fix' a match in the Italian league. Some 11 weeks later, Rossi was the hero of all Italy. He scored three goals in this vital group qualifying match to eliminate the favourites, Brazil, two in the semi-final against Poland, and one in the final, when Italy beat West Germany 3–1. His six goals made him the tournament's leading marksman and completed a remarkable comeback for one of the most effective strikers of his generation.

Rossi was still only 24, and Juventus had such faith in him that they paid Perugia £600,000 to buy him while he had a year of the ban to run. He had always protested his innocence – and his demonic efforts to regain match fitness, plus his finishing, took Italy to a merited success after they had managed only three draws in their initial qualifying group.

Brazil began against Italy needing only a draw to reach the semi-finals, and should have achieved it with some ease. But their two brilliant goals encouraged them to keep on attacking and their over-stretched defence made too many errors against a forward in such inspired mood as Rossi, the man who came back, and perhaps the best team in the competition were out.

The consolation of the finest goal of the game, however, went to Brazilian midfielder Paulo Roberto Falcao – driving a thunderous shot past Dino Zoff for the equalizer at 2-2 after his team-mates' dummy runs pulled the Italian defence all over the place and left Zoff and the goal at his mercy.

West Germany vs. France 1982

July 8, 1982
Sanchez Pizjuan, Seville
World Cup semi-final

West Germany 3

(Littbarski 18, Rummenigge 102, Fischer 107)

France 3

(Platini 27 pen, Trésor 92, Giresse 98) aet

Half Time:	***90 Minutes:***	***Penalties:***
1–1	1–1	5–4

Attendance:

63,000

Referee:

C. Corver (Holland)

West Germany:

Schumacher, Kaltz, Forster, K.-H., Stielike, Briegel (Rummenigge), Forster, B., Dremmler, Breitner, Littbarski, Magath

France:

Ettori, Amoros, Janvion, Bossis, Tigana, Trésor, Genghini (Battiston, Lopez), Giresse, Platini, Rocheteau, Six.

The first World Cup finals match to be decided on penalties was resolved because indomitable German spirit proved just too much for French skill. But West Germany were lucky to go through after an appalling foul by goalkeeper Harald Schumacher on French substitute Patrick Battiston. Schumacher's headlong charge left Battiston unconscious for several minutes. A penalty? A sending-off? Not even a booking. The referee, in his wisdom, allowed Schumacher to remain, staring cold-eyed as Battiston was carried away.

France recovered so well after a poor opening that they might well have won inside 90 minutes. Then two quick goals in extra time seemed to have made them safe, and delighted all neutrals. Yet the Germans, again showing remarkable spirit in adversity, pulled the game round.

Karl-Heinz Rummenigge, their captain, went on as a substitute, although far from fit, and scored almost at once. Then, with Rummenigge this time the creator, an overhead hook from centre-forward Klaus Fischer levelled the scores.

Even then France should have won. They won the toss to decide who took the first penalty of the shoot-out, which usually proves a mental advantage, and when Uli Stielike missed Germany's third attempt, France led 3–2. But Didier Six failed with his and, after West Germany had levelled at 4–4, Schumacher made himself even less popular with the world at large by parrying a weak effort from Maxime Bossis. Hrubesch promptly hit the winner.

West Germany vs. England 1990

July 4, 1990
Delle Alpe, Turin
World Cup semi-final

West Germany 1

(Brehme 59)

England 1

(Lineker 80) aet

Half Time:	**90 Minutes:**	**Penalties:**
0–0	1–1	4–3

Attendance:

62,628

Referee:

J R Wright (Brazil)

West Germany:

Illgner, Brehme, Kohler, Augenthaler, Buchwald, Berthold, Matthäus, Hässler (Reuter), Thom, Völler (Riedle), Klinsmann.

England:

Shilton, Wright, Parker, Butcher (Steven), Walker, Pearce, Beardsley, Platt, Gascoigne, Waddle, Lineker.

Two of soccer's oldest rivals served up a magnificent match, sadly decided by what was then FIFA's only solution to draws after 120 minutes: penalties. England went so very, very close to reaching the final for only the second time. Despite all the trials and tribulations besetting their manager, Bobby Robson, and despite the lack of class players – in the English game at large, let alone in the squad – there was only the merest fraction between the teams at the end. The splendid spirit in which the match was contested was another bonus. So, on a more personal level, was the flood of tears released by the England enigma, Paul Gascoigne, which made him a media and public darling overnight and earned him a wallet of gold to go with his later-revealed feet of clay.

This was a night with many heroes, perhaps none more so than the referee, Jose Roberto Wright, who let the game run without the nit-picking fussiness of so many other officials. The Germans, often wanting to referee as well as play, were none too keen on Wright's firm hand, but that suited England perfectly and helped them to play above themselves. Only a freak goal by Andy Brehme, deflected high over Peter Shilton by Paul Parker's attempted interception, put Germany in front. The indomitable Gary Lineker pounced on a half-chance to level and from then on penalties seemed the only solution. The Germans scored all the four they needed to take whereas Stuart Pearce and Chris Waddle missed England's last two. No arguing with that – only with the system.

Denmark vs. Germany 1992

June 26, 1992
Ullevi, Gothenburg
European Championship Final

Denmark 2

(Jensen 18, Vilfort 78)

Germany 0

Half Time:

1–0

Attendance:

37,800

Referee:

B. Galler (Switzerland)

Denmark:

Schmeichel, Piechnik, Olsen L., Nielsen, Sivebaek (Christiansen 68), Vilfort,Jensen, Larsen, Christofte, Laudrup B., Povlsen.

Germany:

Illgner, Reuter, Kohler, Helmer, Buchwald, Brehme, Hässler, Effenberg (Thom 80), Sammer (Doll 46), Klinsmann, Riedle.

Germany or Holland seemed the likely winners of the ninth European Championship. France and perhaps even England looked likely to have a good run. As for Denmark, they had not even qualified for the finals and got in only when war-ravaged Yugoslavia had to withdraw after topping their qualifying group, a point ahead of the Danes.

When Denmark began by drawing with England and losing to Sweden they seemed lost beyond retrieval. Many of the players had been on holiday and out of training when the call came for them to sweat off the pounds and make the trip to Sweden. Manager Richard Moller Nielsen was in the middle of decorating his kitchen and most of the fine team from the 1980s were no longer in the reckoning – Michael Laudrup having squabbled with Moller Nielsen – while several of the squad were injured during the event. Despite all that, the Danes showed spirit and considerable skill and discipline. A late goal against France made them second in their group and meant a semi-final against the Dutch, who snatched a late equalizer but lost on penalties – the decisive kick being wasted by Marco Van Basten, of all people.

So Denmark went through to meet Germany in what was expected to be a one-sided final – except that nobody had told the Danes. From Schmeichel to Povlsen, they all played their parts to perfection on an evening when little the Germans did went right. Vilfort, who scored the deciding goal (did he handle the ball first?) had just returned to the squad after going home because of his daughter's illness. Hans Christian Andersen could not have written a finer fairytale.

England vs. Germany 1996

June 30, 1996
Wembley, London, European Championship semi-final

England 1

(Shearer 2)

Germany 1

(Kuntz 16) After golden goal extra-time

Half Time:	***Full Time:***	***Penalties:***
1–1	1–1	5–6

Attendance:

75,862

Referee:

S. Puhl (Hungary)

England:

Seaman, Southgate, Adams, Pearce, Anderton, Platt, Ince, Gascoigne, McManaman, Sheringham, Shearer.

Germany:

Köpke, Reuter, Babbel, Sammer, Helmer (Bode 95), Ziege, Scholl (Hässler 76), Eilts, Möller, Freund (Strunz 104), Kuntz.

Germany won the European Championship for a record third time but hosts England were indirect winners as well for the staging of the most prestigious European event, mixing drama on the pitch with enthusiastic, welcoming support off it as well as a national team which rose to the occasion in magnificent style to reach the semi-finals.

As in the 1990 World Cup, England and Germany could only then be separated by a penalty shoot-out after a night of exciting intensity which a 76,000 crowd at Wembley and 26 million domestic television viewers will never forget.

England secured a magnificent start, Shearer heading home in the second minute. Germany, with only one fit striker, responded with courage and invention and that lone raider, Stefan Kuntz, equalized in the 16th minute.

The game was an emotional roller-coaster and produced one of the most thrilling extra time spectacles Wembley has witnessed thanks to the introduction of the golden goal rule. Darren Anderton was an inch from the vital strike when he hit a post, then Germany thought they had it as Kuntz headed past Seaman, only for referee Sandor Puhl to penalize the German for pushing.

And so to penalties. Both teams converted their five regulation efforts. Then Gareth Southgate ran up, only to push his kick low into the grateful arms of German keeper Andy Köpke. Andy Möller ran up for Germany… and shot them into the final. German coach Berti Vogts had plainly written the script, saying later: "I told my players in which order they would take the penalties – and I told Möller he would shoot the winner."

The Famous Stadiums

A football stadium is a simple thing: a mixture of concrete, steel, stone and plastic which serves a similarly simple purpose: to allow thousands of like-minded people to watch 22 men play football. Yet the great stadia of the world have long since taken on personalities of their own – the power of their presence offering strength and confidence to the footballers who call the ground "home."

Real Madrid, for instance, were never beaten at the mighty Bernabéu stadium in the first seven dominant years of their command of European club football. But even Madrid were set on the defensive by the challenge of playing in Barcelona's Nou Camp or the Meazza stadium at San Siro, Milan – a ground whose terraces rise like the steepest, noisiest cliffs above the tempestuous football sea at their feet. The stadia of different countries offer contrasts. England boasts the most recently redeveloped stadia in Europe, although Italy, Spain and Germany boast grounds with bigger capacities. Most capital cities possess a proud, monolithic structure to show off their football prowess. Many of these stadia serve a dual purpose, possessing the pitch-side facilities for other sports. Thus Rome, Berlin and Moscow have all played host to the Olympic Games as well as top-level international football. One stadium has played host twice to the World Cup Final itself – the Azteca in Mexico City, lately renamed in memory of top local soccer director, Guillermo Canedo. The Maracana in Rio, which once welcomed 200,000 at the 1950 World Cup, has had its capacity cut for security reasons. But it is still Brazil's home – and playing there or in any one of these other great stadia remains a status symbol among footballers the world over.

Nou Camp

Barcelona, Spain

Capacity:
115,000

Opened:
1957

Club:
FC Barcelona

Hosted:
1982 World Cup Opening Match (Belgium 1, Argentina 0); 1992 Olympic Final (Spain 3, Poland 2); 1989 European Cup Final (Milan 4, Steaua Bucharest 0); 1982 European Cup-winners' Cup Final (Barcelona 2, Standard Liège 1)

Higher and higher, bigger and better could be the motto of Barcelona's towering and breathtaking Nou Camp, "the new ground", which opened its doors on September 24, 1957 and was financed to the tune of 66 million pesetas by club members. In Europe today only Benfica's Estadio da Luz can claim to be larger. Sport, it has been said, is the acceptable substitute for war, and Barcelona, the football team (*see* page 37) has always been a vehicle for the fervent nationalism of Catalonia. The rivalry with Madrid is intense, and the Nou Camp's continual improvements and expansion have much to do with the desire to outdo Real's Bernabéu stadium.

Barcelona, formed in 1899, outgrew their old Les Corts ground in the 1940s and moved to the new stadium, in an area of allotments to the west, in 1957. When Nou Camp was inaugurated with a match against Legia Warsaw, plans had already been laid to increase capacity to 150,000.

An indoor sports hall, connected to Nou Camp by a concourse, was opened in 1971 and houses the club's basketball, handball and volleyball teams. Ice hockey is held in the adjacent Ice Palace. Even more remarkably, there is a walkway over a road leading to another football stadium, the 16,500 capacity Mini-Estad, opened in 1982 and used by Barcelona's nursery team in the Spanish Second Division as well as by the club's top amateur side.

Capacity increase

The first major redevelopment of the main stadium was in the early 1980s, when the addition of a third tier increased capacity to 120,000 in time for Nou Camp to host the opening ceremony of the 1982 World Cup. When the old ground was opened in 1922, "Barça" had a membership of 5,000. When Pope John Paul II visited the Nou Camp in World Cup year he was enrolled as member no. 108,000. Since then membership has passed 110,000, making Barcelona the largest club in the world. The work never stops. For the 1992 Olympic Games in Barcelona, two more tiers were installed above the previous roof line, with a suspended cantilevered roof soaring overhead.

Olympia-stadion

Berlin, Germany

Capacity:
76,006
Opened:
1936
Clubs:
Hertha BSC, Blau-Weiss 90
Hosted:
1936 Olympic Final (Italy 2, Austria 1); 1974 World Cup group matches

Berlin's historic – or notorious – stadium may be considered not so much a theatre of dreams, more a monument to the nightmarish world of Adolf Hitler and his national socialism. It was here that Hitler opened the 1936 Olympics, a giant propaganda exercise, to Wagnerian strains before an ecstatic 100,000 crowd. And it was here, much to his chagrin, that the black American athlete Jesse Owens won four gold medals to challenge the myth of Aryan superiority. Two years later the England team played Germany and avenged the politically-engineered demand that they give the Nazi salute by winning 6–3 (*see* page 168).

The Olympiapark, of which the Olympiastadion is the neo-classical centre-piece, had its origins before the First World War since Germany had been chosen to stage the Games in 1916. The unused facilities, adjacent to the Grunewald racecourse, were taken over when Hitler came to power in 1933. His grand plan involved the 86,000 capacity stadium on a 131-hectare sports field which also included hockey, riding and swimming stadia plus an open-air amphitheatre. These were all linked to the vast Maifeld, used by the Nazis for mass rallies.

East vs. West

The stadium suffered from Allied bombing but was repaired by the mid-1960s, when Hertha Berlin drew 70,000 crowds in the early years of the Bundesliga, the new national championship of West Germany. The stadium was renovated for the 1974 World Cup when it staged three group matches. The use of the Olympiastadion in the first place had caused political tension between East and West, and its incorporation in the World Cup programme at all was a triumph for German football chief Hermann Neuberger.

The unique political problems of Berlin meant that the stadium was underused for years. It was the home of both Hertha and Blau-Weiss Berlin but that meant mainly Second Division football. Now, since reunification, the Olympiastadion has regained its status as a focal point for German football and it is once again the permanent home of the German cup final.

Monumental

Buenos Aires, Argentina

Capacity:
76,000

Opened:
1938

Club:
River Plate

Hosted:
1978 World Cup Final (Argentina 3, Holland 1 aet); 1946, 1959 and 1987 South American Championships

There were many misgivings about holding the 1978 World Cup in Argentina, not the least of which concerned the political climate. Ultimately, the ruling military junta invested huge sums in the renovation of the Monumental, which had been the home of the national side and of one of the world's great clubs, River Plate (*see* page 65). Several of River's own players, including skipper Daniel Passarella (Argentina's manager for the 1998 World Cup in France), goalkeeper Ubaldo Fillol and forwards Leopoldo Luque and Oscar Ortiz, featured in the side which defeated the Netherlands 3–1 in the final amid a paper snowstorm which tumbled down the Monumental and set the scene for the coming 90 minutes.

Work had begun on the Monumental on September 27, 1936 and it was ready for the River team to move in by May 1938. The dressing-rooms and offices were of a standard then unique in South America, while the three-sided horseshoe boasted an original capacity of 100,000, with the potential of a third tier which would lift it to 150,000. Needless to say, that third tier was never needed.

The opening game, a 3–1 win over the Uruguayan champions Peñarol, was watched by a crowd of 70,000. But the stadium itself was not completed, even in its initial phase, for many years, until 1957, when River invested much of the then world record fee of £97,000 they had received from Italy's Juventus for their inside-forward Omar Sivori.

Another World Cup?

Apart from the 1978 World Cup, the Monumental has played host to many internationals and South American club ties, as well as key games when Argentina have taken their turn to host the Copa America (the South American Championship).

Major redevelopment work has been under consideration for some time both to assist crowd control after increasing problems of hooliganism in Argentine soccer but also because the Monumental will be the centre-piece of the projected bid to host the World Cup once again.

Hampden Park

Glasgow, Scotland

Capacity:

50,000

Opened:

1903

Club:

Queen's Park

Hosted:

1960 European Cup Final (Real Madrid 7, Eintracht Frankfurt 3), 1976 (Bayern Munich 1, Saint-Etienne 0); 1961 European Cup-winners' Cup (Fiorentina 2, Rangers 0), 1962 (Atlético Madrid 1, Fiorentina 1, replay in Stuttgart), 1966 (Borussia Dortmund 2, Liverpool 1); 1989 World Under-17 Championship Final (Saudi Arabia 1, Scotland 1 aet: Saudi Arabia 5–4 on pens).

As early as 1908, Glasgow had three of the largest grounds in the world: Ibrox, home of Protestant Rangers, Celtic Park, home of Catholic Celtic, and Hampden, owned by amateurs Queens Park. Hampden was already the national stadium, never more vibrant than when hosting games against the old enemy England, whom Scotland had met in the first-ever international in 1872. It was the largest stadium in the world until the Maracana opened in 1950 and still holds several attendance records. In 1937, 149,415 paid to see the Scots beat England, a record for a match in Europe. A week later, a European club record 147,365 saw Celtic beat Aberdeen for the Scottish Cup.

Ten-goal Final

In 1960, 135,000 watched Real Madrid trounce Eintracht Frankfurt 7–3 in the European Cup Final (*see* page 176). That record was bettered five years later, when 136,505 saw Celtic's semi-final with Leeds. Since then there has been major redevelopment. First came a £3 million refurbishment in 1975 then a £12 million remodelling in the early 1990s. Hampden was shut again after the 1996 Scottish Cup Final for the construction of an 18,000-capacity new South Stand. Considering all the work carried out, it is remarkable that Hampden has not staged a European club final for more than 20 years.

While it remains easily the most famous soccer stadium in Scotland, Hampden has faced a challenge from the major redevelopment projects undertaken at both of Glasgow's other big grounds, Ibrox and Celtic Park.

It remains, fortunately, the one stadium in the city where fans of both the Old Firm clubs can meet on neutral territory.

Estádio Da Luz

Lisbon, Portugal

Capacity:
130,000

Opened:
1954

Club:
Benfica

Hosted:
1991 World Youth Cup Final (Portugal 0, Brazil 0: Portugal 4–2 on pens); 1967 European Cup Final (Celtic 2, Internazionale 1); 1992 European Cup-Winners' Cup Final (Werder Bremen 2, Monaco 0)

Although the 'Stadium of Light' is one of the most evocatively named arenas in the world, it takes its name not from the power of its floodlighting but from the nearby Lisbon district of Luz. Yet one of the most dazzling players in history, the 'Black Pearl' Eusebio (*see* page 104), led Benfica to unparalleled heights here during the 1960s and 1970s when 14 league titles, two European Cup wins (1960 and 1961) and three more final appearances established Benfica among the aristocracy of European football.

In 1992, a statue of their greatest son was unveiled to celebrate his fiftieth birthday, before a match with old British rivals Manchester United, and this now greets visitors as they arrive at the entrance of the stadium.

Porto Keep Winning

Benfica, or Sport Lisboa Benfica (*see* page 39)as they are officially named, were formed in 1908, and by the 1950s had long outgrown their fifth ground at Campo Grande. Plans for the 60,000 capacity Estádio da Luz were drawn up by a former Benfica athlete in 1951 and the original two–tiered stadium was opened in 1954. Porto won the inaugural game 3–0, and Portugal's first floodlit game, again won by Porto, took place four years later. By 1960 a third tier had been added to increase the capacity to 75,000, and by the late 1970s the Estádio Da Luz, all white and bright, seated 130,000, and was a legend in Europe.

The stadium was filled to this capacity only once, however, when Portugal defeated Brazil in a penalty shoot-out in the 1991 World Youth Cup final. UEFA restrictions on standing and security, introduced in the wake of various crowd disasters around the world, meant reducing the available match day capacity to its current limit, which is around 100,000.

Wembley Stadium

London, England

Capacity:
80,000

Opened:
1923

Club:
None

Hosted:
1948 Olympic Final (Sweden 3, Yugoslavia 1); 1966 World Cup Final (England 4, West Germany 2 aet); 1996 European Championship; 1963 European Cup Final (Milan 2, Benfica 1), 1968 (Manchester United 4, Benfica 1 aet), 1971 (Ajax 2, Panathinaikos 0), 1978 (Liverpool 1, Brugge 0), 1992 (Barcelona 1, Sampdoria 0 aet); 1965 Cup-Winners Cup Final (West Ham 2, Munich 1860 0); 1993 (Parma 3, Antwerp 1)

Wembley may be the ageing grande dame of stadia but, steeped in history and with its distinctive twin towers, it remains the Mecca of English football and is revered by players and fans throughout the world. Wembley is synonymous with England internationals, the FA Cup Final and the epic World Cup Final of 1966\.

Unusually for a major stadium, Wembley is privately owned and financed by its staging of major soccer, greyhound racing, rugby league, showpiece American football games, and ancillary sporting activities at the nearby 9,000-seater Arena. In the 1920s the green fields of Wembley Park were chosen as the site for the 1923 Empire Exhibition. The then Empire Stadium was built between January 22 and April 23. It was hailed as the largest monumental building of reinforced concrete in the world, and a troop of soldiers marched up and down the terracing in a unique safety check.

Since a crowd of "only" 53,000 had turned up for the 1922 FA Cup Final at Stamford Bridge, the authorities were concerned that Bolton and West Ham might not fill the new 126,000 capacity ground the following year. But on April 28 more than 200,000 people besieged Wembley, and that Bolton were eventually able to defeat West Ham 2–0 was due in no small part to the good nature of the crowd in the presence of King George V and a celebrated policeman on his white horse (*see* page 166). The Wembley legend was born.

Wembley has moved with the times. The surrounding exhibition centre was redeveloped while the stadium was remodelled in the 1980s. Adapting to all-seater demands meant a capacity reduction from 100,000. The addition of an Olympic Gallery beneath the roof edge kept an 80,000 level at which Wembley took centre stage in England's hosting of the 1996 European Championship.

Santiago Bernabéu

Madrid, Spain

Capacity:
105,000

Opened:
1947

Club:
Real Madrid

Hosted:
1982 World Cup Final (Italy 3, West Germany 2); 1964 European Championship Final (Spain 2, Soviet Union 1); 1957 European Cup Final (Real Madrid 2, Fiorentina 0), 1969 (Milan 4, Ajax 1), 1980 (Nottingham Forest 1, Hamburg 0).

It is thanks to the visionary foresight of long-time president Santiago Bernabéu that Real Madrid (*see* page 63) boast an imposing edifice on Madrid's most prestigious street, the Castellana, housing one of the world's foremost clubs and a trophy room bulging with silverware and displaying more than 5,000 items. The ground, which began life as the Nuevo Chamartin Stadium in 1944 on five hectares of prime land, was Bernabéu's brainchild. He was a lawyer who had been, in turn, player, captain, club secretary, coach and then, from 1942, president. The old stadium had been ravaged during the Spanish Civil War of the 1930s and Bernabéu decided that a super new stadium was needed if the club were to raise the funds needed to build a super new team. Real Madrid, who now include the King and Queen of Spain and President of the International Olympic Committee Juan Antonio Samaranch among their members, raised an astonishing 41 million pesetas by public subscription to finance the land purchase and first stage of building. The stadium was opened, with a 75,000 capacity, for a testimonial match for veteran player Jesus Alonso against Portuguese club Belenenses of Lisbon in December, 1947.

In the 1950s the finance raised by Real's dominance of the fledgeling European Cup enabled capacity within the distinctive white towers to be extended to 125,000. The name Estadio Santiago Bernabéu was adopted in 1955 and the floodlights were switched on in 1957 for the European Cup Final.

Bernabéu, who died in 1978, had plans for another new stadium north of the city but for once did not get his way and, instead, Spain's hosting of the 1982 World Cup led to more improvements to the original stadium. A total of 345,000 people watched three group matches and an outstanding World Cup Final in a stadium offering 30,200 seats and standing room for 60,000. Ten years on, the improvements continue. A third tier has been completed and further remodelling has increased the seating to 65,000 within a total capacity of 105,000.

Estadio Guillermo Canedo

Mexico City, Mexico

Capacity:
110,000

Opened:
1960

Club:
America (but others for big matches)

Hosted:
1968 Olympic Final (Hungary 4, Bulgaria 1); 1970 World Cup Final (Brazil 4, Italy 1); 1986 World Cup Final (Argentina 3, West Germany 2)

Better know as the Azteca, the pride and joy of Mexican football has been the venue for some of the most memorable World Cup matches in history. It is also one of the most enjoyable, passionate and colourful stadiums in which to watch a game since its lower tier is only 30 feet from the pitch, thus providing fans there with a sense of immediacy while those in the upper tier benefit from the steep, cliff-like design. The Azteca was the first stadium to have staged two World Cup Final matches and the 1970 tournament also produced an incredible semi-final between West Germany and Italy. The drama was won 4–3 by the talented Italians who were, in turn, swept aside 4–1 in the final by a Brazilian side, rated as the finest to take the field in the history of the competition.

Some 16 years later Mexico stepped in at short notice to beat the United States and Canada to the right to host the finals after Colombia pulled out. In the final Argentina, led by Diego Maradona at the height of his creative footballing powers, lifted the crown for a second time against West Germany.

The stadium, built on scrubland to the south-west of the sprawling mass which is Mexico City, required 100,000 tons of concrete, four times more than was used to build Wembley Stadium in London. It was planned for the 1968 Olympics and opened in June 1966 with a match betweeen Mexico and Turin, but the first major internationals came during the 1968 Games. Since then, club sides America, Atlante, Necaxa and Cruz Azul have all used the the three-tiered Azteca for important games.

In 1997 the stadium was renamed in memory of the late Guillermo Canedo who had been Mexico's top football official for more than 20 years – as well as a vice-president of FIFA.

Giuseppe Meazza

Milan, Italy

Capacity:
83,107

Opened:
1926

Club:
Milan, Internazionale

Hosted:
1965 European Cup Final (Internazionale 1, Benfica 0), 1970 (Feyenoord 2, Celtic 1 aet); 1990 World Cup opening and group matches.

Fantastic is a much misused word, but it seems appropriate to describe the home of two of Europe's leading clubs in the city which can claim to be the continent's premier soccer centre. The cylindrical towers which allowed builders to construct a third tier and roof in advance of the 1992 World Cup have become just as much a trademark as the ramp system which gave access to the original two tiers of what used to be known as the San Siro. The cost of the remodelling came close to £50 million – even before the extra expense of sorting out problems with the pitch caused by shutting out both light and breeze.

San Siro, named after the suburb, was originally the home of Milan (*see* page 53), formed in 1899 by the Englishman Alfred Edwards. They outgrew their original ground in the mid-1920s, and the site of their new stadium was bought by their wealthy president, Piero Pirelli of tyre fame. It was Inter (*see* page 47) of all teams who ruined the opening party at the 35,000 capacity Stadio Calcistico San Siro by beating their rivals 6–3 in a local derby in September 1926.

The stadium was bought from Milan by the local council and was gradually enlarged until a 65,000 crowd were able to watch Italy play their Axis partners Germany in 1940. Inter had outgrown their own Stadio Arena by 1947; but the proposed groundshare needed an even larger stadium. The San Siro reopened in 1955 with an increased capacity of 82,000 as the home ground for two teams who have been bettered in domestic football by Juventus and Torino but are second to none in European success.

The San Siro was renamed Stadio Giuseppe Meazza in 1979 to honour the memory of one of the only two players to appear in both Italy's 1934 and 1938 World Cup-winning sides. The inside-forward had been hero-worshipped while playing for both Milan clubs.

Centenario

Montevideo, Uruguay

Capacity:
76,609

Opened:
1930

Club:
Peñarol, Nacional

Hosted:
1930 World Cup Final (Uruguay 4, Argentina 2); 1942, 1956, 1967, 1983 and 1995 South American Championships

The Centenario holds a special place in football history, having been the stage for the first World Cup Final in 1930 when Uruguay (*see* page 29), then Olympic champions and enjoying their golden age in international football, defeated Argentina, their old rivals from across the River Plate, by 4–2 after being 2–1 down at half-time. But it was a close call for Montevideo's magnificent new stadium, which was being built especially for the fledgeling world championship and to celebrate 100 years of the country's independence. Work continued throughout the first days of the tournament to have it ready for the final.

It has since become the regular venue for internationals, the South American Championship (the world's longest running international competition since the demise of the British Home Championship in 1984), the World Club Championship, the South American club championship (Copa Libertadores), Supercopa and Recopa. Uruguay's most recent international success came in the 1995 South American Championship, when Brazil were beaten on penalties in the Centenario after a 1–1 draw.

Football in Uruguay is really all about football in Montevideo and the Centenario is home to two of the leading clubs, Peñarol (*see* page 58) and Nacional (*see* page 57), who dominated the Copa Libertadores in its early years. From 1960, when Peñarol defeated Olimpia of Paraguay 1–0 in the Centenario and 2–1 on aggregate, they and Nacional were involved in 10 of the first 11 finals, and in 1968 the stadium was full to see Estudiantes beat Palmeiras 2–0 in a final play-off.

Peñarol entertained Real Madrid in the first World Club Championship in 1960, but were held to a goalless draw and lost 5–0 away. They took their revenge by beating Benfica the following season in a play-off, and Real, by 2–0 both home and away, in 1966.

Luzhniki

Moscow, Russia

Capacity:
100,000
Opened:
1956
Club:
Spartak Moscow
Hosted:
1980 Olympic Final (Czechoslovakia 1, East Germany 0)

A statue of Vladimir Ilyich Lenin, the now discredited father of the Russian Revolution, for years welcomed the visitor to the Centralny Stadion Lenina on the banks of the Moscow River, which is the site of possibly the largest and most popular sports complex in the world. There are 140 separate sports centres, including a Palace of Sports, an open-air swimming centre, a multi-purpose hall, 22 smaller halls, 11 football pitches, four athletics tracks, three skating rinks and 55 tennis courts. Many countries cannot offer as much. The all-seater football stadium plays host to the capital's most popular club, Spartak (*see* page 56), and internationals. It is built on the site of the old Red Stadium where Spartak, then called Moscow Sports Club, were founded in 1922. They adopted the present name in 1935 after affiliating to the trade unions for producers' co-operatives.

The new stadium opened in 1956 with the first All Union Spartakia, which brought together 34,000 athletes to celebrate Communist sport. But the history of the Luzhniki is darkened by one of soccer's major disasters: in 1982, Spartak were playing Haarlem of Holland in a UEFA Cup tie. Most of the crowd were leaving just before the end when Spartak scored a late goal. As fans tried to get back up the icy steps a fatal crush occurred.

The Soviet people only learned of the tragedy seven years later, and then the official death toll was way below the 300 estimated at the time. The stadium was closed for much of 1996 and 1997 for major redevelopment. The first major international it should have staged was then the Russia vs. Italy play-off first leg in the 1998 World Cup qualifying competition.

Unfortunately, the new pitch had deteriorated so rapidly that the game had to be switched to the Dynamo stadium.

Olympia-stadion

Munich, Germany

Capacity:
74,000
Opened:
1972
Club:
Bayern Munich
Hosted:
1972 Olympic Final (Poland 2, Hungary 1); 1974 World Cup Final (West Germany 2, Holland 1); 1988 European Championship Final (Holland 2, Soviet Union 0); 1979 European Cup Final (Nottingham Forest 1, Malmo 0), 1993 (Marseille 1, Milan 0), 1997 (Borussia Dortmund 3, Juventus 1)

Descriptions of the individualistic Olympiastadion vary from a futuristic Bedouin tent to a steel and glass spider's web – although the desert analogy can feel rather tenuous in the depths of a Bavarian winter on the site of the airfield to which Neville Chamberlain flew in 1938 for his infamous ("Peace in our time") meeting with Hitler. The tragic shadow of history fell across the stadium again at the end of the 1972 Olympics for which it had been built, when Arab terrorists took hostage and murdered Israeli athletes competing at the Games.

The bill for Behnisch and Otto's staggering creation at the centre of the green and pleasant Olympiapark came to 137 million marks. It was money well spent. The Park has become Germany's leading tourist attraction and a stunning venue for major events.

Bayern Munich (*see* page 38), about to establish themselves as European giants with players such as Franz Beckenbauer (*see* page 92), Paul Breitner and Gerd Müller (*see* page 138), moved into the new stadium in 1972, two seasons before they lifted the first of their three successive European Champions Cups. Müller had helped to celebrate the opening by scoring all four goals in West Germany's 4–1 win over the Soviet Union in 1972. Two years later the stocky striker's place in soccer's hall of fame was assured by his winning goal against Holland in the 1974 World Cup Final in front of his home fans.

The Dutch took happier memories away from the 1988 European Championship Final when they overcame the Soviets 2–0. Most recently Borussia Dortmund shocked Juventus by defeating them 3–1 in the Champions Cup Final in 1997.

San Paolo

Naples, Italy

Capacity:
65,102
Opened:
1960
Club:
Napoli
Hosted:
1968 European Championship semi-final (Italy 2, Soviet Union 1); 1980 European Championship finals venue; 1990 World Cup semi-final (Italy 1, Argentina 1: Argentina 4–3 on pens)

Regarded purely as a stadium, the concrete bowl of San Paolo, complete with roof since the 1992 World Cup, is unremarkable. But on match days it is transformed into a vibrant, uninhibited place by the local *tifosi*, some of the most colourful, eccentric and volatile fans (hence the moat and fences) in the world.

San Paolo represents the third home for Napoli, a club formed in 1904 with the help of English sailors and looked upon with some disdain by the more sophisticated clubs of Turin and Milan, though one of them, Juventus, deigned to come south to play the first match in the new stadium in the Olympic year of 1960.

Napoli, despite the largesse of millionaire president and shipping owner Achille Lauro, had little success until the arrival of the Argentine superstar Diego Maradona in the mid-1980s. He filled San Paolo as it had never been filled before. The size of the stadium enabled Napoli to sell 70,000 season tickets, an Italian record, and thus not only pay Barcelona the then world record transfer fee of five million for Maradona, but afford his wages and bring in other superstars, such as Brazil's Careca, into the bargain.

Sadly, the club has recently been embroiled in controversy, first over links with the Camorra (the local version of the Mafia) and then over the misuse and misappropriation of funds set aside for development work in and around the stadium for the 1990 World Cup. Long-serving club president Corrado Ferlaino was forced to step down at one stage but he later took command again – only to be assailed by a consortium seeking to bring back Maradona as chief executive cum player-coach.

Parc des Princes

Paris, France

Capacity:

48,700

Opened:

1887 (rebuilt 1932, 1972)

Club:

Paris Saint-Germain, Racing Club

Hosted:

1984 European Championship Final (France 2, Spain 0); 1956 European Cup Final (Real Madrid 4, Reims 3), 1975 (Bayern Munich 2, Leeds 0), 1981 (Liverpool 1, Real Madrid 0); 1978 European Cup-winners' Cup Final (Anderlecht 4, FK Austria 0); 1994 European Cup-winners' Cup Final (Zaragoza 2, Arsenal 1)

The award of the 1998 World Cup to France has spelled the beginning of the end of the chequered career of the Parc des Princes as a major soccer venue. The all-concrete near-50,000 capacity stadium designed by Roger Taillibert for soccer and rugby union in the early 1970s fails to meet FIFA's minimum capacity of 80,000 for a final, and the French government has spent £300 million on a new, 80,000-capacity stadium in the northern suburb of St Denis.

The Parc des Princes lies in the south-west and, as the name suggests, before the Revolution it was a pleasure ground for royalty. The stadium began life as a velodrome at the end of the last century and, until 1967, was the finish for the Tour de France.

When professional football was introduced in 1932 it became home to Racing Club de France, but they enjoyed only limited success and the Stade Colombes remained the favourite ground for internationals and the 1938 World Cup. Until the current stadium was built, one of the biggest soccer matches staged was the first European Cup Final in 1956, when a sell-out 38,000 crowd saw Real Madrid beat Stade Reims 4–3. Paris, sad to say, is the great capital under-achiever in soccer terms.

The creation of the Périphérique, the Paris ring road, led to the new two-tiered state-of-the-art stadium being built. It was the first in Europe with integral floodlighting and closed-circuit television. Problems with the pitch dogged its early years, but these ills were cured by the time the Parc was needed to host three group matches and the final of the 1984 European Championship, won in style by France's finest ever team, led by Michel Platini.

Racing Club went out of professional soccer business in 1964, and Paris Saint-Germain, an amalgamation of Paris FC and Saint-Germain, moved into the new stadium in 1973. They drew 20,000 crowds, became only the second Paris club to win the Championship and dominated the domestic game in the mid-1990s.

Rose Bowl

Pasadena, United States

Capacity:
102,083

Opened:
1922

Hosted:
1984 Olympic Final (France 2, Brazil 0); 1994 World Cup Final (Brazil 0, Italy 0 – Brazil win 3–2 on penalties).

The Rose Bowl, synonymous with American football, came into its own as a soccer venue at the 1994 World Cup when it served as a home from home for the United States. The stadium, far better equipped for the occasion than the more famous Los Angeles Coliseum, hosted three matches in the opening round, including the hosts' 2–1 victory over Colombia.

Later it staged one second round match (Romania 3 Argentina 2), a semi-final (Brazil 1 Sweden 0), the third place match (Sweden 4 Bulgaria 0) and the final itself. That brought Pasadena a place in soccer history as venue for the only World Cup Final ever decided in a penalty shoot-out, with Brazil defeating Italy after Franco Baresi and Roberto Baggio missed decisive kicks.

The rose-covered stadium, based in the leafy city of Pasadena seven miles north-west of downtown Los Angeles, cut its teeth on soccer in the 1984 Olympics, when the tournament drew massive crowds. Yugoslavia versus Italy was attended by 100,374 spectators. France's semi-final against Yugoslavia 97,451, and 101,799 watched France defeat Brazil in the final. That topped the record attendance for grid-iron football's Superbowl XVII in 1983, when 101,063 watched the Washington Redskins defeat the Miami Dolphins.

The Rose Bowl has hosted five Super Bowls but is best known as the home of UCLA and the annual Rose Bowl game on New Year's Day.

It has also become home of the Los Angeles Galaxy, the club set up as the local entrant into Major League Soccer, the new professional championship set up in the wake of the success of the 1994 World Cup finals. Drawing heavily on the enthusiasm for soccer among the local Latin American element, Galaxy regularly draw crowds of more than 30,000 for their big games.

Mario Filho/ Maracana

Rio de Janeiro, Brazil

Capacity:
120,000

Opened:
1950

Club:
Botofago, Vasco da Gama, Flamengo, Fluminense

Hosted:
1950 World Cup Final (Uruguay 2, Brazil 1); 1989 South American Championship

What Wembley is to the old world, the Maracana is to the new. This architectural marvel is the largest stadium in the world and the spiritual home to Brazil's second religion, football. However, it has spent much of the last few years out of commission while work has been carried out to renovate a bowl which had started, literally, to fall apart.

The Maracana, which takes its name from the little river that runs close by, was begun outside the city in 1948 in preparation for the 1950 World Cup, but was not completed until 1965. What has become Brazil's national stadium was originally intended to replace Vasco da Gama's club ground and was built and is still owned by the city, being formally named after the mayor, Mario Filho, who carried the project through. It was officially opened in June 1950 with a game beween Rio and São Paulo, the first goal being scored by Didi.

The first great matches were staged in the fourth World Cup, which culminated in the hosts losing to old rivals Uruguay before a world record crowd of 199,850. Like Hampden Park in Glasgow, the Maracana sets and holds attendance records. In 1963, 177,656 watched a league match between Flamengo (*see* page 44) and and Fluminense (*see* page 45), a world club record attendance. Internationals have drawn crowds of 180,000, and league matches in the 1980s were watched regularly by 130,000. Santos even flew north to use Maracana for their World Club Cup Final ties against Benfica and Milan in 1962 and 1963.

The stadium is oval in shape and topped by a breathtaking cantilevered roof while a moat separates the fans from the pitch. Like Wembley and the Olympiastadion in Munich, the Maracana has become a major tourist attraction and is held in such esteem that several smaller versions have been built throughout Brazil. Next to the stadium is the Maracanazinho, a scaled down indoor version which stages boxing, tennis, festivals and concerts.

Olimpico

Rome, Italy

Capacity:
60,000
Opened:
1953
Club:
Roma, Lazio
Hosted:
1960 Olympic Final (Yugoslavia 3, Denmark 1); 1990 World Cup Final (West Germany 1, Argentina 0); 1968 European Championship Final (Italy 1, Yugoslavia 1; replay, Italy 2, Yugoslavia 0), 1980 (West Germany 2, Belgium 1); 1977 European Cup Final (Liverpool 3, Borussia Mönchengladbach 1), 1984 (Liverpool 1, Roma 1: Liverpool 4–2 on pens) 1996 (Juventus 1, Ajax 1: Juventus 4–2 on pens)

Benito Mussolini was bad news for Italy. But allegedly he did make the trains run on time, and he also left the beautiful Foro Italico sports complex at the foot of Monte Mario as a legacy. His original plan was to stage the 1944 Olympics there, much as Hitler used Berlin for propaganda purposes in 1936. Then the Second World War intervened. The stadium was originally called Stadio dei Cipressi, but was inaugurated in 1953 as the Olimpico by the legendary Hungarian team who beat Italy 3–0 in front of an 80,000 crowd. The stadium became the focal point of the 1960 Olympic Games, a home to both Roma and Lazio, and the scene of a home triumph in the 1968 European Championship when Italy overcame Yugoslavia in a replay.

All roads led to Rome for Liverpool in 1977, when they turned the stadium into a sea of red celebrating the first of their four European Cup triumphs. They returned for the 1984 Final to beat Roma, playing on their own ground but unable to take advantage. Liverpool eventually won on penalties.

To allow the stadium to stage the 1990 World Cup, individual seating had to be increased to 80,000 and a roof added to give two-thirds cover. Only in Italy could the wrangling and talking have gone on until May 1988. A year later the roof design was ditched, costs had risen to £75 million, and the odds shifted against the stadium being ready.

FIFA's threat to move the final to Milan eventually saw to it that this beautiful venue was ready for West Germany's revenge over Argentina: a gracious setting for what proved to be an uninspiring contest.

Morumbi

São Paulo, Brazil

Capacity:
150,000

Opened:
1978

Club:
São Paulo FC, Corinthians

Hosted:
1992 Copa Libertadores (South American club championship) Final 2nd leg (São Paulo 1, Newells Old Boys 0: agg 2–1)

The rivalry between Rio de Janeiro and São Paulo provides much of the dynamic rivalry which fires domestic football within Brazil. Fans from the respective cities consider "their" state championships – the Carioca and the Paulista – as the best and most important, and fail to understand why players from the other city should ever be preferred to any of their favourites for the national team.

They are equally partisan about their stadia. Just as Rio de Janeiro boasts the Maracana – venue for the 1950 World Cup Final and host to a world record soccer attendance – so São Paulo football centres on the magnificent Morumbi.

The name, in fact, is that of the local suburb of São Paulo, and the stadium is formally entitled the Estadio Cicero Pompeu de Toledo – explaining, perhaps, why it is generally known by the much shorter name 'barrio'.

The Morumbi is effectively Brazil's biggest stadium since a failure to maintain the Maracana has led to its capacity being steadily reduced for security and safety reasons. Other 100,000–plus stadia include the Castelao at Fortaleza and the Mineirao at Belo Horizonte.

São Paulo FC and Corinthians both play all their big games in the Morumbi, though Corinthians did have to move out briefly for a South American club tie in 1993 when the date clashed with a pop concert. International club matches, such as ties in the three South American club tournaments, are guaranteed to draw big crowds but domestic matches are not such crowd-pullers. In particular, the problems associated with the organization of the Brazilian national championship has meant that even the Morumbi has seen only four-figure crowds on occasion – underlining media criticism about a surfeit of football in Brazil.

National Olympic Stadium

Tokyo, Japan

Capacity:
62,000

Opened:
1972

Club:
None

Hosted:
1979 World Youth Cup Final (Argentina 3, Soviet Union 1); World Club Cup finals (every year since 1980)

Soccer is the 1990s growth sport in Japan, and it was natural that the stadium built to host the 1964 Olympics should serve as the home of the national team and launch the successful professional J-League in 1993. Japan's appetite for big-time soccer was whetted in 1980 when Tokyo became the permanent home of the World Club Cup Final sponsored by Toyota.

This previously two-leg affair between the European and South American Club Champions had become progressively discredited since its inception in 1960, often degenerating into violence. But the decision to change the format to a one-off game in front of an excitable but well-behaved Japanese crowd, beginning with Nacional of Uruguay's 1–0 defeat of Nottingham Forest in 1980, has transformed it into a popular fixture in the international calendar early each December.

The stadium proved one of the points of weakness, however, in the Japanese bid to gain the right to host the 2002 World Cup finals. The city of Tokyo and the government failed to agree on how best to share funding for redevelopment work which would have been necessary to bring it up to World Cup standard. That meant that Japan did not have an obvious capital city main venue in their World Cup proposals – despite the state-of-the-art construction of a new stadium in the nearby port of Yokohama. In due course South Korea made excellent propaganda use of the presence in Seoul of their Olympic stadium – and that certainly helped them catch the Japanese in the bid process. Ultimately, of course, FIFA decided that the 2002 finals should be co-hosted – though it still seems there may be no place in the tournament for the stadium which has played such a key role in soccer development in Japan.

Ernst-Happel-Stadion

Vienna, Austria

Capacity:

62,958

Opened:

1931

Club:

No permanent club

Hosted:

1964 European Cup Final (Internazionale 3, Real Madrid 1), 1987 (Porto 2, Bayern Munich 1), 1990 (Milan 1, Benfica 0), 1995 (Ajax 1, Milan 0); 1970 European Cup-winners' Cup Final (Manchester City 2, Gornik Zarbrze 1)

Long known as the Prater, the Ernst Happel stadium gained its new name in memory of the late Austrian international defender and coach. It overlooks the pleasure grounds forever associated with Orson Welles and *The Third Man*, but Austrian fans associate it more with the Hugo Meisl (*see* page 77) "Wunderteam" of the 1930s, which counted England among their victims in 1936. The stadium was used as a troop headquarters during the latter stages of the Second World War and suffered severe bomb damage. This was rapidly repaired and the Prater regularly welcomed capacity 70,000 crowds throughout the 1950s and early 1960s.

It has been transformed in recent years into one of Europe's leading venues, the original open two-tiered amphitheatre topped by a remarkable roof which was erected in 10 months during 1985 at a cost of £17.5 million. The original 60,000-capacity stadium, a legacy of the socialist-controlled city administration, opened in July 1931 with a match appropriately between two workers teams, and hosted athletics championships and the long forgotten Workers Olympiad.

After the Anschluss, the stadium became an army barracks, and staged wartime internationals while serving as a staging post for Austrian Jews on their way to concentration camps. Though badly damaged by Allied troops, the stadium was quickly restored after the war. Rapid (*see* page 62) played Real Madrid under floodlights in 1955 and a record 90,593 watched Austria play Spain in 1960. In the 1970s, the of an all-weather track cut capacity to 72,000.

No club has used it permanently for league matches since FK Austria moved out in 1982. But Rapid, FK Austria and even Casino Salzburg have all used it intermittently for important European cup-ties.

The Statistics

Statistics are what make the football world go round. Who won what when and who scored the winning goal. From Amsterdam to Athens and Seoul to São Paulo, football fans are always on a quest to discover yet more information about the world's most 'beautiful game'.

The international programme has grown in piecemeal fashion since the first match between Scotland and England in 1872. Now there are myriad tournaments, ranging from the World Cup, the planet's most popular sporting event, to the well-established club competitions such as the European Champions Cup and the South American Copa Libertadores. All results and statistics, from all the major competitions, are covered in comprehensive detail.

Key: WCQ = World Cup Qualifier;
WCF = World Cup Final
ECQ = European Championship Qualifier
ECF = European Championship Finals
UT = Umbro Tournament;
TdF = Tournoi de France

The World Cup

1930 World Cup

Pool 1

France	4	Mexico	1
Argentina	1	France	0
Chile	3	Mexico	0
Chile	1	France	0
Argentina	6	Mexico	3
Argentina	3	Chile	1

Teams	P	W	D	L	F	A	Pts
Argentina	3	3	0	0	10	4	6
Chile	3	2	0	1	5	3	4
France	3	1	0	2	4	3	2
Mexico	3	0	0	3	4	13	0

Pool 2

Yugoslavia	2	Brazil	1
Yugoslavia	4	Bolivia	0
Brazil	4	Bolivia	0

Teams	P	W	D	L	F	A	Pts
Yugoslavia	2	2	0	0	6	1	4
Brazil	2	1	0	1	5	2	2
Bolivia	2	0	0	2	0	8	0

Pool 3

Romania	3	Peru	1
Uruguay	1	Peru	0
Uruguay	4	Romania	0

Teams	P	W	D	L	F	A	Pts
Uruguay	2	2	0	0	5	0	4
Romania	2	1	0	1	3	5	2
Peru	2	0	0	2	1	4	0

Pool 4

USA	3	Belgium	0
USA	3	Paraguay	0
Paraguay	1	Belgium	0

Teams	P	W	D	L	F	A	Pts
USA	2	2	0	0	6	0	4
Paraguay	2	1	0	1	1	3	2
Belgium	2	0	0	2	0	4	0

Semi-finals

Argentina	6	USA	1
Uruguay	6	Yugoslavia	1

Final

Uruguay	(1)4	Argentina	(2)2
Dorado, Cea		*Peucelle,*	
Iriarte, Castro		*Stabile*	

Leading scorers:

8 Stabile (Argentina); 5 Cea (Uruguay).

Uruguay:

Ballesteros, Nasazzi (capt.), Mascheroni, Andrade, Fernandez, Gestido, Dorado, Scarone, Castro, Cea, Iriarte.

Argentina:

Botasso, Della Torre, Paternoster, Evaristo J., Monti, Suarez, Peucelle, Varallo, Stabile, Ferreira (capt.), Evaristo M.

1934 World Cup

First round

Italy	7	USA	1
Czech.	2	Romania	1
Germany	5	Belgium	2
Austria	3	France	2*
Spain	3	Brazil	1
Switzerland	3	Holland	2
Sweden	3	Argentina	2
Hungary	4	Egypt	2

Second round

Germany	2	Sweden	1
Austria	2	Hungary	1
Italy	1	Spain	1*
Italy	1	Spain	0
Czech.	3	Switzerland	2

Semi-finals

Czech.	3	Germany	1
Italy	1	Austria	0

Third place match

Germany	3	Austria	2

Final

Italy	(0)2	Czech.	(0)1*
Orsi, Schiavio		*Puc*	

Italy:

Combi (capt.), Monzeglio, Allemandi, Ferraris IV, Monti, Bertolini, Guaita, Meazza, Schiavio, Ferrari, Orsi.

Czechoslovakia:

Planicka (capt.), Zenisek, Ctyroky, Kostalek, Cambal, Kreil, Junek, Svoboda, Sobotka, Nejedly, Puc.

Leading scorers:

4 Nejedly (Czechoslovakia), Schiavio (Italy), Conen (Germany).

1938 World Cup

First round

Switzerland	1	Germany	1*
Switzerland	4	Germany	2 (r)
Cuba	3	Romania	3*
Cuba	2	Romania	1 (r)
Hungary	6	Dutch E.Ind.	0
France	3	Belgium	1
Czech.	3	Holland	0*
Brazil	6	Poland	5*
Italy	2	Norway	1*

Second round

Sweden	8	Cuba	0
Hungary	2	Switzerland	0
Italy	3	France	1
Brazil	1	Czech.	1*
Brazil	2	Czech.	1*

Semi-finals

Italy	2	Brazil	1
Hungary	5	Sweden	1

Third place match

Brazil	4	Sweden	2

Final

Italy	(3)4	Hungary	(1)2
Colaussi (2), Piola (2)		*Titkos, Sarosi*	

Italy:

Olivieri, Foni, Rava, Serantoni, Andreolo, Locatelli, Biavati, Meazza (capt.), Piola, Ferrari, Colaussi.

Hungary:

Szabo, Polgar, Biro, Szalay, Szucs, Lazar, Sas, Vincze, Sarosi (capt.), Szengeller, Titkos.

Leading scorers

8 Leonidas (Brazil); 7 Szengeller (Hungary); 5 Piola (Italy).

1950 World Cup

Pool 1

Brazil	4	Mexico	0
Yugoslavia	3	Switzerland	0
Yugoslavia	4	Mexico	1
Brazil	2	Switzerland	2
Brazil	2	Yugoslavia	0
Switzerland	2	Mexico	1

Teams	P	W	D	L	F	A	Pts
Brazil	3	2	1	0	8	2	5
Yugoslavia	3	2	0	1	7	3	4
Switzerland	3	1	1	1	4	6	3
Mexico	3	0	0	3	2	10	0

Pool 2

Spain	3	USA	1
England	2	Chile	0
USA	1	England	0
Spain	2	Chile	0
Spain	1	England	0
Chile	5	USA	2

Teams	P	W	D	L	F	A	Pts
Spain	3	3	0	0	6	1	6
England	3	1	0	2	2	2	2
Chile	3	1	0	2	5	6	2
USA	3	1	0	2	4	8	2

Pool 3

Sweden	3	Italy	2
Sweden	2	Paraguay	2
Italy	2	Paraguay	0

Teams	P	W	D	L	F	A	Pts
Sweden	2	1	1	0	5	4	3
Italy	2	1	0	1	4	3	2
Paraguay	2	0	1	1	2	4	1

Pool 4

Uruguay	8	Bolivia	0

Teams	P	W	D	L	F	A	Pts
Uruguay	1	1	0	0	8	0	2
Bolivia	1	0	0	1	0	8	0

Final pool

Uruguay	2	Spain	2
Brazil	7	Sweden	1
Uruguay	3	Sweden	2
Brazil	6	Spain	1
Sweden	3	Spain	1
Uruguay	2	Brazil	1

Teams	P	W	D	L	F	A	Pts
Uruguay	3	2	1	0	7	5	5
Brazil	3	2	0	1	14	4	4
Sweden	3	1	0	2	6	11	2
Spain	3	0	1	2	4	11	1

Deciding match

Uruguay	(0)2	Brazil	(0)1
Schiaffino, Ghiggia		*Friaca*	

Uruguay:

Maspoli, Gonzales, M., Tejera, Gambetta, Varela, Andrade, Ghiggia, Perez, Miguez, Schiaffino, Moran.

Brazil:

Barbosa, Augusto, Juvenal, Bauer, Danilo, Bigode, Friaca, Zizinho, Ademir, Jair, Chico.

Leading scorers:

9 Ademir (Brazil); 6 Schiaffino (Uruguay); 5 Zarra (Spain).

1954 World Cup

Pool 1

Yugoslavia	1	France	0
Brazil	5	Mexico	0
France	3	Mexico	2
Brazil	1	Yugoslavia	1

Teams	P	W	D	L	F	A	Pts
Brazil	2	1	1	0	6	1	3
Yugoslavia	2	1	1	0	2	1	3
France	2	1	0	1	3	3	2
Mexico	2	0	0	2	2	8	0

Pool 2

Hungary	9	Korea	0
W. Germany	4	Turkey	1
Hungary	8	W.Germany	3
Turkey	7	Korea	0

Teams	P	W	D	L	F	A	Pts
Hungary	2	2	0	0	17	3	4
W. Germany	2	1	0	1	7	9	2
Turkey	2	1	0	1	8	4	2
Korea	2	0	0	2	0	16	0

Play-off

W. Germany	7	Turkey	2

Pool 3

Austria	1	Scotland	0
Uruguay	2	Czech.	0
Austria	5	Czech.	0
Uruguay	7	Scotland	0

Teams	P	W	D	L	F	A	Pts
Uruguay	2	2	0	0	9	0	4
Austria	2	2	0	0	6	0	4
Czech.	2	0	0	2	0	7	0
Scotland	2	0	0	2	0	8	0

Pool 4

England	4	Belgium	4
England	2	Switzerland	0
Switzerland	2	Italy	1
Italy	4	Belgium	1

Teams	P	W	D	L	F	A	Pts
England	2	1	1	0	6	4	3
Italy	2	1	0	1	5	3	2
Switzerland	2	1	0	1	2	3	2
Belgium	2	0	1	1	5	8	1

Play-off

Switzerland	4	Italy	1

Quarter-finals

W. Germany	2	Yugoslavia	0
Hungary	4	Brazil	2
Austria	7	Switzerland	5
Uruguay	4	England	2

Semi-finals

W. Germany	6	Austria	1
Hungary	4	Uruguay	2

Third-place match

Austria	3	Uruguay	1

Final

W. Germany	(2)3	Hungary	(2)2
Morlock, Rahn (2)		*Puskas, Czibor*	

Leading scorers

11 Kocsis (Hungary); 8 Morlock (W. Germany); 6 Probst (Austria), Hügi (Switzerland).

West Germany:

Turek, Posipal, Kohlmeyer, Eckel, Liebrich, Mai, Rahn, Morlock, Walter O., Walter F (capt.), Schäfer.

Hungary:

Grosics, Buzansky, Lantos, Bozsik, Lorant, Zakarias, Czibor, Kocsis, Hidegkuti, Puskas (capt.), Toth J.

1958 World Cup

Pool 1

W. Germany	3	Argentina	1
N. Ireland	1	Czech.	0
W. Germany	2	Czech.	2
Argentina	3	N. Ireland	1
W. Germany	2	N. Ireland	2
Czech.	6	Argentina	1

Teams	P	W	D	L	F	A	Pts
W. Germany	3	1	2	0	7	5	4
Czech.	3	1	1	1	8	4	3
N. Ireland	3	1	1	1	4	5	3
Argentina	3	1	0	2	5	10	2

Play-off

N. Ireland 2 Czech. 1

Pool 2

France	7	Paraguay	3
Yugoslavia	1	Scotland	1
Yugoslavia	3	France	2
Paraguay	3	Scotland	2
France	2	Scotland	1
Yugoslavia	3	Paraguay	3

Teams	P	W	D	L	F	A	Pts
France	3	2	0	1	11	7	4
Yugoslavia	3	1	2	0	7	6	4
Paraguay	3	1	1	1	9	12	3
Scotland	3	0	1	2	4	6	1

Pool 3

Sweden	3	Mexico	0
Hungary	1	Wales	1
Wales	1	Mexico	1
Sweden	2	Hungary	1
Sweden	0	Wales	0
Hungary	4	Mexico	0

Teams	P	W	D	L	F	A	Pts
Sweden	3	2	1	0	5	1	5
Hungary	3	1	1	1	6	3	3
Wales	3	0	3	0	2	2	3
Mexico	3	0	1	2	1	8	1

Play-off

Wales 2 Hungary 1

Pool 4

England	2	Soviet Union	2
Brazil	3	Austria	0
England	0	Brazil	0
Soviet Union	2	Austria	0
Brazil	2	Soviet Union	0
England	2	Austria	2

Teams	P	W	D	L	F	A	Pts
Brazil	3	2	1	0	5	0	5
England	3	0	3	0	4	4	3
Soviet Union	3	1	1	1	4	4	3
Austria	3	0	1	2	2	7	1

Play-off

Soviet Union 1 England 0

Quarter-finals

France	4	N. Ireland	0
W. Germany	1	Yugoslavia	0
Sweden	2	Soviet Union	0
Brazil	1	Wales	0

Third place match

France 6 W. Germany 3

Leading scorers

13 Fontaine (France); 6 Pele (Brazil), Rahn (W. Germany); 5 Vava (Brazil), McParland (N.Ireland).

Semi-finals

Brazil	5	France	2
Sweden	3	W. Germany	1

Final

Brazil	(2)5	Sweden	(1)2
Vava (2), Pele (2), Zagallo		*Liedholm Simonsson*	

Brazil: Gilmar, Santos D., Santos N., Zito, Bellini (capt.), Orlando, Garrincha, Didi, Vava, Pele, Zagallo.

Sweden: Svensson, Bergmark, Axbom, Boerjesson, Gustavsson, Parling, Hamrin, Gren, Simonsson, Liedholm (capt.), Skoglund.

1962 World Cup

Group 1

Uruguay	2	Colombia	1
Soviet Union	2	Yugoslavia	0
Yugoslavia	3	Uruguay	1
Soviet Union	4	Colombia	4
Soviet Union	2	Uruguay	1
Yugoslavia	5	Colombia	0

Teams	P	W	D	L	F	A	Pts
Soviet Union.	3	2	1	0	8	5	5
Yugoslavia	3	2	0	1	8	3	4
Uruguay	3	1	0	2	4	6	2
Colombia	3	0	1	2	5	11	1

Group 2

Chile	3	Switzerland	1
W. Germany	0	Italy	0
Chile	2	Italy	0
W. Germany	2	Switzerland	1
W. Germany	2	Chile	0
Italy	3	Switzerland	0

Teams	P	W	D	L	F	A	Pts
W. Germany	3	2	1	0	4	1	5
Chile	3	2	0	1	5	3	4
Italy	3	1	1	1	3	2	3
Switzerland	3	0	0	3	2	8	0

Group 3

Brazil	2	Mexico	0
Czech.	1	Spain	0
Brazil	0	Czech.	0
Spain	1	Mexico	0
Brazil	2	Spain	1
Mexico	3	Czech.	1

Teams	P	W	D	L	F	A	Pts
Brazil	3	2	1	0	4	1	5
Czech.	3	1	1	1	2	3	3
Mexico	3	1	0	2	2	3	2
Spain	3	1	0	2	2	3	2

Group 4

Argentina	1	Bulgaria	0
Hungary	2	England	1
England	3	Argentina	1
Hungary	6	Bulgaria	1
Argentina	0	Hungary	0
England	0	Bulgaria	0

Teams	P	W	D	L	F	A	Pts
Hungary	3	2	1	0	8	2	5
England	3	1	1	1	4	3	3
Argentina	3	1	1	1	2	3	3
Bulgaria	3	0	1	2	1	7	1

Quarter-finals

Yugoslavia	1	W. Germany	0
Brazil	3	England	1
Chile	2	Soviet Union	1
Czech.	1	Hungary	0

Third place match

Chile	1	Yugoslavia	0

Leading scorers

4 Garrincha (Brazil), Vava (Brazil), Sanchez L. (Chile), Jerkovic (Yugoslavia), Albert (Hungary), Ivanov V. (USSR); 3 Amarildo (Brazil), Scherer (Czechoslovakia), Galic (Yugoslavia), Tichy (Hungary).

Semi-finals

Brazil	4	Chile	2
Czech.	3	Yugoslavia	1

Final

Brazil	(1)3	Czech.	(1)1
Amarildo, Zito, Vava		*Masopust*	

Brazil: Gilmar, Santos D., Mauro (capt.), Zozimo, Santos N., Zito, Didi, Garrincha, Vava, Amarildo, Zagallo.

Czechoslovakia: Schroiff, Tichy, Novak (capt.), Pluskal, Popluhar, Masopust, Pospichal, Scherer, Kvasniak, Kadraba, Jelinek.

1966 World Cup

Group 1

England	0	Uruguay	0
France	1	Mexico	1
Uruguay	2	France	1
England	2	Mexico	0
Uruguay	0	Mexico	0
England	2	France	0

Teams	P	W	D	L	F	A	Pts
England	3	2	1	0	4	0	5
Uruguay	3	1	2	0	2	1	4
Mexico	3	0	2	1	1	3	2
France	3	0	1	2	2	5	1

Group 2

W. Germany	5	Switzerland	0
Argentina	2	Spain	1
Spain	2	Switzerland	1
Argentina	0	W. Germany	0
Argentina	2	Switzerland	0
W. Germany	2	Spain	1

Teams	P	W	D	L	F	A	Pts
W. Germany	3	2	1	0	7	1	5
Argentina	3	2	1	0	4	1	5
Spain	3	1	0	2	4	5	2
Switzerland	3	0	0	3	1	9	0

Group 3

Brazil	2	Bulgaria	0
Portugal	3	Hungary	1
Hungary	3	Brazil	1
Portugal	3	Bulgaria	0
Portugal	3	Brazil	1
Hungary	3	Bulgaria	1

Teams	P	W	D	L	F	A	Pts
Portugal	3	3	0	0	9	2	6
Hungary	3	2	0	1	7	5	4
Brazil	3	1	0	2	4	6	2
Bulgaria	3	0	0	3	1	8	0

Group 4

Soviet Union	3	North Korea	0
Italy	2	Chile	0
Chile	1	North Korea	1
Soviet Union	1	Italy	0
North Korea	1	Italy	0
Soviet Union	2	Chile	1

Teams	P	W	D	L	F	A	Pts
Soviet Union	3	3	0	0	6	1	6
North Korea	3	1	1	1	2	4	3
Italy	3	1	0	2	2	2	2
Chile	3	0	1	2	2	5	1

Quarter-finals

England	1	Argentina	0
W. Germany	4	Uruguay	0
Portugal	5	North Korea	3
Soviet Union	2	Hungary	1

Third place match

Portugal	2	Soviet Union	1

Leading scorers

9 Eusebio (Portugal); 5 Haller (West Germany); 4 Beckenbauer (West Germany), Hurst (England), Bene (Hungary), Porkujan (USSR).

Semi-finals

W. Germany	2	Soviet Union	1
England	2	Portugal	1

Final

England	(1)4	W. Germany	(1)2*
Hurst (3), Peters		*Haller, Weber*	

England: Banks, Cohen, Wilson, Stiles, Charlton J., Moore (capt.), Ball, Hurst, Hunt, Charlton R., Peters.

West Germany: Tilkowski, Höttges, Schülz, Weber, Schnellinger, Haller, Beckenbauer, Overath, Seeler (capt.), Held, Emmerich.

1970 World Cup

Group 1

Mexico	0	Soviet Union	0
Belgium	3	El Salvador	0
Soviet Union	4	Belgium	1
Mexico	4	El Salvador	0
Soviet Union	2	El Salvador	0
Mexico	1	Belgium	0

Teams	P	W	D	L	F	A	Pts
Soviet Union	3	2	1	0	6	1	5
Mexico	3	2	1	0	5	0	5
Belgium	3	1	0	2	4	5	2
El Salvador	3	0	0	3	0	9	0

Group 2

Uruguay	2	Israel	0
Italy	1	Sweden	0
Uruguay	0	Italy	0
Sweden	1	Israel	1
Sweden	1	Uruguay	0
Italy	0	Israel	0

Teams	P	W	D	L	F	A	Pts
Italy	3	1	2	0	1	0	4
Uruguay	3	1	1	1	2	1	3
Sweden	3	1	1	1	2	2	3
Israel	3	0	2	1	1	3	2

Group 3

England	1	Romania	0
Brazil	4	Czech.	1
Romania	2	Czech.	1
Brazil	1	England	0
Brazil	3	Romania	2
England	1	Czech.	0

Teams	P	W	D	L	F	A	Pts
Brazil	3	3	0	0	8	3	6
England	3	2	0	1	2	1	4
Romania	3	1	0	2	4	5	2
Czech.	3	0	0	3	2	7	0

Group 4

Peru	3	Bulgaria	2
W. Germany	2	Morocco	1
Peru	3	Morocco	0
W. Germany	5	Bulgaria	2
W. Germany	3	Peru	1
Morocco	1	Bulgaria	1

Teams	P	W	D	L	F	A	Pts
W. Germany	3	3	0	0	10	4	6
Peru	3	2	0	1	7	5	4
Bulgaria	3	0	1	2	5	9	1
Morocco	3	0	1	2	2	6	1

Quarter-finals

W. Germany	3	England	2*
Brazil	4	Peru	2
Italy	4	Mexico	1
Uruguay	1	Soviet Union	0

Third place match

W. Germany	1	Uruguay	0

Semi-finals

Italy	4	W. Germany	3*
Brazil	3	Uruguay	1

Final

Brazil	4	Italy	1
Pele, Gerson, Jairzinho, Carlos Alberto		*Boninsegna*	

Brazil: Felix, Carlos Alberto (capt.), Brito, Piazza, Everaldo, Clodoaldo, Gerson, Jairzinho, Tostao, Pele, Rivelino.
Italy: Albertosi, Cera, Burgnich, Bertini (Juliano), Rosato, Facchetti (capt.), Domenghini, Mazzola, De Sisti, Boninsegna (Rivera), Riva.

Leading scorers

9 Müller (West Germany); 7 Jairzinho (Brazil); 4 Pele (Brazil), Cubillas (Peru), Byscevietz (USSR), Seeler (West Germany).

1974 World Cup

Group 1

W. Germany	1	Chile	0
E. Germany	2	Australia	0
W. Germany	3	Australia	0
E. Germany	1	Chile	1
E. Germany	1	W. Germany	0
Chile	0	Australia	0

Teams	P	W	D	L	F	A	Pts
E. Germany	3	2	1	0	4	1	5
W. Germany	3	2	0	1	4	1	4
Chile	3	0	2	1	1	2	1
Australia	3	0	1	2	0	5	1

Group 2

Brazil	0	Yugoslavia	0
Scotland	2	Zaire	0
Brazil	0	Scotland	0
Yugoslavia	9	Zaire	0
Scotland	1	Yugoslovia	1
Brazil	3	Zaire	0

Teams	P	W	D	L	F	A	Pts
Yugoslavia	3	1	2	0	10	1	4
Brazil	3	1	2	0	3	0	4
Scotland	3	1	2	0	3	1	4
Zaire	3	0	0	3	0	14	0

Group 3

Holland	2	Uruguay	0
Sweden	0	Bulgaria	0
Holland	0	Sweden	0
Bulgaria	1	Uruguay	1
Holland	4	Bulgaria	1
Sweden	3	Uruguay	0

Teams	P	W	D	L	F	A	Pts
Holland	3	2	1	0	6	1	5
Sweden	3	1	2	0	3	0	4
Bulgaria	3	0	2	1	2	5	2
Uruguay	3	0	1	2	1	6	1

Group 4

Italy	3	Haiti	1
Poland	3	Argentina	2
Italy	1	Argentina	1
Poland	7	Haiti	0
Argentina	4	Haiti	1
Poland	2	Italy	1

Teams	P	W	D	L	F	A	Pts
Poland	3	3	0	0	12	3	6
Argentina	3	1	1	1	7	5	3
Italy	3	1	1	1	5	4	3
Haiti	3	0	0	3	2	14	0

Group A

Brazil	1	E. Germany	0
Holland	4	Argentina	0
Holland	2	E. Germany	0
Brazil	2	Argentina	1
Holland	2	Brazil	0
Argentina	1	E. Germany	1

Teams	P	W	D	L	F	A	Pts
Holland	3	3	0	0	8	0	6
Brazil	3	2	0	1	3	3	4
E. Germany	3	0	1	2	1	4	1
Argentina	3	0	1	2	2	7	1

Group B

Poland	1	Sweden	0
W. Germany	2	Yugoslavia	0
Poland	2	Yugoslavia	1
W. Germany	4	Sweden	2
Sweden	2	Yugoslavia	1
W. Germany	1	Poland	0

Teams	P	W	D	L	F	A	Pts
W. Germany	3	3	0	0	7	2	6
Poland	3	2	0	1	3	2	4
Sweden	3	1	0	2	4	6	2
Yugoslovia	3	0	0	3	2	6	0

Third place match

Poland	1	Brazil	0

Final

W. Germany	(2)2	Holland	(1)1*
Breitner, Müller		*Neeskens (pen)*	

Leading scorers

7 Lato (Poland); 5 Neeskens (Holland), Szarmach (Poland).

1978 World Cup

Group 1

Argentina 2 Hungary 1
Italy 2 France 1
Argentina 2 France 1
Italy 3 Hungary 1
Italy 1 Argentina 0
France 3 Hungary 1

Teams	P	W	D	L	F	A	Pts
Italy	3	3	0	0	6	2	6
Argentina	3	2	0	1	4	3	4
France	3	1	0	2	5	5	2
Hungary	3	0	0	3	3	8	0

Group 2

W. Germany 0 Poland 0
Tunisia 3 Mexico 1
Poland 1 Tunisia 0
W. Germany 6 Mexico 0
Poland 3 Mexico 1
W. Germany 0 Tunisia 0

Teams	P	W	D	L	F	A	Pts
Poland	3	2	1	0	4	1	5
W. Germany	3	1	2	0	6	0	4
Tunisia	3	1	1	1	3	2	3
Mexico	3	0	0	3	2	12	0

Group 3

Austria 2 Spain 1
Sweden 1 Brazil 1
Austria 1 Sweden 0
Brazil 0 Spain 0
Spain 1 Sweden 0
Brazil 1 Austria 0

Teams	P	W	D	L	F	A	Pts
Austria	3	2	0	1	3	2	4
Brazil	3	1	2	0	2	1	4
Spain	3	1	1	1	2	2	3
Sweden	3	0	1	2	1	3	1

Group 4

Peru 3 Scotland 1
Holland 3 Iran 1
Scotland 1 Iran 1
Holland 0 Peru 0
Peru 4 Iran 1
Scotland 3 Holland 2

Teams	P	W	D	L	F	A	Pts
Peru	3	2	1	0	7	2	5
Holland	3	1	1	1	5	3	3
Scotland	3	1	1	1	5	6	3
Iran	3	0	1	2	2	8	1

Group A
Group A

Italy 0 W. Germany 0
Holland 5 Austria 1
Italy 1 Austria 0
Austria 3 W. Germany 2
Holland 2 Italy 1
Holland 2 W. Germany 2

Teams	P	W	D	L	F	A	Pts
Holland	3	2	1	0	9	4	5
Italy	3	1	1	1	2	2	3
W. Germany	3	0	2	1	4	5	2
Austria	3	1	0	2	4	8	2

Group B

Argentina 2 Poland 0
Brazil 3 Peru 0
Argentina 0 Brazil 0
Poland 1 Peru 0
Brazil 3 Poland 1
Argentina 6 Peru 0

Teams	P	W	D	L	F	A	Pts
Argentina	3	2	1	0	8	0	5
Brazil	3	2	1	0	6	1	5
Poland	3	1	0	2	2	5	2
Peru	3	0	0	3	0	10	0

Final

Argentina (1)3 Holland (0)1*
Kempes (2), Bertoni — *Nanninga*

Third place match

Brazil 2 Italy 1

Leading scorers

6 Kempes (Argentina); 5 Rensenbrink (Holland), Cubillas (Peru).

1982 World Cup

Group 1

Italy	0	Poland	0
Peru	0	Cameroon	0
Italy	1	Peru	1
Poland	0	Cameroon	0
Poland	5	Peru	1
Italy	1	Cameroon	1

Teams	P	W	D	L	F	A	Pts
Poland	3	1	2	0	5	1	4
Italy	3	0	3	0	2	2	3
Cameroon	3	0	3	0	1	1	3
Peru	3	0	2	1	2	6	2

Group 2

Algeria	2	W. Germany	1
Austria	1	Chile	0
W. Germany	4	Chile	1
Austria	2	Algeria	1
Algeria	3	Chile	2
W. Germany	1	Austria	0

Teams	P	W	D	L	F	A	Pts
W. Germany	3	2	0	1	6	3	4
Austria	3	2	0	1	3	1	4
Algeria	3	2	0	1	5	5	4
Chile	3	0	0	3	3	8	0

Group 3

Belgium	1	Argentina	0
Hungary	10	El Salvador	1
Argentina	4	Hungary	1
Belgium	1	El Salvador	0
Belgium	1	Hungary	1
Argentina	2	El Salvador	0

Teams	P	W	D	L	F	A	Pts
Belgium	3	2	1	0	3	1	5
Argentina	3	2	0	1	6	2	4
Hungary	3	1	1	1	12	6	3
El Salvador	3	0	0	3	1	13	3

Group 4

England	3	France	1
Czech.	1	Kuwait	1
England	2	Czech.	0
France	4	Kuwait	1
France	1	Czech.	1
England	1	Kuwait	0

Teams	P	W	D	L	F	A	Pts
England	3	3	0	0	6	1	6
France	3	1	1	1	6	5	3
Czech.	3	0	2	1	2	4	2
Kuwait	3	0	1	2	2	6	1

Group 5

Spain	1	Honduras	1
N. Ireland	0	Yugoslavia	0
Spain	2	Yugoslavia	1
N. Ireland	1	Honduras	1
Yugoslavia	1	Honduras	0
N. Ireland	1	Spain	0

Teams	P	W	D	L	F	A	Pts
N. Ireland	3	1	2	0	2	1	4
Spain	3	1	1	1	3	3	3
Yugoslavia	3	1	1	1	2	2	3
Honduras	3	0	2	1	2	3	2

Group 6

Brazil	2	Soviet Union	1
Scotland	5	New Zealand	2
Brazil	4	Scotland	1
Soviet Union	3	New Zealand	0
Scotland	2	Soviet Union	2
Brazil	4	New Zealand	0

Teams	P	W	D	L	F	A	Pts
Brazil	3	3	0	0	10	2	6
Soviet Un.	3	1	1	1	6	4	3
Scotland	3	1	1	1	8	8	3
New Zealand	3	0	0	3	2	12	0

Group A

Poland	3	Belgium	0
Soviet Union	1	Belgium	0
Soviet Union	0	Poland	0

Teams	P	W	D	L	F	A	Pts
Poland	2	1	1	0	3	0	3
Soviet Un.	2	1	1	0	1	0	3
Belgium	2	0	0	2	0	4	0

Group B

W. Germany	0	England	0
W. Germany	2	Spain	1
England	0	Spain	0

Teams	P	W	D	L	F	A	Pts
W.Germany	2	1	1	0	2	1	3
England	2	0	2	0	0	0	2
Spain	2	0	1	1	1	2	1

Group C

Italy	2	Argentina	1
Brazil	3	Argentina	1
Italy	3	Brazil	2

Teams	P	W	D	L	F	A	Pts
Italy	2	2	0	0	5	3	4
Brazil	2	1	0	1	5	4	2
Argentina	2	0	0	2	2	5	0

Group D

France	1	Austria	0
N. Ireland	2	Austria	2
France	4	N. Ireland	1

Teams	P	W	D	L	F	A	Pts
France	2	2	0	0	5	1	4
Austria	2	O	1	1	2	3	1
N. Ireland	2	0	1	1	3	6	1

Semi-finals

Italy	2	Poland	0
W. Germany	3	France	3*

(West Germany won 5–4 on pens)

Italy: Zoff (capt.), Bergomi, Cabrini, Collovati, Scirea, Gentile, Oriale, Tardelli, Conti, Graziani (Altobelli; Causio), Rossi.

West Germany: Schumacher, Kaltz, Förster K., Stielike, Förster B., Breitner, Dremmler (Hrubesch), Littbarski, Briegel, Fischer (Müller, H.), Rummenigge (capt.).

Third place match

Poland	3	France	2

Final

Italy	(0)3	W. Germany	(0)1
Rossi, Tardelli		*Breitner*	
Altobelli			

Leading scorers

6 Rossi (Italy); 5 Rummenigge (West Germany); 4 Zico (Brazil), Boniek (Poland).

1986 World Cup

Group A

Bulgaria	1	Italy	1
Argentina	3	South Korea	1
Italy	1	Argentina	1
Bulgaria	1	South Korea	1
Argentina	2	Bulgaria	0
Italy	3	South Korea	2

Teams	P	W	D	L	F	A	Pts
Argentina	3	2	1	O	6	2	5
Italy	3	1	2	0	5	4	4
Bulgaria	3	0	2	1	2	4	2
South Korea	3	0	1	2	4	7	1

Group B

Mexico	2	Belgium	1
Paraguay	1	Iraq	0
Mexico	1	Paraguay	1
Belgium	2	Iraq	1
Paraguay	2	Belgium	2
Mexico	1	Iraq	0

Teams	P	W	D	L	F	A	Pts
Mexico	3	2	1	0	4	2	5
Paraguay	3	1	2	0	4	3	4
Belgium	3	1	1	1	5	5	4
Iraq	3	0	0	3	1	4	0

Group C

Soviet Union	6	Hungary	0
France	1	Canada	0
Soviet Union	1	France	1
Hungary	2	Canada	0
France	3	Hungary	0
Soviet Union	2	Canada	0

Teams	P	W	D	L	F	A	Pts
Soviet Union	3	2	1	0	9	1	5
France	3	2	1	0	5	1	5
Hungary	3	1	0	2	2	9	2
Canada	3	0	0	3	0	5	0

Group D

Brazil	1	Spain	0
N. Ireland	1	Algeria	1
Spain	2	N. Ireland	1
Brazil	1	Algeria	0
Spain	3	Algeria	0
Brazil	3	N. Ireland	0

Teams	P	W	D	L	F	A	Pts
Brazil	3	3	0	0	5	0	6
Spain	3	2	0	1	5	2	4
N. Ireland	3	0	1	2	2	6	1
Algeria	3	0	1	2	1	5	1

Group E

W. Germany	1	Uruguay	1
Denmark	1	Scotland	0
Denmark	6	Uruguay	1
W. Germany	2	Scotland	1
Scotland	0	Uruguay	0
Denmark	2	W.Germany	0

Teams	P	W	D	L	F	A	Pts
Denmark	3	3	0	0	9	1	6
W. Germany	3	1	1	1	3	4	3
Scotland	3	0	2	1	1	3	2
Uruguay	3	0	2	1	2	7	2

Group F

Morocco	0	Poland	0
Portugal	1	England	0
England	0	Morocco	0
Poland	1	Portugal	0
England	3	Poland	0
Morocco	3	Portugal	1

Teams	P	W	D	L	F	A	Pts
Morocco	3	1	2	0	3	1	4
England	3	1	1	1	3	1	3
Poland	3	1	1	1	1	3	3
Portugal	3	1	0	2	2	4	2

Second round

Knock-out phase comprising the top two teams from each group plus the four best third-placed teams.

Mexico	2	Bulgaria	0
Belgium	4	Soviet Union	3*
Brazil	4	Poland	0
Argentina	1	Uruguay	0
France	2	Italy	0
W.Germany	1	Morocco	0
England	3	Paraguay	0
Spain	5	Denmark	1

Third place match

France	4	Belgium	2

Leading scorers

6 Lineker (England); 5 Butragueno (Spain), Careca (Brazil), Maradona (Argentina); 4 Altobelli (Italy), Belanov (USSR), Elkjaer (Denmark), Valdano (Argentina).

Quarter-finals

France	1	Brazil	1*
(France won 4–3 on pens)			
W.Germany	0	Mexico	0*
(W. Germany won 4–1 on pens)			
Argentina	2	England	1
Spain	1	Belgium	1*
(Belgium won 5–4 on pens)			

Semi-finals

Argentina	2	Belgium	0
W. Germany	2	France	0

Final

Argentina	(1)3	W. Germany	(0)2
Brown, Valdano, Burruchaga		*Rummenigge, Völler*	

Argentina: Pumpido, Cuciuffo, Olarticoechea, Ruggeri, Brown, Giusti, Burruchaga (Trobbiani), Batista, Valdano, Maradona (capt.), Enrique.

West Germany: Schumacher, Berthold, Briegel, Jakobs, Förster, Eder, Brehme, Matthäus, Allofs (Völler), Magath (Hoeness, D.), Rummenigge (capt.).

1990 World Cup

Group A

Italy	1	Austria	0
Czech.	5	USA	1
Italy	1	USA	0
Czech.	1	Austria	0
Italy	2	Czech.	0
Austria	2	USA	1

Teams	P	W	D	L	F	A	Pts
Italy	3	3	0	0	4	0	6
Czech.	3	2	0	1	6	3	4
Austria	3	1	0	2	2	3	2
USA	3	0	0	3	2	8	0

Group B

Cameroon	1	Argentina	0
Romania	2	Soviet Union	0
Argentina	2	Soviet Union	0
Cameroon	2	Romania	1
Argentina	1	Romania	1
Soviet Union	4	Cameroon	0

Teams	P	W	D	L	F	A	Pts
Cameroon	3	2	0	1	3	5	4
Romania	3	1	1	1	4	3	3
Argentina	3	1	1	1	3	2	3
Soviet Union	3	1	0	2	4	4	2

Group C

Brazil	2	Sweden	1
Costa Rica	1	Scotland	0
Brazil	1	Costa Rica	0
Scotland	2	Sweden	1
Brazil	1	Scotland	0
Costa Rica	2	Sweden	1

Teams	P	W	D	L	F	A	Pts
Brazil	3	3	0	0	4	1	6
Costa Rica	3	2	0	1	3	2	4
Scotland	3	1	0	2	2	3	2
Sweden	3	0	0	3	3	6	0

Group D

Colombia	2	UAE	0
W. Germany	4	Yugoslavia	1
Yugoslavia	1	Colombia	0
W. Germany	5	UAE	1
W. Germany	1	Colombia	1
Yugoslavia	4	UAE	1

Teams	P	W	D	L	F	A	Pts
W.Germany	3	2	1	0	10	3	5
Yugoslavia	3	2	0	1	6	5	4
Colombia	3	1	1	1	3	2	3
UAE	3	0	0	3	2	11	0

Group E

Belgium	2	South Korea	0
Uruguay	0	Spain	0
Belgium	3	Uruguay	1
Spain	3	South Korea	1
Spain	2	Belgium	1
Uruguay	1	South Korea	0

Teams	P	W	D	L	F	A	Pts
Spain	3	2	1	0	5	2	5
Belgium	3	2	0	1	6	3	4
Uruguay	3	1	1	1	2	3	3
Sth. Korea	3	0	0	3	1	6	0

Group F

England	1	Rep. Ireland	1
Holland	1	Egypt	1
England	0	Holland	0
Egypt	0	Rep. Ireland	0
England	1	Egypt	0
Holland	1	Rep. Ireland	1

Teams	P	W	D	L	F	A	Pts
England	3	1	2	0	2	1	4
Rep. Ireland	3	0	3	0	2	2	3
Holland	3	0	3	0	2	2	3
Egypt	3	0	2	1	1	2	2

Second phase

Knock-out phase comprising the top two teams from each group plus the four best third-placed teams

Cameroon	2	Colombia	1*
Czech.	4	Costa Rica	1
Argentina	1	Brazil	0
W. Germany	2	Holland	1
Rep. Ireland	0	Rumania	0*
(Rep. Ireland won 5–4 on pens)			
Italy	2	Uruguay	0
Yugoslavia	2	Spain	1*
England	1	Belgium	0*

Third place match

Italy	2	England	1

Quarter-finals

Argentina	0	Yugoslavia	0*
(Argentina won 3–2 on pens)			
Italy	1	Rep. Ireland	0
W. Germany	1	Czech.	0
England	3	Cameroon	2*

Semi-finals

Argentina	1	Italy	1*
(Argentina won 4–3 on pens)			
W. Germany	1	England	1*
(West Germany won 4–3 on pens)			

Leading scorers

6 Schillaci (Italy); 5 Skuhravy (Czechoslovakia); 4 Michel (Spain), Milla (Cameroon), Matthäus (West Germany), Lineker (England).

Final

W.Germany	(0)1	Argentina	(0)0
Brehme (pen)			

West Germany: Illgner, Berthold (Reuter), Kohler, Augenthaler, Buchwald, Brehme, Littbarski, Hässler, Matthäus (capt.), Völler, Klinsmann.

Argentina: Goycochea, Lorenzo, Serrizuela, Sensini, Ruggeri (Monzon), Simon, Basualdo, Burruchaga (Calderon), Maradona (capt.), Troglio, Dezotti.

1994 World Cup

Group A

USA	1	Switzerland	1
Colombia	1	Romania	3
USA	2	Colombia	1
Romania	1	Switzerland	4
USA	0	Romania	1
Switzerland	0	Colombia	2

Teams	P	W	D	L	F	A	Pts
Romania	3	2	0	1	5	5	6
Switzerland	3	1	1	1	5	4	4
USA	3	1	1	1	3	3	4
Colombia	3	1	0	2	4	5	3

Group B

Cameroon	2	Sweden	2
Brazil	2	Russia	0
Brazil	3	Cameroon	0
Sweden	3	Russia	1
Russia	6	Cameroon	1
Brazil	1	Sweden	1

Teams	P	W	D	L	F	A	Pts
Brazil	3	2	1	0	6	1	7
Sweden	3	1	2	0	6	4	5
Russia	3	1	0	2	7	6	3
Cameroon	3	0	1	2	11	1	1

Group C

Germany	1	Bolivia	0
Spain	2	South Korea	2
Germany	1	Spain	1
South Korea	0	Bolivia	0
Bolivia	1	Spain	3
Germany	3	South Korea	2

Teams	P	W	D	L	F	A	Pts
Germany	3	2	1	0	5	3	7
Spain	3	1	2	0	6	4	5
South. Korea	3	0	2	1	4	5	2
Bolivia	3	0	1	2	1	4	1

Group D

Argentina	4	Greece	0
Nigeria	3	Bulgaria	0
Argentina	2	Nigeria	1
Bulgaria	4	Greece	0
Greece	0	Nigeria	2
Argentina	0	Bulgaria	2

Teams	P	W	D	L	F	A	Pts
Nigeria	3	2	0	1	6	2	6
Bulgaria	3	2	0	1	6	3	6
Argentina	3	2	0	1	6	3	6
Greece	3	0	0	3	10	1	0

Group E

Italy	0	Rep. Ireland	1
Norway	1	Mexico	0
Italy	1	Norway	0
Mexico	2	Rep. Ireland	1
Rep of Ireland	0	Norway	0
Italy	1	Mexico	1

Teams	P	W	D	L	F	A	Pts
Mexico	3	1	1	1	3	3	4
Rep. Ireland	3	1	1	1	2	2	4
Italy	3	1	1	1	2	2	4
Norway	3	1	1	1	1	1	4

Group F

Belgium	1	Morocco	0
Holland	2	Saudi Arabia	1
Belgium	1	Holland	0
Saudi Arabia	2	Morocco	1
Morocco	1	Holland	2
Belgium	0	Saudi Arabia	1

Teams	P	W	D	L	F	A	Pts
Holland	3	2	0	1	4	3	6
Saudi Arabia	3	2	0	1	4	3	6
Belgium	3	2	0	1	2	1	6
Morocco	3	0	0	3	2	5	0

Second phase

Germany	3	Belgium	2
Spain	3	Switzerland	0
Saudi Arabia	1	Sweden	3
Romania	3	Argentina	2
Holland	2	Rep. Ireland	0
Brazil	1	USA	0
Nigeria	1	Italy	2*
Mexico	1	Bulgaria	1*

(Bulgaria won 3–1 on pens)

Third place match

Sweden	4	Bulgaria	0

Leading scorers

6 Salenko (Russia), Stoichkov (Bulgaria); 5 K. Andersson (Sweden), R. Baggio (Italy), Klinsmann (Germany), Romario (Brazil); 4 Batistuta (Argentina), Dahlin (Sweden), Raducioiu (Romania)

Quarter-finals

Italy	2	Spain	1
Holland	2	Brazil	3
Germany	1	Bulgaria	2
Sweden	2	Romania	2*

(Sweden won 5–4 on pens)

Semi-finals

Brazil	1	Sweden	0
Italy	2	Bulgaria	1

Final

Brazil	0	Italy	0*

(Brazil won 3–2 on pens)

Brazil:

Taffarel, Jorginho (Cafu 20), Aldair, Marcio Santos, Branco, Mazinho (Viola 106), Dunga (capt.), Mauro Silva, Zinho, Romario, Bebeto.

Italy:

Pagliuca, Mussi (Apolloni 34), Maldini, Baresi (capt.), Benarrivo, Berti, Albertini, D. Baggio (Evani 94), Donadoni, R. Baggio, Massaro.

FIFA Under-20 World Championship

Finalists

1977

Soviet Union	2	Mexico	2

(Soviet Union won 9–8 on penalties)

1979

Argentina	3	Soviet Union	1

1981

W. Germany	4	Qatar	0

1983

Brazil	1	Argentina	0

1985

Brazil	1	Spain	0

1987

Yugoslavia	1	W. Germany	1

(Yugoslavia won 5–4 on penalties)

1989

Portugal	2	Nigeria	0

1991

Portugal	0	Brazil	0

(Portugal won 4–2 on penalties)

1993

Brazil	2	Ghana	1

1995

Argentina	2	Brazil	0

1997

Argentina	2	Uruguay	1

Women's World Championship

Finalists

1991

USA	2	Norway	1

1995

Norway	2	Germany	0

Copa America (South American Championship)

Winners

1910 Buenos Aires:
1st Argentina
2nd Uruguay*

1916 Buenos Aires:
1st Uruguay
2nd Argentina*

1917 Montevideo:
1st Uruguay
2nd Argentina

1919 Rio de Janeiro (play-off):

Brazil	1	Uruguay	0

Friedenreich
Att: 28,000

1920 Vina del Mar:
1st Uruguay
2nd Argentina

1921 Buenos Aires:
1st Argentina
2nd Brazil

1922 Rio de Janeiro (play-off):

Brazil	3	Paraguay	1

Formiga (2), Neco Rivas G.
Att: 20,000

1923 Montevideo:
1st Uruguay
2nd Argentina

1924 Montevideo:
1st Uruguay
2nd Argentina

1925 Buenos Aires:
1st Argentina
2nd Brazil

1926 Santiago:
1st Uruguay
2nd Argentina

1927 Lima:
1st Argentina
2nd Uruguay

1929 Buenos Aires:
1st Argentina
2nd Paraguay

1935 Lima:
1st Uruguay
2nd Argentina*

1937 Buenos Aires (play-off):

Argentina	2	Brazil	0

De la Mata (2)

Att: 80,000

1939 Lima:

1st Peru
2nd Uruguay

1941 Santiago:

1st Argentina
2nd Uruguay*

1942 Montevideo:

1st Uruguay
2nd Argentina

1945 Santiago:

1st Argentina
2nd Brazil*

1946 Buenos Aires:

1st Argentina
2nd Brazil*

1947 Guayaquil:

1st Argentina
2nd Paraguay

1949 Rio de Janeiro (play-off):

Brazil 7 Paraguay 0
Ademir Menezes (3), Tesourinha (2), Jair R. Pinto (2)
Att: 55,000

1953 Lima (play-off):

Paraguay 3 Brazil 2
Lopez A., Gavilan, Fernandez — *Baltazar (2)*
Att: 35,000

1955 Santiago:

1st Argentina
2nd Chile

1956 Montevideo:

1st Uruguay
2nd Chile*

1957 Lima:

1st Argentina
2nd Brazil

1959 Buenos Aires:

1st Argentina
2nd Brazil*

1959 Guayaquil:

1st Uruguay
2nd Argentina

1963 Bolivia:

1st Bolivia
2nd Paraguay

1967 Montevideo:

1st Uruguay
2nd Argentina

1975 Bogota (1st leg):

Colombia 1 Peru 0
Castro P.
Att: 50,000

1975 Lima (2nd leg):

Peru 2 Colombia 0
Oblitas, Ramirez O.
Att: 50,000

1975 Caracas (play-off):

Peru 1 Colombia 0
Sotil
Att: 30,000

1979 Asuncion (1st leg):

Paraguay 3 Chile 0
Romero C. (2), Morel M.

1979 Santiago (2nd leg):

Chile 1 Paraguay 0
Rivas
Att: 55,000

1979 Buenos Aires (play-off):

Paraguay 0 Chile 0
Att: 6,000
(Paraguay won on goal difference)

1983 Montevideo (1st leg):

Uruguay 2 Brazil 0
Francescoli, Diogo
Att: 65,000

1983 Salvador (2nd leg):

Brazil 1 Uruguay 1
Jorginho — *Aguilera*
Att: 95,000

1987 Buenos Aires:

Uruguay 1 Chile 0
Bengochea
Att: 35,000

1989 Brazil:

1st Brazil
2nd Uruguay

1991 Chile

1st Argentina
2nd Brazil

1993 Guayaquil:

Argentina 2 Mexico 1
Batistuta (2) — *Galindo (pen.)*
Att: 40,000

1995 Montevideo:

Uruguay 1 Brazil 1
Bengoechea 48 — *Tulio 30*
Att: 58,000
(Uruguay 5-3 on pens)

1997 La Paz:

Brazil 3 Bolivia 1
Edmundo 37, Ronaldo 79, Ze Roberto 90 — *Irwin Sanchez 45*
Att: 45,000

Notes:

Details of final matches or championship play-offs have been given where applicable. For all other tournaments, played on a league basis, only the first and second have been listed
** unofficial "extraordinarios" tournaments*

FIFA Confederations Cup

Winners

1997

Brazil	6	Australia	0

European Championship

Winners

1960:

Soviet Union	2	Yugoslavia	1
Metreveli, Ponedelnik		*Galic*	

Att: 18,000 *(Paris)*

1964:

Spain	2	Soviet Union	1
Pereda, Marcelino		*Khusainov*	

Att: 105,000 *(Madrid, Bernabéu)*

1968:

Italy	1	Yugoslavia	1
Domenghini		*Dzajic*	

Att: 85,000 *(Rome)*

1968 replay:

Italy	2	*Yugoslavia*	*0*
Riva, Anastasi			

Att: 85,000 *(Rome)*

1972:

W. Germany	3	Soviet Union	0
Müller G. (2), Wimmer			

Att: 65,000 *(Brussels)*

1976:

Czech.	2	W. Germany	2*
Svehlik, Dobias		*Müller D., Holzenbein*	

(Czechoslovakia 5–4 on penalties)
Att: 45,000 *(Belgrade)*

1980:

W. Germany	2	Belgium	1
Hrubesch (2)		*Vandereycken*	

Att: 48,000 *(Rome)*

1984:

France	2	Spain	0
Platini, Bellone			

Att: 47,000 *(Paris)*

1988:

Holland	2	Soviet Union	0
Gullit, Van Basten			

Att: 72,000 *(Munich)*

1992:

Denmark	2	Germany	0
Jensen, Vilfort			

Att: 37,000 *(Gothenburg)*

1996:

Germany	2	Czech Rep.	1
Bierhoff (2)		*Berger (pen)*	

Att: 73,611 *(Wembley)*
Germany win on golden goals rule

European Under-21 Championship

Winners

1978	Yugoslavia
1980	Soviet Union
1982	England
1984	England
1986	Spain
1988	France
1990	Soviet Union
1992	Italy
1994	Portugal
1996	Italy

European Youth Championship

Winners

1948	England
1949	France
1950	Austria
1951	Yugoslavia
1952	Spain
1953	Hungary
1954	Spain
1957	Austria
1958	Italy
1959	Bulgaria
1960	Hungary
1961	Portugal
1962	Romania
1963	England

1964	England
1965	East Germany
1966	Soviet Union/Italy
1967	Soviet Union
1968	Czechoslovakia
1969	Bulgaria
1970	East Germany
1971	England
1972	England
1973	England
1974	Bulgaria
1975	England
1976	Soviet Union
1977	Belgium
1978	Soviet Union
1979	Yugoslavia
1980	England
1981	West Germany
1982	Scotland
1983	France
1984	Hungary
1986	East Germany
1988	Soviet Union
1990	Soviet Union
1992	Turkey
1993	England
1994	Portugal
1995	Spain
1996	France
1997	France

African Nations Cup

Finalists

1957:

Egypt 4 Ethiopia 0
El Diba (4)
Att: 20,000 *(Khartoum)*

1959:

1st Egypt
2nd Sudan *(in Cairo)*

1962:

Ethiopia 4 Egypt 2*
Girma, Menguitsou (2), Italo — *Badawi 2*
Att: 50,000 *(Addis Ababa)*

1963:

Ghana 3 Sudan 0
Aggrey-Fynn, Mfum (2)
Att: 80,000 *(Accra)*

1965:

Ghana 3 Tunisia 2*
Odoi (2), Kofi — Chetali, Chaibi
Att: 50,000 *(Tunis)*

1968:

Congo Kinshasa (Zaire) 1 Ghana 0
Kalala
Att: 80,000 *(Accra)*

1970:

Sudan 1 Ghana 0
El Issed
Att: 12,000 *(Khartoum)*

1972:

Congo 3 Mali 2
M'Bono (2), M'Pele — *Diakhite, Traore M.*
Att: 20,000 *(Yaounde)*

1974:

Zaire 2 Zambia 2*
Ndaye (2) — *Kaushi, Sinyangwe*
Att: 15,000 *(Cairo)*

1974 replay:

Zaire 2 Zambia 0
Ndaye (2)
Att: 1,000 *(Cairo)*

1976:

1st Morocco
2nd Guinea
(in Addis Ababa)

1978:

Ghana 2 Uganda 0
Afriye (2)
Att: 40,000 *(Accra)*

1980:

Nigeria 3 Algeria 0
Odegbami (2), Lawal
Att: 80,000 *(Lagos)*

1982:

Ghana 1 Libya 1*
Al Hassan — *Beshari*
(Ghana 7–6 on penalties)
Att: 50,000 *(Tripoli)*

1984:

Cameroon 3 Nigeria 0
Ndjeya, Abega, Ebongue
Att: 50,000 *(Abidjan)*

1986:

Egypt 0 Cameroon 0*
(Egypt 5–4 on penalties)
Att: 100,000 *(Cairo)*

1988:

Cameroon 1 Nigeria 0
Kunde
Att: 50,000 *(Casablanca)*

1990:

Algeria 1 Nigeria 0
Oudjani
Att: 80,000 *(Algiers)*

1992:

Ivory Coast	0	Ghana	0*

(Ghana 11–10 on penalties.)
Att: 60,000 *(Dakar)*

1994:

Nigeria	2	Zambia	1
Amunike (2)		*Litana*	

Att: 25,000 *(Tunis)*

1996:

South Africa	2	Tunisia	0
Williams (2)			

Att: 80,000 *(Johannesburg)*

Asian Cup

Winners

1956:			
South Korea	2	Israel	1
1960:			
South Korea	3	Israel	0
1964:			
Israel 2		India	0
1968:			
Iran	3	Burma	1
1972:			
Iran	2	South Korea	1
1976:			
Iran	1	Kuwait	0
1980:			
Kuwait	3	South Korea	0
1984:			
Saudi Arabia	2	China	0
1988:			
Saudi Arabia	0	South Korea	0
(Saudia Arabia 4–3 on penalties)			
1992:			
Japan 1		Saudi Arabia	0
1996:			
Saudi Arabia	0	U.A.E.	0
(Saudia Arabia 4–2 on penalties)			

Asian Games

Winners

1951			
India	1	Iran	0
1954			
Taiwan	5	South Korea	2
1958			
Taiwan	3	South Korea	2
1962			
India	2	South Korea	1
1966			
Burma	1	Iran	0
1970			
Burma	0	South Korea	0
1974			
Iran	1	Israel	0
1978			
North Korea	0	South Korea	0
1982			
Iraq	1	Kuwait	0
1986			
South Korea	2	Saudi Arabia	0
1990			
Iran	0	North Korea	0
(Iran 4–1 on penalties)			
1994			
Uzbekistan	4	China	2

Note:
The trophy was shared in 1970 and 1978

CONCACAF Championship

Winners

1941	Costa Rica
1943	El Salvador
1946	Costa Rica
1948	Costa Rica
1951	Panama
1953	Costa Rica
1955	Costa Rica
1957	Haiti
1960	Costa Rica
1961	Costa Rica
1963	Costa Rica
1965	Mexico
1967	Guatemala
1969	Costa Rica
1971	Mexico
1973	Haiti
1977	Mexico
1981	Honduras
1985	Canada
1989	Costa Rica
1991	USA
1993	Mexico
1996	Mexico

World Club Cup

Finalists

1960 Montevideo:
Peñarol 0 — Real Madrid 0
Att: 75,000

Madrid:
Real Madrid 5 — Peñarol 1
Puskas (2), Di Stefano, Herrera, Gento — *Borges*
Att: 125,000

1961 Lisbon:
Benfica 1 — Peñarol 0
Coluna
Att: 50,000

Montevideo:
Peñarol 5 — Benfica 0
Sasia, Joya (2), Spencer (2)
Att: 56,000

Montevideo (play-off):
Peñarol 2 — Benfica 1
Sasia (2) — *Eusebio*
Att: 62,000

1962 Rio de Janeiro:
Santos 3 — Benfica 2
Pele (2), Coutinho — *Santana (2)*
Att: 90,000

Lisbon:
Benfica 2 — Santos 5
Eusebio, Santana — *Pele (3), Coutinho, Pepe*
Att: 75,000

1963 Milan:
Milan 4 — Santos 2
Trapattoni, Amarildo (2), Mora — *Pele (2)*
Att: 80,000

Rio de Janeiro:
Santos 4 — Milan 2
Pepe (2), Almir, Lima — *Altafini, Mora*
Att: 150,000

Rio de Janeiro (play-off):
Santos 1 — Milan 0
Dalmo
Att: 121,000

1964 Avellanada:
Independiente 1 — Internazionale 0
Rodriguez
Att: 70,000

Milan:
Internazionale 2 — Independiente 0
Mazzola, Corso
Att: 70,000

Milan (play-off):
Internazionale 1 — Independiente 0*
Corso
Att: 45,000

1965 Milan:
Internazionale 3 — Independiente 0
Peiro, Mazzola (2)
Att: 70,000

Avellanada:
Independiente 0 — Internazionale 0
Att: 70,000

1966 Montevideo:
Penarol 2 — Real Madrid 0
Spencer (2)
Att: 70,000

Madrid:
Real Madrid 0 — Penarol 2
Rocha, Spencer
Att: 70,000

1967 Glasgow:
Celtic 1 — Racing Club 0
McNeill
Att: 103,000

Avellanada:
Racing Club 2 — Celtic 1
Raffo, Cardenas — *Gemmell*
Att: 80,000

Montevideo (play-off):
Racing Club 1 — Celtic 0
Cardenas
Att: 65,000

1968 Buenos Aires:
Estudiantes 1 — Man. United 0
Conigliaro
Att: 65,000

Manchester:
Manchester Utd 1 — Estudiantes 1
Morgan — *Veron*
Att: 60,000

1969 Milan:
Milan 3 — Estudiantes 0
Sormani (2), Combin
Att: 80,000

Buenos Aires:
Estudiantes 2 — Milan 1
Conigliaro, Aguirre-Suarez — *Rivera*
Att: 65,000
Milan won 4–2 on aggregate

1970 Buenos Aires:
Estudiantes 2 — Feyenoord 2
Echecopar, Veron — *Van Hanegem Kindvall,*
Att: 65,000

Rotterdam:
Feyenoord 1 — Estudiantes 0

Van Deale
Att: 70,000
Feyenoord won 3–2 on aggregate

1971 Athens:

Panathinaikos	1	Nacional (Uru)	1
Filakouris		*Artime*	

Att: 60,000

Montevideo:

Nacional	2	Panathinaikos	1
Artime (2)		*Filakouris*	

Att: 70,000.
Nacional won 3–2 on aggregate

1972 Avellanada:

Independiente	1	Ajax	1
Sa		*Cruyff*	

Att: 65,000

Amsterdam:

Ajax	3,	Independiente	0
Neeskens, Rep (2)			

Att: 60,000
Ajax won 4–1 on aggregate

1973 Rome (single match):

Independiente	1	Juventus	0
Bochini 40			

Att: 35,000

1974 Buenos Aires:

Independiente	1	Atletico Madrid	0
Balbuena 33			

Att: 60,000

Madrid:

Atletico Madrid	2	Independiente	0
Irureta 21, Ayala 86			

Att: 45,000.
Atletico won 2–1 on aggregate

1975 not played

1976 Munich:

Bayern Munich	2	Cruzeiro	0
Müller, Kapellmann			

Att: 22,000

Belo Horizonte:

Cruzeiro	0	Bayern Munich	0

Att: 114,000.
Bayern won 2–0 on aggregate

1977 Buenos Aires:

Boca Juniors	2	Mönchengladbach	2
Mastrangelo, Ribolzi		*Hannes, Bonhof*	

Att: 50,000

Karlsruhe:

Mönchengladbach	0	Boca Juniors	3
		Zanabria, Mastrangelo, Salinas	

Att: 21,000
Boca Juniors won 5–2 on aggregate

1978 not played

1979 Malmö:

Malmö	0	Olimpia	1
		Isasi	

Att: 4,000

Asuncion:

Olimpia	2	Malmö	1
Solalinde, Michelagnoli		*Earlandsson*	

Att: 35,000
Olimpia won 3–1 on aggregate

1980 Tokyo:

Nacional (Uru)	1	Notts. Forest	0
Victorino			

Att: 62,000

1981 Tokyo:

Flamengo	3	Liverpool	0
Nunes (2), Adilio			

Att: 62,000

1982 Tokyo:

Peñarol	2	Aston Villa	0
Jair, Charrua			

Att: 62,000

1983 Tokyo:

Gremio	2	Hamburg SV	1
Renato (2)		*Schroder*	

Att: 62,000

1984 Tokyo:

Independiente	1	Liverpool	0
Percudani			

Att: 62,000

1985 Tokyo:

Juventus	2	Argentinos Juniors	2*
Platini, Laudrup M.		*Ereros, Castro*	

Att: 62,000
Juventus won 4–2 on penalties

1986 Tokyo:

River Plate	1	Steaua Bucharest	0
Alzamendi			

Att: 62,000

1987 Tokyo:

FC Porto	2	Peñarol	1*
Gomes, Madjer		*Viera*	

Att: 45,000

1988 Tokyo:

Nacional (Uru)	2	PSV Eindhoven	2*
Ostolaza (2)		*Romario, Koeman R*	

Att: 62,000
Nacional won 7–6 on penalties

1989 Tokyo:

Milan	1	Nacional (Col)	0
Evani			

Att: 62,000

1990 Tokyo:

Milan	3	Olimpia	0
Rijkaard (2), Stroppa			
Att: 60,000			

1991 Tokyo:

Red Star Belgrade	3	Colo Colo	0
Jugovic (2), Pancev			
Att: 60,000			

1992 Tokyo:

São Paulo	2	Barcelona	1
Rai (2)		*Stoichkov*	
Att: 80,000			

1993 Tokyo:

São Paulo	3	Milan	2
Palinha, Cerezo, Müller		*Massaro, Papin*	
Att: 52,000			

1994 Tokyo:

Velez Sarsfield	2	Milan	0
Trott, Abad			
Att: 65,000			

1995 Tokyo:

Ajax	0	Gremio	0
Att: 62,000			
Ajax won 4–3 on penalties			

1996 Tokyo:

Juventus	1	River Plate	0
Del Piero			
Att: 55,000			

1997 Tokyo:

Borussia Dortmund	2	Cruzeiro	0
Zorc, Herrlich			
Att: 60,000			

Note:

From 1960 to 1979 the World Club Cup was decided on points, not goal difference. Since 1980 it has been a one-off match in Tokyo

Copa Libertadores (South American Club Cup)

Finalists

1960 Montevideo:

Peñarol	1	Olimpia	0
Spencer			
Att: 80,000			

Asuncion:

Olimpia	1	Peñarol	1
Recalde		*Cubilla*	
Att: 35,000			

Winners:

Peñarol

1961 Montevideo:

Peñarol	1	Palmeiras	0
Spencer			
Att: 50,000			

São Paulo:

Palmeiras	1	Peñarol	1
Nardo		*Sasia*	
Att: 40,000.			

Winners:

Peñarol

1962 Montevideo:

Peñarol	1	Santos	2
Spencer		*Coutinho (2)*	
Att:50,000			
Santos	2	Peñarol	3
Dorval, Mengalvio		*Spencer, Sasia (2)*	

Play-off – Buenos Aires:

Santos	3	Peñarol	0
Coutinho, Pele (2)			
Att: 36,000			

1963 Rio de Janeiro:

Santos	3	Boca Juniors	2
Coutino 2, Lima		*Sanfilippo (2)*	
Att: 55,000			

Buenos Aires:

Boca Juniors	1	Santos	2
Sanfilippo		*Coutinho, Pele*	
Att: 50,000			

Winners:

Santos.

1964 Montevideo:

Nacional (Uru)	0	Independiente	0
Att: 75,000			

Avellaneda:

Independiente	1	Nacional (Uru)	0
Rodriguez			
Att: 60,000			

Winners:

Independiente.

1965 Avellaneda:

Independiente	1	Peñarol	0
Bernao			
Att: 55,000			
Peñarol	3	Independiente	1
Goncalvez, Reznik, Rocha		*De la Mata*	
Att: 65,000			

Play-off – Santiago:

Independiente	4	Peñarol	1
Acevedo, Bernao, Avallay, Mura		*Joya*	
Att: 25,000			

1966 Montevideo:

Peñarol	2	River Plate	0
Abaddie, Joya			
Att: 49,000			

Buenos Aires:

River Plate	3	Peñarol	2
E Onega, D Onega, Sarnari		*Rocha, Spencer*	
Att: 60,000.			

Play-off – Santiago:

Peñarol	4	River Plate	2
Spencer (2), Rocha, Abbadie		*D Onega, Solari*	
Att: 39,000.			

1967 Avellaneda:

Racing Club	0	Nacional (Uru)	0
Att: 54,000			

Montevideo:

Nacional (Uru)	0	Racing Club	0
Att: 54,000			

Play-off – Santiago:

Racing Club	2	Nacional (Uru)	1
Cardozo, Raffo		*Esparrago*	
Att: 25,000			

1968 La Plata:

Estudiantes	2	Palmeiras	1
Veron, Flores		*Servillio*	
Att: 40,000			

Sao Paulo:

Palmeiras	3	Estudiantes	1
Tupazinho (2), Reinaldo		*Veron*	
Att: 75,000			

Play-off – Montevideo:

Estudiantes	2	Palmeiras	0
Ribaudo, Veron			
Att: 30,000			

1969 Montevideo:

Nacional (Uru)	0	Estudiantes	1
		Flores 66	
Att:50,000			

La Plata:

Estudiantes	2	Nacional (Uru)	0
Flores 31, Conigliaro 37			
Att: 30,000			

Winners:
Estudiantes.

1970 La Plata:

Estudiantes	1	Peñarol	0
Togneri 87			
Att: 36,000			

Montevideo:

Peñarol	0	Estudiantes	0
Att: 50,000.			

Winners:
Estudiantes.

1971 La Plata:

Estudiantes	1	Nacional (Uru)	0
Romeo			
Att: 32,000			
Nacional (Uru)	1	Estudiantes	0
Masnik 17			
Att: 62,000			

Play-off – Lima:

Nacional (Uru)	2	Estudiantes	0
Esparrago 22, Artime 65			
Att: 42,000			

1972 Lima:

Universitario	0	Independiente	0
Att: 45,000			

Avellaneda:

Independiente	2	Universitario	1
Maglioni (2)		*Rojas*	
Att: 65,000			

1973 Avellaneda:

Independiente	1	Colo Colo	1
Mendoza 75		*Sa og 71*	
Att: 65,000			

Santiago:

Colo Colo	0	Independiente	0
Att: 77,000			

Play-off – Montevideo:

Independiente 2		Colo Colo	1
Mendoza 25, Giachello 107		*Caszely 39*	
Att: 45,000			

1974 São Paulo:

Sao Paulo	2	Independiente	1
Rocha 48, Mirandinha 50		*Saggioratto 28*	
Att: 51,000			

Avellaneda:

Independiente	2	São Paulo	0
Bochini 34, Balbuena 48			
Att: 48,000			

Play-off – Santiago:

Independiente	1	São Paulo	0

Pavoni 37			
Att: 27,000			

1975 Santiago:

Union Espanola	1	Independiente	0
Ahumada 87			
Att:43,000			

Avellaneda:

Independiente	3	Union Espanola	1
Rojas 1, Pavoni 58, Bertoni 83		*Las Heras*	
Att: 52,000			

Play-off – Asuncion (play-off):

Independiente	2	Union Espanola	0
Ruiz Moreno 29, Bertoni 65			
Att: 45,000			

1976 Belo Horizonte:

Cruzeiro	4	River Plate	1
Nelinho, Palinha 2, Waldo		*Mas*	
Att:58,000			

Buenos Aires:

River Plate	2	Cruzeiro	1
J Lopez, Gonzalez		*Palinha*	
Att: 45,000			

Play-off – Santiago:

Cruzeiro	3	River Plate	2
Nelinho, Ronaldo, Joazinho		*Mas, Urquiza*	
Att: 35,000			

1977 Buenos Aires:

Boca Juniors	1	Cruzeiro	0
Veglio 3			
Att: 50,000			
Cruzeiro	1	Boca Juniors	0
Nelinho 76			
Att: 55,000			

Play-off – Montevideo:

Boca Juniors	0	Cruzeiro	0
Att: 45,000			

1978 Cali:

Deportivo Cali	0	Boca Juniors	0

Buenos Aires:

Boca Juniors	4	Deportivo Cali	0
Perotti 15, 85, Mastrangelo 60, Salinas 71			

Winners:
Boca Juniors

1979 Asuncion:

Olimpia	2	Boca Juniors	0
Aquino 3, Piazza.		Att: 45,000	

Buenos Aires:

Boca Juniors	0	Olimpia	0
Att: 50,000			

Winners:
Olimpia

1980 Porto Alegre:

Internacional P A (Brz)	0	Nacional (Uru)	0
Att: 80,000			

Montevideo:

Nacional (Uru)	1	Internacional PA	0
Victorino 35			
Att: 75,000			

Winners:
Nacional

1981 Rio de Janeiro:

Flamengo	2	Cobreloa	1
Zico 12, 30		*Merello 65*	
Att: 114,000			

Santiago:

Cobreloa	1	Flamengo	0
Merello 79			
Att: 61,000			

Play-off – Montevideo:

Flamengo	2	Cobreloa	0
Zico 18, 79			
Att: 35,000			

1982 Montevideo:

Pñnarol	0	Cobreloa	0
Att: 70,000			

Santiago:

Cobreloa	0	Peñarol	1
		Morena 89	
Att: 70,000			

Winners:
Peñarol

1983 Montevideo:

Penarol	1	Gremio	1
Morena 35		*Tita 12*	
Att: 65,000			

Porto Alegre:

Gremio	2	Penarol	1
Caio 9, Cesar 87		*Morena 70*	
Att: 75,000			

Winners:
Gremio

1984 Porto Alegre:

Gremio	0	Independiente	1
		Burruchaga 24	
Att: 55,000			

Avellaneda:

Independiente	0	Gremio	0

Winners:
Independiente

1985 Buenos Aires:
Argentinos Juniors 1 America Cali 0
Comisso 40
Att: 50,000

Cali:
America Cali 1 Argentinos J. 0
Ortiz 3
Att: 50,000

Play-off – Asuncion:
Argentinos Juniors 1 America Cali 1
Comizzo 37 *Gareca 42*
Att: 35,000
Argentinos Juniors 5-4 on penalties

1986 Cali:
America Cali 1 River Plate 2
Cabanas 47 *Funes 22, Alonso 25*
Att: 55,000

Buenos Aires:
River Plate 1 America Cali 0
Funes 70
Att: 85,000

Winners:
River Plate

1987 Cali:
America Cali 2 Penarol 0
Bataglia, Cabanas
Att: 45,000.

Montevideo:
Penarol 2 America Cali 1
Aguirre 58, Villar 86 *Cabanas 19*
Att: 70,000

Play-off – Santiago:
Penarol 1 America Cali 0
Aguirre 119
Att: 30,000

1988 Rosario:
Newell's Old Boys 1 Nacional (Uru) 0
Gabrich 60
Att: 45,000

Montevideo:
Nacional (Uru) 3 Newell's OB 0
Vargas 10, Ostolaza 30, De Leon 81
Att: 75,000
Nacional 3-1 on agg

1989 Asuncion:
Olimpia 2 Atlético Nacional 0
Bobadilla 36, Sanabria 60
Att: 50,000

Bogota:
Atlético Nacional 2 Olimpia 0
Mano og 46, Usurriaga 64
Att: 50,000
Atletico Nacional 5-4 on pens, agg 2-2

1990 Asuncion:
Olimpia 2 Barcelona 0
Amarilla 47, Samaniego 65
Att: 35,000

Guayaquil:
Barcelona 1 Olimpia 1
Trobbiani 61 *Amarilla 80*
Att: 55,000
Olimpia 3-1 on agg

1991 Asuncion:
Olimpia 0 Colo Colo 0
Att: 48,000

Santiago:
Colo Colo 3 Olimpia 0
Perez 13, 18, Herrera 85
Att: 64,000
Colo Colo 3-0 on agg

1992 Rosario:
Newell's Old Boys 1 São Paulo 0
Berizzo 38
Att: 45,000

São Paulo:
Sao Paulo 1 Newell's OBs 0
Rai 65
Att: 105,000
São Paulo 3-2 on pens, 1-1 agg

1993 São Paulo:
São Paulo 5 Catolica 1
Lopez, og Dinho, Gilmar, Rai, Muller *Almada*
Att: 99,000

Santiago:
Catolica 2 São Paulo 0
Lunari, Almada
Att: 50,000
São Paulo 5-3 on agg

1994 Buenos Aires:
Velez Sarsfield 1 Sao Paulo 0

Asad
Att: 48,000

Sao Paulo:

Sao Paulo	1	Velez Sarsfield	0
Muller			

Velez Sarsfield 5-3 on pens, 1-1 agg

1995 Porto Alegre:

Gremio	3	Atletico Nacional	1
Marulanda og, Jardel, Paulo Nunes		*Angel*	

Att: 50,000

Medellin:

Atletico Nacional	1	Gremio	1
Aristizabal		*Dinho (pen)*	

Att: 52,000
Gremio 4-2 on agg

1996 Cali:

America	1	River Plate	0
De Avila			

Att: 55,000

Buenos Aires:

River Plate	2	America	0
Crespo (2)			

Att: 68,000
River Plate 2-1 on agg

1997 Lima:

Sporting Cristal	0	Cruzeiro	0

Att: 45,000

Belo Horizonte:

Cruzeiro	1	Sporting Cristal	0
Elivelton 75			

Att: 65,000
Cruzeiro 1-0 on agg

South American Recopa

Winners

1988	Nacional
1989	Boca Juniors
1990	Olimpia
1991	Colo Colo
1992	São Paulo
1993	São Paulo
1994	São Paulo
1995	Independiente
1996	Gremio
1997	Lanus

South American Super Cup

Winners

1988	Racing Club
1989	Boca Juniors
1990	Olimpia
1991	Cruzeiro
1992	Cruzeiro
1993	Botafogo
1994	Independiente
1995	Independiente
1996	Velez Sarsfield
1997	River Plate

European Champions Club Cup (now UEFA Champions League)

Finalists

1956 Paris:
Real Madrid 4 – Stade de Reims 3
Di Stefano, Rial (2), Marquitos – *Leblond, Templin, Hidalgo*
Att: 38,000

1957 Madrid:
Real Madrid 2 – Fiorentina 0
Di Stefano, Gento
Att: 124,000

1958 Brussels:
Real Madrid 3 – Milan 2*
Di Stefano, Rial, Gento – *Schiaffino, Grillo*
Att: 67,000

1959 Stuttgart:
Real Madrid 2 – Stade de Reims 0
Mateos, Di Stefano
Att: 80,000

1960 Glasgow:
Real Madrid 7 – Eintracht Frankfurt 3
Di Stefano (3), Puskas (4) – *Kress, Stein (2)*
Att: 127,621

1961 Berne:
Benfica 3 – Barcelona 2
Aguas, o.g., Coluna 2 – *Kocsis, Czibor*
Att: 33,000

1962 Amsterdam:
Benfica 5 – Real Madrid 3
Aguas, Cavem, Coluna, Eusebio (2) – *Puskas (3)*
Att: 68,000

1963 Wembley:
Milan 2 – Benfica 1
Altafini (2) – *Eusebio*
Att: 45,000

1964 Vienna:
Internazionale 3 – Real Madrid 1
Mazzola (2), Milani – *Felo*
Att: 72,000

1965 Milan:
Internazionale 1 – Benfica 0
Jair
Att: 80,000

1966 Brussels:
Real Madrid 2 – Partizan Belgrade 1
Amancio, Serena – *Vasovic*
Att: 55,000

1967 Lisbon:
Celtic 2 – Internazionale 1
Gemmell, Chalmers – *Mazzola*
Att: 55,000

1968 Wembley:
Man. United 4 – Benfica 1*
Charlton (2), Best, Kidd – *Graca*
Att: 100,000

1969 Madrid:
Milan 4 – Ajax 1
Prati (3), Sormani – *Vasovic*
Att: 50,000

1970 Milan:
Feyenoord 2 – Celtic 1*
Israel, Kindvall – *Gemmell*
Att: 53,187

1971 Wembley:
Ajax 2 – Panathinaikos 0
Van Dijk, Haan
Att: 90,000

1972 Rotterdam:
Ajax 2 – Internazionale 0
Cruyff (2)
Att: 61,000

1973 Belgrade:
Ajax 1 – Juventus 0
Rep
Att: 93,500

1974 Brussels:
Bayern Munich 1 – Atlético Madrid 1*
Schwartzenbeck – *Luis*
Att: 65,000

Brussels (replay):
Bayern Munich 4 – Atlético Madrid 0
Hoeness (2), Müller (2)
Att: 23,000

1975 Paris:
Bayern Munich 2 – Leeds United 0
Roth, Müller
Att: 48,000

1976 Glasgow:
Bayern Munich 1 – St Etienne 0
Roth
Att: 54,684

1977 Rome:
Liverpool 3 – Borussia Mönchengladbach 1
McDermott, Smith, Neal – *Simonsen*
Att: 57, 000

1978 Wembley:
Liverpool 1 Club Brugge 0
Dalglish
Att: 92,000

1979 Munich:
Notts Forest 1 Malmö 0
Francis
Att: 57,500

1980 Madrid:
Notts Forest 1 Hamburg 0
Robertson
Att: 51,000

1981 Paris:
Liverpool 1 Real Madrid 0
Kennedy A.
Att: 48,360

1982 Rotterdam:
Aston Villa 1 Bayern Munich 0
Withe
Att: 46,000

1983 Athens:
Hamburg 1 Juventus 0
Magath
Att: 80,000

1984 Rome:
Liverpool 1 AS Roma 1*
Neal *Pruzzo*
Att: 69,693
Liverpool 4–2 on penalties

1985 Brussels:
Juventus 1 Liverpool 0
Platini
Att: 58,000

1986 Seville:
Steaua Bucharest 0 Barcelona 0*
Att: 70,000
Steaua 2–0 on penalties

1987 Vienna:
FC Porto 2 Bayern Munich 1
Madjer, Juary *Kogl*
Att: 56,000

1988 Stuttgart:
PSV Eindhoven 0 Benfica 0*
Att: 55,000
PSV 6–5 on penalties

1989 Barcelona:
Milan 4 Steaua Bucharest 0
Gullit (2),
Van Basten (2)
Att: 97,000

1990 Vienna:
Milan 1 Benfica 0
Rijkaard
Att: 56,000

1991 Bari:
Red Star Belgrade 0 Marseille 0*
Att: 50,000
Red Star 5–3 on penalties

1992 Wembley:
Barcelona 1 Sampdoria 0*
Koeman R.
Att: 74,000

1993 Munich:
Marseille 1 Milan 0
Boli
Att: 72, 300

1994 Athens:
Milan 4 Barcelona 0
Massaro (2),
Savicevic, Desailly
Att: 76,000

1995 Vienna:
Ajax 1 Milan 0
Kluivert
Att 49,000

1996 Rome:
Juventus 1 Ajax 1
Ravanelli *Litmanen*
Att: 67,000
Juventus 4–2 on penalties

1997 Munich:
Borussia Dortmund 3 Juventus 1
Riedle (2), Ricken *Del Piero*
Att: 55,000

European Cup-Winners Cup

Finalists

1961 Glasgow:
Rangers 0 Fiorentina 2
Milani (2)
Att: 80,000

Florence:
Fiorentina 2 Rangers 1
Milani, Hamrin *Scott*
Att: 50,000
Fiorentina 4–1 on aggregate

1962 Glasgow:
Atlético Madrid 1 Fiorentina 1*
Peiro *Hamrin*
Att: 30,000

Stuttgart (replay):
Atlético Madrid 3 Fiorentina 0
Jones, Mendonca,
Peiro
Att: 39,000

1963 Rotterdam:
Tottenham 5 — Atletico Madrid 1
Greaves (2), White, Dyson (2) — *Collar*
Att: 50,000

1964 Brussels:
Sporting Lisbon 3 — MTK Budapest 3*
Mascaranha, Figueiredo (2) — *Sandor (2), Kuti*
Att: 4,000

Antwerp (replay):
Sporting Lisbon 1 — MTK Budapest 0
Morais
Att: 14,000

1965 Wembley:
West Ham 2 — TSV Munich 0
Sealey (2)
Att: 98,000

1966 Glasgow:
Borussia Dortmund 2 — Liverpool 1*
Held, Libuda — *Hunt*
Att: 42,000

1967 Nuremberg:
Bayern Munich 1 — Rangers 0*
Roth
Att: 70,000

1968 Rotterdam:
Milan 2 — Hamburg SV 0
Hamrin (2)
Att: 54,000

1969 Basle:
Slovan Bratislava 3 — Barcelona 2
Cvetler, Hrivnak, Jan Capkovic — *Zaldua, Rexach*
Att: 40,000

1970 Vienna:
Man. City 2 — Gornik Zabrze 1
Young, Lee — *Oslizlo*
Att: 10,000

1971 Athens:
Chelsea 1 — Real Madrid 1*
Osgood — *Zoco*
Att: 42,000

Athens (replay):
Chelsea 2 — Real Madrid 1
Dempsey, Osgood — *Fleitas*
Att: 24,000

1972 Barcelona:
Rangers 3 — Moscow Dynamo 2
Stein, Johnston (2) — *Estrekov, Makovikov*
Att: 35,000

1973 Salonika:
Milan 1 — Leeds United 0
Chiarugi
Att: 45,000

1974 Rotterdam:
FC Magdeburg 2 — Milan 0
o.g., Seguin
Att: 5,000

1975 Basle:
Kiev Dynamo 3 — Ferencvaros 0
Onischenko (2), Blokhin
Att: 13,000

1976 Brussels:
Anderlecht 4 — West Ham 2
Rensenbrink (2), Van der Elst (2) — *Holland, Robson*
Att: 58,000

1977 Amsterdam:
Hamburg SV 2 — Anderlecht 0
Volkert, Magath
Att: 65,000

1978 Paris:
Anderlecht 4 — FK Austria 0
Rensenbrink (2), Van Binst (2)
Att: 48,679

1979 Basle:
Barcelona 4 — Fortuna Düsseldorf 3*
Sanchez, Asensi, Rexach, Krankl — *Allofs K., Seel (2)*
Att: 58,000

1980 Brussels:
Valencia 0 — Arsenal 0*
Att: 40,000
Valencia 5–4 on penalties

1981 Düsseldorf:
Dynamo Tbilisi 2 — Carl Zeiss Jena 1
Gutsayev, Daraselia — *Hoppe*
Att: 9,000

1982 Barcelona:
Barcelona 2 — Standard Liège 1
Simonsen, Quini — *Vandermissen*
Att: 100,000

1983 Gothenburg:
Aberdeen 2 — Real Madrid 1*
Black , Hewitt — *Juanito*
Att: 17,804

1984 Basle:
Juventus 2 — FC Porto 1
Vignola, Boniek — *Sousa*
Att: 60,000

1985 Rotterdam:
Everton 3 — Rapid Vienna 1
Gray, Steven, Sheedy — *Krankl*
Att: 50,000

1986 Lyons:
Kiev Dynamo 3 — Atlético Madrid 0
Zavarov, Blokhin, Yevtushenko
Att: 57,000

1987 Athens:

Ajax 1 Lokomotiv Leipzig 0
Van Basten
Att: 35,000

1988 Strasbourg:

Mechelen 1 Ajax 0
De Boer
Att: 39,446

1989 Berne:

Barcelona 2 Sampdoria 0
Salinas, Recarte
Att: 45,000

1990 Gothenburg:

Sampdoria 2 Anderlecht 0*
Vialli (2)
Att: 20,103

1991 Rotterdam:

Man. United 2 Barcelona 1
Hughes (2) — *Koeman*
Att: 42,000

1992 Lisbon:

Werder Bremen 2 Monaco 0
Allofs K., Rufer
Att: 16,000

1993 Wembley:

Parma 3 Antwerp 1
Minotti, Melli, Cuoghi — *Severeyns*
Att: 37,393

1994 Copenhagen:

Arsenal 1 Parma 0
Smith
Att: 33,765

1995 Paris:

Zaragoza 2 Arsenal 1
Esnaider, Nayim — *Hartson*
Att: 48,000

1996 Brussels:

PSG 1 Rapid Vienna 0
N'Gotty
Att: 37,500

1997 Rotterdam:

Barcelona 1 PSG 0
Ronaldo
Att: 50,000

UEFA/Fairs Cup

Finalists

Inter-cities Industrial Fairs Cup

1958:

London Select XI 2 Barcelona 2
Greaves 5, Langley 83 — *Tejada 4, Martinez 43*
Att: 45,000

Barcelona 6 London Select XI 0
Suarez 6, 8, Evaristo 52, 75, Martinez 43, Verges 63
Att: 62,000
Barcelona 8-2 on agg

1960:

Birmingham City 0 Barcelona 0
Att: 40,000

Barcelona:

Barcelona 4 Birmingham City 1
Martinez 3, Czibor 6, 48, Coll 78 — *Hooper 82*
Att: 70,000
Barcelona 4-1 on agg

1961:

Birmingham City 2 Roma 2
Hellawell 78, Orritt 85 — Manfredini 30, 56
Att:21,000

Roma 2 Birmingham City 0
o.g 56, Pestrin 90
Att: 60,000
Roma 4-2 on agg

1962:

Valencia 6 Barcelona 2
Yosu 14, 42, Guillot 35, 54, 67, Nunez 74 — *Kocsis 4, 20*
Att: 65,000

Barcelona:

Barcelona 1 Valencia 1
Kocsis 46 — *Guillot 87*
Att: 60,000
Valencia 7-3 on agg

1963:

Dinamo Zagreb 1 Valencia 2
Zambata 13 — *Waldo 64, Urtiaga 67*
Att: 40,000

Valencia 2 Dinamo Zagreb 0
Manio 68, Nunez 78
Att: 55,000
Valencia 4-1 on agg

1964:

Zaragoza 2 Valencia 1

Villa 40,		*Urtiaga 42*	
Marcelino 83			

Att: 50,000 (in Barcelona)

1965:

Ferencvaros	1	Juventus	0
Fenyvesi 74			

Att: 25,000 (in Turin)

1966:

Barcelona	0	Zaragoza	1
		Canario 30	

Att: 35,000

Zaragoza	2	Barcelona	4*
Marcelino 24, 87		*Pujol 3, 86, 119, Zaballa 89*	

Att: 70,000
Barcelona 4-3 on agg

1967:

Dinamo Zagreb	2	Leeds	0
Cercek 39, 59			

Att: 40,000

Leeds	0	Dinamo Zagreb	0

Att: 35,000
Dinamo Zagreb 2-0 on agg

1968:

Leeds	1	Ferencvaros	0
Jones 41			

Att: 25,000

Ferencvaros	0	Leeds	0

Att: 76,000
Leeds 1-0 on agg

1969:

Newcastle	3	Ujpest Dozsa	0
Moncur 63, 72, Scott 83			

Att: 60,000

Ujpest Dozsa	2	Newcastle	3
Bene 31, Gorocs 44		*Moncur 46, Arentoft 50, Foggon 74*	

Att: 37,000
Newcastle 6-2 on agg

1970:

Anderlecht	3	Arsenal	1
Devrindt 25, Mulder 30, 74		*Kennedy 82*	

Att: 37,000

Arsenal	3	Anderlecht	0
Kelly 25, Radford 75, Sammels 76			

Att: 51,000
Arsenal 4-3 on agg

1971:

Juventus	2	Leeds Utd	2
Bettega 27, Capello 55		*Madeley 48, Bates 77*	

Att: 65,000

Leeds Utd	1	Juventus	1
Clark 12		*Anastasi 20*	

Att: 42,000
Leeds Utd on away goals, 3-3 agg

UEFA Cup

Finalists

1972:

Wolverhampton	1	Tottenham	2
McCalliog 72		*Chivers 57, 87*	

Att: 38,000

Tottenham	1	Wolverhampton	1
Mullery 30		*Wagstaffe 41*	

Att: 54,000
Tottenham 3-2 on agg

1973:

Liverpool	0	Borussia Möenchengladbach	0

abandoned after 27min, rain

Replay:

Liverpool	3	Borussia Mg	0
Keegan 21, 32, Lloyd 61			

Att: 41,000

Borussia Mg	2	Liverpool	0
Heynckes 29, 40			

Att: 35,000
Liverpool 3-2 on agg

1974:

Tottenham	2	Feyenoord	2
England 39, Van Daele og 64		*Van Hanegem 43, De Jong 85*	

Att: 46,000

Feynoord	2	Tottenham	0
Rijsbergen 43, Ressel 84			

Att: 59,000
Feyenoord 4-2 on agg

1975:
Borussia Mg 0 Twente Enschede 0
Att: 42,000 (in Dusseldorf)
Twente Enschede 1 Borussia Mg 5
Drost 76 *Simonsen 2, 86, Heynckes 9, 50, 60*
Att: 21,000
Borussia Mg 5-1 on agg

1976:
Liverpool 3 Club Brugge 2
Kennedy 59, Case 61, Keegan 65 *Lambert 5, Cools 15*
Att: 49,000
Club Brugge 1 Liverpool 1
Lambert 11 *Keegan 15*
Att: 32,000
Liverpool 4-3 on agg

1977:
Juventus 1 Athletic Bilbao 0
Tardelli 15
Att: 75,000
Athletic Bilbao 2 Juventus 1
Churruca 11, Carlos 78 *Bettega 7*
Att: 43,000
Juventus on away goals rule, 2-2 agg

1978:
Bastia 0 PSV Eindhoven 0
Att: 15,000
PSV Eindhoven 3 Bastia 0
Van der Kerkhof W 24, Deijkers 67, Van der Kuijlen 69
Att: 27,000
PSV 3-0 on agg

1979:
Red Star Belgrade 1 Borussia Mg 1
Sestic 21 *Jurisic og 60*
Att: 87,000
Borussia Mg 1 Red Star Belgrade 0
Simonsen 15
Att: 45,000 (in Dusseldorf)
Borussia Mg 2-1 on agg

1980:
Borussia Mg 3 Eintracht Frankfurt 2
Kulik 44, 88, 76 *Karger 37, Matthaus Holzenbein 71*
Att: 25,000
Eintracht Frankfurt 1 Borussia Mg 0
Schaub 81
Att: 59,000
Eintracht Frankfurt on away goals, 3-3 agg

1981:
Ipswich Town 3 AZ67 Alkmaar 0
Wark 28, Thijssen 46, Mariner 56
Att: 27,000
AZ67 Alkmaar 4 Ipswich Town 2
Welzl 7, Metgod 25, Tol 40, Jonker 74 *Thijssen 4, Wark 32*
Att: 28,000
Ipswich 5-4 on agg

1982:
IFK Gothenburg 1 Hamburg SV 0
Tord Holmgren 87
Att: 42,000
Hamburg SV 0 IFK Gothenburg 3
Corneliusson 26, Nilsson 61, Fredriksson 63
Att: 60,000
IFK 4-0 on agg

1983:
Anderlecht 1 Benfica 0
Brylle 29
Att: 55,000
Benfica 1 Anderlecht 1
Sheu 36 *Lozano 38*
Att: 80,000
Anderlecht 2-1 on agg

1984:
Anderlecht 1 Tottenham 1
Olsen 85 *Miller 57*
Att: 35,000
Tottenham 1 Anderlecht 1*
Roberts 84 *Czerniatynski 60*
Att: 46,000.
Tottenham 4-3 on pens, 2-2 agg

1985:
Videoton 0 Real Madrid 3
Michel 31, Santilana 77, Valdano 89
Att: 30,000 (in Szekesfehervar)
Real Madrid 0 Videoton 1
Majer 86
Att: 90,000
Real Madrid 3-1 on agg

1986:
Real Madrid 5 FC Koln 1
Sanchez 38, Gordillo 42, Valdano 51, 84, *Allofs 29*

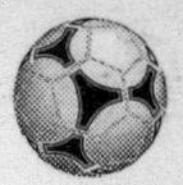

Santillana 89
Att: 85,000
FC Koln 2 Real Madrid 0
Bein 22,
Geilenkirchen 72
Att: 15,000 (in West Berlin)
Real Madrid 5-3 on agg

1987:
IFK Gothenburg 1 Dundee United 0
Pettersson 38
Att: 50,000
Dundee United 1 IFK Gothenburg 1
Clark 60 *Nilsson L. 22*
Att: 21,000
IFK 2-1 on agg

1988:
Espanol 3 Bayer Leverkusen 0
Losada 45, 56,
Soler 49
Att: 42,000 (in Barcelona)
Bayer Leverkusen 3 Espanol 0*
Tita 57, Gotz 63,
Cha 81
Att: 22,000
Leverkusen 3-2 on penalties, agg 3-3

1989:
Napoli 2 VfB Stuttgart 1
Maradona 68, *Gaudino 17*
Careca 87
Att: 83,000
VfB Stuttgart 3 Napoli 3
Klinsmann 27, *Alemao 18,*
De Napoli og 70, *Ferrera 39,*
Schmaler O. 89 *Careca 62*
Att: 67,000
Napoli 5-4 on agg

1990:
Juventus 3 Fiorentina 1
Galia 3, Casiraghi 59, *Buso 10*
De Agostini 73
Att: 45,000
Fiorentina 0 Juventus 0
Att: 32,000 (in Avellino)
Juventus 3-1 on agg

1991:
Internazionale 2 Roma 0
Matthaus 55,
Berti 67
Att: 75,000
Roma 1 Internazionale 0
Rizzitelli 81
Att: 71,000 *Internazionale 2-1 on agg*

1992:
Torino 2 Ajax 2
Casagrande 65, 82 *Jonk 17, Pettersson 73*
Att: 65,000
Ajax 0 Torino 0
Att: 42,000
Ajax on away goals, 2-2 agg

1993:
Borussia Dortmund 1 Juventus 3
M Rummenigge 2 *Baggio D. 27,*
Baggio R. 31, 74
Att: 37,000
Juventus 3 B. Dortmund 0
Baggio D. 5, 40,
Moller 65
Att: 60,000
Juventus 6-1 on agg

1994:
Austria Salzburg 0 Internazionale 1
Berti 35
Att: 47,000
Internazionale 1 Austria Salzburg 0
Jonk 63
Att: 80,000
Internazionale 2-0 on agg

1995:
Parma 1 Juventus 0
Baggio D. 5
Att: 22,000
Juventus 1 Parma 1
Vialli 33 *Baggio D. 54*
Att: 80,000
Parma 2-1 on agg

1996:
Bayern Munich 2 Bordeaux 0
Helmer 35,
Scholl 60
Att: 62,500
Bordeaux 1 Bayern Munich 3
Dutuel 75 *Scholl 53,*
Kostadinov 65,
Klinsmann 79
Att: 36,000
Bayern Munich 5-1 on agg

1997:
Schalke 1 Internazionale 0
Wilmots 69
Att: 56,824
Internazionale 1 Schalke 0*
Zamorano 84
Att: 81,675
Schalke 4-1 on pens, 1-1 agg

European Super Cup

Winners

1972	Ajax
1973	Ajax
1974	not contested
1975	Kiev Dynamo
1976	Anderlecht
1977	Liverpool
1978	Anderlecht
1979	Nottingham Forest
1980	Valencia
1981	not contested
1982	Aston Villa
1983	Aberdeen
1984	Juventus
1985	not contested
1986	Steaua
1987	FC Porto
1988	Mechelen
1989	Milan
1990	Milan
1991	Manchester Utd
1992	Barcelona
1993	Parma
1994	Milan
1995	Ajax
1996	Juventus

African Champions Cup

Winners

1964	Oryx Douala (Cameroon)
1965	not held
1966	Stade Abidjan (Ivory Coast)
1967	TP Englebert (Zaire)
1968	TP Englebert (Zaire)
1969	Al Ismaili (Egypt)
1970	Asante Kotoko (Ghana)
1971	Canon Yaounde (Cameroon)
1972	Hafia Conakry (Ghana)
1973	AS Vita Kinshasa (Zaire)
1974	CARA Brazzaville (Congo)
1975	Hafia Conakry (Ghana)
1976	MC Algiers (Algeria)
1977	Hafia Conakry (Gha)
1978	Canon Yaounde (Cam)
1979	Union Douala (Cam)
1980	Canon Yaounde (Cam)
1981	JE Tizi-Ouzou (Alg)
1982	Al Ahly (Egy)
1983	Asant Kotoko (Gha)
1984	Zamalek (Egy)
1985	FAR Rabat (Morocco)
1986	Zamalek (Egy)
1987	Al Ahly (Egy)
1988	EP Setif (Alg)
1989	Raja Casablanca (Mor)
1990	JS Kabylie (Alg)
1991	Club Africain (Alg)
1992	Wydad Casablanca (Mor)
1993	Zamalek (Egy)
1994	Esperance (Tunisia)
1995	Orlando Pirates (S Africa)
1996	Zamalek (Egy)
1997	Raja Casablanca (Mor)

African Cup-winners Cup

Winners

1975	Tonnerre Yaounde (Cam)
1976	Shooting Stars (Nigeria)
1977	Enugu Rangers (Nig)
1978	Horoya Conakry (Gui)
1979	Canon Yaounde (Cam)
1980	TP Mazembe (Zai)
1981	Union Douala (Cam)
1982	Al Mokaoulum (Egy)
1983	Al Mokaoulum (Egy)
1984	Al Ahly (Egy)
1985	Al Ahly
1986	Al Ahly
1987	Gor Mahia (Kenya)
1988	CA Bizerte (Tun)
1989	Al Merreikh (Sudan)
1990	BCC Lions (Nig)
1991	Power Dynamos (Zam)
1992	Africa Sports (IC)
1993	Al Ahly (Egypt)
1994	Daring Club (Zaire)
1995	J S Kabyle (Alg)
1996	Arab Contractors (Egypt)
1997	Etoile Sahel (Tun)

CAF Cup

Winners

1992	Shooting Stars (Nig)
1993	Stella Abidjan (Ivory Coast)
1994	Bendel Insurance (Nigeria)
1995	Etoile Sahel (Tunisia)
1996	Kawkab (Morocco)
1997	Esperance (Tun)

CONCACAF Champions Cup

Winners

1962	Guadalajara CD (Mexico)
1963	Racing Club (Haiti)
1964	Not completed
1965	Not completed
1966	Not held
1967	Alianza (El Salvador)
1968	Toluca (Mex)
1969	Cruz Azul (Mex)
1970	Cruz Azul, Mex (North), Deportivo Saprissa (Central), Transvaal, Sur (Caribbean)
1971	Cruz Azul (Mex)
1972	Olimpia (Honduras)
1973	Transvaal (Surinam)
1974	Municipal (Guatemala)
1975	Atletico Espanol (Mex)
1976	Aguila (El Salvador)
1977	America (Mex)
1978	Univ Guadalajara, Mex (North), Comunicaciones (Central), Defence Force, Trin (Caribbean)
1979	Deportivo FAS (El Salvador)
1980	UNAM (Mex)
1981	Transvaal (Surinam)
1982	UNAM (Mex)
1983	Atlante (Mex)
1984	Violette (Haiti
1985	Defence Force (Trinidad)
1986	LD Alajuelense (Costa Rica)
1987	America (Mex)
1988	Olimpia (Hond)
1989	UNAM (Mex)
1990	America (Mex)
1991	Puebla (Mex)
1992	America (Mex)
1993	Deportivo Saprissa (CR)
1994	Cartagines (CR)
1995	Dep Saprissa (CR)

Inter-American Cup

Winners

1968	Estudiantes (Arg)
1971	Nacional (Uru)
1972	Independiente (Arg)
1973	Independiente (Arg)
1974	Independiente (Arg)
1976	Independiente (Arg)
1977	America (Mex)
1979	Olimpia (Hon)
1980	UNAM (Mex)
1985	Argentinos Juniors (Arg)
1986	River Plate (Arg)
1988	Nacional (Uru)
1989	Atletico Nacional (Col)
1990	America (Mex)
1992	Colo Colo (Chile)
1993	Un Catolica (Chile)
1994	Velez Sarsfield (Arg)

ENGLAND

Football League

Winners

Season	Champions	Pts	Runners–up	Pts
1888–89	Preston NE	40	Aston Villa	29
1889–90	Preston NE	33	Everton	31
1890–91	Everton	29	Preston NE	27
1891–92	Sunderland	42	Preston NE	37

First Division

Winners

Season	Champions	Pts	Runners–up	Pts
1892–93	Sunderland	48	Preston NE	37
1893–94	Aston Villa	44	Sunderland	38
1894-95	Sunderland	47	Everton	42
1895–96	Aston Villa	45	Derby County	41
1896–97	Aston Villa	47	Sheffield Utd	36
1897–98	Sheffield Utd	42	Sunderland	37
1898–99	Aston Villa	45	Liverpool	43
1899–00	Aston Villa	50	Sheffield Utd	48
1900–01	Liverpool	45	Sunderland	43
1901–02	Sunderland	44	Everton	41
1902–03	Sheffield Wed	42	Aston Villa	41
1903–04	Sheffield Wed	47	Manchester C	44
1904–05	Newcastle Utd	48	Everton	47
1905–06	Liverpool	51	Preston NE	47
1906–07	Newcastle Utd	51	Bristol City	48
1907–08	Manchester Utd	52	Aston Villa*	43
1908–09	Newcastle Utd	53	Everton	46
1909–10	Aston Villa	53	Liverpool	48
1910–11	Manchester Utd	52	Aston Villa	51
1911–12	Blackburn R	49	Everton	46
1912–13	Sunderland	54	Aston Villa	50
1913–14	Blackburn R	51	Aston Villa	44
1914–15	Everton	46	Oldham Ath	45
1919–20	WBA	60	Burnley	51
1920–21	Burnley	59	Manchester C	54
1921–22	Liverpool	57	Tottenham H	51
1922–23	Liverpool	60	Sunderland	54
1923–24	Huddersfield T*	57	Cardiff C	57
1924–25	Huddersfield T	58	WBA	56
1925–26	Huddersfield T	57	Arsenal	52
1926–27	Newcastle Utd	56	Huddersfield T	51
1927–28	Everton	53	Huddersfield T	51
1928–29	Sheffield Wed	52	Leicester C	51
1929–30	Sheffield Wed	60	Derby County	50
1930–31	Arsenal	66	Aston Villa	59
1931–32	Everton	56	Arsenal	54
1932–33	Arsenal	58	Aston Villa	54
1933–34	Arsenal	59	Huddersfield T	56
1934–35	Arsenal	58	Sunderland	54
1935–36	Sunderland	56	Derby County	48
1936–37	Manchester C	57	Charlton Ath	54
1937–38	Arsenal	52	Wolves	51
1938–39	Everton	59	Wolves	55
1946–47	Liverpool	57	Manchester Utd*	56
1947–48	Arsenal	59	Manchester Utd*	52
1948–49	Portsmouth	58	Manchester Utd*	53
1949–50	Portsmouth*	53	Wolves	53
1950–51	Tottenham H	60	Manchester Utd	56
1951–52	Manchester Utd	57	Tottenham H	53
1952–53	Arsenal*	54	Preston NE	54
1953–54	Wolves	57	WBA	53
1954–55	Chelsea	52	Wolves	48
1955–56	Manchester Utd	60	Blackpool*	49
1956–57	Manchester Utd	64	Tottenham H*	56
1957–58	Wolves	64	Preston NE	59
1958–59	Wolves	61	Manchester Utd	55
1959–60	Burnley	55	Wolves	54
1960–61	Tottenham H	66	Sheffield Wed	58
1961–62	Ipswich T	56	Burnley	53
1962–63	Everton	61	Tottenham H	55
1963–64	Liverpool	57	Manchester Utd	53
1964–65	Manchester Utd*	61	Leeds Utd	61
1965–66	Liverpool	61	Leeds Utd*	55
1966–67	Manchester Utd	60	Nottm Forest*	56
1967–68	Manchester C	58	Manchester Utd	56
1968–69	Leeds Utd	67	Liverpool	61
1969–70	Everton	66	Leeds Utd	57
1970–71	Arsenal	65	Leeds Utd	64
1971–72	Derby County	58	Leeds Utd*	57
1972–73	Liverpool	60	Arsenal	57
1973–74	Leeds Utd	62	Liverpool	57
1974–75	Derby County	53	Liverpool*	51
1975–76	Liverpool	60	QPR	59
1976–77	Liverpool	57	Manchester C	56
1977–78	Nottm Forest	64	Liverpool	57
1978–79	Liverpool	68	Nottm Forest	60
1979–80	Liverpool	60	Manchester Utd	58
1980–81	Aston Villa	60	Ipswich T	56
1981–82	Liverpool	87	Ipswich T	83
1982–83	Liverpool	82	Watford	71
1983–84	Liverpool	80	Southampton	77
1984–85	Everton	90	Liverpool*	77
1985–86	Liverpool	88	Everton	86
1986–87	Everton	86	Liverpool	77
1987–88	Liverpool	90	Manchester Utd	81
1988–89	Arsenal*	76	Liverpool	76
1989–90	Liverpool	79	Aston Villa	70
1990–91	Arsenal+	83	Liverpool	76
1991–92	Leeds Ud	82	Manchester Utd	78

Notes: * Position decided by goal average or goal difference, + 2 points deducted

FA Premier League

Winners

Season	Champions	Pts	Runners-up	Pts
1992–93	Manchester Utd	84	Aston Villa	74
1993–94	Manchester Utd	92	Blackburn R	84
1994–95	Blackburn R	89	Manchester Utd	88
1995–96	Manchester Utd	82	Newcastle Utd	78
1996–97	Manchester Utd	75	Newcastle Utd	68

Football League Cup

Winners

Year	Winners	Runners-up	Result
1961	Aston Villa	Rotherham Utd	0–2, 3–0*
1962	Norwich C	Rochdale	3–0, 1–0
1963	Birmingham C	Aston Villa	3–1, 0–0
1964	Leicester C	Stoke C	1–1, 3–2
1965	Chelsea	Leicester C	3–2, 0–0
1966	WBA	West Ham Utd	1–2, 4–1
1967+	QPR	WBA	3–2
1968	Leeds Utd	Arsenal	1–0
1969	Swindon T	Arsenal	3–1*
1970	Manchester C	WBA	2–1*
1971	Tottenham H	Aston Villa	2–0
1972	Stoke C	Chelsea	2–1
1973	Tottenham H	Norwich C	1–0
1974	Wolves	Manchester C	2–1
1975	Aston Villa	Norwich C	1–0
1976	Manchester C	Newcastle Utd	2–1
1977	Aston Villa	Everton	0–0*, 1–1*, 3–2*
1978	Nottm Forest	Liverpool	0–0*, 1–0
1979	Nottm Forest	Southampton	3–2
1980	Wolves	Nottm Forest	1–0
1981	Liverpool	West Ham Utd	1–1*, 2–1
1982	Liverpool	Tottenham H	3–1*
1983	Liverpool	Manchester Utd	2–1*
1984	Liverpool	Everton	0–0*, 1–0
1985	Norwich C	Sunderland	1–0
1986	Oxford Utd	QPR	3–0
1987	Arsenal	Liverpool	2–1
1988	Luton Town	Arsenal	3–2
1989	Nottm Forest	Luton Town	3–1
1990	Nottm Forest	Oldham Ath	1–0
1991	Sheffield Wed	Manchester Utd	1–0
1992	Manchester Utd	Nottm Forest	1–0
1993	Arsenal	Sheffield Wed	2–1
1994	Aston Villa	Manchester Utd	3–1
1995	Liverpool	Bolton Wanderers	2–1
1996	Aston Villa	Leeds Utd	3–0
1997	Leicester City	Middlesbrough	1–1*, 1–0*

Notes: * After extra time, + One-leg Final from this year

FA Cup

Winners

Year	Winners	Runners-up	Result
1872	Wanderers	Royal Engineers	1–0
1873	Wanderers	Oxford University	2–0
1874	Oxford University	Royal Engineers	2–0
1875	Royal Engineers	Old Etonians	1–1*, 2–0
1876	Wanderers	Old Etonians	0–0*, 3–0
1877	Wanderers	Oxford University	2–0*
1878+	Wanderers	Royal Engineers	3–1
1879	Old Etonians	Clapham Rovers	1–0
1880	Clapham Rovers	Oxford University	1–0
1881	Old Carthusians	Old Etonians	3–0
1882	Old Etonians	Blackburn R	1–0
1883	Blackburn Olympic	Old Etonians	2–1*
1884	Blackburn R	Queens Park Glasgow	2–1
1885	Blackburn R	Queens Park Glasgow	2–0
1886	Blackburn R	WBA	0–0*, 2–0
1887	Aston Villa	WBA	2–0
1888	WBA	Preston NE	2–1
1889	Preston NE	Wolves	3–0
1890	Blackburn R	Sheffield Wed	6–1
1891	Blackburn R	Notts County	3–1
1892	WBA	Aston Villa	3–0
1893	Wolves	Everton	1–0
1894	Notts County	Bolton W	4–1
1895	Aston Villa	WBA	1–0
1896	Sheffield Wed	Wolves	2–1
1897	Aston Villa	Everton	3–2
1898	Nottm Forest	Derby County	3–1
1899	Sheffield Utd	Derby County	4–1
1900	Bury	Southampton	4–0
1901	Tottenham H	Sheffield Utd	2–2*, 3–1
1902	Sheffield Utd	Southampton	1–1*, 2–1
1903	Bury	Derby County	6–0
1904	Manchester C	Bolton W	1–0
1905	Aston Villa	Newcastle Utd	2–0
1906	Everton	Newcastle Utd	1–0
1907	Sheffield Wed	Everton	2–1
1908	Wolves	Newcastle Utd	3–1
1909	Manchester Utd	Bristol C	1–0
1910	Newcastle Utd	Barnsley	1–1*, 2–0
1911	Bradford C	Newcastle Utd	0–0*, 1–0
1912	Barnsley	WBA	0–0*, 1–0
1913	Aston Villa	Sunderland	1–0
1914	Burnley	Liverpool	1–0

1915	Sheffield Utd	Chelsea	3–0
1920	Aston Villa	Huddersfield T	1–0*
1921	Tottenham H	Wolves	1–0
1922	Huddersfield T	Preston NE	1–0
1923	Bolton W	West Ham Utd	2–0
1924	Newcastle Utd	Aston Villa	2–0
1925	Sheffield Utd	Cardiff C	1–0
1926	Bolton W	Manchester C	1–0
1927	Cardiff C	Arsenal	1–0
1928	Blackburn R	Huddersfield T	3–1
1929	Bolton W	Portsmouth	2–0
1930	Arsenal	Huddersfield T	2–0
1931	WBA	Birmingham C	2–1
1932	Newcastle Utd	Arsenal	2–1
1933	Everton	Manchester C	3–0
1934	Manchester C	Portsmouth	2–1
1935	Sheffield Wed	WBA	4–2
1936	Arsenal	Sheffield Utd	1–0
1937	Sunderland	Preston NE	3–1
1938	Preston NE	Huddersfield T	1–0*
1939	Portsmouth	Wolves	4–1
1946	Derby County	Charlton Ath	4–1*
1947	Charlton Ath	Burnley	1–0*
1948	Manchester Utd	Blackpool	4–2
1949	Wolves	Leicester C	3–1
1950	Arsenal	Liverpool	2–0
1951	Newcastle Utd	Blackpool	2–0
1952	Newcastle Utd	Arsenal	1–0
1953	Blackpool	Bolton W	4–3
1954	WBA	Preston NE	3–2
1955	Newcastle Utd	Manchester C	3–1
1956	Manchester C	Birmingham C	3–1
1957	Aston Villa	Manchester Utd	2–1
1958	Bolton W	Manchester Utd	2–0
1959	Nottm Forest	Luton T	2–1
1960	Wolves	Blackburn R	3–0
1961	Tottenham H	Leicester C	2–0
1962	Tottenham H	Burnley	3–1
1963	Manchester Utd	Leicester C	3–1
1964	West Ham Utd	Preston NE	3–2
1965	Liverpool	Leeds Utd	2–1*
1966	Everton	Sheffield Wed	3–2
1967	Tottenham H	Chelsea	2–1
1968	WBA	Everton	1–0*
1969	Manchester C	Leicester C	1–0
1970	Chelsea	Leeds Utd	2–2*, 2–1*
1971	Arsenal	Liverpool	2–1*
1972	Leeds Utd	Arsenal	1–0
1973	Sunderland	Leeds Utd	1–0
1974	Liverpool	Newcastle Utd	3–0
1975	West Ham Utd	Fulham	2–0
1976	Southampton	Manchester Utd	1–0
1977	Manchester Utd	Liverpool	2–1
1978	Ipswich T	Arsenal	1–0
1979	Arsenal	Manchester Utd	3–2
1980	West Ham Utd	Arsenal	1–0
1981	Tottenham H	Manchester C	1–1*, 3–2
1982	Tottenham H	QPR	1–1*, 1–0
1983	Manchester Utd	Brighton & HA	2–2*, 4–0
1984	Everton	Watford	2–0
1985	Manchester Utd	Everton	1–0*
1986	Liverpool	Everton	3–1
1987	Coventry C	Tottenham H	3–2*
1988	Wimbledon	Liverpool	1–0
1989	Liverpool	Everton	3–2*
1990	Manchester Utd	Crystal Palace	3–3*, 1–0
1991	Tottenham H	Nottm Forest	2–1*
1992	Liverpool	Sunderland	2–0
1993	Arsenal	Sheffield Wed	1–1*, 2–1*
1994	Manchester Utd	Chelsea	4–0
1995	Everton	Manchester Utd	1–0
1996	Manchester Utd	Liverpool	1–0
1997	Chelsea	Middlesbrough	2–0

Notes: * After extra time;
+ Cup won outright but restored to the FA;

England Internationals 1872–99

Results

Date	Opponents	Venue	Score
30/11/72	Scotland	Glasgow	0–0
8/3/73	Scotland	Kennington Oval	4–2
7/3/74	Scotland	Glasgow	1–2
6/3/75	Scotland	Kennington Oval	2–2
4/3/76	Scotland	Glasgow	0–3
3/3/77	Scotland	Kennington Oval	1–3
2/3/78	Scotland	Glasgow	2–7
18/1/79	Wales	Kennington Oval	2–1
5/4/79	Scotland	Kennington Oval	5–4
13/3/80	Scotland	Glasgow	4–5
15/3/80	Wales	Wrexham	3–2
26/2/81	Wales	Blackburn	0–1
12/3/81	Scotland	Kennington Oval	1–6
18/2/82	Ireland	Belfast	13–0
11/3/82	Scotland	Glasgow	1–5
13/3/82	Wales	Wrexham	3–5
3/2/83	Wales	Kennington Oval	5–0
24/2/83	Ireland	Liverpool	7–0
10/3/83	Scotland	Sheffield	2–3
25/2/84	Ireland	Belfast	8–1
15/3/84	Scotland	Glasgow	0–1
17/3/84	Wales	Wrexham	4–0
28/2/85	Ireland	Manchester	4–0
14/3/85	Wales	Blackburn	1–1
21/3/85	Scotland	Kennington Oval	1–1

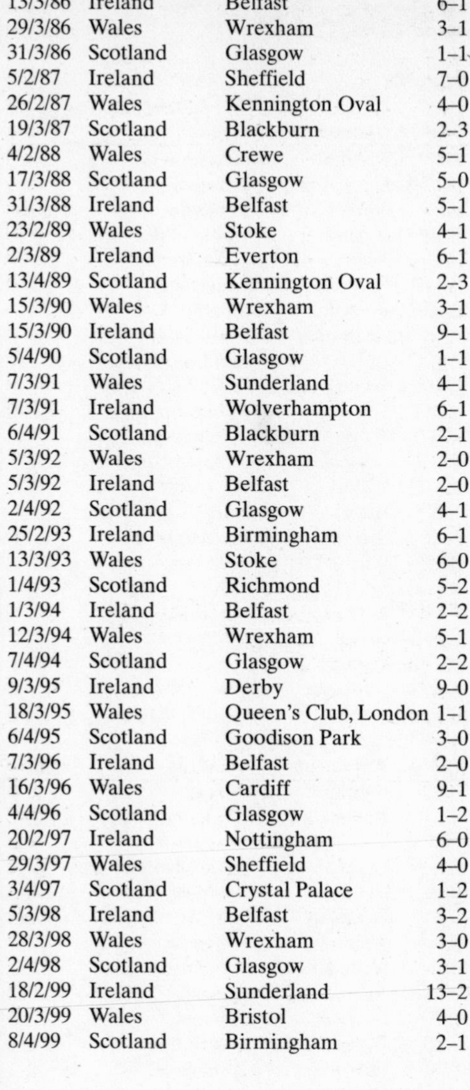

13/3/86	Ireland	Belfast	6–1
29/3/86	Wales	Wrexham	3–1
31/3/86	Scotland	Glasgow	1–1
5/2/87	Ireland	Sheffield	7–0
26/2/87	Wales	Kennington Oval	4–0
19/3/87	Scotland	Blackburn	2–3
4/2/88	Wales	Crewe	5–1
17/3/88	Scotland	Glasgow	5–0
31/3/88	Ireland	Belfast	5–1
23/2/89	Wales	Stoke	4–1
2/3/89	Ireland	Everton	6–1
13/4/89	Scotland	Kennington Oval	2–3
15/3/90	Wales	Wrexham	3–1
15/3/90	Ireland	Belfast	9–1
5/4/90	Scotland	Glasgow	1–1
7/3/91	Wales	Sunderland	4–1
7/3/91	Ireland	Wolverhampton	6–1
6/4/91	Scotland	Blackburn	2–1
5/3/92	Wales	Wrexham	2–0
5/3/92	Ireland	Belfast	2–0
2/4/92	Scotland	Glasgow	4–1
25/2/93	Ireland	Birmingham	6–1
13/3/93	Wales	Stoke	6–0
1/4/93	Scotland	Richmond	5–2
1/3/94	Ireland	Belfast	2–2
12/3/94	Wales	Wrexham	5–1
7/4/94	Scotland	Glasgow	2–2
9/3/95	Ireland	Derby	9–0
18/3/95	Wales	Queen's Club, London	1–1
6/4/95	Scotland	Goodison Park	3–0
7/3/96	Ireland	Belfast	2–0
16/3/96	Wales	Cardiff	9–1
4/4/96	Scotland	Glasgow	1–2
20/2/97	Ireland	Nottingham	6–0
29/3/97	Wales	Sheffield	4–0
3/4/97	Scotland	Crystal Palace	1–2
5/3/98	Ireland	Belfast	3–2
28/3/98	Wales	Wrexham	3–0
2/4/98	Scotland	Glasgow	3–1
18/2/99	Ireland	Sunderland	13–2
20/3/99	Wales	Bristol	4–0
8/4/99	Scotland	Birmingham	2–1

1900–29

Results

Date	Opponents	Venue	Score
17/3/00	Ireland	Dublin	2–0
26/3/00	Wales	Cardiff	1–1
7/4/00	Scotland	Glasgow	1–4
9/3/01	Ireland	Southampton	3–0
18/3/01	Wales	Newcastle	6–0
30/3/01	Scotland	Crystal Palace	2–2
3/3/02	Wales	Wrexham	0–0
22/3/02	Ireland	Belfast	1–0
3/5/02	Scotland	Birmingham	2–2
14/2/03	Ireland	Wolverhampton	4–0
2/3/03	Wales	Portsmouth	2–1
4/4/03	Scotland	Sheffield	1–2
29/2/04	Wales	Wrexham	2–2
12/3/04	Ireland	Belfast	3–1
9/4/04	Scotland	Glasgow	1–0
25/2/05	Ireland	Middlesbrough	1–1
27/3/05	Wales	Liverpool	3–1
1/4/05	Scotland	Crystal Palace	1–0
17/2/06	Ireland	Belfast	5–0
19/3/06	Wales	Cardiff	1–0
7/4/06	Scotland	Glasgow	1–2
16/2/07	Ireland	Goodison Park	1–0
18/3/07	Wales	Fulham	1–1
6/4/07	Scotland	Newcastle	1–1
15/2/08	Ireland	Belfast	3–1
16/3/08	Wales	Wrexham	7–1
4/4/08	Scotland	Glasgow	1–1
6/6/08	Austria	Vienna	6–1
8/6/08	Austria	Vienna	11–1
10/6/08	Hungary	Budapest	7–0
13/6/08	Bohemia	Prague	4–0
13/2/09	Ireland	Bradford	4–0
15/3/09	Wales	Nottingham	2–0
3/4/09	Scotland	Crystal Palace	2–0
29/5/09	Hungary	Budapest	4–2
31/5/09	Hungary	Budapest	8–2
1/6/09	Austria	Vienna	8–1
12/2/10	Ireland	Belfast	1–1
14/3/10	Wales	Cardiff	1–0
2/4/10	Scotland	Glasgow	0–2
11/2/11	Ireland	Derby	2–1
13/3/11	Wales	Millwall	3–0
1/4/11	Scotland	Goodison Park	1–1
10/2/12	Ireland	Dublin	6–1
11/3/12	Wales	Wrexham	2–0
23/3/12	Scotland	Glasgow	1–1
15/2/13	Ireland	Belfast	1–2
17/3/13	Wales	Bristol	4–3
5/4/13	Scotland	Stamford Bridge	1–0
14/2/14	Ireland	Middlesbrough	0–3

16/3/14	Wales	Cardiff	2–0
4/4/14	Scotland	Glasgow	1–3
25/10/19	Ireland	Belfast	1–1
15/3/20	Wales	Highbury	1–2
10/4/20	Scotland	Sheffield	5–4
23/10/20	Ireland	Sunderland	2–0
14/3/21	Wales	Cardiff	0–0
9/4/21	Scotland	Glasgow	0–3
21/5/21	Belgium	Brussels	2–0
22/10/21	Ireland	Belfast	1–1
13/3/22	Wales	Anfield	1–0
8/4/22	Scotland	Birmingham	0–1
21/10/22	Ireland	West Bromwich	2–0
5/3/23	Wales	Cardiff	2–2
19/3/23	Belgium	Highbury	6–1
14/4/23	Scotland	Glasgow	2–2
10/5/23	France	Paris	4–1
21/5/23	Sweden	Stockholm	4–2
24/5/23	Sweden	Stockholm	3–1
20/10/23	Ireland	Belfast	1–2
1/11/23	Belgium	Antwerp	2–2
3/3/24	Wales	Blackburn	1–2
12/4/24	Scotland	Wembley	1–1
17/5/24	France	Paris	3–1
22/10/24	Ireland	Anfield	3–1
8/12/24	Belgium	West Bromwich	4–0
28/2/25	Wales	Swansea	2–1
4/4/25	Scotland	Glasgow	0–2
21/5/25	France	Paris	3–2
24/10/25	Ireland	Belfast	0–0
1/3/26	Wales	Selhurst Park	1–3
17/4/26	Scotland	Manchester	0–1
24/4/26	Belgium	Antwerp	5–3
20/10/26	Ireland	Anfield	3–3
12/2/27	Wales	Wrexham	3–3
2/4/27	Scotland	Glasgow	2–1
11/5/27	Belgium	Brussels	9–1
21/5/27	Luxembourg	Luxembourg	5–2
26/5/27	France	Paris	6–0
22/10/27	Ireland	Belfast	0–2
28/11/27	Wales	Burnley	1–2
31/3/28	Scotland	Wembley	1–5
17/5/28	France	Paris	5–1
19/5/28	Belgium	Antwerp	3–1
22/10/28	Ireland	Anfield	2–1
17/11/28	Wales	Swansea	3–2
13/4/29	Scotland	Glasgow	0–1
9/5/29	France	Paris	4–1
11/5/29	Belgium	Brussels	5–1
15/5/29	Spain	Madrid	3–4
19/10/29	Ireland	Belfast	3–0
20/11/29	Wales	Stamford Bridge	6–0

1930–39

Results

Date	Opponents	Venue	Score
5/4/30	Scotland	Wembley	5–2
10/5/30	Germany	Berlin	3–3
14/5/30	Austria	Vienna	0–0
20/10/30	Ireland	Sheffield	5–1
22/11/30	Wales	Wrexham	4–0
28/3/31	Scotland	Glasgow	0–2
14/5/31	France	Paris	2–5
16/5/31	Belgium	Brussels	4–1
17/10/31	Ireland	Belfast	6–2
18/11/31	Wales	Anfield	3–1
9/12/31	Spain	Highbury	7–1
9/4/32	Scotland	Wembley	3–0
17/10/32	Ireland	Blackpool	1–0
16/11/32	Wales	Wrexham	0–0
7/12/32	Austria	Stamford Bridge	4–3
1/4/33	Scotland	Glasgow	1–2
13/5/33	Italy	Rome	1–1
20/5/33	Switzerland	Berne	4–0
14/10/33	Ireland	Belfast	3–0
15/11/33	Wales	Newcastle	1–2
6/12/33	France	White Hart Lane	4–1
14/4/34	Scotland	Wembley	3–0
10/5/34	Hungary	Budapest	1–2
16/5/34	Czechoslovakia	Prague	1–2
29/9/34	Wales	Cardiff	4–0
14/11/34	Italy	Highbury	3–2
6/2/35	Ireland	Goodison Park	2–1
6/4/35	Scotland	Glasgow	0–2
18/5/35	Holland	Amsterdam	1–0
19/10/35	Ireland	Belfast	3–1
4/12/35	Germany	White Hart Lane	3–0
5/2/36	Wales	Wolverhampton	1–2
4/4/36	Scotland	Wembley	1–1
6/5/36	Austria	Vienna	1–2
9/5/36	Belgium	Brussels	2–3
17/10/36	Wales	Cardiff	1–2
18/11/36	Ireland	Stoke	3–1
2/12/36	Hungary	Highbury	6–2
17/4/37	Scotland	Glasgow	1–3
14/5/37	Norway	Oslo	6–0
17/5/37	Sweden	Stockholm	4–0
20/5/37	Finland	Helsinki	8–0
23/10/37	Ireland	Belfast	5–1
17/11/37	Wales	Middlesbrough	2–1
1/12/37	Czechoslovakia	White Hart Lane	5–4
9/4/38	Scotland	Wembley	0–1
14/5/38	Germany	Berlin	6–3
21/5/38	Switzerland	Zurich	1–2
26/5/38	France	Paris	4–2
22/10/38	Wales	Cardiff	2–4

26/10/38	FIFA	Highbury	3–0
9/11/38	Norway	Newcastle	4–0
16/11/38	Ireland	Manchester	7–0
15/4/39	Scotland	Glasgow	2–1
13/5/39	Italy	Milan	2–2
18/5/39	Yugoslavia	Belgrade	1–2
24/5/39	Romania	Bucharest	2–0

1940–49

Results

Date	Opponents	Venue	Score
28/9/46	N Ireland	Belfast	7–2
30/9/46	Rep of Ireland	Dublin	1–0
19/10/46	Wales	Maine Road	3–0
27/11/46	Holland	Huddersfield	8–2
12/4/47	Scotland	Wembley	1–1
3/5/47	France	Highbury	3–0
18/5/47	Switzerland	Zurich	0–1
27/5/47	Portugal	Lisbon	10–0
21/9/47	Belgium	Brussels	5–2
18/10/47	Wales	Cardiff	3–0
5/11/47	N Ireland	Goodison Park	2–2
19/11/47	Sweden	Highbury	4–2
10/4/48	Scotland	Glasgow	2–0
16/5/48	Italy	Turin	4–0
26/9/48	Denmark	Copenhagen	0–0
9/10/48	N Ireland	Belfast	6–2
10/11/48	Wales	Villa Park	1–0
1/12/48	Switzerland	Highbury	6–0
9/4/48	Scotland	Wembley	1–3
13/5/49	Sweden	Stockholm	1–3
18/5/49	Norway	Oslo	4–1
22/5/49	France	Paris	3–1
21/9/49	Rep of Ireland	Goodison Park	0–2
15/10/49	Wales	Cardiff (WCQ)	4–1
16/11/49	N Ireland	Maine Road(WCQ)	9–2
30/11/49	Italy	White Hart Lane	2–0

1950

Results

Date	Opponents	Venue	Score
15/4	Scotland	Glasgow (WCQ)	1–0
14/5	Portugal	Lisbon	5–3
18/5	Belgium	Brussels	4–1
15/6	Chile	Rio de Janeiro (WCQ)	2–0
29/6	USA	Belo Horizonte (WCQ)	0–1
2/7	Spain	Rio de Janeiro (WCQ)	0–1
7/10	N Ireland	Belfast	4–1
15/11	Wales	Sunderland	4–2
22/11	Yugoslavia	Highbury	2–2

1951

Results

Date	Opponents	Venue	Score
14/4	Scotland	Wembley	2–3
9/5	Argentina	Wembley	2–1
9/5	Portugal	Goodison Park	5–2
3/10	France	Highbury	2–2
20/10	Wales	Cardiff	1–1
14/11	N Ireland	Villa Park	2–0
28/11	Austria	Wembley	2–2

1952

Results

Date	Opponents	Venue	Score
5/4	Scotland	Glasgow	2–1
18/5	Italy	Florence	1–1
25/5	Austria	Vienna	3–2
28/5	Switzerland	Zurich	3–0
4/10	N Ireland	Belfast	2–2
12/11	Wales	Wembley	5–2
26/11	Belgium	Wembley	5–0

1953

Results

Date	Opponents	Venue	Score
18/4	Scotland	Wembley	2–2
17/5	Argentina	Buenos Aires	0–0
	(abandoned after 21 minutes)		
24/5	Chile	Santiago	2–1
31/5	Uruguay	Montevideo	1–2
8/6	USA	New York	6–3
10/10	Wales	Cardiff (WCQ)	4–1
21/10	Rest of Europe	Wembley	4–4
11/11	N Ireland	Goodison Pk (WCQ)	3–1
25/11	Hungary	Wembley	3–6

1954

Results

Date	Opponents	Venue	Score
3/4	Scotland	Glasgow (WCQ)	4–2
16/5	Yugoslavia	Belgrade	0–12
3/5	Hungary	Budapest	1–7
17/6	Belgium	Basle (WCQ)	4–4*
20/6	Switzerland	Berne (WCQ)	2–0
26/6	Uruguay	Basle (WCF)	2–4
2/10	N Ireland	Belfast	2–0
10/11	Wales	Wembley	3–2
1/12	W Germany	Wembley	3–1

1955

Results

Date	Opponents	Venue	Score
2/4	Scotland	Wembley	7–2
18/5	France	Paris	0–1
18/5	Spain	Madrid	1–1
22/5	Portugal	Oporto	1–3
2/10	Denmark	Copenhagen	5–1
22/10	Wales	Cardiff	1–1
2/11	N Ireland	Wembley	3–0
30/11	Spain	Wembley	4–1

1956

Results

Date	Opponents	Venue	Score
14/4	Scotland	Glasgow	1–1
9/5	Brazil	Wembley	4–2
16/5	Sweden	Stockholm	0–0
20/5	Finland	Helsinki	5–1
26/5	West Germany	Berlin	3–1
6/10	N Ireland	Belfast	1–1
14/11	Wales	Wembley	3–1
28/11	Yugoslavia	Wembley	3–0
5/12	Denmark (WCQ)	Wolverhampton	5–2

1957

Results

Date	Opponents	Venue	Score
6/4	Scotland	Wembley	2–1
8/5	Rep of Ireland	Wembley (WCQ)	5–1
15/5	Denmark	Copenhagen (WCQ)	4–1
19/5	Rep of Ireland	Dublin (WCQ)	1–1
19/10	Wales	Cardiff	4–0
6/11	N Ireland	Wembley	2–3
27/11	France	Wembley	4–0

1958

Results

Date	Opponents	Venue	Score
19/4	Scotland	Glasgow	4–0
7/5	Portugal	Wembley	2–1
11/5	Yugoslavia	Belgrade	0–5
18/5	USSR	Moscow	1–1
8/6	USSR	Gothenburg (WCQ)	2–2
11/6	Brazil	Gothenburg (WCQ)	0–0
15/6	Austria	Boras (WCQ)	2–2
17/6	USSR	Gothenburg (WCF)	0–1
4/10	N Ireland	Belfast	3–3
22/10	USSR	Wembley	5–0
26/11	Wales	Villa Park	2–2

1959

Results

Date	Opponents	Venue	Score
11/4	Scotland	Wembley	1–0
6/5	Italy	Wembley	2–2
13/5	Brazil	Rio de Janeiro	0–2
17/5	Peru	Lima	1–4
24/5	Mexico	Mexico C	1–2
28/5	USA	Los Angeles	8–1
17/10	Wales	Cardiff	1–1
28/10	Sweden	Wembley	2–3
18/11	N Ireland	Wembley	2–1

1960

Results

Date	Opponents	Venue	Score
19/4	Scotland	Glasgow	1–1
11/5	Yugoslavia	Wembley	3–3
15/5	Spain	Madrid	0–3
22/5	Hungary	Budapest	0–2
8/10	N Ireland	Belfast	5–2
19/10	Luxembourg	Luxembourg (WCQ)	9–0
26/10	Spain	Wembley	4–2
23/11	Wales	Wembley	5–1

1961

Results

Date	Opponents	Venue	Score
15/4	Scotland	Wembley	9–3
10/5	Mexico	Wembley	8–0
21/5	Portugal	Lisbon (WCQ)	1–1
24/5	Italy	Rome	3–2
27/5	Austria	Vienna	1–3
28/9	Luxembourg	Highbury (WCQ)	4–1
14/10	Wales	Cardiff	1–1
25/10	Portugal	Wembley (WCQ)	2–0
22–11	N Ireland	Wembley	1–1

1962

Results

Date	Opponents	Venue	Score
4/4	Austria	Wembley	3–1
14/4	Scotland	Glasgow	0–2
9/5	Switzerland	Wembley	3–1
20/5	Peru	Lima	4–0
31/5	Hungary	Rancagua (WCQ)	1–2
2/6	Argentina	Rancagua (WCQ)	3–1
7/6	Bulgaria	Rancagua (WCQ)	0–0
10/6	Brazil	Vina del Mar (WCQ)	1–3
3/10	France	Hillsborough (WCQ)	1–1
20/10	N Ireland	Belfast	3–1
21/11	Wales	Wembley	4–0

1963

Results

Date	Opponents	Venue	Score
27/2	France	Paris √ (WCQ)	2–5
6/4	Scotland	Wembley	1–2
8/5	Brazil	Wembley	1–1
20/5	Czechoslovakia	Bratislava	4–2
2/6	East Germany	Leipzig	2–1
5/6	Switzerland	Basle	8–1
12/10	Wales	Cardiff	4–0
23/10	Rest of World	Wembley	2–1
20/11	N Ireland	Wembley	8–3

1964

Results

Date	Opponents	Venue	Score
11/4	Scotland	Glasgow	0–1
6/5	Uruguay	Wembley	2–1
17/5	Portugal	Lisbon	4–3
24/5	Rep of Ireland	Dublin	3–1
27/5	USA	New York	10–0
30/5	Brazil	Rio de Janeiro	1–5
4/6	Portugal	São Paulo	1–1
6/6	Argentina	Rio de Janeiro	0–1
3/10	N Ireland	Belfast	4–3
21/10	Belgium	Wembley	2–2
18/11	Wales	Wembley	2–1
9/12	Holland	Amsterdam	1–1

1965

Results

Date	Opponents	Venue	Score
10/4	Scotland	Wembley	2–2
5/5	Hungary	Wembley	1–0
9/5	Yugoslavia	Belgrade	1–1
12/5	W Germany	Nuremberg	1–0
16/5	Sweden	Gothenburg	2–1
2/10	Wales	Cardiff	0–0
20/10	Austria	Wembley	2–3
10/11	N Ireland	Wembley	2–1
8/12	Spain	Madrid	2–0

1966

Results

Date	Opponents	Venue	Score
5/1	Poland	Anfield	1–1
23/2	W Germany	Wembley	1–0
2/4	Scotland	Glasgow	4–3
4/5	Yugoslavia	Wembley	2–0
26/6	Finland	Helsinki	3–0
29/6	Norway	Oslo	6–1
3/7	Denmark	Copenhagen	2–0
5/7	Poland	Chorzow	1–0
11/7	Uruguay	Wembley (WCF)	0–0
16/7	Mexico	Wembley (WCF)	2–0
20/7	France	Wembley (WCF)	2–0
23/7	Argentina	Wembley (WCF)	1–0
26/7	Portugal	Wembley (WCF)	2–1
30/7	W Germany	Wembley (WCF)	4–2*
22/10	N Ireland	Belfast (ECQ)	2–0
2/11	Czechoslovakia	Wembley	0–0
16/11	Wales	Wembley (ECQ)	5–1

1967

Results

Date	Opponents	Venue	Score
15/4	Scotland	Wembley (ECQ)	2–3
24/5	Spain	Wembley	2–0
27/5	Austria	Vienna	1–0
21/10	Wales	Cardiff (ECQ)	3–0
22/11	N Ireland	Wembley (ECQ)	2–0
6/12	USSR	Wembley	2–2

1968

Results

Date	Opponents	Venue	Score
24/2	Scotland	Glasgow (ECQ)	1–1
3/4	Spain	Wembley (ECQ)	1–0
8/5	Spain	Madrid (ECQ)	2–1
22/5	Sweden	Wembley	3–1
1/6	W Germany	Hanover	0–1
5/6	Yugoslavia	Florence (ECF)	0–1
8/6	USSR	Rome (ECF)	2–0
6/11	Romania	Bucharest	0–0
11/12	Bulgaria	Wembley	1–1

1969

Results

Date	Opponents	Venue	Score
15/1	Romania	Wembley	1–1
12/3	France	Wembley	5–0
3/5	N Ireland	Belfast	3–1
7/5	Wales	Wembley	2–1
10/5	Scotland	Wembley	4–1
1/6	Mexico	Mexico C	0–0
8/6	Uruguay	Montevideo	2–1
12/6	Brazil	Rio de Janeiro	1–2
5/11	Holland	Amsterdam	1–0
10/12	Portugal	Wembley	1–0

1970

Results

Date	Opponents	Venue	Score
14/1	Holland	Wembley	0–0
25/2	Belgium	Brussels	3–1
18/4	Wales	Cardiff	1–1
21/4	N Ireland	Wembley	3–1
25/4	Scotland	Glasgow	0–0
20/5	Colombia	Bogota	4–0
24/5	Ecuador	Quito	2–0
2/6	Romania	Guadalajara (WCF)	1–0
7/6	Brazil	Guadalajara (WCF)	0–1
11/6	Czechoslovakia	Guadalajara (WCF)	1–0
14/6	W Germany	Leon (WCF)	2–3*
25/11	E Germany	Wembley	3–1

1971

Results

Date	Opponents	Venue	Score
3/2	Malta	Valletta (ECQ)	1–0
21/4	Greece	Wembley (ECQ)	4–0
12/5	Malta	Wembley (ECQ)	5–0
15/5	N Ireland	Belfast	1–0
19/5	Wales	Wembley	0–0
22/5	Scotland	Wembley	3–1
13/10	Switzerland	Basle (ECQ)	3–2
10/11	Switzerland	Wembley (ECQ)	1–1
1/12	Greece	Athens (ECQ)	2–0

1972

Results

Date	Opponents	Venue	Score
29/4	W Germany	Wembley (ECQ)	1–3
13/5	W Germany	Berlin (ECQ)	0–0
20/5	Wales	Cardiff	3–0
23/5	N Ireland	Wembley	0–1
27/5	Scotland	Glasgow	1–0
11/10	Yugoslavia	Wembley	1–11
5/11	Wales	Cardiff (WCQ)	1–0

1973

Results

Date	Opponents	Venue	Score
24/1	Wales	Wembley (WCQ)	1–1
14/2	Scotland	Glasgow	5–0
12/5	N Ireland	Anfield	2–1
15/5	Wales	Wembley	3–0
19/5	Scotland	Wembley	1–0
27/5	Czechoslovakia	Prague	1–1
6/6	Poland	Chorzow (WCQ)	0–2
10/6	USSR	Moscow	2–1
14/6	Italy	Turin	0–2
26/9	Austria	Wembley	7–0
17/10	Poland	Wembley (WCQ)	1–1
14/11	Italy	Wembley	0–1

1974

Results

Date	Opponents	Venue	Score
3/4	Portugal	Lisbon	0–0
11/5	Wales	Cardiff	2–0
15/5	N Ireland	Wembley	1–0
18/5	Scotland	Glasgow	0–2
22/5	Argentina	Wembley	2–2
29/5	East Germany	Leipzig	1–1
1/6	Bulgaria	Sofia	1–0
5/6	Yugoslavia	Belgrade	2–2
30/10	Czechoslovakia	Wembley (ECQ)	3–0
20/11	Portugal	Wembley (ECQ)	0–0

1975

Results

Date	Opponents	Venue	Score
12/3	W Germany	Wembley	2–0
16/4	Cyprus	Wembley (ECQ)	5–0
11/5	Cyprus	Limassol (ECQ)	1–0
17/5	N Ireland	Belfast	0–0
21/5	Wales	Wembley	2–2
24/5	Scotland	Wembley	5–1
3/9	Switzerland	Basle	2–1
30/10	Czechoslovakia	Bratislava (ECQ)	1–2
19/11	Portugal	Lisbon (ECQ)	1–1

1976

Results

Date	Opponents	Venue	Score
24/3	Wales	Wrexham	2–1
8/5	Wales	Cardiff	1–0
11/5	N Ireland	Wembley	4–0
15/5	Scotland	Glasgow	1–2
23/5	Brazil	Los Angeles	0–1
28/5	Italy	New York	3–2
13/6	Finland	Helsinki (WCQ)	4–1
8/9	Rep of Ireland	Wembley	1–1
13/10	Finland	Wembley (WCQ)	2–1
17/11	Italy	Rome (WCQ)	0–2

1977

Results

Date	Opponents	Venue	Score
9/2	Holland	Wembley	0–2
30/3	Luxembourg	Wembley (WCQ)	5–0
28/5	N Ireland	Belfast	2–1
31/5	Wales	Wembley	0–1
4/6	Scotland	Wembley	1–2
8/6	Brazil	Rio de Janeiro	0–0
12/6	Argentina	Buenos Aires	1–1
15/6	Uruguay	Montevideo	0–0
7/9	Switzerland	Wembley	0–0
12/10	Luxembourg	Luxembourg (WCQ)	2–0
16/11	Italy	Wembley (WCQ)	2–0

1978

Results

Date	Opponents	Venue	Score
22/2	W Germany	Munich	1–2
19/4	Brazil	Wembley	1–1
13/5	Wales	Cardiff	3–1
16/5	N Ireland	Wembley	1–0
20/5	Scotland	Glasgow	1–0
24/5	Hungary	Wembley	4–1
20/9	Denmark	Copenhagen (ECQ)	4–3
25/10	Rep of Ireland	Dublin (ECQ)	1–1
29/11	Czechoslovakia	Wembley	1–0

1979

Results

Date	Opponents	Venue	Score
7/2	N Ireland	Wembley (ECQ)	4–0
19/5	N Ireland	Belfast	2–0
23/5	Wales	Wembley	0–0
26/5	Scotland	Wembley	3–1
6/6	Bulgaria	Sofia (ECQ)	3–0
10/6	Sweden	Stockholm	0–0
13/6	Austria	Vienna	3–4
12/9	Denmark	Wembley (ECQ)	1–0
17/10	N Ireland	Belfast (ECQ)	5–1
22/11	Bulgaria	Wembley (ECQ)	2–0

1980

Results

Date	Opponents	Venue	Score
6/2	Rep of Ireland	Wembley (ECQ)	2–0
26/3	Spain	Barcelona	2–0
13/5	Argentina	Wembley	3–1
17/5	Wales	Wrexham	1–4
20/5	N Ireland	Wembley	1–1
24/5	Scotland	Glasgow	2–0
31/5	Australia	Sydney	2–1
12/6	Belgium	Turin (ECF)	1–1
15/6	Italy	Turin (ECF)	0–1
18/6	Spain	Naples (ECF)	2–1
10/9	Norway	Wembley (WCQ)	4–0
15/10	Romania	Bucharest (WCQ)	1–2
19/11	Switzerland	Wembley (WCQ)	2–1

1981

Results

Date	Opponents	Venue	Score
25/3	Spain	Wembley	1–2
29/4	Romania	Wembley (WCQ)	0–0
12/5	Brazil	Wembley	0–1
20/5	Wales	Wembley	0–0
23/5	Scotland	Wembley	0–1
30/5	Switzerland	Basle (WCQ)	1–2
6/6	Hungary	Budapest (WCQ)	3–1
9/9	Norway	Oslo (WCQ)	1–2
18/11	Hungary	Wembley (WCQ)	1–0

1982

Results

Date	Opponents	Venue	Score
23/2	N Ireland	Wembley	4–0
25/5	Holland	Wembley	2–0
29/5	Scotland	Glasgow	1–0
2/6	Iceland	Reykjavik	1–1
3/6	Finland	Helsinki	4–1
16/6	France	Bilbao (WCF)	3–1
20/6	Czechoslovakia	Bilbao (WCF)	2–0

25/6	Kuwait	Bilbao (WCF)	1–0
29/6	W Germany	Madrid (WCF)	0–0
5/7	Spain	Madrid (WCF)	0–0
22/9	Denmark	Copenhagen (ECQ)	2–2
13/10	W Germany	Wembley	1–2
17/11	Greece	Salonika (ECQ)	3–0
15/12	Luxembourg	Wembley (ECQ)	9–0

1983

Results

Date	Opponents	Venue	Score
23/2	Wales	Wembley	2–1
30/3	Greece	Wembley (ECQ)	0–0
27/4	Hungary	Wembley (ECQ)	2–0
28/5	N Ireland	Belfast	0–0
1/6	Scotland	Wembley	2–0
12/6	Australia	Sydney	0–0
15/6	Australia	Brisbane	1–0
19/6	Australia	Melbourne	1–1
21/9	Denmark	Wembley (ECQ)	0–1
12/10	Hungary	Budapest (ECQ)	3–0
16/11	Luxembourg	Luxembourg (ECQ)	4–0

1984

Results

Date	Opponents	Venue	Score
29/2	France	Paris	0–2
4/4	N Ireland	Wembley	1–0
2/5	Wales	Wrexham	0–1
26/5	Scotland	Glasgow	1–1
2/6	USSR	Wembley	0–2
10/6	Brazil	Rio de Janeiro	2–0
13/6	Uruguay	Montevideo	0–2
17/6	Chile	Santiago	0–0
12/9	E Germany	Wembley (WCQ)	1–0
17/10	Finland	Wembley	5–0
14/11	Turkey	Istanbul (WCQ)	8–0

1985

Results

Date	Opponents	Venue	Score
27/2	N Ireland	Belfast (WCQ)	1–0
26/3	Rep of Ireland	Wembley	2–1
1/5	Romania	Bucharest (WCQ)	0–0
22/5	Finland	Helsinki (WCQ)	1–1
25/5	Scotland	Glasgow	0–1
6/6	Italy	Mexico C	1–2
9/6	Mexico	Mexico C	0–1
12/6	W Germany	Mexico C	3–0
16/6	USA	Los Angeles	5–0
11/9	Romania	Wembley (WCQ)	1–1
16/10	Turkey	Wembley (WCQ)	5–0
13/11	N Ireland	Wembley (WCQ)	0–0

1986

Results

Date	Opponents	Venue	Score
29/1	Egypt	Cairo	4–0
26/2	Israel	Ramat Gan	2–1
26/3	USSR	Tblisi	1–0
23/4	Scotland	Wembley	2–1
17/5	Mexico	Los Angeles	3–0
24/5	Canada	Burnaby	1–0
3/6	Portugal	Monterrey (WCF)	0–1
6/6	Morocco	Monterrey (WCF)	0–0
11/6	Poland	Monterrey (WCF)	3–0
18/6	Paraguay	Mexico C (WCF)	3–0
22/6	Argentina	Mexico C (WCF)	1–2
10/9	Sweden	Stockholm	0–1
15/10	N Ireland	Wembley (ECQ)	3–0
12/11	Yugoslavia	Wembley (ECQ)	2–0

1987

Results

Date	Opponents	Venue	Score
10/2	Spain	Madrid	4–2
1/4	N Ireland	Belfast (ECQ)	2–0
29/4	Turkey	Izmir (ECQ)	0–0
19/5	Brazil	Wembley	1–1
23/5	Scotland	Glasgow	0–0

9/9	W Germany	Düsseldorf	1–3
14/10	Turkey	Wembley (ECQ)	8–0
11/11	Yugoslavia	Belgrade (ECQ)	4–1

1988

Results

Date	Opponents	Venue	Score
17/2	Israel	Tel Aviv	0–0
23/3	Holland	Wembley	2–2
27/4	Hungary	Budapest	0–0
21/5	Scotland	Wembley	1–0
24/5	Colombia	Wembley	1–1
28/5	Switzerland	Lausanne	1–0
12/6	Rep of Ireland	Stuttgart (ECF)	0–1
15/6	Holland	Düsseldorf (ECF)	1–3
18/6	USSR	Frankfurt (ECF)	1–3
14/9	Denmark	Wembley	1–0
19/10	Sweden	Wembley (WCQ)	0–0
16/11	Saudi Arabia	Riyadh	1–1

1989

Results

Date	Opponents	Venue	Score
8/2	Greece	Athens	2–1
8/3	Albania	Tirana (WCQ)	2–0
26/4	Albania	Wembley (WCQ)	5–0
23/5	Chile	Wembley	0–0
27/5	Scotland	Glasgow	2–0
3/6	Poland	Wembley (WCQ)	3–0
7/6	Denmark	Copenhagen	1–1
6/9	Sweden	Stockholm (WCQ)	0–0
11/10	Poland	Katowice (WCQ)	0–0
15/11	Italy	Wembley	0–0
13/12	Yugoslavia	Wembley	2–1

1990

Results

Date	Opponents	Venue	Score
28/3	Brazil	Wembley	1–0
25/4	Czechoslovakia	Wembley	4–2
15/5	Denmark	Wembley	1–0
22/5	Uruguay	Wembley	1–2
2/6	Tunisia	Tunis	1–1
11/6	Rep of Ireland	Cagliari (WCF)	1–1
16/6	Holland	Cagliari (WCF)	0–0
21/6	Egypt	Cagliari (WCF)	1–0
26/6	Belgium	Bologna (WCF)	1–0
1/7	Cameroon	Naples (WCF)	3–2
4/7	W Germany	Turin	1–1*
	(WCF) *(England lost 3–4 on penalties)*		
7/7	Italy	Bari (WCF)	1–2
12/9	Hungary	Wembley	1–0
17/10	Poland	Wembley (ECQ)	2–0
14/11	Rep of Ireland	Dublin (ECQ)	1–1

1991

Results

Date	Opponents	Venue	Score
6/2	Cameroon	Wembley	2–0
27/3	Rep of Ireland	Wembley (ECQ)	1–1
1/5	Turkey	Izmir (ECQ)	1–0
21/5	USSR	Wembley	3–1
25/5	Argentina	Wembley	2–2
1/6	Australia	Sydney	1–0
3/6	New Zealand	Auckland	1–0
8/6	New Zealand	Wellington	2–0
12/6	Malaysia	Kuala Lumpur	4–2
11/9	Germany	Wembley	0–1
16/10	Turkey	Wembley (ECQ)	1–0
13/11	Poland	Poznan (ECQ)	1–1

1992

Results

Date	Opponents	Venue	Score
19/2	France	Wembley	2–0
25/3	Czechoslovakia	Prague	2–2
29/4	CIS	Moscow	2–2
12/5	Hungary	Budapest	1–0
17/5	Brazil	Wembley	1–1
3/6	Finland	Helsinki	2–1

11/6	Denmark	Malmo (ECF)	0–0
14/6	France	Malmo (ECF)	0–0
17/6	Sweden	Stockholm (ECF)	1–2
9/9	Spain	Santander	0–1
14/10	Norway	Wembley (WCQ)	1–1
18/11	Turkey	Wembley (WCQ)	4–0

1993

Results

Date	Opponents	Venue	Score
17/2	San Marino	Wembley (WCQ)	6–0
31/3	Turkey	Izmir (WCQ)	2–0
28/4	Holland	Wembley (WCQ)	2–2
29/5	Poland	Katowice (WCQ)	1–1
2/6	Norway	Oslo (WCQ)	0–2
9/6	USA	Boston (USC)	0–2
13/6	Brazil	Washington (USC)	1–1
19/6	Germany	Detroit (USC)	1–2
8/9	Poland	Wembley (WCQ)	3–0
13/10	Holland	Rotterdam (WCQ)	0–2
17/11	San Marino	Bologna (WCQ)	7–1

1994

Results

Date	Opponents	Venue	Score
9/3	Denmark	Wembley	1–0
17/5	Greece	Wembley	5–0
22/5	Norway	Wembley	0–0
7/9	United States	Wembley	2–0
16/11	Nigeria	Wembley	1–0

1995

Results

Date	Opponents	Venue	Score
15/2	Rep of Ireland	Dublin	0–1
	(abandoned after 21 minutes)		
29/3	Uruguay	Wembley	0–0
3/6	Japan	Wembley (UT)	2–1
8/6	Sweden	Leeds (UT)	3–3
11/6	Brazil	Wembley (UT)	1–3
6/9	Colombia	Wembley	0–0
11/10	Norway	Oslo	0–0
15/11	Switzerland	Wembley	3–1
12/12	Portugal	Wembley	1–1

1996

Results

Date	Opponents	Venue	Score
27/3	Bulgaria	Wembley	1–0
24/4	Croatia	Wembley	0–0
18/5	Hungary	Wembley	3–0
23/5	China	Beijing	3–0
8/6	Switzerland	Wembley (ECF)	1–1
15/6	Scotland	Wembley (ECF)	2–0
18/6	Holland	Wembley (ECF)	4–1
22/6	Spain	Wembley (ECF)	0–0
	(England won 4–2 on penalties)		
26/6	Germany	Wembley (ECF)	1–1
	(England lost 5–6 on penalties)		
1/9	Moldova	Chisinau (WCQ)	3–0
9/10	Poland	Wembley (WCQ)	2–1
9/11	Georgia	Tbilisi (WCQ)	2–0

1997

Results

Date	Opponents	Venue	Score
12/2	Italy	Wembley (WCQ)	0–1
29/3	Mexico	Wembley	2–0
30/4	Georgia	Wembley (WCQ)	2–0
24/5	South Africa	Old Trafford	2–1
31/5	Poland	Chorzow (WCQ)	2–0
4/6	Italy	Nantes (TdF)	2–0
7/6	France	Montpellier (TdF)	1–0
10/6	Brazil	Paris (TdF)	0–1
10/9	Moldova	Wembley (WCQ)	4–0
11/10	Italy	Rome (WCQ)	0–0
15/11	Cameroon	Wembley	2–0

SCOTLAND

Scottish League First Division

Winners

Season	Champions	Pts	Runners-up	Pts
1890–91	Dumbarton	29	Rangers	29 +
1891–92	Dumbarton	37	Celtic	35
1892–93	Celtic	29	Rangers	28
1893–94	Celtic	29	Hearts	26
1894–95	Hearts	31	Celtic	26
1895–96	Celtic	30	Rangers	26
1896–97	Hearts	28	Hibernian	26
1897–98	Celtic	33	Rangers	29
1898–99	Rangers	36	Hearts	26
1899–00	Rangers	32	Celtic	25
1900–01	Rangers	35	Celtic	29
1901–02	Rangers	28	Celtic	26
1902–03	Hibernian	37	Dundee	31
1903–04	Third Lanark	43	Hearts	39
1904–05	Celtic	41	Rangers	41+
1905–06	Celtic	49	Hearts	43
1906–07	Celtic	55	Dundee	48
1907–08	Celtic	55	Falkirk	51
1908–09	Celtic	51	Dundee	50
1909–10	Celtic	54	Falkirk	52
1910–11	Rangers	52	Aberdeen	48
1911–12	Rangers	51	Celtic	45
1912–13	Rangers	53	Celtic	49
1913–14	Celtic	65	Rangers	59
1914–15	Celtic	65	Hearts	61
1915–16	Celtic	67	Rangers	56
1916–17	Celtic	64	Morton	54
1917–18	Rangers	56	Celtic	55
1918–19	Celtic	58	Rangers	57
1919–20	Rangers	71	Celtic	68
1920–21	Rangers	76	Celtic	66
1921–22	Celtic	67	Rangers	66
1922–23	Rangers	55	Airdrieonians	50
1923–24	Rangers	59	Airdrieonians	50
1924–25	Rangers	60	Airdrieonians	57
1925–26	Celtic	58	Airdrieonians*	50
1926–27	Rangers	56	Motherwell	51
1927–28	Rangers	60	Celtic*	55
1928–29	Rangers	67	Celtic	51
1929–30	Rangers	60	Motherwell	55
1930–31	Rangers	60	Celtic	58
1931–32	Motherwell	66	Rangers	61
1932–33	Rangers	62	Motherwell	59
1933–34	Rangers	66	Motherwell	62
1934–35	Rangers	55	Celtic	52
1935–36	Celtic	66	Rangers*	61
1936–37	Rangers	61	Aberdeen	54
1937–38	Celtic	61	Hearts	58
1938–39	Rangers	59	Celtic	48
1946–47	Rangers	46	Hibernian	44
1947–48	Hibernian	48	Rangers	46
1948–49	Rangers	46	Dundee	45
1949–50	Rangers	50	Hibernian	49
1950–51	Hibernian	48	Rangers*	38
1951–52	Hibernian	45	Rangers	41
1952–53	Rangers*	43	Hibernian	43
1953–54	Celtic	43	Hearts	38
1954–55	Aberdeen	49	Celtic	46
1955–56	Rangers	52	Aberdeen	46
1956–57	Rangers	55	Hearts	53
1957–58	Hearts	62	Rangers	49
1958–59	Rangers	50	Hearts	48
1959–60	Hearts	54	Kilmarnock	50
1960–61	Rangers	51	Kilmarnock	50
1961–62	Dundee	54	Rangers	51
1962–63	Rangers	57	Kilmarnock	48
1963–64	Rangers	55	Kilmarnock	49
1964–65	Kilmarnock*	50	Hearts	50
1965–66	Celtic	57	Rangers	55
1966–67	Celtic	58	Rangers	55
1967–68	Celtic	63	Rangers	61
1968–69	Celtic	54	Rangers	49
1969–70	Celtic	57	Rangers	45
1970–71	Celtic	56	Aberdeen	54
1971–72	Celtic	60	Aberdeen	50
1972–73	Celtic	57	Rangers	56
1973–74	Celtic	53	Hibernian	49
1974–75	Rangers	56	Hibernian	49

Premier Division

Winners

Season	Champions	Pts	Runners-up	Pts
1975–76	Rangers	54	Celtic	48
1976–77	Celtic	55	Rangers	46
1977–78	Rangers	55	Aberdeen	53
1978–79	Celtic	48	Rangers	45
1979–80	Aberdeen	48	Celtic	47
1980–81	Celtic	56	Aberdeen	49
1981–82	Celtic	55	Aberdeen	53
1982–83	Dundee Utd	56	Celtic*	55
1983–84	Aberdeen	57	Celtic	50
1984–85	Aberdeen	59	Celtic	52
1985–86	Celtic*	50	Hearts	50
1986–87	Rangers	69	Celtic	63
1987–88	Celtic	72	Hearts	62
1988–89	Rangers	56	Aberdeen	50
1989–90	Rangers	51	Aberdeen*	44
1990–91	Rangers	55	Aberdeen	53

1991–92	Rangers	72	Hearts	63
1992–93	Rangers	73	Aberdeen	64
1993–94	Rangers	58	Aberdeen	55
1994–95	Rangers	69	Motherwell	54
1995–96	Rangers	87	Celtic	83
1996–97	Rangers	80	Celtic	75

Notes: * On goal average/difference; + Championship held jointly

Scottish League Cup

Finalists

Season	Winners	Runners-up	Score
1946–47	Rangers	Aberdeen	4–0
1947–48	East Fife	Falkirk	0–0, 4–1
1948–49	Rangers	Raith Rovers	2–0
1949–50	East Fife	Dunfermline Ath	3–0
1950–51	Motherwell	Hibernian	3–0
1951–52	Dundee	Rangers	3–2
1952–53	Dundee	Kilmarnock	2–0
1953–54	East Fife	Partick T	3–2
1954–55	Hearts	Motherwell	4–2
1955–56	Aberdeen	St Mirren	2–1
1956–57	Celtic	Partick T	0–0, 3–0
1957–58	Celtic	Rangers	7–1
1958–59	Hearts	Partick T	5–1
1959–60	Hearts	Third Lanark	2–1
1960–61	Rangers	Kilmarnock	2–0
1961–62	Rangers	Hearts	1–1, 3–1
1962–63	Hearts	Kilmarnock	1–0
1963–64	Rangers	Morton	5–0
1964–65	Rangers	Celtic	2–1
1965–66	Celtic	Rangers	2–1
1966–67	Celtic	Rangers	1–0
1967–68	Celtic	Dundee	5–3
1968–69	Celtic	Hibernian	6–2
1969–70	Celtic	St Johnstone	1–0
1970–71	Rangers	Celtic	1–0
1971–72	Partick T	Celtic	4–1
1972–73	Hibernian	Celtic	2–1
1973–74	Dundee	Celtic	1–0
1974–75	Celtic	Hibernian	6–3
1975–76	Rangers	Celtic	1–0
1976–77	Aberdeen	Celtic	2–1
1977–78	Rangers	Celtic	2–1
1978–79	Rangers	Aberdeen	2–1
1979–80	Dundee Utd	Aberdeen	0–0, 3–0
1980–81	Dundee Utd	Dundee	3–0
1981–82	Rangers	Dundee Utd	2–1
1982–83	Celtic	Rangers	2–1
1983–84	Rangers	Celtic	3–2
1984–85	Rangers	Dundee Utd	1–0
1985–86	Aberdeen	Hibernian	3–0
1986–87	Rangers	Celtic	2–1
1987–88	Rangers	Aberdeen	3–3
	Rangers won 5–3 on penalties		
1988–89	Rangers	Aberdeen	3–2
1989–90	Aberdeen	Rangers	2–1
1990–91	Rangers	Celtic	2–1
1991–92	Hibernian	Dunfermline A	2–0
1992–93	Rangers	Aberdeen	2–1
1993–94	Rangers	Hibernian	2–1
1994–95	Raith Rovers	Celtic	0–0
	(Raith Rovers won 6–5 on penalties)		
1995–96	Aberdeen	Dundee	2–0
1996–97	Rangers	Hearts	4–3
1997–98	Celtic	Dundee Utd	2–0

Scottish FA Cup

Finalist

Year	Winners	Runners-up	Score
1874	Queen's Park	Clydesdale	2–0
1875	Queen's Park	Renton	3–0
1876	Queen's Park	Third Lanark	1–1, 2–0
1877	Vale of Leven	Rangers	0–0, 1–1, 3–2
1878	Vale of Leven	Third Lanark	1–0
1879	Vale of Leven	Rangers	
Rangers failed to appear for replay after 1–1 draw. Vale awarded Cup			
1880	Queen's Park	Thornlibank	3–0
1881	Queen's Park	Dumbarton	3–1
1882	Queen's Park	Dumbarton	2–2, 4–1
1883	Dumbarton	Vale of Leven	2–2, 2–1
1884	Queen's Park	Vale of Leven	
Vale of Leven failed to appear. Queen's Park awarded Cup			
1885	Renton	Vale of Leven	0–0, 3–1
1886	Queen's Park	Renton	3–1
1887	Hibernian	Dumbarton	2–1
1888	Renton	Cambuslang	6–1
1889	Third Lanark	Celtic	3–0+, 2–1
+Replay ordered because of playing conditions in the first game			
1890	Queen's Park	Vale of Leven	1–1, 2–1
1891	Hearts	Dumbarton	1–0
1892	Celtic	Queen's Park	5–1
After mutually protested game which Celtic won 1–0			
1893	Queen's Park	Celtic	2–1
1894	Rangers	Celtic	3–1
1895	St Bernard's	Renton	2–1
1896	Hearts	Hibernian	3–1
1897	Rangers	Dumbarton	5–1
1898	Rangers	Kilmarnock	2–0
1899	Celtic	Rangers	2–0
1900	Celtic	Queen's Park	4–3

1901	Hearts	Celtic	4–3
1902	Hibernian	Celtic	1–0
1903	Rangers	Hearts	1–1, 0–0, 2–0
1904	Celtic	Rangers	3–2
1905	Third Lanark	Rangers	0–0, 3–1
1906	Hearts	Third Lanark	1–0
1907	Celtic	Hearts	3–0
1908	Celtic	St Mirren	5–1
1909	Celtic	Rangers	2–2, 1–1
Owing to riot, the cup was withheld after two drawn games			
1910	Dundee	Clyde	2–2, 0–0, 2–1
1911	Celtic	Hamilton A	0–0, 2–0
1912	Celtic	Clyde	2–0
1913	Falkirk	Raith R	2–0
1914	Celtic	Hibernian	0–0, 4–1
1920	Kilmarnock	Albion R	3–2
1921	Partick T	Rangers	1–0
1922	Morton	Rangers	1–0
1923	Celtic	Hibernian	1–0
1924	Airdrieonians	Hibernian	2–0
1925	Celtic	Dundee	2–1
1926	St Mirren	Celtic	2–0
1927	Celtic	East Fife	3–1
1928	Rangers	Celtic	4–0
1929	Kilmarnock	Rangers	2–0
1930	Rangers	Partick T	0–0, 2–1
1931	Celtic	Motherwell	2–2, 4–2
1932	Rangers	Kilmarnock	1–1, 3–0
1933	Celtic	Motherwell	1–0
1934	Rangers	St Mirren	5–0
1935	Rangers	Hamilton A	2–1
1936	Rangers	Third Lanark	1–0
1937	Celtic	Aberdeen	2–1
1938	East Fife	Kilmarnock	1–1, 4–2
1939	Clyde	Motherwell	4–0
1947	Aberdeen	Hibernian	2–1
1948	Rangers	Morton	1–1, 1–0
1949	Rangers	Clyde	4–1
1950	Rangers	East Fife	3–0
1951	Celtic	Motherwell	1–0
1952	Motherwell	Dundee	4–0
1953	Rangers	Aberdeen	1–1, 1–0
1954	Celtic	Aberdeen	2–1
1955	Clyde	Celtic	1–1, 1–0
1956	Hearts	Celtic	3–1
1957	Falkirk	Kilmarnock	1–1, 2–1
1958	Clyde	Hibernian	1–0
1959	St Mirren	Aberdeen	3–1
1960	Rangers	Kilmarnock	2–0
1961	Dunfermline A	Celtic	0–0, 2–0
1962	Rangers	St Mirren	2–0
1963	Rangers	Celtic	1–1, 3–0
1964	Rangers	Dundee	3–1
1965	Celtic	Dunfermline A	3–2
1966	Rangers	Celtic	0–0, 1–0
1967	Celtic	Aberdeen	2–0
1968	Dunfermline A	Hearts	3–1
1969	Celtic	Rangers	4–0
1970	Aberdeen	Celtic	3–1
1971	Celtic	Rangers	1–1, 2–1
1972	Celtic	Hibernian	6–1
1973	Rangers	Celtic	3–2
1974	Celtic	Dundee Utd	3–0
1975	Celtic	Airdrieonians	3–1
1976	Rangers	Hearts	3–1
1977	Celtic	Rangers	1–0
1978	Rangers	Aberdeen	2–1
1979	Rangers	Hibernian	0–0, 0–0, 3–2
1980	Celtic	Rangers	1–0
1981	Rangers	Dundee Utd	0–0, 4–1
1982	Aberdeen	Rangers	4–1*
1983	Aberdeen	Rangers	1–0*
1984	Aberdeen	Celtic	2–1*
1985	Celtic	Dundee Utd	2–1
1986	Aberdeen	Hearts	3–0
1987	St Mirren	Dundee Utd	1–0 *
1988	Celtic	Dundee Utd	2–1
1989	Celtic	Rangers	1–0
1990	Aberdeen	Celtic	0–0*
	(Aberdeen won 9–8 on penalties)		
1991	Motherwell	Dundee Utd	4–3*
1992	Rangers	Airdrieonians	2–1
1993	Rangers	Aberdeen	2–1
1994	Dundee Utd	Rangers	1–0
1995	Celtic	Airdrieonians	1–0
1996	Rangers	Hearts	5–1
1997	Kilmarnock	Falkirk	1–0

Scotland Internationals 1872–99

Results

Date	*Opponents*	*Venue*	*F–A*
30/11/72	England	Glasgow	0–0
8/3/73	England	London	2–4
7/3/74	England	Glasgow	2–1
6/3/75	England	London	2–2
4/3/76	England	Glasgow	3–0
25/3/76	Wales	Glasgow	4–0
3/3/77	England	London	3–1
5/3/77	Wales	Wrexham	2–0
2/3/78	England	Glasgow	7–2
23/3/78	Wales	Glasgow	9–0

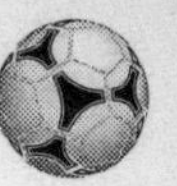

7/4/79	Wales	Wrexham	3–0
5/4/79	England	London	4–5
13/3/80	England	Glasgow	5–4
27/3/80	Wales	Glasgow	5–1
12/3/81	England	London	6–1
14/3/81	Wales	Wrexham	5–1
11/3/82	England	Glasgow	5–1
25/3/82	Wales	Glasgow	5–0
10/3/83	England	Sheffield	3–2
12/3/83	Wales	Wrexham	3–0
26/1/84	Ireland	Belfast	5–0
15/3/84	England	Glasgow	1–0
29/3/84	Wales	Glasgow	4–1
14/3/85	Ireland	Glasgow	8–2
21/3/85	England	London	1–1
23/3/85	Wales	Wrexham	8–1
20/3/86	Ireland	Belfast	7–2
31/3/86	England	Glasgow	1–1
10/4/86	Wales	Glasgow	4–4
19/2/87	Ireland	Glasgow	4–1
19/3/87	England	Blackburn	3–2
21/3/87	Wales	Wrexham	2–0
10/3/88	Wales	Edinburgh	5–1
17/3/88	England	Glasgow	0–5
24/3/88	Ireland	Belfast	10–2
9/3/89	Ireland	Glasgow	7–0
13/4/89	England	London	3–2
15/4/89	Wales	Wrexham	0–0
22/3/90	Wales	Glasgow	5–0
29/3/90	Ireland	Belfast	4–1
5/4/90	England	Glasgow	1–1
21/3/91	Wales	Wrexham	4–3
28/3/91	Ireland	Glasgow	2–1
6/4/91	England	Blackburn	1–2
19/3/92	Ireland	Belfast	3–2
26/3/92	Wales	Edinburgh	6–1
2/4/92	England	Glasgow	1–4
18/3/93	Wales	Wrexham	8–0
25/3/93	Ireland	Glasgow	6–1
1/4/93	England	Richmond	2–5
24/3/94	Wales	Kilmarnock	5–2
31/3/94	Ireland	Belfast	2–1
7/4/94	England	Glasgow	2–2
23/3/95	Wales	Wrexham	2–2
30/3/95	Ireland	Glasgow	3–1
6/4/95	England	Liverpool	0–3
21/3/96	Wales	Dundee	4–0
28/3/96	Ireland	Belfast	3–3
4/4/96	England	Glasgow	2–1
20/3/97	Wales	Wrexham	2–2
27/3/97	Ireland	Glasgow	5–1
3/4/97	England	London	2–1
19/3/98	Wales	Motherwell	5–2
26/3/98	Ireland	Belfast	3–0
2/4/98	England	Glasgow	1–3
18/3/99	Wales	Wrexham	6–0
25/3/99	Ireland	Glasgow	9–1
8/4/99	England	Birmingham	1–2

1900–09

Results

Date	Opponents	Venue	F–A
3/2/00	Wales	Aberdeen	5–2
3/3/00	Ireland	Belfast	3–0
7/4/00	England	Glasgow	4–1
23/2/01	Ireland	Glasgow	11–0
2/3/01	Wales	Wrexham	1–1
30/3/01	England	London	2–2
1/3/02	Ireland	Belfast	5–1
15/3/02	Wales	Greenock	5–1
3/5/02	England	Birmingham	2–2
9/3/03	Wales	Cardiff	1–0
21/3/03	Ireland	Glasgow	0–2
4/4/03	England	Sheffield	2–1
12/3/04	Wales	Dundee	1–1
26/3/04	Ireland	Dublin	1–1
9/4/04	England	Glasgow	0–1
6/3/05	Wales	Wrexham	1–3
18/3/05	Ireland	Glasgow	4–0
1/4/05	England	London	0–1
3/3/06	Wales	Edinburgh	0–2
17/3/06	Ireland	Dublin	1–0
7/4/06	England	Glasgow	2–1
4/3/07	Wales	Wrexham	0–1
16/3/07	Ireland	Glasgow	3–0
6/4/07	England	Newcastle	1–1
7/3/08	Wales	Dundee	2–1
14/3/08	Ireland	Dublin	5–0
4/4/08	England	Glasgow	1–1
1/3/09	Wales	Wrexham	2–3
15/3/09	Ireland	Glasgow	5–0
3/4/09	England	London	0–2

1910–14

Results

Date	Opponents	Venue	F–A
5/3/10	Wales	Kilmarnock	1–0
19/3/10	Ireland	Belfast	0–1
2/4/10	England	Glasgow	2–0
6/3/11	Wales	Cardiff	2–2
18/3/11	Ireland	Glasgow	2–0
1/4/11	England	Liverpool	1–1
2/3/12	Wales	Edinburgh	1–0
16/3/12	Ireland	Belfast	4–1
23/3/12	England	Glasgow	1–1
3/3/13	Wales	Wrexham	0–0
15/3/13	Ireland	Dublin	2–1
5/4/13	England	Stamford Bridge	0–1
28/2/14	Wales	Glasgow	0–0
14/3/14	Ireland	Belfast	1–1
4/4/14	England	Glasgow	3–1

1920–29

Results

Date	Opponents	Venue	F–A
26/2/20	Wales	Cardiff	1–1
13/3/20	Ireland	Glasgow	3–0
10/4/20	England	Sheffield	4–5
12/2/21	Wales	Aberdeen	2–1
26/2/21	Ireland	Belfast	2–0
9/4/21	England	Glasgow	3–0
4/2/22	Wales	Wrexham	1–2
4/3/22	Ireland	Glasgow	2–1
8/4/22	England	Birmingham	1–0
3/3/23	Ireland	Belfast	1–0
17/3/23	Wales	Glasgow	2–0
14/4/23	England	Glasgow	2–2
16/2/24	Wales	Cardiff	0–2
1/3/24	Ireland	Glasgow	2–0
12/4/24	England	Wembley	1–1
14/2/25	Wales	Edinburgh	3–1
28/2/25	Ireland	Belfast	3–0
4/4/25	England	Glasgow	2–0
31/10/25	Wales	Cardiff	3–0
27/2/26	Ireland	Glasgow	4–0
17/4/26	England	Manchester	1–0
30/10/26	Wales	Glasgow	3–0
26/2/27	Ireland	Belfast	2–0
2/4/27	England	Glasgow	1–2
29/10/27	Wales	Wrexham	2–2
25/2/28	Ireland	Glasgow	0–1
31/3/28	England	Wembley	5–1
27/10/28	Wales	Glasgow	4–2
23/2/29	Ireland	Belfast	7–3
13/4/29	England	Glasgow	1–0
26/5/29	Norway	Bergen	7–3
1/6/29	Germany	Berlin	1–1
4/6/29	Holland	Amsterdam	2–0
26/10/29	Wales	Cardiff	4–2

1930–39

Results

Date	Opponents	Venue	F–A
22/2/30	Ireland	Glasgow	3–1
5/4/30	England	Wembley	2–5
18/5/30	France	Paris	2–0
25/10/30	Wales	Glasgow	1–1
21/2/31	Ireland	Belfast	0–0
28/3/31	England	Glasgow	2–0
16/5/31	Austria	Vienna	0–5
20/5/31	Italy	Rome	0–3
24/5/31	Switzerland	Geneva	3–2
19/9/31	Ireland	Glasgow	3–1
31/10/31	Wales	Wrexham	3–2
9/4/32	England	Wembley	0–3
8/5/32	France	Paris	3–1
19/9/32	Ireland	Belfast	4–0
26/10/32	Wales	Edinburgh	2–5
1/4/33	England	Glasgow	2–1
16/9/33	Ireland	Glasgow	1–2
4/10/33	Wales	Cardiff	2–3
29/11/33	Austria	Glasgow	2–2
14/4/34	England	Wembley	0–3
20/10/34	Ireland	Belfast	1–2
21/11/34	Wales	Aberdeen	3–2
6/4/35	England	Glasgow	2–0
5/10/35	Wales	Cardiff	1–1
13/11/35	Ireland	Edinburgh	2–1
4/4/36	England	Wembley	1–1
14/10/36	Germany	Glasgow	2–0
31/10/36	Ireland	Belfast	3–1
2/12/36	Wales	Dundee	1–2
17/4/37	England	Glasgow	3–1
9/5/37	Austria	Vienna	1–1
22/5/37	Czechoslovakia	Prague	3–1
30/10/37	Wales	Cardiff	1–2
10/11/37	Ireland	Aberdeen	1–1
8/12/37	Czechoslovakia	Glasgow	5–0
9/4/38	England	Wembley	1–0
21/5/38	Holland	Amsterdam	3–1

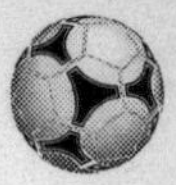

8/10/38	Ireland	Belfast	2–0
9/11/38	Wales	Edinburgh	3–2
7/12/38	Hungary	Glasgow	3–1
15/4/39	England	Glasgow	1–2

1940–49

Results

Date	Opponents	Venue	F–A
19/10/46	Wales	Wrexham	1–3
27/11/46	N Ireland	Glasgow	0–0
12/4/47	England	Wembley	1–1
18/5/47	Belgium	Brussels	1–2
24/5/47	Luxembourg	Luxembourg	6–0
4/10/47	N Ireland	Belfast	0–2
12/11/47	Wales	Glasgow	1–2
10/4/48	England	Glasgow	0–2
28/4/48	Belgium	Glasgow	2–0
17/5/48	Switzerland	Berne	1–2
23/5/48	France	Paris	0–3
23/10/48	Wales	Cardiff	3–1
17/11/48	N Ireland	Glasgow	3–2
9/4/49	England	Wembley	3–1
27/4/49	France	Glasgow	2–0
1/10/49	N Ireland	Belfast (WCQ)	8–2
9/11/49	Wales	Glasgow (WCQ)	2–0

1950–59

Results

Date	Opponents	Venue	F–A
15/4/50	England	Glasgow (WCQ)	0–1
26/4/50	Switzerland	Glasgow	3–1
25/5/50	Portugal	Lisbon	2–2
27/5/50	France	Paris	1–0
21/10/50	Wales	Cardiff	3–1
1/11/50	N Ireland	Glasgow	6–1
13/12/50	Austria	Glasgow	0–1
14/4/51	England	Wembley	3–2
12/5/51	Denmark	Glasgow	3–1
16/5/51	France	Glasgow	1–0
20/5/51	Belgium	Brussels	5–0
27/5/51	Austria	Vienna	0–4
6/10/51	N Ireland	Belfast	3–0
28/11/51	Wales	Glasgow	0–1
5/4/52	England	Glasgow	1–2
30/4/52	USA	Glasgow	6–0
25/5/52	Denmark	Copenhagen	2–1
30/5/52	Sweden	Stockholm	1–3
15/10/52	Wales	Cardiff	2–1
5/11/52	N Ireland	Glasgow	1–1
18/4/53	England	Wembley	2–2
6/5/53	Sweden	Glasgow	1–2
3/10/53	N Ireland	Belfast (WCQ)	3–1
4/11/53	Wales	Glasgow (WCQ)	3–3
3/4/54	England	Glasgow (WCQ)	2–4
5/5/54	Norway	Glasgow	1–0
19/5/54	Norway	Oslo	1–1
25/5/54	Finland	Helsinki	2–1
16/6/54	Austria	Zurich (WCF)	0–1
19/6/54	Uruguay	Basle (WCF)	0–7
16/10/54	Wales	Cardiff	1–0
3/11/54	N Ireland	Glasgow	2–2
8/12/54	Hungary	Glasgow	2–4
2/4/55	England	Wembley	2–7
16/5/55	Portugal	Glasgow	3–0
15/5/55	Yugoslavia	Belgrade	2–2
19/5/55	Austria	Vienna	4–1
29/5/55	Hungary	Budapest	1–3
8/10/55	N Ireland	Belfast	1–2
9/11/55	Wales	Glasgow	2–0
14/4/56	England	Glasgow	1–1
2/5/56	Austria	Glasgow	1–1
20/10/56	Wales	Cardiff	2–2
7/11/56	N Ireland	Glasgow	1–0
21/11/56	Yugoslavia	Glasgow	2–0
6/4/57	England	Wembley	1–2
8/5/57	Spain	Glasgow (WCQ)	4–2
19/5/57	Switzerland	Basle (WCQ)	2–1
22/5/57	W Germany	Stuttgart	3–1
26/5/57	Spain	Madrid (WCQ)	1–4
5/10/57	N Ireland	Belfast	1–1
6/11/57	Switzerland	Glasgow (WCQ)	3–2
13/11/57	Wales	Glasgow	1–1
19/4/58	England	Glasgow	0–4
7/5/58	Hungary	Glasgow	1–1
1/6/58	Poland	Warsaw	2–1
8/6/58	Yugoslavia	Vasteras (WCF)	1–1
11/6/58	Paraguay	Norrköping (WCF)	2–3
15/6/58	France	Örebro (WCF)	1–2
18/10/58	Wales	Cardiff	3–0
5/11/58	N Ireland	Glasgow	2–2
11/4/59	England	Wembley	0–1
6/5/59	W Germany	Glasgow	3–2
27/5/59	Holland	Amsterdam	2–1
3/6/59	Portugal	Lisbon	0–1
3/10/59	N Ireland	Belfast	4–0
14/11/59	Wales	Glasgow	1–1

1960

Results

Date	Opponents	Venue	F–A
9/4	England	Glasgow	1–1
4/5	Poland	Glasgow	2–3
29/5	Austria	Vienna	1–4
5/6	Hungary	Budapest	3–3
8/6	Turkey	Ankara	2–4
22/10	Wales	Cardifff	0–2
9/11	N Ireland	Glasgow	5–2

1961

Results

Date	Opponents	Venue	F–A
15/4	England	Wembley	3–9
3/5	Rep of Ireland	Glasgow (WCQ)	4–1
7/5	Rep of Ireland	Dublin (WCQ)	3–0
14/5	Czechoslovakia	Bratislava (WCQ)	0–4
26/9	Czechoslovakia	Glasgow (WCQ)	3–2
7/10	N Ireland	Belfast	6–1
8/11	Wales	Glasgow	2–0
29/11	Czechoslovakia	Brussels (WCQ)	2–4

1962

Results

Date	Opponents	Venue	F–A
14/4	England	Glasgow	2–0
2/5	Uruguay	Glasgow	2–3
20/10	Wales	Cardiff	3–2
7/11	N Ireland	Glasgow	5–1

1963

Results

Date	Opponents	Venue	F–A
6/4	England	Wembley	2–1
8/5	Austria	Glasgow	4–1
4/6	Norway	Bergen	3–4
9/6	Rep of Ireland	Dublin	0–1
13/6	Spain	Madrid	6–2
12/10	N Ireland	Belfast	1–2
7/11	Norway	Glasgow	6–1
20/11	Wales	Glasgow	2–1

1964

Results

Date	Opponents	Venue	F–A
11/4	England	Glasgow	1–0
12/5	W Germany	Hanover	2–2
3/10	Wales	Cardiff	2–3
21/10	Finland	Glasgow (WCQ)	3–1
25/11	N Ireland	Glasgow	3–2

1965

Results

Date	Opponents	Venue	F–A
10/4	England	Wembley	2–2
8/5	Spain	Glasgow	0–0
23/5	Poland	Chorzow (WCQ)	1–1
27/5	Finland	Helsinki (WCQ)	2–1
2/10	N Ireland	Belfast	2–3
13/10	Poland	Glasgow (WCQ)	1–2
9/11	Italy	Glasgow (WCQ)	1–0
24/11	Wales	Glasgow	4–1
7/12	Italy (WCQ)	Naples (WCQ)	0–3

1966

Results

Date	Opponents	Venue	F–A
/4	England	Glasgow	3–4
1/5	Holland	Glasgow	0–3
8/6	Portugal	Glasgow	0–1
5/6	Brazil	Glasgow	1–1
2/10	Wales	Cardiff (ECQ)	1–1
6/11	N Ireland	Glasgow (ECQ)	2–1

1967

Results

Date	Opponents	Venue	F–A
5/4	England	Wembley (ECQ)	3–2
0/5	USSR	Glasgow	0–2
1/10	N Ireland	Belfast (ECQ)	0–1
2/11	Wales	Glasgow (ECQ)	3–2

1968

Results

Date	Opponents	Venue	F–A
4/2	England	Glasgow (ECQ)	1–1
0/5	Holland	Amsterdam	0–0
6/10	Denmark	Copenhagen	1–0
/11	Austria	Glasgow (WCQ)	2–1
1/12	Cyprus	Nicosia (WCQ)	5–0

1969

Results

Date	Opponents	Venue	F–A
6/4	W Germany	Glasgow (WCQ)	1–1
/5	Wales	Wrexham	5–3
/5	N Ireland	Glasgow (ECQ)	1–1
0/5	England	Wembley	1–4
2/5	Cyprus	Glasgow (WCQ)	8–0
21/9	Rep of Ireland	Dublin	1–1
22/10	W Germany	Hamburg (WCQ)	2–3
5/11	Austria	Vienna (WCQ)	0–2

1970

Results

Date	Opponents	Venue	F–A
18/4	N Ireland	Belfast	1–0
22/4	Wales	Glasgow	0–0
25/4	England	Glasgow	0–0
11/11	Denmark	Glasgow (ECQ)	1–0

1971

Results

Date	Opponents	Venue	F–A
3/2	Belgium	Liège (ECQ)	0–3
21/4	Portugal	Lisbon (ECQ)	0–2
15/5	Wales	Cardiff	0–0
18/5	N Ireland	Glasgow	0-1
22/5	England	Wembley	1–3
9/6	Denmark	Copenhagen	0–1
14/6	USSR	Moscow	0–1
13/10	Portugal	Glasgow (ECQ)	2–1
10/11	Belgium	Aberdeen (ECQ)	1–0
1/12	Holland	Rotterdam	1–2

1972

Results

Date	Opponents	Venue	F–A
26/4	Peru	Glasgow	2–0
20/5	N Ireland	Glasgow	2–0
24/5	Wales	Glasgow	1–0
27/5	England	Glasgow	0–1
29/6	Yugoslavia	Belo Horizonte	2–2

2/7	Czechoslovakia	Porto Alegre	0–0
5/7	Brazil	Rio de Janeiro	0–1
18/10	Denmark	Copenhagen (WCQ)	4–1
15/11	Denmark	Glasgow (WCQ)	2–0

1973

Results

Date	Opponents	Venue	F–A
14/2	England	Glasgow	0–5
12/5	Wales	Wrexham	2–0
16/5	N Ireland	Glasgow	1–2
19/5	England	Wembley	0–1
22/6	Switzerland	Berne	0–1
30/6	Brazil	Glasgow	0–1
26/9	Czechoslovakia	Glasgow (WCQ)	2–1
17/10	Czechoslovakia	Bratislava (WCQ)	0–1
14/11	W Germany	Glasgow	1–1

1974

Results

Date	Opponents	Venue	F–A
27/3	W Germany	Frankfurt	1–2
11/5	N Ireland	Glasgow	0–1
14/5	Wales	Glasgow	2–0
18/5	England	Glasgow	2–0
2/6	Belgium	Brussels	1–2
6/6	Norway	Oslo	2–1
14/6	Zaire	Dortmund (WCF)	2–0
18/6	Brazil	Frankfurt (WCF)	0–0
22/6	Yugoslavia	Frankfurt (WCF)	1–1
30/10	E Germany	Glasgow	3–0
20/11	Spain	Glasgow (ECQ)	1–2

1975

Results

Date	Opponents	Venue	F–A
5/2	Spain	Valencia (ECQ)	1–1
16/4	Sweden	Gothenburg	1–1
13/5	Portugal	Glasgow	1–0
17/5	Wales	Cardiff	2–2
20/5	N Ireland	Glasgow	3–0
24/5	England	Wembley	1–5
1/6	Romania	Bucharest (ECQ)	1–1
3/9	Denmark	Copenhagen (ECQ)	1–0
29/10	Denmark	Glasgow (ECQ)	3–1
17/12	Romania	Glasgow (ECQ)	1–1

1976

Results

Date	Opponents	Venue	F–A
7/4	Switzerland	Glasgow	1–0
6/5	Wales	Glasgow	3–1
8/5	N Ireland	Glasgow	3–0
15/5	England	Glasgow	2–1
8/9	Finalsnd	Glasgow	6–0
13/10	Czechoslovakia	Prague (WCQ)	0–2
17/11	Wales	Glasgow (WCQ)	1–0

1977

Results

Date	Opponents	Venue	F–A
27/4	Sweden	Glasgow	3–1
28/5	Wales	Wrexham	0–0
1/6	N Ireland	Glasgow	3–0
4/6	England	Wembley	2–0
15/6	Chile	Santiago	4–2
18/6	Argentina	Buenos Aires	1–1
23/6	Brazil	Rio de Janeiro	0–2
7/9	E Germany	E Berlin	0–1
21/9	Czechoslovakia	Glasgow (WCQ)	3–1
12/10	Wales	Liverpool (WCQ)	2–0

1978

Results

Date	Opponents	Venue	F–A
22/2	Bulgaria	Glasgow	2–1
13/5	N Ireland	Glasgow	1–1
17/5	Wales	Glasgow	1–1
20/5	England	Glasgow	0–1
3/6	Peru	Cordoba (WCF)	1–3
7/6	Iran	Cordoba (WCF)	1–1
11/6	Holland	Mendoza (WCF)	3–2
20/9	Austria	Vienna (ECQ)	2–3
25/10	Norway	Glasgow (ECQ)	3–2
29/11	Portugal	Lisbon (ECQ)	0–1

1979

Results

Date	Opponents	Venue	F–A
19/5	Wales	Cardiff	0–3
22/5	N Ireland	Glasgow	1–0
26/5	England	Wembley	1–3
2/6	Argentina	Glasgow	1–3
7/6	Norway	Oslo (ECQ)	4–0
12/9	Peru	Glasgow	1–1
17/10	Austria	Glasgow (ECQ)	1–1
21/11	Belgium	Brussels (ECQ)	0–2
19/12	Belgium	Glasgow	1–3

1980

Results

Date	Opponents	Venue	F–A
26/3	Portugal	Glasgow (ECQ)	4–1
16/5	N Ireland	Belfast	0–1
21/5	Wales	Glasgow	1–0
24/5	England	Glasgow	0–2
28/5	Poland	Poznan	0–1
31/5	Hungary	Budapest	1–3
10/9	Sweden	Stockholm (WCQ)	1–0
15/10	Portugal	Glasgow (WCQ)	0–0

1981

Results

Date	Opponents	Venue	F–A
25/2	Israel	Tel Aviv (WCQ)	1–0
25/3	N Ireland	Glasgow (WCQ)	1–1
28/4	Israel	Glasgow (WCQ)	3–1
16/5	Wales	Swansea	0–2
19/5	N Ireland	Glasgow	2–0
23/5	England	Wembley	1–0
9/9	Sweden	Glasgow (WCQ)	2–0
14/10	N Ireland	Belfast (WCQ)	
18/11	Portugal	Lisbon (WCQ)	1–2

1982

Results

Date	Opponents	Venue	F–A
24/2	Spain	Valencia	0–3
23/3	Holland	Glasgow	2–1
28/4	N Ireland	Belfast	1–1
24/5	Wales	Glasgow	1–0
29/5	England	Glasgow	0–1
15/6	New Zealand	Malaga WCF)	5–2
18/6	Brazil	Seville (WCF)	1–4
22/6	USSR	Malaga (WCF)	2–2
13/10	E Germany	Glasgow ECQ)	2–0
17/11	Switzerland	Berne (ECQ)	0–2
15/12	Belgium	Brussels (ECQ)	2–3

1983

Results

Date	Opponents	Venue	F–A
30/3	Switzerland	Glasgow (ECQ)	2–2
24/5	N Ireland	Glasgow	0–0
28/5	Wales	Cardiff	2–0
1/6	England	Wembley	0–2
12/6	Canada	Vancouver	2–0
16/6	Canada	Edmonton	3–0
20/6	Canada	Toronto	2–0
21/9	Uruguay	Glasgow	2–0
12/10	Belgium	Glasgow (ECQ)	1–1

16/11	E Germany	Halle (ECQ)	1–2
13/12	N Ireland	Belfast	0–2

1984

Results

Date	Opponents	Venue	F–A
28/2	Wales	Glasgow	2–1
26/5	England	Glasgow	1–1
1/6	France	Marseille	0–2
12/9	Yugoslavia	Glasgow	6–1
17/10	Iceland	Glasgow (WCQ)	3–0
14/11	Spain	Glasgow (WCQ)	3–1

1985

Results

Date	Opponents	Venue	F–A
27/2	Spain	Seville (WCQ)	0–1
27/3	Wales	Glasgow (WCQ)	0–1
25/5	England	Glasgow	1–0
28/5	Iceland	Reykjavik (WCQ)	1–0
10/9	Wales	Cardiff (WCQ)	1–1
16/10	E Germany	Glasgow	0–0
20/11	Australia	Glasgow (WCQ)	2–0
4/12	Australia	Melbourne (WCQ)	0–0

1986

Results

Date	Opponents	Venue	F–A
28/1	Israel	Tel Aviv	1–0
26/3	Romania	Glasgow	3–0
23/4	England	Wembley	1–2
29/4	Holland	Eindhoven	0–0
4/6	Denmark	Nezahualcoyot (WCF)	0–1
8/6	W Germany	Queretaro (WCF)	1–2
13/6	Uruguay	Nezahualcoyot (WCF)	0–0

10/9	Bulgaria	Glasgow (ECQ)	0–0
15/10	Rep of Ireland	Dublin (ECQ)	0–0
12/11	Luxembourg	Glasgow (ECQ)	3–0

1987

Results

Date	Opponents	Venue	F–A
18/2	Rep of Ireland	Glasgow (ECQ)	0–1
1/4	Belgium	Brussels (ECQ)	1–4
6/5	Brazil	Glasgow	0–2
23/5	England	Glasgow	0–0
9/9	Hungary	Glasgow	2–0
14/10	Belgium	Glasgow (ECQ)	2–0
11/11	Bulgaria	Sofia (ECQ)	1–0
2/12	Luxembourg	Esch (ECQ)	0–0

1988

Results

Date	Opponents	Venue	F–A
17/2	Saudi Arabia	Riyadh	2–2
22/3	Malta	Valletta	1–1
27/4	Spain	Madrid	0–0
17/5	Colombia	Glasgow	0–0
21/5	England	Wembley	0–1
14/9	Norway	Oslo (WCQ)	2–1
19/10	Yugoslavia	Glasgow (WCQ)	1–1
22/12	Italy	Perugia	0–2

1989

Results

Date	Opponents	Venue	F–A
8/2	Cyprus	Limassol (WCQ)	3–2
8/3	France	Glasgow (WCQ)	2–0
26/4	Cyprus	Glasgow (WCQ)	2–1
27/5	England	Glagow	0–2
30/5	Chile	Glasgow	2–0
6/9	Yugoslavia	Zagreb (WCQ)	1–3

11/10	France	Paris (WCQ)	0–3
15/11	Norway	Glasgow (WCQ)	1–1

1990

Results

Date	Opponents	Venue	F–A
28/3	Argentina	Glasgow	1–0
25/4	E Germany	Glasgow	0–1
19/5	Poland	Glasgow	1–1
28/5	Malta	Valletta	2–1
11/6	Costa Rica	Genoa (WCF)	0–1
16/6	Sweden	Genoa (WCF)	2–1
20/6	Brazil	Turin (WCF)	0–1
12/9	Romania	Glasgow (ECQ)	2–1
17/10	Switzerland	Glasgow (ECQ)	2–1
14/11	Bulgaria	Sofia (ECQ)	1–1

1991

Results

Date	Opponents	Venue	F–A
6/2	USSR	Glasgow	0–1
27/3	Bulgaria	Glasgow (ECQ)	1–1
1/5	San Marino	Serravalle (ECQ)	2–0
11/9	Switzerland	Berne (ECQ)	2–2
16/10	Romania	Bucharest (ECQ)	0–1
13/11	San Marino	Glasgow (ECQ)	4–0

1992

Results

Date	Opponents	Venue	F–A
25/3	Finland	Glasgow	1–1
17/5	USA	Denver	1–0
21/5	Canada	Toronto	3–1
3/6	Norway	Oslo	0–0
12/6	Holland	Gothenburg (ECF)	0–1
15/6	Germany	Gothenburg (ECF)	0–2
18/6	CIS	Norrkoping (ECF)	3–0
9/9	Switzerland	Berne (WCQ)	1–3
14/10	Portugal	Glasgow (WCQ)	0–0
18/11	Italy	Glasgow (WCQ)	0–0

1993

Results

Date	Opponents	Venue	F–A
17/2	Malta	Glasgow (WCQ)	3–0
24/3	Germany	Glasgow	0–1
28/4	Portugal	Lisbon (WCQ)	0–5
19/5	Estonia	Tallinn (WCQ)	3–0
2/6	Estonia	Aberdeen (WCQ)	3–1
8/9	Switzerland	Glasgow (WCQ)	1–1
13/10	Italy	Rome (WCQ)	1–3
17/11	Malta	Sliema (WCQ)	2–0

1994

Results

Date	Opponents	Venue	F–A
23/3	Holland	Glasgow	0–1
20/4	Austria	Vienna	–1
27/5	Holland	Utrecht	1–3
7/9	Finland	Helsinki (ECQ)	2–0
12/10	Faroe Islands	Glasgow	5–1
16/11	Russia	Glasgow (ECQ)	1–1
19/12	Greece	Athens (ECQ)	0–1

1995

Results

Date	Opponents	Venue	F–A
29/3	Russia	Moscow (ECQ)	0–0
26/4	San Marino	Serravalle (ECQ)	2–0
21/5	Japan	Hiroshima	0–0

24/5	Ecuador	Toyama, Japan	2–1
7/6	Faroe Islands	Toftir (ECQ)	2–0
16/8	Greece	Glasgow (ECQ)	1–0
6/9	Finland	Glasgow (ECQ)	1–0
11/10	Sweden	Stockholm	0–2
15/11	San Marino	Glasgow (ECQ)	5–0

1996

Results

Date	Opponents	Venue	F–A
27/3	Australia	Glasgow	1–0
24/4	Denmark	Copenhagen	0–2
26/5	United States	New Britain, Conn	1–2
29/5	Colombia	Miami	0–1
10/6	Holland	Birmingham (ECF)	0–0
15/6	England	Wembley (ECF)	0–2
18/6	Switzerland	Birmingham (ECF)	1–0

1997

Results

Date	Opponents	Venue	F–A
11/2	Estonia	Monaco (WCQ)	0–0
29/3	Estonia	Kilmarnock (WCQ)	2–0
2/4	Austria	Glasgow (WCQ)	2–0
30/4	Sweden	Gothenburg (WCQ)	1–2
27/5	Wales	Kilmarnock	0–1
1/6	Malta	Valletta	3–2
8/6	Belarus	Minsk (WCQ)	1–0
7/9	Belarus	Aberdeen (WCQ)	4–1
11/10	Latvia	Glasgow (WCQ)	2–0
12/11	France	Saint-Etienne	1–2

WALES

League of Wales

Winners

1993	Cwmbran Town
1994	Bangor C
1995	Bangor C
1996	Barry T
1997	Barry T

League of Wales Cup

Finalists

Year	Winners	Runners-up	Score
1993	Caersws	Afan Lido	Penalties
1994	Afan Lido	Bangor	1–0
1995	Llansantffraid	Ton Pentre	2–1
1996	Connah's Quay	Ebbw Vale	1–0
1997	Barry Town	Bangor City	2–2

(Barry Town won 4–2 on penalties)

Welsh Cup Finals

Finalists

Year	Winners	Runners-up	Score
1878	Wrexham	Druids	1–0
1879	Newtown	Wrexham	1–0
1880	Druids	Ruthin	2–1
1881	Druids	Newtown White Stars	2–0
1882	Druids	Northwich	2–1
1883	Wrexham	Druids	1–0
1884	Oswestry	Druids	3–2
1885	Druids	Oswestry	2–0
1886	Druids	Newtown	5–0
1887	Chirk	Davenham	4–2
1888	Chirk	Newtown	5–0
1889	Bangor	Northwich	2–1
1890	Chirk	Wrexham	1–0
1891	Shrewsbury T	Wrexham	5–2
1892	Chirk	Westminster R	2–1
1893	Wrexham	Chirk	2–1
1894	Chirk	Westminster R	2–0
1895	Newtown	Wrexham	3–2
1896	Bangor	Wrexham	3–1

1897	Wrexham	Newtown	2–0
1898	Druids	Wrexham	1–1, 2–1
1899	Druids	Wrexham	2–2, 1–0
1900	Aberystwyth	Druids	3–0
1901	Oswestry	Druids	1–0
1902	Wellington	Wrexham	1–0
1903	Wrexham	Aberaman	8–0
1904	Druids	Aberdare	3–2
1905	Wrexham	Aberdare	3–0
1906	Wellington	Whitchurch	3–2
1907	Oswestry	Whitchurch	2–0
1908	Chester	Connah's Quay	3–1
1909	Wrexham	Chester	1–0
1910	Wrexham	Chester	2–1
1911	Wrexham	Connah's Quay	6–1
1912	Cardiff C	Pontypridd	0–0, 3–0
1913	Swansea	Pontypridd	0–0, 1–0
1914	Wrexham	Llanelly	1–1, 3–0
1915	Wrexham	Swansea	0–0, 1–0
1920	Cardiff C	Wrexham	2–1
1921	Wrexham	Pontypridd	1–1, 3–1
1922	Cardiff C	Ton Pentre	2–0
1923	Cardiff C	Aberdare	3–2
1924	Wrexham	Merthyr	2–2, 1–0
1925	Wrexham	Flint	3–1
1926	Ebbw Vale	Swansea	3–2
1927	Cardiff C	Rhyl	0–0, 4–2
1928	Cardiff C	Bangor	2–0
1929	Connah's Quay	Cardiff C	3–0
1930	Cardiff C	Rhyl	0–0, 4–2
1931	Wrexham	Shrewsbury	7–0
1932	Swansea	Wrexham	1–1, 2–0
1933	Chester	Wrexham	2–0
1934	Bristol C	Tranmere R	1–1, 3–0
1935	Tranmere R	Chester	1–0
1936	Crewe	Chester	2–0
1937	Crewe	Rhyl	1–1, 3–1
1938	Shrewsbury	Swansea	2–1
1939	S Liverpool	Cardiff C	2–1
1940	Welling T	Swansea	4–0
1947	Chester	Merthyr Tydfil	0–0, 5–1
1948	Lovells Ath	Shrewsbury T	3–0
1949	Merthyr Tydfil	Swansea T	2–0
1950	Swansea T	Wrexham	4–1
1951	Merthyr Tydfil	Cardiff C	1–1, 3–2
1952	Rhyl	Merthyr Tydfil	4–3
1953	Rhyl	Chester	2–1
1954	Flint T Utd	Chester	2–0
1955	Barry T	Chester	1–1, 4–3
1956	Cardiff C	Swansea T	3–2
1957	Wrexham	Swansea T	2–1
1958	Wrexham	Chester	1–1, 2–0
1959	Cardiff C	Lovells Ath	2–0
1960	Wrexham	Cardiff C	0–0, 1–0
1961	Swansea T	Bangor C	3–1
1962	Bangor C	Wrexham	3–1
1963	Borough Utd	Newport Co	2–1 *
1964	Cardiff C	Bangor C	5–3 *
1965	Cardiff C	Wrexham	8–2 *
1966	Swansea T	Chester	2–1
1967	Cardiff C	Wrexham	2–1 *
1968	Cardiff C	Hereford Utd	6–1 *
1969	Cardiff C	Swansea T	5–1 *
1970	Cardiff C	Chester	5–0
1971	Cardiff C	Wrexham	4–1 *
1972	Wrexham	Cardiff C	3–2 *
1973	Cardiff C	Bangor C	5–1 *
1974	Cardiff C	Stourbridge	2–0 *
1975	Wrexham	Cardiff C	5–2 *
1976	Cardiff C	Hereford Utd	6–5 *
1977	Shrewsbury T	Cardiff C	4–2 *
1978	Wrexham	Bangor C	3–1 *
1979	Shrewsbury T	Wrexham	2–1 *
1980	Newport Co	Shrewsbury T	5–1 *
1981	Swansea C	Hereford Utd	2–1 *
1982	Swansea C	Cardiff C	2–1 *
1983	Swansea C	Wrexham	4–1 *
1984	Shrewsbury T	Wrexham	2–0 *
1985	Shrewsbury T	Bangor C	5–1 *
1986	Kidderminster H	Wrexham	1–1, 2–1
1987	Merthyr Tydfil	Newport Co	2–2, 1–0
1988	Cardiff C	Wrexham	1–0
1989	Swansea C	Kidderminster H	5–0
1990	Hereford Utd	Wrexham	2–1
1991	Swansea C	Wrexham	2–0
1992	Cardiff C	Hednesford T	1–0
1993	Cardiff C	Rhyl	5–0
1994	Barry T	Cardiff C	2–1
1995	Wrexham	Cardiff C	2–1
1996	Llansantffraid	Barry T	3–3
	(Llansantffraid won 3–2 on penalties)		
1997	Barry T	Cwmbran T	2–1

* Aggregate score

Welsh Internationals 1876–99

Results

Date	Opponents	Venue	F–A
25/3/76	Scotland	Glasgow	0–4
5/3/77	Scotland	Wrexham	0–2
23/3/78	Scotland	Glasgow	0–9
18/1/79	England	London	1–2
7/4/79	Scotland	Wrexham	0–3
15/3/80	England	Wrexham	2–3

27/3/80	Scotland	Glasgow	1–5
26/2/81	England	Blackburn	1–0
14/3/81	Scotland	Wrexham	1–5
25/2/82	Ireland	Wrexham	7–1
15/3/82	England	Wrexham	5–3
25/3/82	Scotland	Glasgow	0–5
3/2/83	England	London	0–5
12/3/83	Scotland	Wrexham	0–3
17/3/83	Ireland	Belfast	1–1
9/2/84	Ireland	Wrexham	6–0
17/3/84	England	Wrexham	0–4
29/3/84	Scotland	Glasgow	1–4
14/3/85	England	Blackburn	1–1
23/3/85	Scotland	Wrexham	1–8
11/4/85	Ireland	Belfast	8–2
27/2/86	Ireland	Wrexham	5–0
29/3/86	England	Wrexham	1–3
10/4/86	Scotland	Glasgow	1–4
26/2/87	England	London	0–4
12/3/87	Ireland	Belfast	1–4
21/3/87	Scotland	Wrexham	0–2
4/2/88	England	Crewe	1–5
3/3/88	Ireland	Wrexham	11–0
10/3/88	Scotland	Edinburgh	1–5
23/2/89	England	Stoke	1–4
15/4/89	Scotland	Wrexham	0–0
27/4/89	Ireland	Belfast	3–1
8/2/90	Ireland	Shrewsbury	5–2
15/3/90	England	Wrexham	1–3
22/3/90	Scotland	Glasgow	0–5
7/2/91	Ireland	Belfast	2–7
7/3/91	England	Sunderland	1–4
21/3/91	Scotland	Wrexham	3–4
27/2/92	Ireland	Bangor	1–1
5/3/92	England	Wrexham	0–2
26/3/92	Scotland	Edinburgh	1–6
13/3/93	England	Stoke-on-Trent	0–6
18/3/93	Scotland	Wrexham	0–8
5/4/93	Ireland	Belfast	3–4
24/2/94	Ireland	Swansea	4–1
12/3/94	England	Wrexham	1–5
24/3/94	Scotland	Kilmarnock	2–5
16/3/95	Ireland	Belfast	2–2
18/3/95	England	London	1–1
23/3/95	Scotland	Wrexham	2–2
29/2/96	Ireland	Wrexham	6–1
16/3/96	England	Cardiff	1–9
21/3/96	Scotland	Dundee	0–4
6/3/97	Ireland	Belfast	3–4
20/3/97	Scotland	Wrexham	2–2
29/3/97	England	Sheffield	0–4
19/2/98	Ireland	Llandudno	0–1
19/3/98	Scotland	Motherwell	2–5
28/3/98	England	Wrexham	0–3
4/3/99	Ireland	Belfast	0–1
18/3/99	Scotland	Wrexham	0–6
20/3/99	England	Bristol	0–4

1900–19

Results

Date	Opponents	Venue	F–A
3/2/00	Scotland	Aberdeen	2–5
24/2/00	Ireland	Llandudno	2–0
26/3/00	England	Cardiff	1–1
2/3/01	Scotland	Wrexham	1–1
18/3/01	England	Newcastle	0–6
23/3/01	Ireland	Belfast	1–0
22/2/02	Ireland	Cardiff	0–3
3/3/02	England	Wrexham	0–0
15/3/02	Scotland	Greenock	1–5
2/3/03	England	Portsmouth	1–2
9/3/03	Scotland	Cardiff	0–1
28/3/03	Ireland	Belfast	0–2
29/2/04	England	Wrexham	2–2
12/3/04	Scotland	Dundee	1–1
21/3/04	Ireland	Bangor	0–1
6/3/05	Scotland	Wrexham	3–1
27/3/05	England	Liverpool	1–5
8/4/05	Ireland	Belfast	2–2
3/3/06	Scotland	Edinburgh	2–0
19/3/06	England	Cardiff	0–1
2/4/06	Ireland	Wrexham	4–4
23/2/07	Ireland	Belfast	3–2
4/3/07	Scotland	Wrexham	1–0
18/3/07	England	Fulham	1–1
7/3/08	Scotland	Dundee	1–2
16/3/08	England	Wrexham	1–7
11/4/08	Ireland	Aberdare	0–1
1/3/09	Scotland	Wrexham	3–2
15/3/09	England	Nottingham	0–2
20/3/09	Ireland	Belfast	3–2
5/3/10	Scotland	Kilmarnock	0–1
14/3/10	England	Cardiff	0–1
11/4/10	Ireland	Wrexham	4–1
28/1/11	Ireland	Belfast	2–1
6/3/11	Scotland	Cardiff	2–2
13/3/11	England	London	0–3
2/3/12	Scotland	Edinburgh	0–1
11/3/12	England	Wrexham	0–2
13/4/12	Ireland	Cardiff	2–3
18/1/13	Ireland	Belfast	1–0
3/3/13	Scotland	Wrexham	0–0
17/3/13	England	Bristol	3–4
19/1/14	Ireland	Wrexham	1–2
28/2/14	Scotland	Glasgow	0–0
16/3/14	England	Cardiff	0–2

1920–29

Results

Date	Opponents	Venue	F–A
14/2/20	Ireland	Belfast	2–2
26/2/20	Scotland	Cardiff	1–1
15/3/20	England	London	2–1
12/2/21	Scotland	Aberdeen	1–2
16/3/21	England	Cardiff	0–0
9/4/21	Ireland	Swansea	2–1
4/2/22	Scotland	Wrexham	2–1
13/3/22	England	Liverpool	0–1
1/4/22	Ireland	Belfast	1–1
5/3/23	England	Cardiff	2–2
17/3/23	Scotland	Glasgow	0–2
14/4/23	Ireland	Wrexham	0–3
16/2/24	Scotland	Cardiff	2–0
3/3/24	England	Blackburn	2–1
15/3/24	Ireland	Belfast	1–0
14/2/25	Scotland	Edinburgh	1–3
28/2/25	England	Swansea	1–2
18/4/25	Ireland	Wrexham	0–0
31/10/25	Scotland	Cardiff	0–3
13/2/26	Ireland	Belfast	0–3
1/3/26	England	London	3–1
30/10/26	Scotland	Glasgow	0–3
14/2/27	England	Wrexham	3–3
9/4/27	Ireland	Cardiff	2–2
29/10/27	Scotland	Wrexham	2–2
28/11/27	England	Burnley	2–1
4/2/28	Ireland	Belfast	2–1
27/10/28	Scotland	Glasgow	2–4
17/11/28	England	Swansea	2–3
2/2/29	Ireland	Wrexham	2–2
26/10/29	Scotland	Cardiff	2–4
20/11/29	England	London	0–6

1930–39

Results

Date	Opponents	Venue	F–A
1/2/30	Ireland	Belfast	0–7
25/10/30	Scotland	Glasgow	1–1
22/11/30	England	Wrexham	0–4
22/4/31	Ireland	Wrexham	3–2
31/10/31	Scotland	Wrexham	2–3
18/11/31	England	Liverpool	1–3
5/12/31	Ireland	Belfast	0–4
26/10/32	Scotland	Edinburgh	5–2
16/11/32	England	Wrexham	0–0
7/12/32	Ireland	Wrexham	4–1
25/5/33	France	Paris	1–1
4/10/33	Scotland	Cardiff	3–2
4/11/33	Ireland	Belfast	1–1
15/11/33	England	Newcastle	2–1
29/9/34	England	Cardiff	0–4
21/11/34	Scotland	Aberdeen	2–3
27/3/35	Ireland	Wrexham	3–1
5/10/35	Scotland	Cardiff	1–1
5/2/36	England	Wolverhampton	2–1
11/3/36	Ireland	Belfast	2–3
17/10/36	England	Cardiff	2–1
2/12/36	Scotland	Dundee	2–1
17/3/37	Ireland	Wrexham	4–1
30/10/37	Scotland	Cardiff	2–1
17/11/37	England	Middlesbrough	1–2
16/3/38	Ireland	Belfast	0–1
22/10/38	England	Cardiff	4–2
9/11/38	Scotland	Edinburgh	2–3
15/3/39	Ireland	Wrexham	3–1
20/5/39	France	Paris	1–2

1940–49

Results

Date	Opponents	Venue	F–A
19/10/46	Scotland	Wrexham	3–1
13/11/46	England	Manchester	0–3
16/4/47	N Ireland	Belfast	1–2
18/10/47	England	Cardiff	0–3
12/11/47	Scotland	Glasgow	2–1
10/3/48	N Ireland	Wrexham	2–0
23/10/48	Scotland	Cardiff	1–3
10/11/48	England	Villa Park	0–1
9/3/49	N Ireland	Belfast	2–0
15/5/49	Portugal	Lisbon	2–3
23/5/49	Belgium	Liege	1–3
26/5/49	Switzerland	Berne	0–4
15/10/49	England	Cardiff (WCQ)	1–4
9/11/49	Scotland	Glasgow (WCQ)	0–2
23/11/49	Belgium	Cardiff	5–1

1950–59

Results

Date	Opponents	Venue	F–A
8/3/50	N Ireland	Wrexham (WCQ)	0–0
21/10/50	Scotland	Cardiff	1–3
15/11/50	England	Sunderland	2–4
7/3/51	N Ireland	Belfast	2–1
12/5/51	Portugal	Cardiff	2–1
16/5/51	Switzerland	Wrexham	3–2
20/10/51	England	Cardiff	1–1
20/11/51	Scotland	Glasgow	1–0
5/12/51	Rest of UK	Cardiff	3–2
19/3/52	N Ireland	Swansea	3–0
18/10/52	Scotland	Cardiff	1–2
12/11/52	England	Wembley	2–5
15/4/53	N Ireland	Belfast	3–2
14/5/53	France	Paris	1–6
21/5/53	Yugoslavia	Belgrade	2–5
10/10/53	England	Cardiff (WCQ)	1–4
4/11/53	Scotland	Glasgow (WCQ)	3–3
31/3/54	N Ireland	Wrexham (WCQ)	1–2
9/5/54	Austria	Vienna (ECQ)	0–2
22/9/54	Yugoslavia	Cardiff	1–3
16/10/54	Scotland	Cardiff	0–1
10/11/54	England	Wembley	2–3
20/4/55	N Ireland	Belfast	3–2
22/10/55	England	Cardiff	2–1
9/11/55	Scotland	Glasgow	0–2
23/11/55	Austria	Wrexham (ECQ)	1–2
11/4/56	N Ireland	Cardiff	1–1
20/10/56	Scotland	Cardiff	2–2
14/11/56	England	Wembley	1–3
10/4/57	N Ireland	Belfast	0–0
1/5/57	Czechoslovakia	Cardiff (WCQ)	1–0
19/5/57	E Germany	Leipzig (WCQ)	1–2
26/5/57	Czechoslovakia	Prague (WCQ)	0–2
25/9/57	E Germany	Cardiff (WCQ)	4–1
19/10/57	England	Cardiff	0–4
13/11/57	Scotland	Glasgow	1–1
15/1/58	Israel	Tel Aviv (WCQ)	2–0
5/2/58	Israel	Cardiff (WCQ)	2–0
16/4/58	N Ireland	Cardiff	1–1
8/6/58	Hungary	Sandviken (WCF)	1–1
11/6/58	Mexico	Stockholm (WCF)	1–1
15/6/58	Sweden	Stockholm (WCF)	0–0
17/6/58	Hungary	Stockholm (WCF)	2–1
19/6/58	Brazil	Gothenburg (WCF)	0–1
18/10/58	Scotland	Cardiff	0–3
26/11/58	England	Villa Park	2–2
22/4/59	N Ireland	Belfast	1–4
17/10/59	England	Cardiff	1–1
4/11/59	Scotland	Glasgow	1–1

1960–69

Results

Date	Opponents	Venue	F–A
6/4/60	N Ireland	Wrexham	3–2
28/9/60	Rep of Ireland	Dublin	3–2
22/10/60	Scotland	Cardiff	2–0
23/11/60	England	Wembley	1–5
12/4/61	N Ireland	Belfast	5–1
19/4/61	Spain	Cardiff (WCQ)	1–2
18/5/61	Spain	Madrid (WCQ)	1–1
28/5/61	Hungary	Budapest	2–3
14/10/61	England	Cardiff	1–1
8/11/61	Scotland	Glasgow	0–2
11/4/62	N Ireland	Cardiff	4–0
12/5/62	Brazil	Rio de Janeiro	1–3
16/5/62	Brazil	São Paulo	1–3
22/5/62	Mexico	Mexico City	1–2
20/10/62	Scotland	Cardiff	2–3
7/11/62	Hungary	Budapest (ECQ)	1–3
21/11/62	England	Wembley	0–4
20/3/63	Hungary	Cardiff (ECQ)	1–1
3/4/63	N Ireland	Belfast	4–1
12/10/63	England	Cardiff	0–4
20/11/63	Scotland	Glasgow	1–2
15/4/64	N Ireland	Swansea	2–3
3/10/64	Scotland	Cardiff	3–2
21/10/64	Denmark	Copenhagen (WCQ)	0–1
18/11/64	England	Wembley	1–2
9/12/64	Greece	Athens (WCQ)	0–2
17/2/65	Greece	Cardiff (WCQ)	4–1
31/3/65	N Ireland	Belfast	5–0
1/5/65	Italy	Florence	1–4
30/5/65	USSR	Moscow (WCQ)	1–2
2/10/65	England	Cardiff	0–0
27/10/65	USSR	Cardiff (WCQ)	2–1
24/11/65	Scotland	Glasgow (ECQ)	1–4
1/12/65	Denmark	Wrexham (WCQ)	4–2
30/3/66	N Ireland	Cardiff	1–4
14/5/66	Brazil	Rio de Janeiro	1–3
18/5/66	Brazil	Belo Horizonte	0–1
22/5/66	Chile	Santiago	0–2
22/10/66	Scotland	Cardiff (ECQ)	1–1
16/11/66	England	Wembley (ECQ)	1–5
12/4/67	N Ireland	Belfast (ECQ)	0–0
21/10/67	England	Cardiff (ECQ)	0–3
22/11/67	Scotland	Glasgow	2–3
28/2/68	N Ireland	Wrexham (ECQ)	2–0
8/5/68	W Germany	Cardiff	1–1
23/10/68	Italy	Cardiff (WCQ)	0–1
26/3/69	W Germany	Frankfurt	1–1
16/4/69	E Germany	Dresden (WCQ)	1–2
3/5/69	Scotland	Wrexham	3–5
7/5/69	England	Wembley	1–2

10/5/69	N Ireland	Belfast	0–0
28/7/69	Rest of UK	Cardiff	0–1
22/10/69	E Germany	Cardiff (WCQ)	1–3
4/11/69	Italy	Rome (WCQ)	1–4

1970

Results

Date	Opponents	Venue	F–A
18/4	England	Cardiff	1–1
22/4	Scotland	Glasgow	0–0
25/4	N Ireland	Swansea	1–0
11/11	Romania	Cardiff (ECQ)	0–0

1971

Results

Date	Opponents	Venue	F–A
21/4	Czechoslovakia	Swansea (ECQ)	1–3
15/5	Scotland	Cardiff	0–0
18/5	England	Wembley	0–0
22/5	N Ireland	Belfast	0–1
26/5	Finland	Helsinki (ECQ)	1–0
13/10	Finland	Swansea (ECQ)	3–0
27/10	Czechoslovakia	Prague (ECQ)	0–1
24/11	Romania	Bucharest (ECQ)	0–2

1972

Results

Date	Opponents	Venue	F–A
20/5	England	Cardiff	0–3
24/5	Scotland	Glasgow	0–1
27/5	N Ireland	Wrexham	0–0
15/11	England	Cardiff (WCQ)	0–1

1973

Results

Date	Opponents	Venue	F–A
24/1	England	Wembley (WCQ)	1–1
28/3	Poland	Cardiff (WCQ)	2–0
12/5	Scotland	Wrexham	0–2
15/5	England	Wembley	0–3
19/5	N Ireland	Liverpool	0–1
26/9	Poland	Chorzow (WCQ)	0–3

1974

Results

Date	Opponents	Venue	F–A
11/5	England	Cardiff	0–2
14/5	Scotland	Glasgow	0–2
18/5	N Ireland	Wrexham	1–0
4/9	Austria	Vienna (ECQ)	1–2
30/10	Hungary	Cardiff (ECQ)	2–0
20/11	Luxembourg	Swansea (ECQ)	5–0

1975

Results

Date	Opponents	Venue	F–A
16/4	Hungary	Budapest (ECQ)	2–1
1/5	Luxembourg	Luxembourg (ECQ)	3–1
17/5	Scotland	Cardiff	2–2
21/5	England	Wembley	2–2
23/5	N Ireland	Belfast	0–1
19/11	Austria	Wrexham (ECQ)	1–0

1976

Results

Date	Opponents	Venue	F–A
24/3	England	Wrexham	1–2
24/4	Yugoslavia	Zagreb (ECQ)	0–2
6/5	Scotland	Glasgow	1–3
8/5	England	Cardiff	0–1
14/5	N Ireland	Swansea	1–0
22/5	Yugoslavia	Cardiff (ECQ)	1–1
6/10	W Germany	Cardiff	0–2
17/11	Scotland	Glasgow (WCQ)	0–1

1977

Results

Date	Opponents	Venue	F–A
30/3	Czechoslovakia	Wrexham (WCQ)	3–0
28/5	Scotland	Wrexham	0–0
31/5	England	Wembley	1–0
3/6	N Ireland	Belfast	1–1
6/9	Kuwait	Wrexham	0–0
20/9	Kuwait	Kuwait	0–0
12/10	Scotland	Liverpool (WCQ)	0–2
16/11	Czechoslovakia	Prague (WCQ)	0–1
14/12	W Germany	Dortmund	1–1

1978

Results

Date	Opponents	Venue	F–A
18/4	Iran	Teheran	1–0
13/5	England	Cardiff	1–3
17/5	Scotland	Glasgow	1–1
19/5	N Ireland	Wrexham	1–0
25/10	Malta	Wrexham (ECQ)	7–0
29/11	Turkey	Wrexham (ECQ)	1–0

1979

Results

Date	Opponents	Venue	F–A
2/5	W Germany	Wrexham (ECQ)	0–2
19/5	Scotland	Cardiff	3–0
23/5	England	Wembley	0–0
25/5	N Ireland	Belfast	1–1
2/6	Malta	Valetta (ECQ)	2–0
11/9	Rep of Ireland	Swansea	2–1
17/10	W Germany	Cologne (ECQ)	1–5
21/11	Turkey	Izmir (ECQ)	0–1

1980

Results

Date	Opponents	Venue	F–A
17/5	England	Wrexham	4–1
21/5	Scotland	Glasgow	0–1
23/5	N Ireland	Cardiff	0–1
2/6	Iceland	Reykjavic (WCQ)	4–0
15/10	Turkey	Cardiff (WCQ)	4–0
19/11	Czechoslovakia	Cardiff (WCQ)	1–0

1981

Results

Date	Opponents	Venue	F–A
24/2	Rep of Ireland	Dublin	3–1
25/3	Turkey	Ankara (WCQ)	1–0
16/5	Scotland	Swansea	2–0
20/5	England	Wembley	0–0
30/5	USSR	Wrexham (WCQ)	0–0
9/9	Czechoslovakia	Prague (WCQ)	0–2
14/10	Iceland	Swansea (WCQ)	2–2
18/11	USSR	Tbilisi(WCQ)	0–3

1982

Results

Date	Opponents	Venue	F–A
24/3	Spain	Valencia	1–1
27/4	England	Cardiff	0–1
24/5	Scotland	Glasgow	0–1
27/5	N Ireland	Wrexham	3–0
2/6	France	Toulouse	1–0
22/9	Norway	Swansea (ECQ)	1–0
15/12	Yugoslavia	Titograd (ECQ)	4–4

1983

Results

Date	Opponents	Venue	F–A
23/2	England	Wembley	1–2
27/4	Bulgaria	Wrexham (ECQ)	1–0
28/5	Scotland	Cardiff	0–2
31/5	N Ireland	Belfast	1–0
12/6	Brazil	Cardiff	1–1
21/9	Norway	Oslo (ECQ)	0–0
12/10	Romania	Wrexham	5–0
16/11	Bulgaria	Sofia (ECQ)	0–1
14/12	Yugoslavia	Cardiff (ECQ)	1–1

1984

Results

Date	Opponents	Venue	F–A
28/2	Scotland	Glasgow	1–2
2/5	England	Wrexham	1–0
22/5	N Ireland	Swansea	1–1
6/6	Norway	Trondheim	0–1
10/6	Israel	Tel Aviv	0–0
12/9	Iceland	Reykjavik (WCQ)	0–1
17/10	Spain	Seville (WCQ)	0–3
14/11	Iceland	Cardiff (WCQ)	2–1

1985

Results

Date	Opponents	Venue	F–A
26/2	Norway	Wrexham	1–1
27/3	Scotland	Glasgow (WCQ)	1–0
30/4	Spain	Wrexham (WCQ)	3–0
5/6	Norway	Bergen	2–4
10/9	Scotland	Cardiff (WCQ)	1–1
16/10	Hungary	Cardiff	0–3

1986

Results

Date	Opponents	Venue	F–A
25/2	Saudi Arabia	Dhahran	2–1
26/3	Rep of Ireland	Dublin	1–0
21/4	Uruguay	Cardiff	0–0
10/5	Canada	Toronto	0–2
20/5	Canada	Vancouver	3–0
10/9	Finland	Helsinki (ECQ)	1–1

1987

Results

Date	Opponents	Venue	F–A
18/2	USSR	Swansea	0–0
1/4	Finland	Wrexham (ECQ)	4–0
29/4	Czechoslovakia	Wrexham (ECQ)	1–1
9/9	Denmark	Cardiff (ECQ)	1–0
14/10	Denmark	Copenhagen (ECQ)	0–1
11/11	Czechoslovakia	Prague (ECQ)	0–2

1988

Results

Date	Opponents	Venue	F–A
23/3	Yugoslavia	Swansea	1–2
27/4	Sweden	Stockholm	1–4
1/6	Malta	Valletta	3–2
4/6	Italy	Brescia	1–0
14/9	Holland	Amsterdam (WCQ)	0–1
19/10	Finland	Swansea (WCQ)	2–2

1989

Results

Date	Opponents	Venue	F–A
8/2	Israel	Tel Aviv	3–3
26/4	Sweden	Wrexham	0–2
31/5	W Germany	Cardiff (WCQ)	0–0
6/9	Finland	Helsinki (WCQ)	0–1
11/10	Holland	Wrexham (WCQ)	1–2
15/11	W Germany	Cologne (WCQ)	1–2

1990

Results

Date	Opponents	Venue	F–A
28/3	Rep of Ireland	Dublin	0–1
25/4	Sweden	Stockholm	2–4
20/5	Costa Rica	Cardiff	1–0
1/9	Denmark	Copenhagen	0–1
17/10	Belgium	Cardiff(ECQ) 3–1 14/11	
Luxembourg		Luxembourg (ECQ)	1–0

1991

Results

Date	Opponents	Venue	F–A
6/2	Rep of Ireland	Wrexham	0–3
27/3	Belgium	Brussels (ECQ)	1–1
1/5	Iceland	Cardiff	1–0
29/5	Poland	Radom	0–0
5/6	W Germany	Cardiff (ECQ)	1–0
11/9	Brazil	Cardiff	1–0
16/10	W Germany	Nüremberg (ECQ)	1–4
13/11	Luxembourg	Cardiff (ECQ)	1–0

1992

Results

Date	Opponents	Venue	F–A
19/2	Rep of Ireland	Dublin	1–0
29/4	Austria	Vienna	1–1
20/5	Romania	Bucharest (WCQ)	1–5
30/5	Holland	Utrecht	0–4
3/6	Argentina	Tokyo	0–1
7/6	Japan	Matsuyama	1–0
9/9	Faeroes	Cardiff (WCQ)	6–0
14/10	Cyprus	Limassol (WCQ)	1–0
18/11	Belgium	Brussels (WCQ)	0–2

1993

Results

Date	Opponents	Venue	F–A
17/2	Rep of Ireland	Dublin	1–2
31/3	Belgium	Cardiff (WCQ)	2–0
28/4	Czechoslovakia	Ostrava (WCQ)	1–1
6/6	Faeroes	Toftir (WCQ)	3–0
8/9	RCS*	Cardiff (WCQ)	2–2
13/10	Cyprus	Cardiff (WCQ)	2–0
17/11	Romania	Cardiff (WCQ)	1–2

* Representation of Czechs & Slovaks (was Czechoslovakia).

1994

Results

Date	Opponents	Venue	F–A
9/3	Norway	Cardiff	1–3
20/4	Sweden	Wrexham	0–2
23/5	Estonia	Tallinn	2–1
7/9	Albania	Cardiff (ECQ)	2–0
12/10	Moldova	Chislau (ECQ)	2–3
16/11	Georgia	Tbilisi (ECQ)	0–5
14/12	Bulgaria	Cardiff (ECQ)	0–3
7/9	Albania	Cardiff (ECQ)	2–0

1995

Results

Date	Opponents	Venue	F–A
29/3	Bulgaria	Sofia (ECQ)	1–3
26/4	Germany	Düsseldorf (ECQ)	1–1
7/6	Georgia	Cardiff (ECQ)	0–1
6/9	Moldova	Cardiff (ECQ)	1–0
11/10	Germany	Cardiff (ECQ)	1–2
15/11	Albania	Tirana (ECQ)	1–1

1996

Results

Date	Opponents	Venue	F–A
24/1	Italy	Terni	0–3
24/4	Switzerland	Lugano	0–2
2/6	San Marino	Sarravalle (WCQ)	5–0
31/8	San Marino	Cardiff (WCQ)	6–0
5/10	Holland	Cardiff	1–3
9/11	Holland	Eindhoven (WCQ)	1–7
14/12	Turkey	Cardiff (WCQ)	0–0

1997

Results

Date	Opponents	Venue	F–A
11/2	Rep of Ireland	Cardiff	0–0
29/3	Belgium	Cardiff (WCQ)	1–2
27/5	Scotland	Kilmarnock	1–0
20/8	Turkey	Istanbul (WCQ)	4–6
11/10	Belgium	Brussels (WCQ)	2–3
11/11	Brazil	Brasilia (WCQ)	0–3

NORTHERN IRELAND

League Champions

Winners

Year	Winners
1891	Linfield
1892	Linfield
1893	Linfield
1894	Glentoran
1895	Linfield
1896	Distillery
1897	Glentoran
1898	Glenfield
1899	Distillery
1900	Belfast Celtic
1901	Distillery
1902	Linfield
1903	Distillery
1904	Linfield
1905	Glentoran
1906	Cliftonville/ Distillery
1907	Linfield
1908	Linfield
1909	Linfield
1910	Cliftonville
1911	Linfield
1912	Glentoran
1913	Glentoran
1914	Linfield
1915	Belfast Celtic
1920	Belfast Celtic
1921	Glentoran
1922	Linfield
1923	Linfield
1924	Queen's Island
1925	Glentoran
1926	Belfast Celtic
1927	Belfast Celtic
1928	Belfast Celtic
1929	Belfast Celtic
1930	Linfield
1931	Glentoran
1932	Linfield
1933	Belfast Celtic
1934	Linfield
1935	Linfield
1936	Belfast Celtic
1937	Belfast Celtic
1938	Belfast Celtic
1939	Belfast Celtic
1940	Belfast Celtic
1948	Belfast Celtic
1949	Linfield
1950	Linfield
1951	Glentoran
1952	Glenavon
1953	Glentoran
1954	Linfield
1955	Linfield
1956	Linfield
1957	Glentoran
1958	Ards
1959	Linfield
1960	Glenavon
1961	Linfield
1962	Linfield
1963	Distillery
1964	Glentoran
1965	Derry City
1966	Linfield
1967	Glentoran
1968	Glentoran
1969	Linfield
1970	Glentoran
1971	Linfield
1972	Glentoran
1973	Crusaders
1974	Coleraine
1975	Linfield
1976	Crusaders
1977	Glentoran
1978	Linfield
1979	Linfield
1980	Linfield
1981	Linfield
1982	Linfield
1983	Linfield
1984	Linfield
1985	Linfield
1986	Linfield
1987	Linfield
1988	Glentoran
1989	Linfield
1990	Portadown
1991	Portadown
1992	Glentoran
1993	Linfield
1994	Linfield
1995	Crusaders
1996	Portadown
1997	Crusaders

Irish Cup Finals

Finalists

Year	Winners	Runners-up	Result
1881	Moyola Park	Cliftonville	1–0
1882	Queen's Island	Cliftonville	2–1
1883	Cliftonville	Ulster	5–0
1884	Distillery	Ulster	5–0
1885	Distillery	Limavady	2–0
1886	Distillery	Limavady	1–0
1887	Ulster	Cliftonville	3–1
1888	Cliftonville	Distillery	2–1
1889	Distillery	YMCA	5–4
1890	Gordon	Cliftonville	2–2, 3–0
1891	Linfield	Ulster	4–2
1892	Linfield	The Black Watch	7–0
1893	Linfield	Cliftonville	5–1
1894	Distillery	Linfield	2–2, 3–2
1895	Linfield	Bohemians	10–1
1896	Distillery	Glentoran	3–1
1897	Cliftonville	Sherwood	3–1
1898	Linfield	St Columbs Hall	2–0
1899	Linfield	Glentoran	1–0
1900	Cliftonville	Bohemians	2–1
1901	Cliftonville	Freebooters, Dublin	1–0
1902	Linfield	Distillery	5–1
1903	Distillery	Bohemians	3–1
1904	Linfield	Derry Celtic	5–0
1905	Distillery	Shelbourne	3–0
1906	Shelbourne	Belfast Celtic	2–0
1907	Cliftonville	Shelbourne	0–0, 1–0
1908	Bohemians	Shelbourne	1–1, 3–1
1909	Cliftonville	Bohemians	0–0, 2–1
1910	Distillery	Cliftonville	1–0
1911	Shelbourne	Bohemians	0–0, 2–1
1912	*Not played: Linfield awarded cup*		
1913	Linfield	Glentoran	2–0
1914	Glentoran	Linfield	3–1
1915	Linfield	Belfast Celtic	1–0
1916	Linfield	Glentoran	1–0
1917	Glentoran	Belfast Celtic	2–0
1918	Belfast Celtic	Linfield	0–0, 0–0, 2–0
1919	Linfield	Glentoran	1–1, 0–0, 2–1
1920	*Not played: Shelbourne awarded cup*		
1921	Glentoran	Glenavon	2–0

1922	Linfield	Glenavon	2–0
1923	Linfield	Glentoran	2–0
1924	Queen's Island	Willowfield	1–0
1925	Distillery	Glentoran	2–1
1926	Belfast Celtic	Linfield	3–2
1927	Ards	Cliftonville	3–2
1928	Willowfield	Larne	1–0
1929	Ballymena Utd	Belfast Celtic	2–1
1930	Linfield	Ballymena United	4–3
1931	Linfield	Ballymena United	3–0
1932	Glentoran	Linfield	2–1
1933	Glentoran	Distillery	1–1, 1–1, 3–1
1934	Linfield	Cliftonville	5–0
1935	Glentoran	Larne	0–0, 0–0, 1–0
1936	Linfield	Derry City	0–0, 2–1
1937	Belfast Celtic	Linfield	3–0
1938	Belfast Celtic	Bangor	0–0, 2–0
1939	Linfield	Ballymena Utd	2–0
1940	Ballymena Utd	Glenavon	2–0
1941	Belfast Celtic	Linfield	1–0
1942	Linfield	Glentoran	3–1
1943	Belfast Celtic	Glentoran	1–0
1944	Belfast Celtic	Linfield	3–1
1945	Linfield	Glentoran	4–2
1946	Linfield	Distillery	3–0
1947	Belfast Celtic	Glentoran	1–0
1948	Linfield	Coleraine	3–0
1949	Derry City	Glentoran	3–1
1950	Linfield	Distillery	2–1
1951	Glentoran	Ballymena Utd	3–1
1952	Ards	Glentoran	1–0
1953	Linfield	Coleraine	5–0
1954	Derry City	Glentoran	1–0
1955	Dundela	Glenavon	3–0
1956	Distillery	Glentoran	1–0
1957	Glenavon	Derry City	2–0
1958	Ballymena Utd	Linfield	2–0
1959	Glenavon	Ballymena Utd	2–0
1960	Linfield	Ards	5–1
1961	Glenavon	Linfield	5–1
1962	Linfield	Portadown	4–0
1963	Linfield	Distillery	2–1
1964	Derry City	Glentoran	2–0
1965	Coleraine	Glenavon	2–1
1966	Glentoran	Linfield	2–0
1967	Crusaders	Glentoran	3–1
1968	Crusaders	Linfield	2–0
1969	Ards	Distillery	4–2
1970	Linfield	Ballymena Utd	2–1
1971	Distillery	Derry City	3–0
1972	Coleraine	Portadown	2–1
1973	Glentoran	Linfield	3–2
1974	Ards	Ballymena Utd	2–1
1975	Coleraine	Linfield	1–1, 0–0, 1–0
1976	Carrick Rangers	Linfield	2–1
1977	Coleraine	Linfield	4–1

1978	Linfield	Ballymena Utd	3–1
1979	Cliftonville	Portadown	3–2
1980	Linfield	Crusaders	2–0
1981	Ballymena Utd	Glenavon	1–0
1982	Linfield	Coleraine	2–1
1983	Glentoran	Linfield	1–1, 2–1
1984	Ballymena Utd	Garrick Rangers	4–1
1985	Glentoran	Linfield	1–1, 1–0
1986	Glentoran	Coleraine	2–1
1987	Glentoran	Larne	1–0
1988	Glentoran	Glenavon	1–0
1989	Ballymena Utd	Larne	1–0
1990	Glentoran	Portadown	3–0
1991	Portadown	Glenavon	2–1
1992	Glenavon	Linfield	2–1
1993	Bangor	Ards	1–1, 1–1, 1–0
1994	Linfield	Bangor	2–0
1995	Linfield	Carrick Rangers	3–1
1996	Glentoran	Glenavon	1–0
1997	Glenavon	Cliftonville	1–0

Northern Ireland Internationals 1882–00

Results

Date	Opponents	Venue	F–A
18/2/82	England	Belfast	0–13
25/2/82	Wales	Wrexham	1–7
24/2/83	England	Liverpool	0–7
17/3/83	Wales	Belfast	1–1
26/1/84	Scotland	Belfast	0–5
9/2/84	Wales	Wrexham	0–6
23/2/84	England	Belfast	1–8
28/2/85	England	Manchester	0–4
14/3/85	Scotland	Glasgow	2–8
11/4/85	Wales	Belfast	2–8
27/2/86	Wales	Wrexham	0–5
13/3/86	England	Belfast	1–6
20/3/86	Scotland	Belfast	2–7
5/2/87	England	Sheffield	0–7
19/2/87	Scotland	Glasgow	1–4
12/3/87	Wales	Belfast	4–1
3/3/88	Wales	Wrexham	0–11
24/3/88	Scotland	Belfast	2–10
7/4/88	England	Belfast	1–5
2/3/89	England	Liverpool	1–6
9/3/89	Scotland	Glasgow	0–7
27/4/89	Wales	Belfast	1–3
8/2/90	Wales	Shrewsbury	2–5

15/3/90	England	Belfast	1–9
29/3/90	Scotland	Belfast	1–4
7/2/91	Wales	Belfast	7–2
7/3/91	England	Wolverhampton	1–6
28/3/91	Scotland	Glasgow	1–2
27/2/92	Wales	Bangor	1–1
5/3/92	England	Belfast	0–2
19/3/92	Scotland	Belfast	2–3
25/2/93	England	Birmingham	1–6
25/3/93	Scotland	Glasgow	1–6
5/4/93	Wales	Belfast	4–3
24/2/94	Wales	Swansea	1–4
3/3/94	England	Belfast	2–2
31/3/94	Scotland	Belfast	1–2
9/3/95	England	Derby	0–9
16/3/95	Wales	Belfast	2–2
30/3/95	Scotland	Glasgow	1–3
29/2/96	Wales	Wrexham	1–6
7/3/96	England	Belfast	0–2
28/3/96	Scotland	Belfast	3–3
20/2/97	England	Nottingham	0–6
6/3/97	Wales	Belfast	4–3
27/3/97	Scotland	Glasgow	1–5
19/2/98	Wales	Llandudno	1–0
5/3/98	England	Belfast	2–3
26/3/98	Scotland	Belfast	0–3
18/2/99	England	Sunderland	2–13
4/3/99	Wales	Belfast	1–0
25/3/99	Scotland	Glasgow	1–9

1900–09

Results

Date	Opponents	Venue	F–A
24/2/00	Wales	Llandudno	0–2
3/3/00	Scotland	Belfast	0–3
17/3/00	England	Dublin	0–2
23/2/01	Scotland	Glasgow	0–11
9/3/01	England	Southampton	0–3
23/3/01	Wales	Belfast	0–1
22/2/02	Wales	Cardiff	3–0
1/3/02	Scotland	Belfast	1–3
22/3/02	England	Belfast	0–1
14/2/03	England	Wolverhampton	0–4
21/3/03	Scotland	Glasgow	2–0
28/3/03	Wales	Belfast	2–0
12/3/04	England	Belfast	1–3
21/3/04	Wales	Bangor	1–0
26/3/04	Scotland	Dublin	1–1
25/2/05	England	Middlesbrough	1–1
18/3/05	Scotland	Glasgow	0–4
8/4/05	Wales	Belfast	2–2
17/2/06	England	Belfast	0–5
17/3/06	Scotland	Dublin	0–1
2/4/06	Wales	Wrexham	4–4
16/2/07	England	Liverpool	0–1
23/2/07	Wales	Belfast	2
16/3/07	Scotland	Glasgow	0–3
15/2/08	England	Belfast	1–3
14/3/08	Scotland	Dublin	0–5
11/4/08	Wales	Aberdare	1–0
13/2/09	England	Bradford	0–4
15/3/09	Scotland	Glasgow	0–5
20/3/09	Wales	Belfast	2–3

1900–09

Results

Date	Opponents	Venue	F–A
12/2/10	England	Belfast	1–1
19/3/10	Scotland	Belfast	1–0
11/4/10	Wales	Wrexham	1–4
28/1/11	Wales	Belfast	1–2
11/2/11	England	Derby	1–2
18/3/11	Scotland	Glasgow	0–2
10/2/12	England	Dublin	1–6
16/3/12	Scotland	Belfast	1–4
13/4/12	Wales	Cardiff	3–2
18/1/13	Wales	Belfast	0–1
15/2/13	England	Belfast	2–1
15/3/13	Scotland	Dublin	1–2
19/1/14	Wales	Wrexham	2–1
14/2/14	England	Middlesbrough	3–0
14/3/14	Scotland	Belfast	1–1
25/10/19	England	Belfast	1–1

1920–29

Results

Date	Opponents	Venue	F–A
14/2/20	Wales	Belfast	2–2
13/3/20	Scotland	Glasgow	0–3
23/10/20	England	Sunderland	0–2
26/2/21	Scotland	Belfast	0–2
9/4/21	Wales	Swansea	1–2
22/10/21	England	Belfast	1–1

4/3/22	Scotland	Glasgow	1–2
1/4/22	Wales	Belfast	1–1
21/10/22	England	West Bromwich	0–2
3/3/23	Scotland	Belfast	0–1
14/4/23	Wales	Wrexham	3–0
20/10/23	England	Belfast	2–1
1/3/24	Scotland	Glasgow	0–2
15/3/24	Wales	Belfast	0–1
22/10/24	England	Liverpool	1–3
28/2/25	Scotland	Belfast	0–3
18/4/25	Wales	Wrexham	0–0
24/10/25	England	Belfast	0–0
13/2/26	Wales	Belfast	3–0
27/2/26	Scotland	Glasgow	0–4
20/10/26	England	Liverpool	3–3
26/2/27	Scotland	Belfast	0–2
19/4/27	Wales	Cardiff	2–2
22/10/27	England	Belfast	2–0
4/2/28	Wales	Belfast	1–2
25/2/28	Scotland	Glasgow	1–0
22/10/28	England	Liverpool	1–2
2/2/29	Wales	Wrexham	2–2
23/2/29	Scotland	Belfast	3–7
19/10/29	England	Belfast	0–3

1930–39

Results

Date	Opponents	Venue	F–A
1/2/30	Wales	Belfast	0–7
22/2/30	Scotland	Glagow	1–3
20/10/30	England	Sheffield	1–5
21/2/31	Scotland	Belfast	0–0
22/4/31	Wales	Wrexham	2–3
19/9/31	Scotland	Glasgow	1–3
17/10/31	England	Belfast	2–6
5/12/31	Wales	Belfast	4–0
12/9/32	Scotland	Belfast	0–4
17/10/32	England	Blackpool	0–1
7/12/32	Wales	Wrexham	1–4
16/9/33	Scotland	Glasgow	2–1
14/10/33	England	Belfast	0–3
4/11/33	Wales	Belfast	1–1
20/10/34	Scotland	Belfast	2–1
6/2/35	England	Liverpool	1–2
27/3/35	Wales	Wrexham	1–3
19/10/35	England	Belfast	1–3
13/11/35	Scotland	Edinburgh	1–2
11/3/36	Wales	Belfast	3–2
31/10/36	Scotland	Belfast	1–3
18/11/36	England	Stoke–on–Trent	1–3
17/3/37	Wales	Wrexham	1–4
23/10/37	England	Belfast	1–5
10/11/37	Scotland	Aberdeen	1–1
16/3/38	Wales	Belfast	1–0
8/11/38	Scotland	Belfast	0–2
16/11/38	England	Manchester	0–7
15/3/39	Wales	Wrexham	1–3

1940–49

Results

Date	Opponents	Venue	F–A
28/9/40	England	Belfast	2–7
27/11/40	Scotland	Glasgow	0–0
16/4/47	Wales	Belfast	2–1
4/10/47	Scotland	Belfast	2–0
5/11/47	England	Everton	2–2
10/3/48	Wales	Wrexham	0–2
9/10/48	England	Belfast	2–6
17/11/48	Scotland	Glasgow	2–3
9/3/49	Wales	Belfast	0–2
1/10/49	Scotland	Belfast (WCQ)	2–8
6/11/49	England	Manchester (WCQ)	2–9

1950–59

Results

Date	Opponents	Venue	F–A
8/3/50	Wales	Wrexham (WCQ)	0–0
7/10/50	England	Belfast	1–4
1/11/50	Scotland	Glasgow	1–6
7/3/51	Wales	Belfast	1–2
12/5/51	France	Belfast	2–2
6/10/51	Scotland	Belfast	0–3
20/11/51	England	Villa Park	0–2
19/3/52	Wales	Swansea	0–3
4/10/52	England	Belfast	2–2
5/11/52	Scotland	Glasgow	1–1
11/11/52	France	Paris	1–3
15/4/53	Wales	Belfast	2–3
3/10/53	Scotland	Belfast (WCQ)	1–3
11/11/53	England	Everton (WCQ)	1–3
2/10/54	England	Belfast	0–2

3/11/54	Scotland	Glasgow	2–2
20/4/55	Wales	Belfast	2–3
8/10/55	Scotland	Belfast	2–1
2/11/55	England	Wembley	0–3
11/4/56	Wales	Cardiff	1–1
6/10/56	England	Belfast	1–1
7/11/56	Scotland	Glasgow	0–1
16/1/57	Portugal	Lisbon (WCQ)	1–1
10/4/57	Wales	Belfast	0–0
25/4/57	Italy	Rome (WCQ)	0–1
1/5/57	Portugal	Belfast (WCQ)	3–0
5/10/57	Scotland	Belfast	1–1
6/11/57	England	Wembley	3–2
4/12/57	Italy	Belfast	2–2
15/1/58	Italy	Belfast (WCQ)	2–1
16/4/58	Wales	Cardiff	1–1
11/6/58	Argentina	Halmstad (WCQ)	1–3
15/6/58	West Germany	Malmo	2–2
17/6/58	Czechoslovakia	Malmo (WCQ)	2–1
19/6/58	France	Norrkoping (WCQ)	0–4
4/10/59	England	Belfast	3–3
8/10/58	Czechoslovakia	Halmstad (WCQ)	1–0
15/10/58	Spain	Madrid	2–6
5/11/58	Scotland	Glasgow	2–2
22/4/59	Wales	Belfast	4–1
3/10/59	Scotland	Belfast	0–4
18/11/59	England	Wembley	1–2

1960–69

Results

Date	Opponents	Venue	F–A
6/4/60	Wales	Wrexham	2–3
8/10/60	England	Belfast	2–5
26/10/60	W Germany	Belfast (WCQ)	3–4
9/11/60	Scotland	Glasgow	2–5
12/4/61	Wales	Belfast	1–5
25/4/61	Italy	Bologna	2–3
3/5/61	Greece	Athens (WCQ)	1–2
10/5/61	W Germany	Berlin (WCQ)	1–2
7/10/61	Scotland	Belfast	1–6
17/10/61	Greece	Belfast (WCQ)	2–0
22/11/61	England	Wembley	1–1
11/4/62	Wales	Cardiff	0–4
9/5/62	Holland	Rotterdam	0–4
10/10/62	Poland	Katowice (WCQ)	2–0
20/10/62	England	Belfast	1–3
7/11/62	Scotland	Glasgow	1–5
28/11/62	Poland	Belfast (WCQ)	2–0
3/4/63	Wales	Belfast	1–4
30/5/63	Spain	Bilbao	1–1
12/10/63	Scotland	Belfast	2–1
30/10/63	Spain	Belfast	0–1
20/11/63	England	Wembley	3–8
15/4/6[illegible]	[illegible]	Swansea	3–2
29/4/6[illegible]	[illegible]guay	Belfast	3–0
3/10/64	England	Belfast	3–4
14/10/64	Switzerland	Belfast (WCQ)	1–0
14/11/64	Switzerland	Lausanne (WCQ)	1–2
25/11/64	Scotland	Glasgow	2–3
17/3/65	Holland	Belfast (WCQ)	2–1
31/3/65	Wales	Belfast	0–5
7/4/65	Holland	Rotterdam (WCQ)	0–0
7/5/65	Albania	Belfast (WCQ)	4–1
2/10/65	Scotland	Belfast	3–2
10/11/65	England	Wembley	1–2
24/11/65	Albania	Tirana (WCQ)	1–1
30/3/66	Wales	Cardiff	4–1
7/5/66	W Germany	Belfast	0–2
22/6/66	Mexico	Belfast	4–1
22/10/66	England	Belfast (WCQ)	0–2
16/11/66	Scotland	Glasgow	1–2
12/4/67	Wales	Belfast (WCQ)	0–0
21/10/67	Scotland	Belfast	1–0
22/11/67	England	Wembley (WCQ)	0–2
28/2/68	Wales	Wrexham (ECQ)	0–2
10/9/68	Israel	Jaffa	3–2
23/10/68	Turkey	Belfast (WCQ)	4–1
11/12/68	Turkey	Istanbul (WCQ)	3–0
3/5/69	England	Belfast	1–3
6/5/69	Scotland	Glasgow	1–1
10/5/69	Wales	Belfast	0–0
10/9/69	USSR	Belfast (WCQ)	0–0
22/10/69	USSR	Moscow (WCQ)	0–2

1970

Results

Date	Opponents	Venue	F–A
18/4	Scotland	Belfast	0–1
21/4	England	Wembley	1–3
25/4	Wales	Swansea	0–1
11/11	Spain	Seville (ECQ)	0–3

1971

Results

Date	Opponents	Venue	F–A
3/2	Cyprus	Nicosia (ECQ)	3–0
21/4	Cyprus	Belfast (ECQ)	5–0
15/5	England	Belfast	0–1
18/5	Scotland	Glasgow	1–0
22/5	Wales	Belfast	1–0
22/9	USSR	Moscow (ECQ)	0–1
13/10	USSR	Belfast (ECQ)	1–1

1972

Results

Date	Opponents	Venue	F–A
16/2	Spain	Hull (ECQ)	1–1
20/5	Scotland	Glasgow	0–2
23/5	England	Wembley	1–0
27/5	Wales	Wrexham	0–0
18/10	Bulgaria	Sofia (WCQ)	0–3

1973

Results

Date	Opponents	Venue	F–A
14/2	Cyprus	Nicosia (WCQ)	0–1
28/3	Portugal	Coventry (WCQ)	1–1
8/5	Cyprus	London (WCQ)	3–0
12/5	England	Liverpool	1–2
16/5	Scotland	Glasgow	2–1
19/5	Wales	Liverpool	1–0
26/9	Bulgaria	Hillsborough (WCQ)	0–0
14/11	Portugal	Lisbon (WCQ)	1–1

1974

Results

Date	Opponents	Venue	F–A
11/5	Scotland	Glasgow	1–0
15/5	England	Wembley	0–1
18/5	Wales	Wrexham	0–1
4/9	Norway	Oslo (ECQ)	1–2
30/10	Sweden	Solna (ECQ)	2–0

1975

Results

Date	Opponents	Venue	F–A
16/3	Yugoslavia	Belfast (ECQ)	1–0
17/5	England	Belfast	0–0
20/5	Scotland	Glasgow	0–3
23/5	Wales	Belfast	1–0
3/9	Sweden	Belfast (ECQ)	1–2
29/10	Norway	Belfast (ECQ)	3–0
19/11	Yugoslavia	Belgrade (ECQ)	0–1

1976

Results

Date	Opponents	Venue	F–A
24/3	Israel	Tel Aviv	1–1
8/5	Scotland	Glasgow	0–3
11/5	England	Wembley	0–4
14/5	Wales	Swansea	0–1
13/10	Holland	Rotterdam (WCQ)	2–2
10/11	Belgium	Liège (WCQ)	0–2

1977

Results

Date	Opponents	Venue	F–A
27/4	W Germany	Cologne	0–5
28/5	England	Belfast	1–2
1/6	Scotland	Glasgow	0–2
3/6	Wales	Belfast	1–1
11/6	Iceland	Reykjavik (WCQ)	0–1
21/9	Iceland	Belfast (WCQ)	2–0
12/10	Holland	Belfast (WCQ)	0–1
16/11	Belgium	Belfast (WCQ)	3–0

1978

Results

Date	Opponents	Venue	F–A
13/5	Scotland	Glasgow	1–1
16/5	England	Wembley	0–1
19/5	Wales	Wrexham	0–1
20/9	Rep of Ireland	Dublin (ECQ)	0–0
25/10	Denmark	Belfast (ECQ)	2–1
29/11	Bulgaria	Sofia (ECQ)	2–0

1979

Results

Date	Opponents	Venue	F–A
7/2	England	Wembley (ECQ)	0–4
2/5	Bulgaria	Belfast (ECQ)	2–0
19/5	England	Belfast	0–2
22/5	Scotland	Glasgow	0–1
25/5	Wales	Belfast	1–1
6/6	Denmark	Copenhagen (ECQ)	0–4
17/10	England	Belfast (ECQ)	1–5
21/11	Rep of Ireland	Belfast (ECQ)	1–0

1980

Results

Date	Opponents	Venue	F–A
26/3	Israel	Tel Aviv (WCQ)	0–0
16/5	Scotland	Belfast	1–0
20/5	England	Wembley	1–1
23/5	Wales	Cardiff	1–0
11/6	Australia	Sydney	2–1
15/6	Australia	Melbourne	1–1
18/6	Australia	Adelaide	2–1
15/10	Sweden	Belfast (WCQ)	3–0
19/11	Portugal	Lisbon (WCQ)	0–1

1981

Results

Date	Opponents	Venue	F–A
25/3	Scotland	Glasgow (WCQ)	1–1
29/4	Portugal	Belfast (WCQ)	1–0
19/5	Scotland	Glasgow	0–2
3/6	Sweden	Stockholm (WCQ)	0–1
14/10	Scotland	Belfast (WCQ)	0–0
18/11	Israel	Belfast (WCQ)	1–0

1982

Results

Date	Opponents	Venue	F–A
23/2	England	Wembley	0–4
24/3	France	Paris	0–4
28/4	Scotland	Belfast	1–1
27/5	Wales	Wrexham	0–3
17/6	Yugoslavia	Zaragoza (WCF))	0–0
21/6	Honduras	Zaragoza (WCF)	1–1
25/6	Spain	Valencia (WCF)	1–0
1/7	Austria	Madrid (WCF)	2–2
4/7	France	Madrid (WCF)	1–4
13/10	Austria	Vienna (ECQ)	0–2
17/11	W Germany	Belfast (ECQ)	1–0
15/12	Albania	Tirana (ECQ)	0–0

1983

Results

Date	Opponents	Venue	F–A
30/3	Turkey	Belfast (ECQ)	2–1
27/4	Albania	Belfast (ECQ)	1–0
24/5	Scotland	Glasgow (ECQ)	0–0
28/5	England	Belfast	0–0
31/5	Wales	Belfast	0–1
21/9	Austria	Belfast (ECQ)	3–1
12/10	Turkey	Ankara (ECQ)	0–1
16/11	W Germany	Hamburg (ECQ)	1–0
13/12	Scotland	Belfast	2–0

1984

Results

Date	Opponents	Venue	F–A
4/4	England	Wembley	0–1
22/5	Wales	Swansea	1–1
27/5	Finland	Pori (WCQ)	0–1
12/9	Romania	Belfast (WCQ)	3–2
16/10	Israel	Belfast	3–0
14/11	Finland	Belfast (WCQ)	2–1

1985

Results

Date	Opponents	Venue	F–A
27/2	England	Belfast (WCQ)	0–1
27/3	Spain	Palma	0–0
1/5	Turkey	Belfast (WCQ)	2–0
11/9	Turkey	Izmir (WCQ)	0–0
16/10	Romania	Bucharest (WCQ)	1–0
13/11	England	Wembley (WCQ)	0–0

1986

Results

Date	Opponents	Venue	F–A
26/2	France	Paris	0–0
26/3	Denmark	Belfast	1–1
23/4	Morocco	Belfast	2–1
3/6	Algeria	Guadalajara (WCF)	1–1
7/6	Spain	Guadalajara (WCF)	1–2
12/6	Brazil	Guadalajara (WCF)	0–3
15/10	England	Wembley (ECQ)	0–3
12/11	Turkey	Izmir (ECQ)	0–0

1987

Results

Date	Opponents	Venue	F–A
18/2	Israel	Tel Aviv	1–1
1/4	England	Belfast (ECQ)	0–2
29/4	Yugoslavia	Belfast (ECQ)	1–2
14/10	Yugoslavia	Sarajevo (ECQ)	0–3
11/11	Turkey	Belfast (ECQ)	1–0

1988

Results

Date	Opponents	Venue	F–A
17/2	Greece	Athens	2–3
23/3	Poland	Belfast	1–1
27/4	France	Belfast	0–0
21/5	Malta	Belfast(WCQ)	3–0
14/9	Rep of Ireland	Belfast (WCQ)	0–0
19/10	Hungary	Budapest (WCQ)	0–1
21/12	Spain	Seville (WCQ)	0–4

1989

Results

Date	Opponents	Venue	F–A
8/2	Spain	Belfast (WCQ)	0–2
26/4	Malta	Valletta (WCQ)	2–0
26/5	Chile	Belfast	0–1
6/9	Hungary	Belfast (WCQ)	1–2
11/10	Rep of Ireland	Dublin (WCQ)	0–3

1990

Results

Date	Opponents	Venue	F–A
27/3	Norway	Belfast	2–3
18/5	Uruguay	Belfast	1–0
12/9	Yugoslavia	Belfast (ECQ)	0–2
17/10	Denmark	Belfast (ECQ)	1–1
14/11	Austria	Vienna (ECQ)	0–0

1991

Results

Date	Opponents	Venue	F–A
5/2	Poland	Belfast	3–1
27/3	Yugoslavia	Belgrade (ECQ)	1–4
1/5	Faeroes	Belfast (ECQ)	1–1
11/9	Faeroes	Landsrona (ECQ)	5–0
16/10	Austria	Belfast (ECQ)	2–1
13/11	Denmark	Odense (ECQ)	1–2

1992

Results

Date	Opponents	Venue	F–A
28/4	Lithuania	Belfast (WCQ)	2–2
2/6	Germany	Bremen	1–1
9/9	Albania	Belfast (WCQ)	3–0
14/10	Spain	Belfast (WCQ)	0–0
18/11	Denmark	Belfast (WCQ)	0–1

1993

Results

Date	Opponents	Venue	F–A
17/2	Albania	Tirana (WCQ)	2–1
31/3	Rep of Ireland	Dublin (WCQ)	0–3
28/4	Spain	Seville (WCQ)	1–3
25/5	Lithuania	Vilnius (WCQ)	1–0
2/6	Latvia	Riga (WCQ)	2–1
8/9	Latvia	Belfast (WCQ)	2–0
13/10	Denmark	Copenhagen (WCQ)	0–1
17/11	Rep of Ireland	Belfast (WCQ)	1–1

1994

Results

Date	Opponents	Venue	F–A
20/4	Liechtenstein	Belfast (ECQ)	4–1
3/6	Colombia	Boston	0–2
12/6	Mexico	Miami	0–3
7/9	Portugal	Belfast (ECQ)	1–2
12/10	Austria	Vienna (ECQ)	2–1
16/11	Rep of Ireland	Belfast (ECQ)	0–4

1995

Results

Date	Opponents	Venue	F–A
29/3	Rep of Ireland	Dublin (ECQ)	1–1
26/4	Latvia	Riga (ECQ)	1–0
22/5	Canada	Edmonton	0–2
25/5	Chile	Edmonton	1–2
7/6	Latvia	Belfast (ECQ)	1–2
26/4	Latvia	Riga	1–0
3/9	Portugal	Lisbon (ECQ)	1–1
11/10	Liechtenstein	Eschen (ECQ)	4–0
15/11	Austria	Belfast (ECQ)	5–3

1996

Results

Date	Opponents	Venue	F–A
27/3	Norway	Belfast	0–2
24/4	Sweden	Belfast	1–2
29/5	Germany	Belfast	1–1
31/8	Ukraine	Belfast (WCQ)	0–1
5/10	Armenia	Belfast (WCQ)	1–1
9/11	Germany	Nüremburg (WCQ)	1–1
14/12	Albania	Belfast (WCQ)	2–0

1997

Results

Date	Opponents	Venue	F–A
29/3	Portugal	Belfast (WCQ)	0–0
2/4	Ukraine	Kiev (WCQ)	1–2
30/4	Armenia	Yerevan (WCQ)	0–0
21/5	Thailand	Bangkok	0–0
2/8	Germany	Belfast (WCQ)	1–3
10/9	Albania	Zurich (WCQ)	0–1
11/10	Portugal	Lisbon (WCQ)	0–1

Football Records

A selection of the biggest and best, smallest and worst. From highest scores to highest attendance, look no further…

CLUB

Highest scores:

Arbroath 36, Bon Accord (Aberdeen) 0 (Scottish Cup 1st Round, September 12, 1885). Dundee Harp 35, Aberdeen Rovers 0 (Scottish Cup 1st Round, September 12, 1885).
First–class match: Arbroath 36, Bon Accord 0 (Scottish Cup 1st Round, September 12, 1885).
International match: Ireland 0, England 13 (February 18, 1882).
FA Cup: Preston North End 26, Hyde United 0 (1st Round, October 15, 1887).
League Cup: West Ham United 10, Bury 0 (2nd Round, 1st Leg, October 25, 1983); Liverpool 10, Fulham 0 (2nd Round, 1st Leg, September 23, 1986).

Record aggregates:

League Cup: Liverpool 13, Fulham 2 (10–0h, 3–2a), September 23–October 7, 1986). West Ham United 12, Bury 1 (2–1a, 10–0h), October 4–25, 1983. Liverpool 11, Exeter City 0 (5–0h, 6–0a), October 7–28, 1981.
Premier League: *(Home)* Manchester United 9, Ipswich Town 0 (March 4, 1995). *(Away)* Sheffield Wednesday 1, Nottingham Forest 7 (April 1, 1995).
First Division: *(Home)* WBA 12, Darwen 0 (April 4, 1892); Nottingham Forest 12, Leicester Fosse 0 (April 21, 1909). *(Away)* Newcastle United 1, Sunderland 9 (December 5, 1908); Cardiff City 1, Wolverhampton Wanderers 9 (September 3, 1955).
Second Division: *(Home)* Newcastle United 13, Newport County 0 (October 5, 1946). *(Away)* Burslem PV 0, Sheffield United 10 (December 10, 1892).
Third Division: *(Home)* Gillingham 10, Chesterfield 0 (September 5, 1987).
(Away) Halifax Town 0, Fulham 8 (September 16, 1969).
Third Division South: *(Home)* Luton Town 12, Bristol Rovers 0 (April 13, 1936).
(Away) Northampton Town 0, Walsall 8 (February 2, 1947).
Third Division North: *(Home)* Stockport County 13, Halifax Town 0 (January 6, 1934).
(Away) Accrington Stanley 0, Barnsley 9 (February 3, 1934).
Fourth Division: *(Home)* Oldham Athletic 11, Southport 0 (December 26, 1962). *(Away)* Crewe Alexandra 1, Rotherham United 8 (September 8, 1973).
Third Division North: Tranmere Rovers 13, Oldham Athletic 4 (December 26, 1935).
Scottish Premier Division: *(Home)* Aberdeen 8, Motherwell 0 (March 26, 1979). *(Away)* Hamilton Academicals 0, Celtic 8 (November 5, 1988).
Scottish Division One: *(Home)* Celtic 11, Dundee 0 (October 26, 1895).
(Away) Airdrieonians 1, Hibernian 11 (October 24, 1950).
Scottish Division Two: *(Home)* Airdrieonians 15, Dundee Wanderers 1 (December 1, 1894).
(Away) Alloa Athletic 0, Dundee 10 (March 8, 1947).

Internationals:

France 0, England 15 (Amateur match, 1906).
Ireland 0, England 13 (February 18, 1882).

England 9, Scotland 3 (April 15, 1961).
Biggest England win at Wembley: England 9, Luxembourg 0 (European Championship qualifier, December 15, 1982). Scotland 11, Ireland 0 (February 23, 1901). Northern Ireland 7, Wales 0 (February 1, 1930). Wales 11, Ireland 0 (March 3, 1888).
Republic of Ireland 8, Malta 0 (European Championship qualifier, November 16, 1983).
Record international defeats: Hungary 7, England 1 (May 23, 1954). England 9, Scotland 3 (April 15, 1961). Ireland 0, England 13 (February 18, 1882).
Scotland 9, Wales 0 (March 23, 1878).
Brazil 7, Republic of Ireland 0 (May 27, 1982).
World Cup qualifying round: Maldives 0, Iran 17 (June 2, 1997).
World Cup Finals: Hungary 10, El Salvador 1 (Spain, June 15, 1982). Hungary 9, South Korea 0 (Switzerland, June 17, 1954).
Yugoslavia 9, Zaire 0 (West Germany, June 18, 1974).

League:

FA Premier League: Manchester United 9, Ipswich Town 0 (March 4, 1995).
Record away win: Sheffield Wednesday 1, Nottingham Forest 7 (April 1, 1995).
Football League (old 1st Division): Aston Villa 12, Accrington 2 (March 12, 1892).
Tottenham Hotspur 10, Everton 4 (October 11, 1958; highest 1st Division aggregate this century).
West Bromwich Albion 12, Darwen 0 (April 4, 1892).
Nottingham Forest 12, Leicester Fosse 0 (April 12, 1909).
Record away wins: Cardiff City 1, Wolverhampton Wanderers 9 (September 3, 1955).
New 1st Division: Bolton Wanderers 7, Swindon Town 0 (March 8, 1997).
Old 2nd Division: Manchester City 11, Lincoln City 3 (March 23, 1895).
Newcastle United 13, Newport County 0 (October 5, 1946). Small Heath 12, Walsall Town Swifts 0 (December 17, 1892). Darwen 12, Walsall 0 (December 26, 1896).
Small Heath 12, Doncaster Rovers 0 (April 11, 1903).
Record away win: Burstem Port Vale 0, Sheffield United 10 (December 10, 1892).
New 2nd Division: Hartlepool 1, Plymouth Argyle 8 (May 7, 1994).
Old 3rd Division: Gillingham 10, Chesterfield 0 (September 5, 1987). Tranmere Rovers 9, Accrington Stanley 0 (April 18, 1959).
Brighton and Hove Albion 9, Southend United 1 (November 22, 1965).
Brentford 9, Wrexham 0 (October 15, 1963).
Record away win: Halifax Town 0, Fulham 8 (September 16, 1969).
New 3rd Division: Torquay United 1, Scunthorpe United 8 (October 28, 1995).
3rd Division (North): Stockport County 13, Halifax Town 0 (January 6, 1934).
Tranmere Rovers 13, Oldham Athletic 4 (December 26, 1935; highest Football League aggregate).
Record away win: Accrington Stanley 0, Barnsley 9 (February 3, 1934).
3rd Division (South): Luton Town 12, Bristol Rovers 0 (April 13, 1936).
Gillingham 9, Exeter City 4 (January 7, 1951).
Record away win: Northampton Town 0, Walsall 8 (April 8, 1947).
Old 4th Division: Oldham Athletic 11, Southport 0 (December 26, 1962). Hartlepool United 10, Barrow 1 (April 4, 1959).
Wrexham 10, Hartlepool United 1 (March 3, 1962).
Record away win: Crewe Alexandra 1, Rotherham United 8 (September 8, 1973).
Scottish Premier Division: Aberdeen 8, Motherwell 0 (March 26, 1979).
Kilmarnock 1, Rangers 8 (September 6, 1980).
Hamilton 0, Celtic 8 (November 5, 1988).
Record aggregate: Celtic 8, Hamilton 3 (January 3, 1987).
Scottish League Division One: Celtic 11, Dundee 0 (October 26, 1895).
Record away win: Airdrie 1, Hibernian 11 (October 24, 1959).
Scottish League Division Two: Airdrieonians 15, Dundee Wanderers 1 (December 1, 1894).
Record British score this century: Stirling Albion 20, Selkirk 0
(Scottish Cup 1st Round, December 8, 1984).

Longest series of consecutive championships:
Three clubs have won the League Championship three years in succession: Huddersfield Town (1923–24, 1924–25, 1925–26), Arsenal (1932–33, 1933–34, 1934–35), and Liverpool (1981–82, 1982–83, 1983–84).
Both Celtic (1965–66, 1966–67, 1967–68, 1968–69, 1969–70, 1970–71, 1971–72, 1972–73, 1973–74) and Rangers (1988–89, 1989–90, 1990–91, 1991–92, 1992–93, 1993–94, 1994–95, 1995–96, 1996–97) have won the Scottish League Championship nine years in succession.

Most goals scored in a season:

Premier League: Newcastle United (82 goals, 42 games, 1993–94).
Division One: Aston Villa (128 goals, 42 games, 1930–31).
Division Two: Middlesbrough (122 goals, 42 games, 1926–27).

Division Three South: Millwall (127 goals, 42 games, 1927–28).
Division Three North: Bradford City (128 goals, 42 games, 1928–29).
Division Three: QPR (111 goals, 46 games, 1961–62).
Division Four: Peterborough United (134 goals, 46 games, 1960–61).
Scottish Premier Division: Rangers (101 goals, 44 games, 1991–92), Dundee United (90 goals, 36 games, 1982–83), Celtic (90 goals, 36 games, 982–83).
Scottish Division One: Hearts (132 goals, 34 games, 1957–58).
Scottish Division Two: Raith Rovers (142 goals, 34 games, 1937–38).
New Division One: Dunfermline Athletic (93 goals, 44 games, 1993–94), Motherwell (93 goals, 39 games, 1981–82).
New Division Two: Ayr United (95 goals, 39 games, 1987–88).
New Division Three: Forfar Athletic (74 goals, 36 games, 1996–97).

Fewest goals scored in a season:

Premier League: Leeds United (28 goals, 38 games, 1996–97).
(Minimum 42 games):
Division One: Stoke City (24 goals, 42 games, 1984–85).
Division Two: Watford (24 goals, 42 games, 1971–72); Leyton Orient (30 goals, 46 games, 1994–95).
Division Three South: Crystal Palace (33 goals, 42 games, 1950–51).
Division Three North: Crewe Alexandra (32 goals, 42 games, 1923–24).
Division Three: Stockport County (27 goals, 46 games, 1969–70).
Division Four: Crewe Alexandra (29 goals, 46 games, 1981–82).
(Minimum 30 games):
Scottish Premier Division: Hamilton Academicals (19 goals, 36 games, 1988–89); Dunfermline Athletic (22 goals, 44 games, 1991–92).
Scottish Division One: Brechin City (30 goals, 44 games, 1993–94); Ayr United (20 goals, 34 games, 1966–67).
Scottish Division Two: Lochgelly United (20 goals, 38 games, 1923–24).
New Division One: Stirling Albion (18 goals, 39 games, 1980–81); Dumbarton (23 goals, 36 games, 1995–96).
New Division Two: Berwick Rangers (22 goals, 36 games, 1994–95).
New Division Three: Alloa Athletic (26 goals, 36 games, 1995–96).

Most goals against in a season:

Premier League: Swindon Town (100 goals, 42 games, 1993–94).
First Division: Blackpool (125 goals, 42 games, 1930–31).
Second Division: Darwen (141 goals, 34 games, 1898–99).
Third Division South: Merthyr Tydfil (135 goals, 42 games, 1929–30).
Third Division North: Nelson (136 goals, 42 games, 1927–28).
Third Division: Accrington Stanley (123 goals, 46 games, 1959–60).
Fourth Division: Hartlepool United (109 goals, 46 games, 1959–60).
Scottish Premier Division: Morton (100 goals, 44 games, 1987–88, and from 36 games, 1984–85).
Scottish Division One: Leith Athletic (137 goals, 38 games, 1931–32).
Scottish Division Two: Edinburgh City (146 goals, 38 games, 1931–32).
New Division One: Queen of the South (99 goals, 39 games, 1988–89); Cowdenbeath (109 goals, 44 games, 1992–93).
New Division Two: Meadowbank Thistle (89 goals, 39 games, 1977–78).
New Division Three: Albion Rovers (82 goals, 36 games, 1994–95).

Fewest goals against in a season:

Premier League: Arsenal (28 goals, 42 games, 1993–94); Manchester United (28 goals, 42 games, 1994–95).
(Minimum 42 games):
First Division: Liverpool (16 goals, 42 games, 1978–79).
Second Division: Manchester United (23 goals, 42 games, 1924–25); West Ham United (34 goals, 46 games, 1990–91).
Third Division South: Southampton (21 goals, 42 games, 1921–22).
Third Division North: Port Vale (21 goals, 46 games, 1953–54).
Third Division: Gillingham (20 goals, 46 games, 1995–96).
Fourth Division: Lincoln City (25 goals, 46 games, 1980–81).

(Minimum 30 games):
Scottish Premier Division: Rangers (19 goals, 36 games, 1989–90); Rangers (23 goals, 44 games, 1986–87); Celtic (23 goals, 44 games, 1987–88).
Scottish Division One: Celtic (14 goals, 38 games, 1913–14).
Scottish Division Two: Morton (20 goals, 38 games, 1966–67).
New Division One: St. Johnstone (23 goals, 36 games, 1996–97); Hibernian (24 goals, 39 games, 1980–81); Falkirk (32 goals, 44 games, 1993–94).
New Division Two: St. Johnstone (24 goals, 39 games, 1987–88);
Stirling Albion (24 goals, 39 games, 1990–91).
New Division Three: Brechin City (21 goals, 36 games, 1995–96).

Most points in a season:

Two points for a win:
First Division: Liverpool (1978–79), 68 points from 42 matches.
Second Division: Tottenham Hotspur (1919–20), 70 points from 42 matches.
Third Division: Aston Villa (1971–72), 70 points from 46 matches.
Third Division South: Nottingham Forest (1950–51) and Bristol City (1954–55), 70 points from 46 matches.
Third Division North: Doncaster Rovers (1946–47), 72 points from 42 matches.
Fourth Division: Lincoln City (1975–76), 74 points from 46 matches.
Scottish Premier Division: Aberdeen (1984–85), 59 points from 36 matches;
Rangers (1992–93), 73 points from 44 matches.
Scottish Division One: Rangers (1920–21), 76 points from 42 matches.
Scottish Division Two: Morton (1966–67), 69 points from 38 matches.
New Division One: St. Mirren (1976–77), 62 points from 39 matches;
Falkirk (1993–94), 66 points from 44 matches.
New Division Two: Forfar Athletic (1983–84), 63 points from 39 matches.
Three points for a win:
Premier League: Manchester United (1993–94), 92 points from 42 matches.
Old First Division: Everton (1984–85), 90 points from 42 matches;
Liverpool (1987–88), 90 points from 40 matches.
New First Division: Bolton Wanderers (1996–97), 98 points from 46 matches.
Old Second Division: Chelsea (1988–89), 99 points from 46 matches.
New Second Division: Stoke City (1992–93), 93 points from 46 matches.
Old Third Division: Bournemouth (1986–87), 97 points from 46 matches.
New Third Division: Carlisle United (1994–95), 91 points from 42 matches.
Fourth Division: Swindon Town (1985–86), 102 points from 46 matches.
Scottish Premier Division: Rangers (1995–96), 87 points from 36 matches.
Scottish Division One: St. Johnstone (1996–97), 80 points from 36 matches.
Scottish Division Two: Stirling Albion (1995–96), 81 points from 36 matches.
Scottish Division Three: Forfar Athletic (1994–95), 80 points from 36 matches.

Fewest points in a season:

Premier League: Ipswich Town (1994–95), 27 points from 42 matches.
(Minimum 34 games):
First Division: Stoke Coity (1984–85), 17 points from 42 matches.
Second Division: Doncaster Rovers (1904–05), 8 points from 34 matches; Loughborough Town (1899–1900), 8 points from 34 matches;
Walsall (1988–89), 31 points from 46 matches.
Third Division: Rochdale (1973–74), 21 points from 46 matches;
Cambridge United (1984–85), 21 points from 46 matches.
Third Division South: Merthyr Tydfil (1924–25, and 1929–30), 21 points from 42 matches;
QPR (1925–26), 21 points from 42 matches.
Third Division North: Rochdale (1931–32), 11 points from 40 matches.
Fourth Division: Workington (1976–77), 19 points from 46 matches.
(Minimum 30 games):
Scottish Premier Division: St. Johnstone (1975–76), 11 points from 36 matches;
Morton (1987–88), 16 points from 44 matches.
Scottish Division One: Stirling Albion (1954–55), 6 points from 30 matches.
Scottish Division Two: Edinburgh City (1936–37), 7 points from 34 matches.
New Division One: Queen of the South (1988–89), 10 points from 39 matches;
Cowdenbeath (1992–93), 13 points from 44 matches.
New Division Two: Berwick Rangers (1987–88), 16 points from 39 matches;
Stranraer (1987–88), 16 points from 39 matches.
New Division Three: Albion Rovers (1994–95), 18 points from 36 matches.

Most wins in a season:

Premier League: Manchester United (1993–94) and Blackburn Rovers (1994–95), 27 wins from 42 matches.
First Division: Tottenham Hotspur (1960–61), 31 wins from 42 matches.
Second Division: Tottenham Hotspur (1919–20), 32 wins from 42 matches.
Third Division South: Millwall (1927–28), Plymouth Argyle (1929–30) and Cardiff City (1946–47), 30 wins from 42 matches; Nottingham Forest (1950–51) and Bristol City (1954–55), 30 wins from 46 matches.
Third Division North: Doncaster Rovers (1946–47), 33 wins from 42 matches.
Third Division: Aston Villa (1971–72), 32 wins from 46 matches.
Fourth Division: Lincoln City (1975–76) and Swindon Town (1985–86), 32 wins from 46 matches.
Scottish Premier Division: Rangers (1995–96) and Aberdeen (1984–85), 27 wins from 36 matches; Rangers (1991–92 and 1992–93), 33 wins from 44 matches.
Scottish Division One: Rangers (1920–21), 35 wins from 42 matches.
Scottish DIvision Two: Morton (1966–67), 33 wins from 38 matches.
New Division One: Morthwell (1981–82), 26 wins from 39 matches.
New Division Two: Forfar Athletic (1983–84) and Ayr United (1987–88), 27 wins from 39 matches.
New Division Three: Forfar Athletic (1994–95), 25 wins from 36 matches.

Most home wins in a season: Five clubs have won every home League match in a season: Liverpool (14 games, in 1893–94), Bury (15, 1894–95), Sheffield Wednesday (17, 1899–1900) and Birmingham City (17, 1902–03), all in the old Second Division, and Brentford in Division Three South (21 games, 1929–30).
Undefeated sequences (at home): Liverpool went 85 competitive first–team games unbeaten at home between January 23, 1978 (2–3 v Birmingham) and January 31, 1981 (1–2 v Leicester), comprising 63 in the League, 9 in the League Cup, 7 in European competition and 6 in the FA Cup.
Millwall were unbeaten at home in the League for 59 consecutive matches from 1964–67.
Bradford Park Avenue hold the record for most consecutive home victories, winning 25 successive home games in Division Three North: the last 18 in 1926–27 and the first 7 the following season.
The longest run of home wins in the top division is 21 by Liverpool: the last 9 of 1971–72 and the first 12 of 1972–73.

Undefeated sequences (at home and away): Nottingham Forest went 42 League matches unbeaten, spanning the last 26 games of the 1977–78 season, and the first 16 of 1978–79, from November 1977 to the 2–0 defeat to Liverpool on December 9, 1978.
The sequence comprised 21 wins and 21 draws.
In all competitions, Forest went 40 games unbeaten between March and December 1978, comprising 21 wins and 19 draws in 29 League matches, 6 League Cup, 4 European Cup and 1 Charity Shield.
Forest also hold the record unbeaten run in the Premiership, going 25 matches undefeated (15 wins, 10 draws), between February and November 1995, before losing 7–0 to Blackburn Rovers.
The longest unbeaten start to a League season is 29 matches, achieved by Leeds United (Division One, 1973–74: 19 wins, 10 draws, goals 51–16) and Liverpool (Division One, 1987–88: 22 wins, 7 draws, goals 67–13).
Burnley hold the record for the most consecutive League matches unbeaten in a season, with 30 First Division games between September 6, 1920 and March 25, 1921 (21 wins, 9 draws, goals 68–17).
Sequences without a win (at home): In the 1931–32 season, Rochdale went eight home League games without a win in the Third Division North.
Between November 1958 and October 1959, Portsmouth drew 2 and lost 14 out of 16 consecutive home games.
Sequences without a win (at home and away): Cambridge United went 31 matches (21 lost, 10 drawn) without a League win in the 1983–84 season, between October 8 and April 23, on the way to finishing bottom of the Second Division.
The record for the most consecutive League defeats is held by Darwen in the 1898–99 Division One season.
In Division Two in 1988–89, Walsall suffered 15 successive League defeats.
The longest non–winning start to a League season is 25 matches (4 draws, 21 defeats) by Newport County, Division Four (August 15, 1970 to January 9, 1971).
Since then, the record is 16 games: Burnley (9 draws, 7 defeats in Division Two, 1979–80); Hull City (10 draws, 6 defeats in Division Two, 1989–90); Sheffield United (4 draws, 12 defeats in Division One, 1990–91).
The worst start to a Premier League season was made by Swindon Town in 1993–94, who went 15 matches without a win (6 draws, 9 defeats).
The worst losing start to a League season was made by Manchester United in 1930–31, who suffered 12 consecutive defeats in Division One.
Most away wins in a season: Doncaster Rovers won 18 of the 21 League fixtures as Division Three North champions in 1946–47.

Fewest wins in a season:

Premier League: Swindon Town (1993–94), 5 wins from 42 matches.
First Division: Stoke City (1889–90), 3 wins from 22 matches;
Woolwich Arsenal (1912–13), 3 wins from 38 matches;
Stoke City (1984–85), 3 wins from 42 matches.
Second Division: Loughborough Town (1899–1900), 1 win from 34 matches.
Third Division South: Merthyr Tydfil (1929–30) and QPR (1925–26), 6 wins from 42 matches.
Third Division North: Rochdale (1931–32), 4 wins from 40 matches.
Third Division: Rochdale (1931–32), 2 wins from 46 matches.
Fourth Division: Southport (1976–77), 3 wins from 46 matches.
Scottish Premier Division: St. Johnstone (1975–76) and Kilmarnock (1982–83), 3 wins from 36 matches;
Morton (1987–88), 3 wins from 44 matches.
Scottish Division One: Vale of Leven (1891–92), 0 wins from 22 matches.
Scottish Division Two: East Stirlingshire (1905–06), 1 win from 22 matches; Forfar Athletic (1974–75), 1 win from 38 matches.
New Division One: Queen of the South (1988–89), 2 wins from 39 matches;
Cowdenbeath (1992–93), 3 wins from 44 matches.
New Division Two: Forfar Athletic (1975–76), 4 wins from 26 matches;
Stranraer (1987–88), 4 wins from 39 matches.
New Division Three: Albion Rovers (1994–95), 5 wins from 36 matches.

Most defeats in a season:

Premier League: Ipswich Town (1994–95), 29 defeats in 42 matches.
First Division: Stoke City (1984–85), 31 defeats in 42 matches.
Second Division: Tranmere Rovers (1938–39), 31 defeats on 42 matches;
Chester City (1992–93), 33 defeats im 46 matches.
Third Division South: Merthyr Tydfil (1924–25), 29 defeats in 42 matches; Walsall (1952–53 and 1953–54), 29 defeats in 46 matches.
Third Division North: Rochdale (1931–32), 33 defeats in 40 matches.
Third Division: Cambridge United (1984–85), 33 defeats in 46 matches.
Fourth Division: Newport County (1987–88), 33 defeats in 46 matches.
Scottish Premier Division: Morton (1984–85), 29 defeats in 36 matches.
Scottish Division One: St. Mirren (1920–21), 31 defeats in 42 matches.
Scottish Division Two: Brechin City (1962–63), 30 defeats on 36 matches;
Lochgelly (1923–24), 30 defeats in 38 matches.
New Division One: Queen of the South (1988–89), 29 defeats in 39 matches;
Dumbarton (1995–96), 31 defeats in 36 matches;
Cowdenbeath (1992–93), 34 defeats in 44 matches.
New Division Two: Berwick Rangers (1987–88), 29 defeats in 39 matches.
New Division Three: Albion Rovers (1994–95), 28 defeats in 36 matches.

Fewest defeats in a season:

Premier League: Manchester United (1993–94), 4 defeats in 42 matches.
First Division: Preston North End (1888–89), 0 defeats in 22 matches;
Arsenal (1990–91), 1 defeat in 38 matches;
Liverpool (1987–88), 2 defeats in 40 matches;
Leeds United (1968–69), 2 defeats in 42 matches.
Second Division: Liverpool (1893–94), 0 defeats in 28 matches; Burnley (1897–98), 2 defeats in 30 matches; Bristol City (1905–06), 2 defeats in 38 matches; Leeds United (1963–64), 3 defeats in 42 matches; Chelsea (1988–89), 5 defeats in 46 matches.
Third Division: QPR (1966–67) and Bristol Rovers (1989–90), 5 defeats in 46 matches.
Third Division South: Southampton (1921–22) and Plymouth Argyle (1929–30), 4 defeats in 42 matches.
Third Division North: Port Vale (1953–54), 3 defeats in 46 matches;
Doncaster Rovers (1946–47) and Wolverhampton Wanderers (1923–24), 3 defeats in 42 matches.
Fourth Division: Lincoln City (1975–76),
Sheffield United (1981–82),
Bournemouth (1981–82), 4 defeats in 46 matches.
Scottish Premier Division: Rangers (1995–96), 3 defeats in 36 matches;
Celtic (1987–88), 3 defeats in 44 matches.
Scottish Division One: Rangers (1898–99), 0 defeats in 18 matches; Rangers (1920–21), 1 defeat in 42 matches.
Scottish Division Two: Clyde (1956–57),
Morton (1962–63) and St. Mirren (1967–68), 1 defeat in 36 matches.
New Division One: Partick Thistle (1975–76), 2 defeats in 26 matches; St. Mirren (1976–77), 2 defeats in 39 matches; Raith Rovers (1992–93) and Falkirk (1993–94), 4 defeats in 44 matches.
New Division Two: Raith Rovers (1975–76), 1 defeat in 26 matches; Clydebank (1975–76), 3 defeats in 26 matches; Forfar Athletic (1983–84) and Raith Rovers

(1986–87), 3 defeats in 39 matches;
Livingston (1995–96), 6 defeat in 36 matches.
New Division Three: Forfar Athletic (1994–95) and Inverness T (1996–97), 6 defeats in 36 matches.

Most drawn games in a season:

Premier League: Manchester City (1993–94), Sheffield United (1993–94) and Southampton (1994–95), 18 draws in 42 matches.
First Division: Norwich City (1978–79), 23 draws in 42 matches.
Fourth Division: Exeter City (1986–87), 23 draws in 46 matches.
Scottish Premier Division: Aberdeen (1993–94), 21 draws in 44 matches.
New Division One: East Fife (1986–87), 21 draws in 44 matches.

Most League Championships: Liverpool, 18 (1900–01, 1905–06, 1921–22, 1922–23, 1946–47, 1963–64, 1965–66, 1972–73, 1975–76, 1976–77, 1978–79, 1979–80, 1981–82, 1982–83, 1983–84, 1985–86, 1987–88, 1989–90).
Most Premier League Championships: Manchester United, 4 (1992–93, 1993–94, 1995–96, 1996–97).
Most Division Two titles: 6, by Leicester City (1924–25, 1936–37, 1953–54, 1956–57, 1970–71, 1979–80) and Manchester City (1898–99, 1902–03, 1909–10, 1927–28, 1946–47, 1965–66).
Most Division Three titles: 2, by Portsmouth (1961–62, 1982–83) and Oxford United (1967–68, 1983–84).
Most Division Four titles: 2, by Chesterfield (1969–70, 1984–85),
Doncaster Rovers (1965–66, 1968–69) and Peterborough United (1960–61, 1973–74).
Most Division Three South titles: Bristol City, 3 (1922–23, 1926–27, 1954–55).
Most Division Three North titles: 3, by Barnsley (1933–34, 1938–39, 1954–55),
Doncaster Rovers (1934–35, 1946–47, 1949–50) and Lincoln City (1931–32, 1947–48, 1951–52).
Most Scottish League Championships: Rangers, 47.
Most FA Cup victories: Manchester United, 9 (1909, 1948, 1963, 1977, 1983, 1985, 1990, 1994, 1996).
Most Scottish FA Cup victories: Celtic, 30.
Most League Cup victories: 5, by Aston Villa (1961, 1975, 1977, 1994 and 1996) and Liverpool (1981, 1982, 1983, 1984 and 1995).
Most Scottish League Cup victories: Rangers, 20.

INDIVIDUAL

Most goals in a game:

International: Sofus Nielsen (Denmark), 10 goals v France, at White City (Olympics, October 22, 1908);
Gottfried Fuchs (Germany), 10 goals v Russia, in Stockholm (Olympics, July 1, 1912).
World Cup: Gary Cole (Australia), 7 goals v Fiji, (August 14, 1981);
Karim Bagheri (Iran), 7 goals v Maldives, (June 2, 1997).
World Cup Final: Geoff Hurst (England), 3 goals v West Germany, 1966.
Major European Cup game: Lothar Emmerich (Borussia Dortmund), 6 goals v Floriana (Cup Winners' Cup, 1965).
Premier League: Andy Cole (Manchester United), 5 goals v Ipswich Town (March 4, 1995).
Old First Division: Ted Drake (Arsenal), 7 goals v Aston Villa (December 14, 1935);
James Ross (Preston North End), 7 goals v Stoke City (October 6, 1888).
First Division: John Durnin (Oxford United), 4 goals v Luton Town (1992–93);
Guy Whittingham (Portsmouth), 4 goals v Bristol Rovers (1992–93);
Craig Russell (Sunderland), 4 goals v Millwall (1995–96).
Old Second Division: Tommy Briggs (Blackburn Rovers), 7 goals v Bristol Rovers (February 5, 1955);
Neville Coleman (Stoke City), 7 goals v Lincoln City (away, February 23, 1957).
Second Division: Paul Barnes (Burnley), 5 goals v Stockport County (1996–97).
Third Division South: Joe Payne (Luton Town), 10 goals v Bristol Rovers (April 13, 1936).
Third Division North: Bunny Bell (Tranmere Rovers), 9 goals v Oldham Athletic (December 26, 1935).
Old Third Division: Steve Earle (Fulham), 5 goals v Halifax Town (September 16, 1969);
Barrie Thomas (Scunthorpe United), 5 goals v Luton Town (April 24, 1965);
Keith East (Swindon Town), 5 goals v Mansfield Town (November 20, 1965);
Alf Wood (Shrewsbury Town), 5 goals v Blackburn Rovers (October 2, 1971);
Tony Caldwell (Bolton Wanderers), 5 goals v Walsall (September 10, 1983);
Andy Jones (Port Vale), 5 goals v Newport County (May 4, 1987);
Steve Wilkinson (Mansfield Town), 5 goals v Birmingham City (April 3, 1990).
Third Division: Tony Naylor (Crewe Alexandra), 5 goals v Colchester United (1992–93); Steve Butler (Cambridge United), 5 goals v Exeter City (1993–94).
Fourth Division: Bert Lister (Oldham Athletic), 6 goals v Southport (December 26, 1962).

FA Cup: Ted MacDougall (Bournemouth), 9 goals v Margate (1st Round, November 20, 1971).
FA Cup Final: Billy Townley (Blackburn Rovers), 3 goals v Sheffield Wednesday (Kennington Oval, 1890); Jimmy Logan (Notts County), 3 goals v Bolton Wanderers (Everton, 1894);
Stan Mortensen (Blackpool), 3 goals v Bolton Wanderers (Wembley, 1953).
League Cup: Frankie Bunn (Oldham Athletic), 6 goals v Scarborough (October 25, 1989).
Scottish Premier Division: Paul Sturrock (Dundee United), 5 goals v Morton (November 17, 1984).
Scottish Division One: Jimmy McGrory (Celtic), 8 goals v Dunfermline Athletic (September 14, 1928).
Scottish Division Two: Owen McNally (Arthurlie), 8 goals v Armadale (October 1, 1927);
Jim Dyet (King's Park), 8 goals v Forfar Athletic (January 2, 1930);
John Calder (Morton), 8 goals v Raith Rovers (April 18, 1936);
Norman Hayward (Raith Rovers), 8 goals v Brechin City (August 20, 1937).
Scottish Cup: John Petrie (Arbroath), 13 goals v Bon Accord (1st Round, September 12, 1885);
Gerry Baker (St. Mirren), 10 goals v Glasgow University (1st Round, January 30, 1960);
Joe Baker (Hibernian, Gerry's brother), 9 goals v Peebles Rovers (2nd Round, February 11, 1961).
Scottish League Cup: Jim Fraser (Ayr United), 5 goals v Dumbarton (August 13, 1952);
Jim Forrest (Rangers), 5 goals v Stirling Albion (August 17, 1966).

Most League goals in a season:

Premier League: Andy Cole (Newcastle United, 1993–94), 34 goals in 40 matches; Alan Shearer (Blackburn Rovers, 1994–95), 34 goals in 42 matches.
Old First Division: Dixie Dean (Everton, 1927–28), 60 goals in 39 matches.
First Division: Guy Whittingham (Portsmouth, 1992–93), 42 goals in 46 matches.
Old Second Division: George Camsell (Middlesbrough, 1926–27), 59 goals in 37 matches.
Second Division: Jimmy Quinn (Reading, 1993–94), 35 goals in 46 matches.
Third Division South: Joe Payne (Luton Town, 1936–37), 55 goals in 39 matches.
Third Division North: Ted Harston (Mansfield Town, 1936–37), 55 goals in 41 matches.
Old Third Division: Derek Reeves (Southampton, 1959–60), 39 goals in 46 matches.
Third Divisioin: Graeme Jones (Wigan Athletic, 1996–97), 31 goals in 40 matches.
Fourth Division: Terry Bly (Peterborough United, 1960–61), 52 goals in 46 matches.
FA Cup: Sandy Brown (Tottenham Hotspur, 1900–01), 15 goals in 8 matches.
League Cup: Clive Allen (Tottenham Hotspur, 1986–87), 12 goals in 9 matches.
Scottish Premier Division: Brian McClair (Celtic, 1986–87), 35 goals.
Scottish Division One: William McFayden (Motherwell, 1931–32), 53 goals in 34 matches.
Scottish Division Two: Jim Smith (Ayr United, 1927–28), 66 goals in 38 matches.

Most League goals:

Football League:
Arthur Rowley

Club	***Goals***	***Matches***	***Seasons***
WBA	4	24	1946–48
Fulham	27	56	1948–50
Leicester City	251	303	1950–58
Shrewsbury Town	152	236	1958–65
Totals	434	619	

Scottish League:
Jimmy McGrory

Club	***Goals***	***Matches***	***Seasons***
Celtic	1	3	1922–23
Clydebank	13	30	1923–24
Celtic	396	375	1924–38
Totals	410	408	

Most League goals for one club:
349 – Dixie Dean (Everton, 1925–37).

Most Cup goals:

Pre–war: Henry Cursham, 48 (Notts County).
Post–war: Ian Rush, 43 (Liverpool and Newcastle United).
Most FA Cup final goals: 5, Ian Rush (Liverpool): 1986 (2), 1989 (2), 1992 (1).

Penalties:

Most in a season (individual): Francis Lee (Manchester City, 1971–72), 13 goals.
Most awarded in one game: Five – Crystal Palace (4–1 scored, 3 missed) v Brighton and Hove Albion (1 scored), Division 2, 1988–89.
Most saved in a season: 8 out of 10, Paul Cooper (Ipswich Town, 1979–80).

Most League appearances (750 + matches):

1005, Peter Shilton (286 Leicester City, 110 Stoke City, 202 Nottingham Forest, 188 Southampton, 175 Derby County, 34 Plymouth Argyle, 1 Bolton Wanderers, 9 Leyton Orient), 1966–97.
863, Tommy Hutchison (165 Blackpool, 314 Coventry City, 46 Manchester City, 92 Burnley, 178 Swansea City, 68 Alloa), 1965–91.
824, Terry Paine (713 Southampton, 111 Hereford United), 1957–77.
782, Robbie James (484 Swansea City, 48 Stoke City, 87 QPR, 23 Leicester City, 89 Bradford City, 51 Cardiff City).
777, Alan Oakes (565 Manchester City, 211 Chester City, 1 Port Vale), 1959–84.
771, John Burridge (27 Workington, 134 Blackpool, 65 Aston Villa, 6 Southend United (loan), 88 Crystal Palace, 39 QPR, 74 Wolverhampton Wanderers, 6 Derby County (loan), 109 Sheffield United, 62 Southampton, 67 Newcastle United, 65 Hibernian, 3 Scarborough, 4 Lincoln City, 3 Aberdeen, 3 Dumbarton, 3 Falkirk, 4 Manchester City, 3 Darlington, 6 Queen of the South), 1968–96.
770, John Trollope (all for Swindon Town), 1960–80 – record for one club.
764, Jimmy Dickson (all for Portsmouth), 1946–65.
761, Roy Sproson (all for Port Vale), 1950–72.
758, Ray Clemence (48 Scunthorpe United, 470 Liverpool, 240 Tottenham Hotspur), 1966–87.
758, Billy Bonds (95 Charlton Athletic, 663 West Ham United).
757, Pat Jennings (48 Watford, 472 Tottenham Hotspur, **237**, Arsenal), 1963–86.
757, Frank Worthington (171 Hudderfield Town, 210 Leicester City, 84 Bolton Wanderers, 75 Birmingham City, 32 Leeds United, 195 Sunderland, 34 Southampton, 31 Brighton and Hove Albion, 59 Tranmere Rovers, 23 Preston North End, 19 Stockport County), 1966–88.
Consecutive: 401, Harold Bell (401 Tranmere Rovers; 459 in all games), 1946–55.
Most FA Cup appearances: 88, Ian Callaghan (79 Liverpool, 7 Swansea City, 2 Crewe Alexandra).
Most senior matches: 1390, Peter Shilton (1005 League, 86 FA Cup, 102 League Cup, 125 internationals, 13 Under–23s, 4 Football League XI, 20 European Cup, 7 Texaco Cup, 5 Simod Cup, 4 European Super Cup, 4 UEFA Cup, 3 Screen Sport Super Cup, 3 Zenith Data Systems Cup, 2 Autoglass Trophy, 2 Charity Shield, 2 Full Members' Cup, 1 Anglo–Italian Cup, 1 Football League play–offs, 1 World Club Championship).

Goalkeeping records: Longest run without conceding a goal:

British record (all competitive games): Chris Woods (Rangers), in 1196 minutes from November 26, 1986, to January 31, 1987.
Football League: Steve Death (Reading), 1103 minutes from March 24 to August 18, 1979.

Youngest players:

Premier League: Neil Finn, 17 years 3 days, West Ham United v Manchester City, January 1, 1996.
Premier League scorer: Andy Turner, 17 years 166 days, Tottenham Hotspur v Everton, September 5, 1992.
Football League: Albert Geldard, 15 years 158 days, Bradford Park Avenue v Millwall, Division Two, September 16, 1929.
Ken Roberts, 15 years 158 days, Wrexham v Bradford Park Avenue, Division Three North, September 1, 1951.
Football League scorer: Ronnie Dix, 15 years 180 days, Bristol Rovers v Norwich City, Division Three South, March 3, 1928.
First Division: Derek Forster, 15 years 158 days, Sunderland v Leicester City, August 22, 1984.
First Division scorer: Jason Dozzell, 16 years 57 days, as substitute, Ipswich Town v Coventry City, February 4, 1984.
First Division hat–tricks: Alan Shearer, 17 years 240 days, Southampton v Arsenal, March 9, 1988.
Jimmy Greaves, 17 years 10 months, Chelsea v Portsmouth, December 25, 1957.
FA Cup (any round): Andy Awford, 15 years 88 days, as substitute, Worcester City v Boreham Wood, 3rd Qualifying Round, October 10, 1987.
FA Cup proper: Scott Endersby, 15 years 288 days, Kettering v Tilbury, 1st Round, November 26, 1977.
FA Cup Final: James Prinsep, 17 years 245 days, Clapham Rovers v Old Etonians, 1879.
FA Cup Final scorer: Norman Whiteside, 18 years 18 days, Manchester United v Brighton and Hove Albion, 1983.
FA Cup Final captain: David Nish, 21 years 212 days, Leicester City v Manchester City, 1969.
League Cup Final scorer: Norman Whiteside, 17 years 324 days, Manchester United v Liverpool, 1983.
League Cup Final captain: Barry Venison, 20 years 7 months 8 days, Sunderland v Norwich City, 1985.

Oldest players:

Football League: Neil McBain, 52 years 4 months, New Brighton v Hartlepool United, Division Three North, March 15, 1947 (McBain was New Brighton's manager and had to play in an emergency).
First Division: Stanley Matthews, 50 years 5 days, Stoke City v Fulham, February 6, 1965.
FA Cup Final: Walter Hampson, 41 years 8 months, Newcastle United v Aston Villa, 1924.
FA Cup: Billy Meredith, 49 years 8 months, Manchester City v Newcastle United, March 29, 1924.

Sendings-off:

Most in a season: 314 (League alone), 1994–95.
Most in a day: 15 (3 League, 12 FA Cup), November 20, 1982.
Most in the League in a day: 13, December 14, 1985.
Most in the League over a weekend: 15, December 22–23, 1990.
FA Cup Final: Kevin Moran, Manchester United v Everton, 1985.
Others at Wembley: Boris Stankovic, Yugoslavia v Sweden (Olympics), 1948; Antonio Rattin, Argentina v England (World Cup), 1966; Billy Bremner (Leeds United) and Kevin Keegan (Liverpool), Charity Shield 1974; Gilbert Dresch, Luxembourg v England (World Cup qualifier), 1977; Mike Henry, Sudbury Town v Tamworth (FA Vase), 1989; Jason Cook, Colchester United v Witton Albion (FA Vase), 1992; Lee Dixon, Arsenal v Tottenham Hotspur (FA Cup semi–final), 1993; Peter Swan, Port Vale v WBA (play–offs), 1993; Andrei Kanchelskis, Manchester United v Aston Villa (Coca–Cola Cup Final), 1994); Michael Wallace and Chris Beaumont (both Stockport County) v Burnley (play–offs), 1994; Tetsuji Hashiratani, Japan v England (Umbro Cup), 1995; Derek Ward, Northwich Victoria v Macclesfield Town (FA Trophy), 1996; Tony Rogers, Dagenham and Redbridge v Woking (FA Trophy), 1997; Brian Statham, Brentford v Crewe Alexandra (play–offs), 1997.
Quickest: 19 seconds, Mark Smith, Crewe Alexandra v Darlington (away), Division Three (March 12, 1994).
Quickest in Premier League: 72 seconds, Tim Flowers, Blackburn Rovers v Leeds United (February 1, 1995).
Quickest in Division One: 85 seconds, Liam O'Brien, Manchester United v Southampton, (January 3, 1987).
Quickest in the FA Cup: 52 seconds, Ian Culverhouse, Swindon Town v Everton (away), 3rd Round (January 5, 1997).
Quickest in European competition: 90 seconds, Sergei Dirkach, Dynamo Moscow v Ghent, UEFA Cup 3rd Round, 2nd Leg (December 11, 1991).
Quickest in the World Cup: 55 seconds, Jose Batista, Uruguay v Scotland (Neza, Mexico; June 13, 1986).
World record: 10 seconds, Giuseppe Lorenzo, Bologna v Parma, Italian Serie A, December 9, 1990.
Most in one game: 4: Northampton Town (0) v Hereford United (4), Division Three (November 11, 1992); Crewe Alexandra (2) v Bradford Park Avenue (2), Division Three North (Janaury 8, 1955); Sheffield United (1) v Portsmouth (3), Division Two (December 13, 1986); Port Vale (2) v Northampton Town (2), Littlewoods Cup (August 18, 1987); Brentford (2) v Mansfield Town (2), Division Three (December 12, 1987).
Most sendings–off in a career: 21 – Willie Johnston (7 Rangers, 6 WBA, 4 Vancouver Whitecaps, 3 Hearts, 1 Scotland).

Record attendances:

Premier League: 55,314 – Manchester United v Wimbledon, January 29, 1997.
Old First Division: 83,260 – Manchester United v Arsenal (Maine Road), January 17, 1948.
First Division: 30,729 – Manchester City v Oldham Athletic, March 8, 1997.
Old Second Division: 70,302 – Tottenham Hotspur v Southampton, February 25, 1950.
Second Division: 18,674 – Bristol City v Bristol Rovers, December 15, 1996.
Old Third Division: 49,309 – Sheffield Wednesday v Sheffield United, December 26, 1979.
Third Division South: 51,621 – Cardiff City v Bristol City, April 7, 1947.
Third Division North: 49,655 – Hull City v Rotherham United, December 25, 1948.
Fourth Division: 37,774 – Crystal Palace v Millwall, March 31, 1961.
Record Football League aggregate (season): 41,271,414 (1948–49) – 88 clubs.
Record Football League aggregate (single day): 1,269,934, December 27, 1949.
Record average home League attendance for season: 57,758, Manchester United, 1967–68.
Last 1 million League crowd aggregate: 1,007,200, December 27, 1971.
Scottish League: 118,567 – Rangers v Celtic (Ibrox Stadium), January 2, 1939.
FA Cup Final: 126,047 – Bolton Wanderers v West Ham United (Wembley), April 28, 1923.
European Cup: 135,826 – Celtic v Leeds United (semi–final at Hampden Park), April 15, 1970.
Scottish Cup: 146,433 – Celtic v Aberdeen (Hampden Park), April 24, 1937.
Record cup–tie aggregate: 265,199, at two matches between Rangers and Morton, Scottish Cup Final, 1947–48.
World Cup: 199,854 – Brazil v Uruguay (Maracana, Rio), July 16, 1950.

HOW TO BOIL AN EGG

. . . and 184 other
recipes fo

KT-432-919

In the same series

Man Alone Cook Book
*The Big Occasion Cook Book
*The Bride's Guide

**By the same author*

Where to find *Right Way*

Elliot *Right Way* take pride in our editorial quality, accuracy and value-for-money. Booksellers everywhere can rapidly obtain any *Right Way* book for you. If you have been particularly pleased with any one title, do please mention this to your bookseller as personal recommendation helps us enormously.

Please send to the address on the back of the title page opposite, a stamped, self-addressed envelope if you would like a copy of our *free catalogue*. Alternatively, you may wish to browse through our extensive range of informative titles arranged by subject on the Internet at **www.right-way.co.uk**

We welcome views and suggestions from readers as well as from prospective authors; do please write to us or e-mail: **info@right-way.co.uk**

HOW TO BOIL AN EGG

. . . and 184 other simple recipes for one

Jan Arkless

Copyright notice

© Jan Arkless MCMLXXXVI
First published in the *Right Way* series © MCMXCVII

All rights reserved. No part of this book may be reproduced, stored in a retrieval system, or transmitted, in any form or by any means, electronic, photocopying, mechanical, recording or otherwise, without the prior permission of the copyright owner.

Conditions of sale
This book shall only be sold, lent, or hired, for profit, trade, or otherwise, in its original binding, except where special permission has been granted by the Publishers.

Whilst care is taken in selecting Authors who are authoritative in their subjects, it is emphasised that their books can reflect their knowledge only up to the time of writing. Information can be superseded and printers' errors can creep in. This book is sold, therefore, on the condition that neither Publisher nor Author can be held legally responsible for the consequences of any error or omission there may be.

Typeset in 10/12pt Times by County Typesetters, Margate, Kent.

Printed and bound in Great Britain by Cox & Wyman Ltd., Reading, Berkshire.

The *Right Way series* is published by Elliot Right Way Books, Brighton Road, Lower Kingswood, Tadworth, Surrey, KT20 6TD, U.K. For information about our company and the other books we publish, visit our web site at www.right-way.co.uk

CONTENTS

For Jon Jon,
whose architectural aspirations
inspired this book.

1
INTRODUCTION

I originally wrote this book to help my son with his cooking when he first went to university. I have since realised that the recipes contained here are not only useful for students but for anyone, of any age, who find themselves alone, and for the first time have to cook for themselves, whether in their own home or in new accommodation.

Other cookery books assume some basic knowledge of cooking techniques but in this book I have assumed none as I wrote it specifically for the person who knows *absolutely nothing* or *very little* about cooking, or meal planning.

The book explains the simple things that one is supposed to know by instinct, such as how to boil an egg or fry sausages, how to prepare and cook vegetables *and* have them ready to eat at the same time as the main course! It includes recipes and suggestions for a variety of snacks and main meals (not all cooked in the frying pan or made from mince), using fish, chicken, beef, lamb and pork. The majority of the meals are quick, easy and economical to make, but there is a 'Sunday Lunch' chapter near the end of the book.

There are just a few recipes for desserts and cakes as you can easily buy biscuits and ready-made or frozen cakes. Remember that yoghurt makes a good, cheap sweet, and that fresh fruit is the best pud you can eat. Also, fresh fruit juice or milk is far better for you than fizzy drinks or alcohol.

Most recipes in other cookery books are geared towards feeding four or six people, but the recipes contained here are designed for the single person living on his or her own. However, this book does include a few recipes which cater for two people. This is because it is easier to cook larger portions of stews and casseroles as very small helpings tend to dry up during cooking.

AMOUNTS TO USE WHEN COOKING FOR ONE

Pasta, Noodles, Shapes, etc.
1 very generous cup (3 oz/75g) of uncooked pasta.

Potatoes
3–4 (8 oz/225g) according to size.

Rice
½ cup (2–3 oz/50–75g) dry uncooked rice.

Vegetables
See the individual vegetables in Chapter 5.

Oily Fish
1 whole fish (trout, mackerel, herring).

White Fish
6–8 oz (175–225g) fillet of cod, haddock, etc.

Roast Beef
Approximately 6 oz (175g) per person. A joint weighing 2½–3 lb (1–1.5kg) should serve 6–8 helpings; remember you can use cold meat for dinner the next day.

Minced Beef
4–6 oz (100–175g).

Beef Steak
6–8 oz (175–225g) is a fair-sized steak.

Stewing Steak
4–6 oz (100–175g).

Chicken
Allow a 6–8 oz (175–225g) chicken joint (leg or breast) per person. A 2½–3 lb (1–1.5kg) chicken serves 3–4 people.

Lamb or Pork Chops
1 per person.

Lamb Cutlets
1–3 according to size and appetite.

Roast Lamb
Because you are buying meat with a bone in, you need to buy a larger joint to account for the bone. A joint weighing about 2½ lb (1kg) will serve 4 people well.

Roast Pork
Approximately 8 oz (225g) per serving. A boneless joint weighing 2½–3 lb (1–1.5kg) will give 5–6 generous helpings.

Pork or Gammon Steaks
1 per person or 6 oz (175g).

USING THE OVEN

Temperatures are given for both gas and electric ovens.

Remember always to heat the oven for a few minutes before cooking food in it, so that the whole of the oven reaches the appropriate temperature.

REHEATING FOOD

One note of warning: be very careful about reheating cooked dishes. If you must do this, always be sure that the food is re-cooked right through, not merely warmed. *Food just reheated can make you extremely ill if not cooked thoroughly, especially pork and chicken – you have been warned!*

FOLLOWING THE RECIPES

I have given 'preparation and cooking' times for the recipes in this book so that, before you start cooking, you will know approximately how much time to set aside for preparing and cooking the meal. Read the recipe right the way through so that you know what it involves.

The ingredients used in each recipe are all readily available and listed in the order they are used in the method. Collect all the specified ingredients *before* you start cooking, otherwise you may find yourself lacking a vital ingredient when you have already prepared half the meal. When the meal is ready, there should be no ingredients left – if there are, you have missed something out!

Measurements

The ingredients are given in both imperial and metric measurements. Follow one type of measurement or the other, but do not combine the two, as the quantities are not exact conversions.

I have used size 2 or 3 eggs in the recipes so you can use whichever you happen to have in stock. Meat, fish and vegetables can be weighed in the shop when you buy them, or will have the weight on the packet. Don't buy more than you need for the recipe; extra bits tend to get left at the back of the cupboard or fridge and wasted. But it is worthwhile buying some goods in the larger size packets – rice, pasta, tomato ketchup, etc. – as they will keep fresh for ages and be on hand when you need them.

In case you don't own kitchen scales many of the measurements are also given in spoonfuls or tea cups (normal drinking size, which approximates to ¼ pint/5 fl oz/ 150ml; it isn't the American measure of a cup). The following measurements may also be helpful:

Butter, margarine or lard, etc.
1 inch cube (2.5cm cube) = 1 oz (25g); it is easy to divide up a new packet and mark it out in squares.

Cheese
1 inch cube (2.5cm cube) = 1 oz (25g) approximately.

Flour, cornflour
1 very heaped tbsp = 1 oz (25g) approximately.

Pasta (shells, bows, etc.)
1 very full cup = 3 oz (75g) approximately.

Rice
½ cup dry uncooked rice = 2 oz (50g) approximately.

Sugar
1 heaped tbsp = 1 oz (25g) approximately.

Sausages
Chipolatas: 8 sausages in an 8 oz (225g) packet.
Thick sausages: 4 sausages in an 8 oz (225g) packet.

Abbreviations

tsp	= teaspoon
dsp	= dessertspoon
tbsp	= tablespoon (serving spoon)
1 spoonful	= 1 slightly rounded spoonful
1 level spoonful	= 1 flat spoonful

1 cupful	= 1 tea cup (drinking size cup) approximately ¼ pint/5 fl oz/150ml (*not* the American measure)
pt	= pint

USEFUL STORES & KITCHEN EQUIPMENT

This section may be particularly useful if you're a student living away from home and cooking for yourself for the first time in your life. Beg or borrow these items from home or try to collect them at the beginning of term, then just replace them during the year as necessary.

Beef, chicken and vegetable stock cubes
Coffee (instant)
Coffee (real)
Cooking oil
Cornflour
Curry powder
Dried mixed herbs
Drinking chocolate
Flour
Garlic powder (or paste)
Gravy granules
Horseradish sauce
Mustard
Milk powder (for coffee)
Orange/lemon squash
Pasta
Pepper
Pickle
Rice (long grain)
Salt
Soy sauce
Sugar
Tabasco sauce
Tea bags
Tomato purée (in a jar or tube)
Tomato sauce
Vinegar
Worcester sauce

Also
Dish cloth, washing-up liquid, tea towels, pan scrubber, oven cleaning powder, oven cloth.

Store sugar, rice, flour, pasta, biscuits and cakes in airtight containers rather than leaving them in open packets on the shelf. This keeps them fresh and clean for much longer and protects them from ants and other insects. Try to collect some storage jars and plastic containers for this purpose. (Large, empty coffee jars with screw lids, and plastic ice-cream cartons are ideal.)

Perishable Foods
These don't keep so long but are useful to have as a start.

Bacon
Biscuits
Bread
Butter
Cereals (such as cornflakes)
Cheese
Chocolate spread
Eggs
Fruit juice
Frozen vegetables
Honey
Jam
Margarine
Marmalade
Milk
Peanut butter
Potatoes

Handy Cans for a Quick Meal
Baked beans
Beans with sausages
Chicken in white sauce
Corned beef
Evaporated milk
Frankfurter sausages
Italian tomatoes
Luncheon meat
Minced beef
Rice pudding
Sardines
Soups (also packet soups)
Spaghetti
Spaghetti hoops
Stewed steak
Sweetcorn
Tinned fruit
Tuna fish
Vegetables (peas, carrots, etc.)

Also
Blancmange powders
Instant whip
Jellies
Pot noodles

Useful Kitchen Equipment
Basin (small)
Bottle opener

Casserole pan (thick heavy ones are the best)
Chopping/bread board
Cling film
Cooking foil
Cooking tongs
Dessertspoons
Fish slice
Frying pan
Grater
Kettle
Kitchen paper
Kitchen scissors
Knives: bread knife with serrated edge;
sharp chopping knife for meat;
vegetable knife
Measuring jug
Oven-proof dish (pyrex-type): 1 pint/0.5 litre size is big enough for one
Plastic storage containers (large ice-cream tubs are useful, to store biscuits, cakes, pasta, etc.)
Saucepans: 1 small; 1 or 2 large ones
Storage jars (large empty coffee jars are ideal)
Tablespoons
Teaspoons
Tin opener
Wooden spoon

Handy but not Essential Kitchen Equipment

Baking tin (for meat)
Baking tins (various)
Basin (large) or bowl
Bread bin
Colander
Egg whisk or egg beater
Electric frying pan/multi cooker (very useful if your cooker is very small, old or unreliable)
Electric kettle

Foil dishes (these are cheap and last for several bakings; useful if you need a tin of a particular shape or size)
Kitchen scales
Liquidiser
Measuring jug (can also be used as a basin)
Mixer or food processor
Potato masher
Saucepans (extra) and/or casserole dishes
Sieve
Toaster

GLOSSARY

Various cooking terms used in the book (some of which may be unfamiliar to you) are explained in this glossary.

Al dente
Refers to pasta that is cooked and feels firm when bitten.

Basting
Spooning fat or butter or meat juices over food that is being roasted (particularly meat and poultry) to keep it moist.

Beating
Mixing food with a wooden spoon or whisk so that the lumps disappear and it becomes smooth.

Binding
Adding eggs, cream or butter to a dry mixture to hold it together.

Blending
Mixing dry ingredients (such as flour) with a little liquid to make a smooth, runny lumpfree mixture.

Boiling
Cooking food in boiling water (i.e. at a temperature of 212°F/100°C) with the water bubbling gently.

Boning
Removing the bones from meat, poultry or fish.

Braising
Frying food in a hot fat so that it is browned, and then cooking it slowly in a covered dish with a little liquid and some vegetables.

Casserole
An oven-proof dish with lid; also a slow-cooked stew.

Chilling
Cooling food in a fridge without freezing.

Colander
A perforated metal or plastic basket used for straining food.

Deep-frying
Immersing food in hot fat or oil and frying it.

Dicing
Cutting food into small cubes.

Dot with butter
Cover food with small pieces of butter.

Flaking
Separating fish into flaky pieces.

Frying
Cooking food in oil or fat in a pan (usually a flat frying pan).

Grilling
Cooking food by direct heat under a grill.

Mixing
Combining ingredients by stirring.

Nest (making a)
Arranging food (such as rice or potatoes) around the outside of a plate to make a circular border and putting other food into the middle of this 'nest'.

Poaching
Cooking food in water which is just below boiling point.

Purée
Food that has been passed through a sieve and reduced to pulp (or pulped in a liquidiser or electric mixer).

Roasting
Cooking food in a hot oven.

Sautéing
Frying food quickly in hot, shallow fat, and turning it frequently in the pan so that it browns evenly.

Seasoning
Adding salt, pepper, herbs and/or spices to food.

Simmering
Cooking food in water which is just below boiling point so that only an occasional bubble appears.

Straining
Separating solid food from liquid by draining it through a sieve or colander, e.g. potatoes, peas, etc., that have been cooked in boiling water.

2
EGGS

Eggs are super value, quick to cook and can make a nourishing snack or main meal in minutes.

In view of the publicity over salmonella in eggs, take care about the eggs you buy and store them sensibly and hygienically – eggs have porous shells and should never be stored where they are in contact with uncooked meat or fish, dust or dirt of any kind. They also absorb smells through the shells, so beware if you are buying fresh fruit, washing powder, household cleaners, firelighters, etc., and keep them in separate shopping bags. Heed the advice on fresh eggs given out by the health authorities: only buy eggs from a reputable supplier and *do not serve raw or lightly cooked egg dishes to babies, pregnant women or the elderly unless you're sure that the eggs are free from bacteria*. There are egg substitutes available in the shops (although you may have to search for them) which you may prefer for safety reasons instead of fresh eggs. Don't panic, but do take reasonable care with egg cookery.

BOILED EGG

Use an egg already at room temperature if possible, not one straight from the fridge as otherwise it may crack. If you prick the top of the shell once with a special gadget or a clean pin, the egg will not crack while cooking (my daughter-in-law Barbara taught me this, and it really does work). Slip the egg carefully into a small saucepan, cover with warm (not boiling) water and add ½ tsp salt (to seal up any cracks). Bring to the boil, note the time and turn down the heat before the egg starts rattling about in the pan. Simmer gently, timing from when the water begins to boil, using the table below:

Size	*Time*	*Description*
Large (sizes 1 or 2)	3 mins.	soft-boiled
Standard (sizes 3 or 4)	2½ mins.	soft-boiled
Large	4 mins.	soft yolk, hard white
Standard	3½ mins.	soft yolk, hard white
Large	10 mins.	hard-boiled
Standard	9 mins.	hard-boiled

SOFT-BOILED

Remove carefully from the pan with a spoon, put into an egg cup and tap the top to crack the shell and stop the egg continuing to cook inside.

HARD-BOILED

Remove the pan from the heat and place under cold, running water to prevent a black ring forming round the yolk. Peel off shell and rinse in cold water to remove any shell still clinging to the egg.

POACHED EGG

Put about 1 in (2.5cm) water into a clean frying pan and bring to the boil. Reduce the heat so that the water is just simmering. Crack the egg carefully into a cup, and slide it into the simmering water. Cook very gently, just simmering in the hot water, for about 3 minutes, until the egg is set to your liking. Lift it out with a slotted spoon or fish slice, being careful not to break the yolk underneath.

FRIED EGG

Heat a small amount of cooking oil, butter or dripping in a frying pan over a moderate heat (not too hot, or the egg white will frazzle). Carefully break the egg into a cup to check that it is not bad, then pour it into the frying pan and fry gently for 2 to 3 minutes. To cook the top of the egg, either baste the egg occasionally by spooning a little of the hot fat over it, or put the lid on the pan and let the heat cook it. You may prefer the egg carefully flipped over when half done to cook on both sides, but be prepared for a broken yolk. Remove the egg from the pan with a fish slice or wide-bladed knife.

SCRAMBLED EGGS

Usually you will want to scramble 2 or more eggs at a time.

Chopped chives are tasty with scrambled eggs. Simply wash them, cut off their roots and chop them.

Beat the egg well with a fork in a basin or large cup. Add salt, pepper and chopped chives. Melt a large knob of butter in a small, preferably thick, saucepan. Turn heat to low, and pour in the beaten egg, stirring all the time, until the egg looks thick and creamy. Do not overcook, as the egg will continue to cook even when removed from the heat. Stir in (if required) 1 to 2 tsp cream or top of the milk, or a small knob of butter (this helps to stop the egg cooking any more).

CHEESY SCRAMBLED EGGS

Add 1 oz (25g) grated or chopped cheese to the beaten eggs, before cooking.

•

PAN SCRAMBLE

If you are cooking sausages or bacon as well as scrambled eggs, fry the meat first and then cook the eggs in the same hot fat.

PIPERADE

Serves 1

Scrambled eggs plus a bit extra.

Preparation and cooking time: 30 minutes.

1 small onion
Small green pepper
2 tomatoes (fresh or tinned)
1 tbsp oil, or knob of butter (for frying)
Pinch of garlic powder
Salt and pepper
2–3 eggs

Peel and slice the onion. Wash, core and chop the green pepper. Wash and chop the fresh tomatoes or drain the tinned tomatoes and chop roughly. Heat the butter or oil in a saucepan and cook the onion and pepper over a medium heat, stirring well, until soft (about 5 minutes).

Add the chopped tomatoes, garlic, salt, pepper and stir. Put a lid on the pan and continue to cook gently over a low heat, stirring occasionally, for about 15 to 20 minutes, to make a thick saucy mixture.

Break the eggs into a small basin or large cup. Lightly beat them with a fork, then pour them into the vegetable mixture, stirring hard with a wooden spoon, until the eggs are just setting. Pour onto a warm plate, and eat with hot buttered toast or crusty fresh bread rolls.

SAVOURY EGGS

Serves 1

A cheap and tasty variation on the bacon 'n egg theme; makes a good, quick supper.

For a change, cooked sliced sausages or slices of salami can be used instead of bacon.

Preparation and cooking time: 25 minutes.

1 small onion
1 small eating apple
1 rasher of bacon
2 tsp cooking oil or large knob of butter (for frying)
Salt and pepper
¼ tsp sugar
2 eggs

Peel and slice the onion. Wash, core and slice the apple. De-rind the bacon and cut into ½ in (1.25cm) pieces. Heat the oil or butter in a frying pan over a moderate heat. Add the bacon, onion and apple, and fry, stirring occasionally, until soft (about 5 minutes). Stir in the salt, pepper and sugar.

Remove from the heat. Break the eggs into a cup, one at a time, and pour on top of the onion mixture. Cover the pan with a lid, and cook for a further 3 to 5 minutes over a very low heat, until the eggs are as firm as you like them.

CHEESY BAKED EGG

Serves 1

Quite delicious, and so easy to make.

Preparation and cooking time: 20 minutes.

3–4 oz (75–100g) cheese
2 eggs
Salt and pepper
Large knob of butter

Heat the oven (350°F/180°C/Gas Mark 4). Grease an oven-proof dish well with some butter.

Grate the cheese and cover the base of the dish with half of the cheese. Break the eggs, one at a time, into a cup, then slide them carefully on top of the cheese. Season well with the salt and pepper, and cover the eggs completely with the rest of the cheese.

Dot with the butter and bake in the hot oven for about 15 minutes, until the cheese is bubbling and the eggs are just set. Serve at once, with crusty French bread, rolls or crisp toast, or a salad.

EGG NESTS

Serves 1

These can be served plain, or with the addition of grated cheese, to make a very cheap lunch or supper.

Preparation and cooking time: 30 minutes.

2–4 potatoes
Large knob of butter
2 oz (50g) cheese (optional)
Salt and pepper
2 eggs

Peel the potatoes, cut into thick slices and cook in boiling, salted water in a saucepan for 10 to 15 minutes, until soft. Drain and mash with a fork, then beat in the large knob of butter, using a wooden spoon. Grate the cheese, if used, and beat half of it into the potato. Season with the salt and pepper.

1. Egg nest

Grease an oven-proof dish. Spread the potato into this, and make a nest for the eggs. Keep it warm. Boil 1 in (2.5cm) water in a clean frying pan and poach the eggs. If making cheesy eggs, heat the grill. Carefully lift the eggs out of the water when cooked and put them into the potato nest. If making plain eggs serve at once, otherwise cover the eggs with the remainder of the grated cheese and brown for a few moments under the hot grill. Can be served with a fresh tomato or a salad.

SICILIAN EGGS

Serves 1

Saucy tomatoes with eggs and bacon. Serve with hot toast.

Preparation and cooking time: 25 minutes.

2 eggs
1 small onion
Knob of butter
1 small tin (8 oz/230g) tomatoes
Salt and pepper
Pinch of sugar
Pinch of dried herbs
2 rashers of bacon (de-rinded)

Hard boil the eggs for 10 minutes. Cool them in cold, running water. Shell them, rinse clean, slice thickly and arrange in a greased, heat-proof dish.

Peel and slice the onion, and fry it in the butter in a small saucepan over a moderate heat, until soft (about 5 minutes). Add the tomatoes, salt, pepper, sugar and herbs, and cook gently for a further 5 minutes. Heat the grill.

Pour the tomato mixture over the eggs, top with the de-rinded bacon rashers and place under the hot grill until the bacon is cooked.

If you do not have a grill, fry the bacon in the pan with the onions, remove it and keep it hot while the tomatoes are cooking, then top the tomato mixture with the hot, cooked bacon.

EGG, CHEESE AND ONION SAVOURY *Serves 1*

Cheap and cheerful, eaten with chunks of hot, crusty bread.

Preparation and cooking time: 30 minutes.

2 eggs
1 onion
Knob of butter (for frying)
1 oz (25g) cheese

For the cheese sauce (you can omit this and just use grated cheese or alternatively use packet sauce mix):
1 oz (25g) cheese
2 tsp flour (or cornflour)
1 cup (¼ pt/150ml) milk
½ oz (12g) butter
Salt and pepper
Pinch of mustard

Hard boil the eggs for 10 minutes. Peel and slice the onion and fry gently in the knob of butter in a small saucepan over a moderate heat, for 4 to 5 minutes, until soft and cooked. Grate the cheese.

For the cheese sauce: EITHER mix the flour or cornflour into a smooth paste with a little of the milk in a small basin. Boil the rest of the milk and pour onto the flour mixture, stirring all the time. Then pour the whole mixture back into the saucepan and stir over the heat until the mixture thickens. Stir in the butter and beat well. Add the 1 oz (25g) grated cheese, salt, pepper and mustard. OR make up the packet sauce mix.

Put the onion into a greased oven-proof dish. Slice the cold, peeled hard-boiled eggs, and arrange on top of the onion. Cover with the cheese sauce and sprinkle with the rest of the grated cheese. Brown under a hot grill for a few minutes, until the cheese is melted, crisp and bubbly.

MURPHY'S EGGS

Serves 1

A cheap and filling supper dish if you have time to wait for it to cook in the oven.

Preparation and cooking time: 1 hour 15 minutes.

½ lb (225g) potatoes (about 3 or 4 according to appetite)
1 onion
1 rasher of bacon
Salt and pepper
½–1 cup (¼ pt/150ml approx.) hot milk
Knob of butter
2 eggs

Peel the potatoes, cut into small ½ in (1.25cm) dice. Peel and slice the onion. De-rind and chop the bacon. Grease an oven-proof dish. Mix the potatoes, onion and bacon in a bowl, and put into the dish, seasoning well with the salt and pepper. Add the hot milk (enough to come halfway up the dish) and dot with the butter.

Bake in a hot oven (400°F/200°C/Gas Mark 6), covered with a lid or foil, for 45 minutes to 1 hour, until the potatoes are cooked and all the milk is absorbed.

Break each egg into a cup. Remove the dish of potatoes from the oven, make two hollows in the top of the potatoes with a spoon, and slip the raw eggs into the hollows. Return the dish to the oven for 6 to 8 minutes until the eggs are set. Serve at once.

EGGY BREAD OR FRENCH TOAST *Serves 1*

A boarding school favourite.

Serve with golden syrup, honey or jam, or sprinkled with white or brown sugar.

Or to make it savoury, sprinkle with salt, pepper, and a blob of tomato sauce. Savoury eggy bread goes well with bacon, sausages and baked beans.

Preparation and cooking time: 15 minutes.

1 egg
1–2 tsp sugar (according to taste)
½ cup milk
3–4 thick slices of white bread
2 oz (50g) butter (for frying)

Break the egg into a basin or a large cup, add the sugar and beat well with a whisk, mixer or fork, gradually adding the milk. Pour this egg mixture into a shallow dish or soup plate, and soak each slice of bread in the egg, until it is all soaked up.

Heat a frying pan over a moderate heat. Melt the butter in the pan and fry the soaked bread slices in the hot butter, turning to cook both sides, until golden brown and crispy. Serve at once as above.

FRENCH OMELETTE *Serves 1*

The best-known type of omelette: light golden egg, folded over into an envelope shape. Served plain or with a wide variety of sweet or savoury fillings, folded inside. There is no need for a special omelette pan (unless you happen to own one, of course). Use any clean, ordinary frying pan.

Preparation and cooking time: 10 minutes.

2–3 eggs
1 tsp cold water per egg
Pinch of salt and pepper (omit for sweet omelettes)
Knob of butter
Filling as required (see opposite)

Prepare the filling (see list opposite). Warm a plate. Break the eggs into a basin or large cup, add the water, salt and pepper and beat with a fork.

Put the butter in a frying pan and heat over a moderate heat until it is just sizzling (but not brown). Place the egg mixture in the pan at once. Carefully, with a wide-bladed knife or wooden spoon, draw the mixture from the middle to the sides of the pan, so that the uncooked egg in the middle can run onto the hot pan and set. Continue until all the egg is very lightly cooked underneath and the top is still running and soft (about one minute). The top will cook in its own heat, when it is folded over.

With the wide-bladed knife or a fish slice loosen the omelette so that you can remove it easily from the pan. Put the filling across the middle of the omelette and fold both sides over it to make an envelope. If using a cold filling, cook for a further minute. Remove from the pan and place on the warm plate. Serve at once, with French bread, bread rolls, sauté or new potatoes, a side salad or just a fresh tomato. Delicious!

OMELETTE AND PANCAKE FILLINGS

For pancakes, see page 183.

Savoury

Asparagus

Use ½ small can (10 oz/298g size) asparagus tips. Heat them through in a small saucepan. Drain and keep hot.

Bacon

Fry 1–2 rashers of bacon in a little oil or fat. Keep hot.

Cheese

1–2 oz (25–50g) grated or finely cubed.

Chicken

2–3 tbsp chopped, cooked chicken. (You can use the pickings from a roast chicken.)

Fresh or Dried Herbs

Add 1 tsp chopped herbs to the beaten eggs, water and seasoning.

Cooked Meat

Chop 1–2 slices cooked ham, salami or garlic sausage, etc.

Mushrooms

Wash and chop 2 oz (50g or 4–5 mushrooms). Cook gently in a small pan, with a knob of butter, for 2–3 minutes, stirring occasionally. Keep hot.

Tomato

Wash 1–2 tomatoes, slice and fry them in a little oil or fat and keep hot.

Sweet

Choose one of the following fillings, then sprinkle the omelettes with 1 tsp icing or granulated sugar, just before serving.

Fruit
Add 2–3 tbsp sliced, tinned fruit (peaches, pineapple or apricot) or 2–3 tbsp sliced fresh fruit (bananas, peaches, strawberries or raspberries).

Honey
Add 2–3 tbsp honey.

Honey and Walnut
Use 2–3 tbsp honey, 1 tbsp chopped walnuts.

Jam
Add 1–2 tbsp jam or bramble jelly. Warm the jam by standing it in a saucepan with 2 in (5cm) hot water, and warming gently over a low heat.

Marmalade
Add 2–3 tbsp orange or ginger marmalade.

SPANISH OMELETTE *Serves 1*

A delicious, filling, savoury omelette. Served flat like a thick pancake, mixed with onion, potato, cooked meat and other vegetables – a good way of using up cold, cooked, leftovers. (A large omelette, made with 4 eggs and some extra vegetables, can be cut in half, serving 2 people.)

Preparation and cooking time: 15 minutes.

EXTRAS (optional):

Bacon: 1–2 rashers of bacon, chopped and fried with the onion
Cooked meat: 1–2 slices of chopped, cooked ham, salami, or garlic sausage, etc.
Green peppers: 1–2 tbsp green peppers, chopped and mixed with the onion
Sausages: 1–2 cold, cooked sausages, sliced

Vegetables: 1–2 tbsp cold cooked vegetables (peas, sweetcorn, green beans, mixed vegetables)

1 small onion
2–3 boiled potatoes
2–3 eggs
1 tsp cold water per egg
Salt and pepper
Pinch of dried herbs (optional)
1 tbsp oil (for frying)

Prepare the 'extras' if used. Peel and chop the onion. Dice the cooked potatoes. Beat the eggs, water, seasoning and herbs lightly with a fork in a small basin.

Heat the oil in an omelette or frying pan over a medium heat, and fry the onion for 3 to 5 minutes, until soft. Add the diced potato and continue frying until the potato is thoroughly heated. Add the extra meat or vegetables (if used) and heat through again. Heat the grill and warm a plate. Pour the beaten egg mixture into the pan, over the vegetables, and cook without stirring until the bottom is firm, but with the top remaining creamy and moist (about 1 to 2 minutes). Shake the pan occasionally to prevent sticking.

Place under the hot grill for ½ minute, until the top is set – beware in case the pan handle gets hot. Slide the omelette flat onto the warm plate and serve at once.

QUICK EGG AND VEGETABLE CURRY *Serves 1*

A fast and easy curry recipe.

Preparation and cooking time: 35 minutes.

1 onion
Knob of butter
1 tsp cooking oil
1 tsp curry powder (or more or less according to taste)
1 tsp flour or cornflour
Small can (10 oz/295g) mulligatawny soup
2 eggs
½ cup (2–3 oz/50-75g) long grain rice
1 cup or 2 oz (50g) frozen mixed vegetables

Peel and chop the onion, and fry in the oil and butter in a saucepan over a medium heat, until soft (about 3 to 4 minutes). Stir in the curry powder and flour, and cook very gently for a further 2 minutes, stirring all the time. Gradually stir in the soup, bring to the boil, reduce the heat to a simmer, put on the lid, and cook gently for about 20 minutes, stirring occasionally, to make a thick sauce.

Hard boil the eggs for 10 minutes. Rinse them under cold, running water, peel them, wash off the shell and cut in half, lengthways. Cook the rice for 10 to 12 minutes in a large pan of boiling salted water (see page 81). Drain and keep hot, fluffing with a fork to stop it going lumpy. Add the mixed vegetables to the curry sauce, bring back to the boil and simmer for a few minutes to cook the vegetables.

Put the rice onto a warm plate, spreading round with a spoon to form a ring. Arrange the eggs in the centre and cover with the vegetable curry sauce. Serve with any side dishes you like (see page 128).

DRINKING EGG OR EGG NOG

Serves 1

A nourishing breakfast for those in a hurry, or an easily-digested meal for those feeling fragile!

Preparation time: 5 minutes.

1 egg
2 tsp sugar
2 cups (½ pt/300ml) milk (cold or warm)
2 tsp brandy, rum or whisky (optional, but not for breakfast!) or 1 tbsp sherry (optional, but not for breakfast!)
Pinch of nutmeg or cinnamon

Break the egg into a basin, beat it lightly with a mixer, egg whisk or fork, adding the sugar and gradually beating in the milk. Add the spirits (if used). Pour into a tall glass, sprinkle nutmeg or cinnamon on top and serve at once.

HOW TO SEPARATE AN EGG

METHOD 1

Have 2 cups or basins ready. Crack the egg carefully, and pull the 2 halves apart, letting the white drain into one basin, and keeping the yolk in the shell, until all the white has drained out. Tip the yolk into the other basin. If the yolk breaks, tip the whole lot into another basin and start again with another egg.

METHOD 2

Carefully break the egg and tip it onto a saucer, making sure the yolk is not broken. Place a glass over the yolk, and gently tip the white into a basin, keeping the yolk on the saucer with the glass.

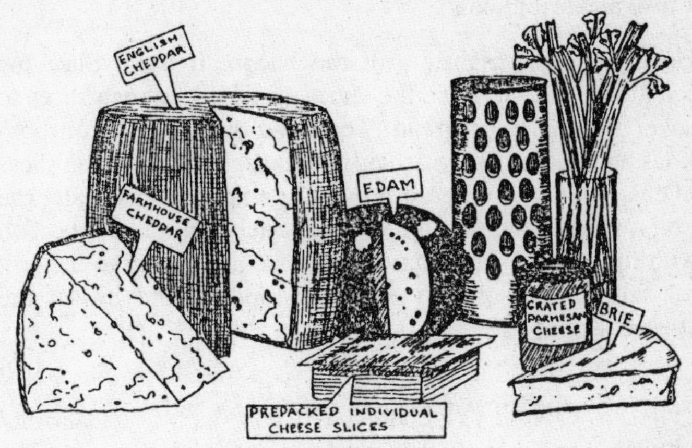

3
CHEESE

Here are some delicious snacks using cheese – they're simple and quick to make.

EASY WELSH RAREBIT (CHEESE ON TOAST)

Serves 1

This is the quickest method of making cheese on toast. It can be served plain, or topped with pickle, sliced tomato or crispy, cooked bacon.

Preparation and cooking time: 5–10 minutes.

1–3 rashers of bacon (optional)
1–2 tomatoes (optional)
2–3 oz (50–75g/2–3 slices) cheese

(continued overleaf)

(Easy Welsh Rarebit continued)

2–3 slices of bread (white or brown)
Butter (for spreading)
1 tbsp pickle (optional)

Heat the grill. Lightly grill the bacon, if used. Slice the tomatoes, if used. Slice the cheese, making enough slices to cover the pieces of bread. Toast the bread lightly on both sides and spread one side with the butter. Arrange the slices of cheese on the buttered side of the toast and put under the grill for 1 to 2 minutes, until the cheese begins to bubble. Top with the tomato slices, bacon or pickle and return to the grill for another minute, to heat the topping and brown the cheese. Eat at once.

TRADITIONAL WELSH RAREBIT *Serves 1*

More soft and creamy than cheese on toast, and only takes a few more minutes to prepare.

Preparation and cooking time: 10 minutes.

1–3 rashers of bacon (optional)
1–2 tomatoes (optional)
2–3 oz (50–75g) cheese
1 tsp milk
Pinch of mustard
Shake of pepper
1 tbsp pickle (optional)
2–3 slices of bread, and butter

Heat the grill. Lightly grill the bacon, if used. Slice the tomatoes, if used. Grate the cheese and mix into a stiff paste with the milk in a bowl, stirring in the mustard and pepper. Lightly toast the bread, and spread one side with butter, then generously cover it with the cheese mixture. Put under the hot grill for 1 to 2 minutes, until the cheese starts to bubble. Top with the bacon, tomato slices or pickle, and return to the grill for another minute, to heat the topping and brown the cheese. Serve at once.

BUCK RAREBIT

Serves 1

Welsh Rarebit with poached eggs. When the toast is covered with the cheese, and ready to pop back under the grill to brown, prepare 1 or 2 poached eggs, by cooking them gently in simmering water for 2 to 3 minutes. While the eggs are cooking, put the toast and cheese slices under the grill to brown. When they are golden and bubbling, and the eggs are cooked, carefully remove the eggs from the water, and slide them onto the hot cheesy toast. Serve immediately.

BOOZY WELSH RAREBIT

Serves 1

Open a can of beer, use a little in the cooking, and drink the rest with your meal.

Preparation and cooking time: 10–15 minutes.

2–3 oz (50–75g) cheese
Knob of butter
1–2 tbsp beer
Shake of pepper
Pinch of mustard
1–2 slices of bread (white or brown)

Grate the cheese and heat the grill. Melt the butter in a small saucepan over a moderate heat. Add the cheese, beer, pepper and mustard, and stir well over the heat, until the cheese begins to melt, and the mixture begins to boil. Remove the saucepan from the heat. Toast the bread lightly on both sides. Carefully pour the cheese mixture onto the toast, and put back under the grill for a few moments, until the cheese is hot, bubbling and golden brown. Serve at once, delicious!

CHEESY FRANKFURTER TOASTS *Serves 1*

A quick snack, made with food from the store cupboard.

Preparation and cooking time: 15 minutes.

2–3 slices of bread
½ oz (12g) butter
2–3 slices of cooked ham, garlic sausage or luncheon meat (optional)
Small can (8 oz/227g; actual weight of sausages 4 oz/163g) Frankfurter sausages
2–3 slices of cheese (pre-packed slices are ideal)

Heat the grill. Lightly toast the bread on one side. Butter the untoasted side of the bread. Lay the ham or garlic sausage on the untoasted side and top with the Frankfurters. Cover with the cheese slices, and cook under the hot grill until the cheese has melted. Eat at once.

If you don't have a grill the bread can be heated in a hot oven (400°F/200°C/Gas Mark 6) for a few minutes, and then buttered. Place the 'toast' with the topping back into the oven, on an oven-proof dish, and cook for 5 to 10 minutes, until the cheese has melted.

CAULIFLOWER CHEESE *Serves 1*

Filling enough for a supper dish with crusty French bread and butter, or serve as a vegetable dish with meat or fish.

Preparation and cooking time: 30 minutes.

1 portion (3–4 florets) cauliflower
1 slice of bread (crumbled or grated into crumbs)
Knob of butter
1 sliced tomato (optional)

For the cheese sauce (alternatively use packet sauce mix or 2 oz/50g grated cheese):
2 oz (50g) cheese
2 tsp cornflour or flour
1 cup (¼ pt/150ml) milk
½ oz (12g) butter or margarine
Salt and pepper
Pinch of mustard

Trim the cauliflower's stalk, divide it into florets and wash thoroughly. Cook it in boiling, salted water for 5 minutes, until just tender. Drain well.

Make the cheese sauce (see page 174).

Put the cauliflower into a greased oven-proof dish. Cover with the cheese sauce, sprinkle the breadcrumbs on top and add a knob of butter and the tomato slices. Place under a hot grill for a few minutes, until golden-brown and crispy. (If you do not have time to make the cheese sauce, cover the cauliflower with 2 oz (50g) grated cheese and grill as above.)

4

SNACKS, SAVOURIES AND SALADS

Just a few ideas and suggestions for quick snacks and packed lunches. Other recipes can be found in Chapters 2 and 3.

SANDWICHES FOR PACKED LUNCHES

Try and ring the changes with different kinds of bread – white, brown, granary, sliced, crusty rolls, soft baps, French bread and Arab bread are a few suggestions. Crisp breads make a change too.

Butter the bread lightly, this stops it going soggy if the

filling is moist, and holds the filling in place (have you ever tried eating unbuttered egg sandwiches?). Wrap the sandwiches in cling film to keep them fresh – it's worth buying a roll if you take sandwiches often – or put them into a polythene bag. A plastic container will stop them getting squashed.

Lettuce, tomato, cucumber, celery and green peppers are a good addition, either sliced in the sandwiches or eaten separately, with them. Treat yourself to some fresh fruit as well, according to what is in season.

Cheese
Slice or grate the cheese.

Cheese and Pickle
As above, and mix with a little pickle or chutney.

Cheese Slices
Quick and easy. Use straight from the packet. Spread pickle on top of the cheese if liked.

Cheese and Tomato
Slice a tomato layer on top of the cheese.

Cheese and Onion
Peel and thinly slice an onion, lay it thinly on top of the sliced cheese.

Cold Meat
Sliced, cooked meat, from the supermarket or delicatessen: ham, tongue, turkey roll, chicken roll, salami, garlic sausage, etc. Buy according to your taste and pocket. Buy fresh as you need it; do not store too long in the fridge.

Cold Meat from the Joint
Beef and mustard or horseradish sauce
Slice the beef thinly, and spread with the mustard or horseradish.

Cold Lamb and Mint Sauce
Slice the meat, cut off any excess fat. Add the mint sauce.

Cold Pork and Apple Sauce and Stuffing
Slice the pork, spread with any leftover apple sauce and stuffing.

Cold Chicken
Use up the fiddly bits from a roast chicken or buy chicken roll slices. Spread with cranberry jelly and stuffing. Do not store for too long in the fridge; buy just a little at a time.

Egg
Cook for 10 minutes in boiling water. Shell, wash and mash with a fork. Mix it either with a little mayonnaise or tomato chutney. One egg will fill two rounds of cut bread sandwiches.

Marmite
Very good for you, especially with a chunk of cheese, or topped with sliced cheese.

Peanut Butter
No need to butter the bread first. Top with seedless jam (jelly) if liked.

Salad
Washed lettuce, sliced tomato, sliced cucumber, layered together.

Salmon
Open a can, drain off any excess juice, and tip the salmon into a bowl. Discard the bones and skin, and mash with a little vinegar and pepper. Spread on the buttered bread, top with cucumber slices or lettuce if liked.

Tuna Fish
Open a can, drain off the oil. Tip the tuna fish into a bowl

and mash with vinegar and pepper, or mayonnaise. Spread on the buttered bread, top with lettuce or cucumber slices.

Liver Pâté
Choose from the numerous smooth or rough pâtés in the supermarket. Brown or granary bread is particularly good with pâté.

Eat with your Packed Lunch:
Cottage Cheese (plain or flavoured)
Eat from the carton with a fresh buttered roll, or an apple if you're slimming. Don't forget to take a spoon.

Yoghurt
Eat from the carton – remember to take a spoon.

Hard-boiled Egg
Hard boil an egg. Shell and wash it. Pop it into a polythene bag and eat with a fresh buttered roll.

Scotch Egg
Buy fresh from the supermarket.

FRIED BREAD *Serves 1*

Best cooked in the frying pan in the fat left from frying bacon or sausages.

Preparation and cooking time: 4–5 minutes.

1–2 slices of bread
Fat left in the pan from cooking sausages or bacon (or 2 tsp cooking oil and large knob of butter)

Remove the sausage or bacon from the pan and keep hot. Cut the bread slices in half, and fry in the hot fat over a moderate heat for 1 to 2 minutes on each side, until golden brown and crispy, adding a little extra butter to the pan if necessary.

FRIED CHEESE SANDWICHES

Serves 1

A very quick and tasty snack.

Preparation and cooking time: 10 minutes.

2–4 slices of bread
½ oz (12g) butter
2–4 thin cheese slices (you can use pre-packed cheese slices if you wish)
1 tbsp cooking oil and a large knob of butter (for frying)

Extra fillings (optional):
1 thinly-sliced tomato
1 tsp pickle
1–2 rashers of crisply fried bacon – fry this ready before you start the sandwiches

Lightly butter the slices of bread. Make them into sandwiches with 1 to 2 slices of cheese in each sandwich, adding any of the optional extras you like.

Heat the oil and knob of butter in a frying pan, over a moderate heat. Put the sandwiches into the hot fat, and fry for a few minutes on each side, until the bread is golden and crispy, and the cheese is beginning to melt.

Remove from the pan, drain on a piece of kitchen paper if they seem a bit greasy. Eat at once while hot.

GARLIC BREAD

Serves 1

A sophisticated alternative to hot bread rolls.

Preparation and cooking time: 18–20 minutes.

1 clove of garlic (or ½ tsp garlic powder or paste)
2 oz (50g) butter
½ French loaf or 1–2 bread rolls (according to appetite)
Large piece of cooking foil (for wrapping)

Peel, chop and crush the garlic clove, if used, until smooth. (You can crush it with a pestle and mortar or garlic press, if you have one, or use the flat side of a knife but this is more fiddly.) Cream together the butter and crushed garlic (or garlic powder or paste), until soft and well-mixed.

Cut the loaf nearly through into 1 in (2.5cm) slices (be careful not to cut the slices completely or the loaf will drop into bits) or cut the rolls in half. Butter the slices of the loaf, or the rolls, generously on both sides with the garlic butter and press the loaf or rolls together again. Wrap the loaf or rolls loosely in the foil. Heat the bread in a hot oven (400°F/ 200°C/Gas Mark 6–7) until hot and crisp (approximately 5 minutes). Serve at once, with the foil unfolded.

HERB BREAD

Serves 1

If you don't like garlic, omit garlic from the above recipe and make a herb loaf, adding a really generous handful of freshly chopped or snipped mixed herbs and a tsp lemon juice to the butter.

BEANS (OR SPAGHETTI) ON TOAST *Serves 1*

If you've never cooked these before, here is the method.

Preparation and cooking time: 5 minutes.

1 oz (25g) cheese (optional)
1 small (8 oz/225g) tin beans, spaghetti, spaghetti hoops, etc.
2–3 slices of bread
Butter

Grate the cheese, or chop it finely (if used).

Put the beans or spaghetti into a small saucepan, and heat slowly over a moderate heat, stirring occasionally. Toast the bread and spread one side of it with butter. When the beans are beginning to bubble, stir gently until they are thoroughly heated.

Put the toast onto a warm plate, and pour the beans on top of the buttered side (some people prefer the toast left at the side of the plate). Sprinkle the cheese on top. Eat at once.

GARLIC MUSHROOMS *Serves 1*

Delicious, but don't breathe over other people after eating these! Serve with fried bacon to make it more substantial.

Preparation and cooking time: 10 minutes.

3–4 oz (75–100g) mushrooms
1 clove of fresh garlic (or garlic powder or garlic paste)
1–2 rashers of bacon (optional)
1 oz (25g) butter with 1 tsp cooking oil
2 thick slices of bread

Wash the mushrooms. Peel, chop and crush the fresh garlic, if used. Fry the bacon and keep hot. Melt the butter and oil in a saucepan over a moderate heat. Add the garlic (fresh, powder or paste) and mushrooms.

Stir well, and fry gently for 3 to 5 minutes, stirring and spooning the garlic-flavoured butter over the mushrooms. While the mushrooms are cooking, toast the bread lightly, cut in half and put onto a hot plate. Spoon the mushrooms onto the toast and pour the remaining garlic butter over the top. Top with bacon, if used. Eat at once.

PIZZA

There are so many makes, shapes and sizes of pizza available now, both fresh and frozen, that it hardly seems worth the effort of making your own. However, these commercial ones are usually improved by adding your own extras during the cooking, either when under the grill or in the oven according to the instructions on the packet.

Add these extras for the last 5 to 10 minutes of cooking time by spreading them on top of the pizza:

Cheese
Use grated or thinly sliced.

Ham
Chop and sprinkle over the pizza.

Salami, Garlic Sausage
Chop or fold slices and arrange on top of the pizza.

Mushrooms
Wash and slice thinly, spread over the pizza.

Tomatoes
Slice thinly, spread over the pizza.

Olives
A few spread on top add colour and flavour.

Anchovies or Sardines
Arrange criss-cross over the pizza.

BASIC GREEN SALAD

Serves 1

Preparation time: 5 minutes.

3–4 washed lettuce leaves
½ small onion
1 tbsp vinaigrette

Leave the lettuce leaves whole if small, or shred as finely as you like. Peel and slice the onion. Put the lettuce and onion into a salad bowl, add the vinaigrette and lightly turn the lettuce over in the dressing, until well mixed.

Other salad vegetables can be added:

Beetroot (cooked, if necessary, and sliced)
Celery (washed, scraped, if necessary, cut into 1 in (2.5cm) lengths)
Cucumber (washed, cut into rings or chunks)
Pepper (washed, cored, cut into rings)
Radishes (with tops cut off, roots removed and washed)
Spring onion (washed, cut off roots and yellow leaves, cut into rings or leave whole)
Tomatoes (washed, sliced or cut into quarters)
Watercress, mustard and cress (washed, sprinkled on top of the other vegetables).

WINTER SALAD

Serves 1

Trim, shred and wash a quarter of a white or green cabbage. Drain well and dry in a salad shaker (if you have one) or put into a clean tea-towel and shake or pat dry. Put the cabbage in a dish, with any other salad vegetables, such as raw, grated carrot, tomato quarters, cucumber, celery, peppers, peeled sliced onion.

It can either be served on its own, or with a dressing made from the following ingredients mixed together thoroughly: 4 tsp salad oil, 2 tsp vinegar, pinch of salt, pepper and sugar.

COLESLAW

Serves 1

A quick and tasty way of using up extra raw cabbage. Serve with cold meat, or with hot dishes.

Preparation time: 15 minutes.

¼ crisp white cabbage
1 small carrot
1 eating apple (red-skinned if possible)
Lemon juice (if possible)
1 small onion
1–2 tbsp mayonnaise
Salt and pepper

Trim off the outer leaves and stalk of the cabbage. Shred it finely, wash it well in cold water. Scrape the carrot. Chop it finely or grate it. Peel and core the apple. Chop it finely or grate it. Sprinkle with a little lemon juice. Peel the onion. Chop or grate it finely. Drain the cabbage well.

Mix all the vegetables together in a bowl. Toss lightly in the mayonnaise until all the ingredients are well-coated. Season to taste.

Many different fruit or vegetables can be used in this recipe. A few chopped salted nuts, a tbsp of washed, dried sultanas, a little chopped green pepper are some ideas you might like to try.

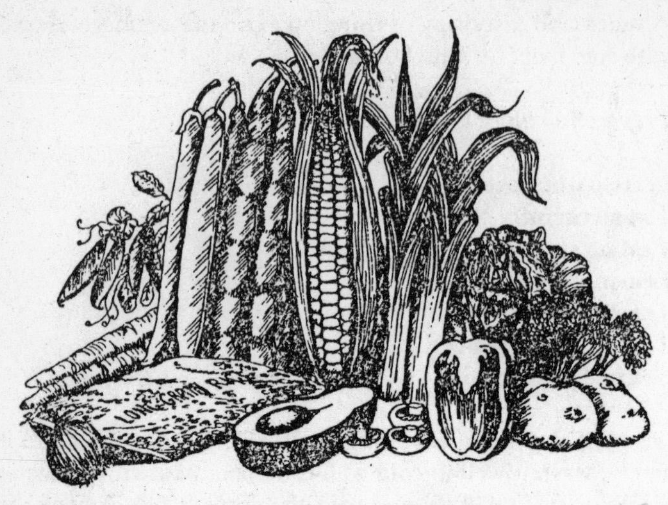

5
VEGETABLES, VEGETABLE DISHES AND RICE

This chapter gives basic instructions on preparing and cooking fresh vegetables (listed in alphabetical order) to be eaten as part of a meal, together with recipes using vegetables which are substantial enough to be used as a lunch or supper dish by themselves.

When cooking vegetables in water, remember that a lot of the goodness and flavour soaks from the vegetables into the cooking water. So do not use too much water or overcook them. When possible, use the vegetable water for making gravy. Frozen vegetables are convenient but are generally dearer than fresh vegetables. Vegetable prices vary tremendously according to the season, so look out for the best buys at the vegetable counter.

GLOBE ARTICHOKES

2. Globe Artichokes

These are the green, leafy type of artichoke. They look large, but as you only eat the bottom tip of each leaf, you do need *a whole artichoke for each person*. As they are expensive, cook them mainly for special occasions.

Cut off the stem of the artichoke to make the base level, snip off the points of the leaves, and wash the artichoke well in cold water. Put in a large saucepan, cover with boiling salted water, and boil for 30 to 40 minutes, until a leaf will pull off easily.

Drain the water from the pan and then turn the artichoke upside down in the pan for a few moments to drain any remaining water. Serve with plenty of butter.

JERUSALEM ARTICHOKES

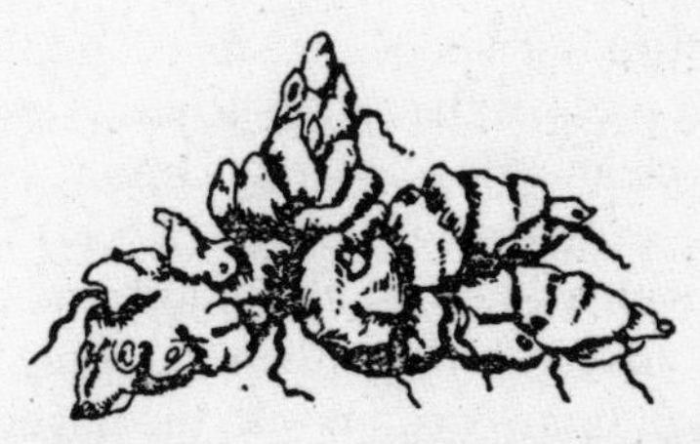

3. Jerusalem Artichokes

These artichokes look like knobbly potatoes. Cook them immediately they are peeled, as they go brown very quickly even in cold water. A little lemon juice in the cooking water helps to keep them white.

8 oz (225g) serves 1–2 portions.

BOILED

Peel the artichokes and cut them into evenly-sized lumps about the size of small potatoes. Boil them in a pan of salted water for 20 to 30 minutes, until tender. Drain and serve with a dab of butter.

BOILED WITH CHICKEN SAUCE

Cook in salted water (as above) until tender. Drain, and put back in the saucepan with ½ can (10 oz/300g size) of condensed chicken soup. Bring back to the boil, stirring occasionally. Tip the artichokes onto a warm plate, pouring the chicken sauce over them.

FRIED

Peel the artichokes and cut them into thick slices or chunks. Put 1 tsp cooking oil and ½ oz (12g) butter into a frying pan, add the artichoke pieces and cook gently, turning frequently, for 15 to 20 minutes, until soft. Tip the artichokes onto a warm plate, pouring the buttery sauce over them.

ASPARAGUS

A very expensive treat! *Usually sold in bundles, enough for 2–4 servings.*

Cut off the woody ends of the stems and then scrape off the white tough parts of the stems. Rinse. Tie the stems into a bundle, with clean string or white cotton, and stand them tips uppermost in a pan with 1 in (2.5cm) boiling water. Cover the pan with a lid or a dome of foil, and boil for 8 to 10 minutes, until tender. Remove them carefully from the pan. Asparagus is traditionally eaten with the fingers. To eat, just dip the tips in butter and leave any woody parts that still remain on the stems.

AUBERGINES

The English name for the aubergine is the 'egg plant'. These lovely, shiny purple-skinned vegetables are best left unpeeled.

Fry 1 medium-sized aubergine per person.

To get rid of any bitter taste before cooking, slice the aubergine into ½ in (1.25cm) pieces. Put into a colander or strainer (if you do not have one, lay the slices on a piece of kitchen paper), sprinkle with salt, press a heavy plate down on top and leave for 30 minutes so that the bitter juices are pressed out. Wash and dry the slices. Heat a little oil in a frying pan, and fry gently until soft (about 5 minutes).

AVOCADO PEARS

Buy avocados when the price is down – the price varies considerably during the year, as they are imported from several countries. They make a nourishing change.

Choose pears that yield slightly when pressed gently. Unripe pears feel very hard.

Slice the avocado in half lengthways, cutting through to the stone. Then separate the two halves by twisting gently. Remove the stone with the tip of the knife, trying not to damage the flesh, which should be soft and buttery in texture.

Cut avocados discolour very quickly, so prepare them just before serving, or rub the cut halves with lemon juice to stop them going brown. Serve avocados plain with a squeeze of lemon juice, with a vinaigrette dressing or with any one of the numerous fillings spooned into the cavity from where the stone was removed. Brown bread and butter is the traditional accompaniment, with a garnish of lettuce, tomato and cucumber.

Some Filling Ideas

Vinaigrette: Mix well 2 tsp oil, 1 tsp vinegar, salt, pepper and a pinch of sugar.

Mayonnaise: 1 tbsp mayonnaise.

Cottage Cheese: Mix well together 2 tbsp cottage cheese (plain or with chives, pineapple, etc.) and 1 tsp mayonnaise.

Prawn or Shrimp: Mix gently together 1–2 tbsp shelled prawns or shrimps (fresh, frozen or canned), 1 tbsp mayonnaise and/or cottage cheese. A sauce can also be made with a mixture of 1 tbsp salad cream and a dash of tomato ketchup.

Egg: Shell and chop 1 hard-boiled egg. Mix gently with 1 tbsp mayonnaise and/or cottage cheese.

Yoghurt: 2 tbsp yoghurt on its own, or mixed with a chopped tomato and a few slices chopped cucumber.

CREAMY AVOCADO TOAST *Serves 1*

Use a soft avocado pear for this. They are often sold off cheaply when they become very ripe and the shop wants to sell them quickly.

Preparation time: 5 minutes.

1 ripe avocado
Salt and pepper
2 thick slices of bread (brown or granary)
Knob of butter

Cut the avocado in half, lengthways and remove the stone. Scoop out the soft flesh with a teaspoon, put it into a small basin, and mash to a soft cream. Season with the salt and pepper.

Toast the bread on both sides, spread one side with butter, then spread the avocado cream thickly on the top. Eat while the toast is hot.

SAVOURY AVOCADO SNACK

Serves 1

If you're a vegetarian and don't want to eat bacon, you may prefer to sprinkle ½ tbsp chopped walnuts on top of the cheese instead.

Preparation and cooking time: 15 minutes.

1–2 rashers of bacon
Oil (for frying)
1 small avocado pear
1 oz (25g) cheese
Chunk of French bread
Knob of butter

De-rind the bacon. Fry it in a little oil in a frying pan over a moderate heat until crisp.

Peel the avocado pear and slice it, removing the stone. Grate or slice the cheese.

Cut the French bread in half lengthways, and spread with the butter. Arrange layers of the avocado and bacon on the bread. Top with the cheese slices or grated cheese.

Grill under a hot grill for a few minutes, until the cheese is golden, bubbling and melted. Eat at once.

BROAD BEANS

Buy 4–8 oz (100–225g) unshelled beans per person, according to the size of the beans. The smaller, younger beans go further, as you can cook them whole, like French beans, whereas older, larger beans need to be shelled.

TINY NEW BROAD BEANS

Top and tail the beans with a vegetable knife or a pair of scissors. Either leave them whole or cut them into shorter lengths (4 in/10cm) depending on their size. Boil them in water for 5 to 10 minutes, according to size, until tender. Drain and serve with a knob of butter.

LARGER BROAD BEANS

Remove the beans from the pods. Cook in boiling water for 5 to 10 minutes, until tender. Drain and serve with a knob of butter, or parsley sauce, if you feel very ambitious.

FROZEN BROAD BEANS

Allow approximately 4 oz (100g) per serving. Cook as instructed on the packet, and serve as above.

FRENCH BEANS

Can be rather expensive, but as there is very little waste you need only buy a small amount. *Allow approximately 4 oz (100g) per serving.*

Top and tail the beans with a vegetable knife or a pair of scissors. Wash the beans and cut the longer beans in half (about 4 in/10cm). Put them into a pan of boiling, salted water and cook for 2 to 5 minutes, until just tender. Drain well and serve them with a knob of butter.

FROZEN WHOLE FRENCH BEANS

Allow approximately 3–4 oz (75–100g) per serving. Cook in boiling, salted water as directed on the packet and serve as above with a knob of butter. Very tasty, but be careful not to overcook them.

RUNNER BEANS

These are sold frozen and ready to cook all year round, but lovely fresh beans are available in August and September. Choose crisp, green beans; limp, pallid ones are not as fresh as they should be. *Allow 4 oz (100g) beans per person.*

Top and tail the beans. Cut down the sides of the large beans to remove any tough stringy bits, and slice the beans evenly into whatever size you prefer, up to 1 in (2.5cm) long. Wash them in cold water. Cook in boiling, salted water for 5 to 10 minutes, according to size, until just tender. Drain well and serve hot.

FROZEN BEANS

Allow 3–4 oz (75–100g) per serving. Cook according to the instructions on the packet, in boiling, salted water.

BEAN SPROUTS

These can be cooked on their own, but are better when cooked with a mixture of stir-fried vegetables. *Allow 4 oz (100g) per portion.* Soak for 10 minutes in cold water, then drain the bean sprouts well. Heat 1 tbsp oil in a frying pan or a wok, add the bean sprouts and fry for 1 to 2 minutes, stirring all the time. Serve at once.

BROCCOLI

Green broccoli and purple sprouting broccoli are both cooked in the same way. *Allow 2–3 pieces or 8 oz (225g) per serving.*

Remove any coarse outer leaves and cut off the ends of the stalks. Wash well in cold water. Boil for 5 to 10 minutes in salted water, until tender. Drain well; press out the water gently with a fork if necessary. Serve with a knob of butter.

FROZEN BROCCOLI

Allow 4–6 oz (100–150g) per serving, according to appetite. Cook as directed on the packet, in boiling, salted water.

BRUSSELS SPROUTS

Try to buy firm, green sprouts of approximately the same size. Yellow outside leaves are a sign of old age.

Allow 4–6 oz (100-150g) per serving.

Cut off the stalk ends, and trim off the outer leaves if necessary. Wash well. Cook in boiling, salted water for 5 to 10 minutes, until tender. Drain well.

FROZEN SPROUTS

Allow 3–4 oz (75–100g) per serving. Cook in boiling, salted water as directed on the packet.

WHITE OR GREEN CABBAGE

A much maligned vegetable, evoking memories of school days. If cooked properly, cabbage is really delicious and much cheaper than a lot of other vegetables. Cabbage goes a very long way, so either buy a *small cabbage* and use it for several meals (cooked, or raw in a winter salad) or *just buy half or a quarter of a cabbage*.

Trim off the outer leaves and the stalk. Cut into quarters and shred, not too finely, removing the central core and cutting that into small pieces. Wash the cabbage. Boil it in salted water for 2 to 5 minutes. Do not overcook. Drain well, serve with a knob of butter, or with a cheese sauce.

To make cabbage cheese, instead of cauliflower cheese, substitute the cabbage for the cauliflower on page 39.

CRISPY CABBAGE CASSEROLE

Serves 1

This is filling enough to serve as a cheap supper dish, with hot bread rolls, butter and a chunk of cheese. It is delicious as a vegetable accompaniment with meat.

Preparation and cooking time: 35 minutes.

1 portion of cabbage (¼ of a cabbage)
1 small onion
1–2 sticks of celery
1 tsp oil and ½ oz (12g) butter (for frying)
1 slice of bread

For the white sauce (or use 1 packet of sauce mix):
2 tsp cornflour (or flour)
1 cup (¼ pt/150ml) milk
½ oz (12g) butter (or margarine)
Salt and pepper

Grease an oven-proof dish or casserole. Trim the outer leaves and stalk from the cabbage. Shred it, not too finely, wash it well and drain. Peel and chop the onion. Scrape and wash the celery and cut into 1 in (2.5cm) lengths. Heat the oil and butter in a frying pan, and fry the onion gently for 2 to 3 minutes until soft. Add the celery and drained cabbage, fry gently for a further 5 minutes, stirring occasionally.

Heat the oven at (400°F/200°C/Gas Mark 6–7). Make the white sauce (see page 174). Put the vegetable mixture into the greased dish. Pour the white sauce over the top. Crumble or grate the bread into crumbs, and sprinkle these on top of the sauce. Dot with a knob of butter. Bake for 15 minutes in the hot oven until the top is crunchy and golden brown.

RED CABBAGE

Serves 1

Usually cooked in a casserole, to make a lovely warming winter vegetable dish. Why not put some jacket potatoes in the oven to eat with it?

Preparation and cooking time: 1 hour (cooked on top of the stove); 1 hour 15 minutes (cooked in the oven).

1 rasher of bacon (optional)
1 small onion
½ small red cabbage
1 eating apple
1 tsp oil
½ oz (12g) butter
Salt and pepper
1 tsp sugar (brown if possible, but white will do)
1 tsp vinegar
½ cup boiling water

Chop the bacon with a sharp knife or a pair of scissors. Peel and chop the onion. Cut off the stalk from the cabbage. Remove any battered outside leaves. Shred the cabbage finely, wash and drain. Peel, core and slice the apple. Melt the oil and butter in a frying pan and fry the bacon until crisp. Remove the bacon, put it on a plate. Add the onion to the pan and fry gently for 2 to 3 minutes, until soft.

PAN METHOD

In a saucepan, put layers of the cabbage, apple, onion and bacon, seasoning each layer with salt, pepper, sugar and vinegar. Pour ½ cup of boiling water over it and lightly sprinkle with sugar. Put on the saucepan lid and simmer gently for 45 minutes, stirring occasionally.

OVEN METHOD

Use a casserole dish (with a lid) that can be put in the oven. Put the vegetables in layers as in the pan method, adding ½ cup of boiling water and the sugar and cook in the oven

(350°F/180°C/Gas Mark 4), stirring occasionally, for about an hour. Jacket potatoes can be cooked with the casserole. Serve hot. Red cabbage cooked in this way is tasty with pork and lamb.

CARROTS

New carrots can simply be scrubbed and cooked whole, like new potatoes. Older, larger carrots should be scraped or peeled, then cut in halves, quarters, slices, rings or dice, as preferred. The smaller the pieces the quicker the carrots will cook.

Allow 4 oz (100g) per serving.

Scrub, peel and slice the carrots as necessary. Boil them in salted water for 5 to 20 minutes, according to their size, until just tender. Serve with a knob of butter.

BUTTERED CARROTS

Prepare the carrots as above: leaving tender, young carrots whole, or slicing old carrots into rings. Put the carrots in a saucepan, with ½ a cup of water, ½ oz (12g) butter, 1 tsp sugar and a pinch of salt. Bring to the boil, then reduce the heat and simmer for 20 minutes, until the carrots are tender. Take the lid off the saucepan, turn up the heat for a few minutes, and let the liquid bubble away until only a little sauce is left. Put the carrots onto a plate, and pour the sauce over them.

FROZEN CARROTS OR MIXED VEGETABLES

Allow 3–4 oz (75–100g) per serving. Cook in boiling, salted water as directed on the packet, and serve as above.

CAULIFLOWER

Most cauliflowers are too large for one person, but they can be cut in half and the remainder kept in the fridge for use in the next few days. Try not to bruise the florets when cutting them, as they will discolour easily. Very small caulis and packets of cauliflower florets are sold in some supermarkets.

Allow 3–4 florets per serving.

Trim off tough stem and outer leaves. The cauli can either be left whole or divided into florets. Wash thoroughly. Cook in boiling, salted water for 5 to 15 minutes, according to size, until just tender. Drain well. Serve hot, with a knob of butter, a spoonful of soured cream, or white sauce (see page 174). For cauliflower cheese, see page 39.

FROZEN CAULIFLOWER

Allow 4–6 oz (100–150g) per serving. Cook as directed on the packet and serve as above.

CELERIAC

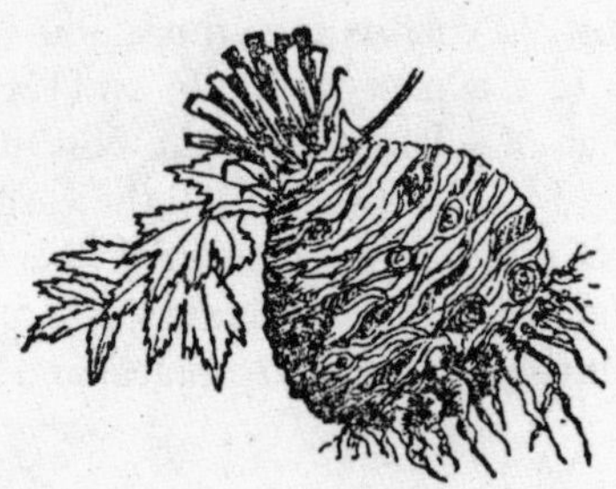

4. Celeriac

The root of a variety of celery, celeriac is one of the more unusual vegetables now available in good greengrocers and larger supermarkets.

Allow 4–8 oz (100–225g) per person.

Peel fairly thickly, and cut into evenly-sized chunks. Put into a saucepan with boiling water, and cook for 30 to 40 minutes. Drain well. Serve with butter, or mash with a potato masher, fork or whisk, with a little butter and top of the milk. Season with salt and pepper.

CELERY

Most popular eaten raw, with cheese, or chopped up in a salad. It can be cooked and served as a hot vegetable; the tougher outer stems can be used for cooking, leaving the tender inner stems to be eaten raw.

Allow 3–4 stalks of celery per serving.

Trim the celery stalk. Divide it into separate stems. Wash each stem well and scrape off any stringy bits with a knife. The celery is now ready to eat raw. To cook, chop the celery into 1 in (2.5cm) lengths. Put it into a saucepan, with boiling, salted water, and cook for 10 minutes, until just tender. Drain well, serve with a knob of butter, or put into a greased, oven-proof dish, top with 1–2 oz (25–50g) grated cheese, and brown under a hot grill.

CHICORY

This can be used raw in salads, or cooked carefully in water and butter, and served hot.

Allow 6–8 oz (175–225g/one head) per serving.

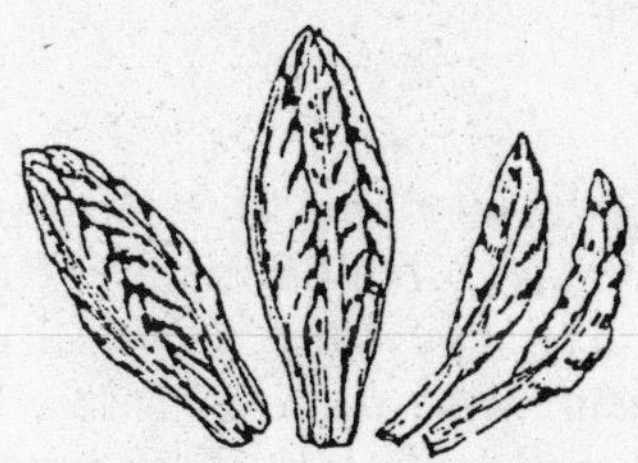

5. Chicory

Remove any damaged outer leaves and trim the stalk. With a pointed vegetable knife, cut a cone-shaped core out of the base, to ensure even cooking and reduce bitterness. Wash in cold water. Put the chicory into a saucepan with a knob of butter, 2–3 tbsp water and a pinch of salt. Cook gently for about 20 minutes, until just tender, making sure that all the liquid does not disappear. Serve with melted butter.

CHINESE LEAVES

These can be used raw in salads. Keep the Chinese leaves in a polythene bag in the fridge to keep them crisp until you want to use them.

Allow ¼–½ small cabbage per serving.

Trim off any spoiled leaves and stalks. Shred finely. Wash and drain well (in a salad shaker or a clean tea-towel). Use in salad with any other salad vegetables (cucumber, tomato, cress, spring onions, raddish etc.) and a vinaigrette dressing (2 tbsp oil, 1 tsp vinegar, pinch of salt, pepper and sugar, all mixed well together).

COURGETTES

These are baby marrows. They are very quick and easy to prepare, and are quite economical as there is almost no waste with them. *Allow 1 or 2 courgettes (4–6 oz/100–175g) per serving, according to size.*

Top and tail very tiny courgettes, and leave them whole. Slice larger ones into rings (½–1 in/1.25–2.5cm) or large dice. Wash well.

BOILED

Prepare the courgettes as above. Boil them gently in salted water for 2 to 5 minutes, until just tender. Drain them very well, as they tend to be a bit watery. (You can get them really dry by shaking them in the pan over a very low heat for a moment.) Serve topped with a knob of butter, or tip them into a greased, oven-proof dish and top with 1 oz (25g) grated cheese, and brown under a hot grill. Courgettes can also be served with white, cheese or parsley sauce.

FRIED

Prepare the courgettes as above. Wash and drain them well and dry on kitchen paper. Melt a little cooking oil and butter in a frying pan, add the courgettes and fry gently for a few minutes, until tender. Drain on kitchen paper. Serve hot.

CUCUMBER

Most widely used as a salad vegetable and eaten raw, although it can be cut in chunks and added to casseroles, or cooked in the same way as courgettes or celery. Cucumbers are usually bought *whole, or cut in half*. They keep best in the fridge, wrapped in a polythene bag.

Wash the cucumber. Peel thinly (if you wish) or leave unpeeled. Cut into thin slices and use with salad, or munch a chunk like an apple, with a ploughman's lunch.

LEEKS

These must be thoroughly washed or they will taste gritty.

Allow 1 or 2 leeks per serving, according to size and appetite.

Cut off the roots and the tough green part, just leaving any green that looks appetising. Slit down one side and rinse well in cold, running water to get rid of all the soil and grit – this is a bit fiddly and it will take a few minutes to get them thoroughly clean. Leave them whole, or cut them into shorter lengths if they are very large, or into rings.

Cook in a very little boiling, salted water for 5 to 10 minutes, according to size, or sauté in a little oil or butter for a few minutes. Drain well. Serve at once, or put into a greased oven-proof dish, cover with 1 oz (25g) grated cheese and brown under a hot grill or serve with white sauce which can be prepared while the leeks are cooking.

LETTUCE

Cheapest and best in spring and summer, when various kinds are available. Choose a lettuce that looks crisp and firm, with a solid heart; if it looks limp and flabby it is old and stale. Lettuce will keep for a few days in a polythene bag or a box in the fridge, but goes slimy if left too long, so buy *a small lettuce* unless you're going to eat a lot of salad.

Cut off the stalk and discard any brown or battered leaves. Pull the leaves off the stem and wash separately in cold, running water. Dry thoroughly in a salad shaker or clean tea-towel. Put into a polythene bag or box in the fridge if not using immediately, to keep it crisp. Serve as a basic green salad or as a garnish with bread rolls, cheese or cold meat, or as a side salad with hot dishes (alone or with a French dressing).

MARROW

Very cheap when in season, during the autumn. *A small marrow* will serve three or four people as a vegetable with meat or fish, or can be stuffed with meat or rice to make a dinner or supper dish.

Wash the marrow in cold water. Peel thinly. Cut into 1 in (2.5cm) rings or cubes, according to size. Boil gently in salted water for 3 to 6 minutes, until just tender. Drain very well, as marrow can be a bit watery. (You can get the pieces really dry by shaking them in the pan over a very low heat for a few moments.) Serve topped with a knob of butter, or tip the pieces into a greased oven-proof dish and top with 1 oz (25g) grated cheese, and brown under a hot grill. Marrow can also be served with white, cheese or parsley sauce.

MUSHROOMS

Buy in small amounts, *2 oz (50g)*, so that they can be eaten fresh. Fresh mushrooms are pale-coloured and look plump and firm; older ones look dried-up and brownish. Keep mushrooms in the fridge. Mushrooms can be fried or grilled with bacon, sausages, chops or steaks. Add them to casseroles or stews or make a tasty snack by cooking them in butter and garlic and serving on toast (see page 46).

Allow 2–3 mushrooms each, according to size, or 1–2 oz (25–50g).

FRIED

Wash the mushrooms in cold water. Leave them whole or slice large ones if you wish. Fry them gently in a little butter and oil for a few minutes, until soft. They can be put in the frying pan with bacon or sausages, or cooked alone in a smaller saucepan.

GRILLED

Put a small knob of butter in each mushroom and grill them for a few minutes in the base of the grill pan. If you are grilling them with bacon, sausages or chops put them under the grill rack; the juice from the meat and mushrooms makes a tasty sauce.

OKRA

6. Okra

Known as Ladies' Fingers, okra consists of curved seed pods. It can be served as a vegetable with meat or curry, or fried with tomatoes, onions and spices with rice as a supper dish.

Allow 2 oz (50g) per serving.

Top and tail the okra. Wash it in cold water. Put 1–2 tbsp cooking oil in a pan, add the okra and cook gently, stirring occasionally for 15 to 20 minutes, until the okra feels tender when tested with a pointed knife. It should have a slightly glutinous texture.

ONIONS

The best way to peel onions without crying is to cut off their tops and tails and then peel off their skins with a vegetable knife under cold running water.

To chop onions evenly, peel them under cold water, then slice them downwards vertically into evenly-sized rings. If you want finely-chopped onion pieces, slice the rings through again horizontally.

ROAST ONION

Allow 1 medium or large onion per person. Spanish onions are good for roasting. Top, tail and peel the onion. Heat a little oil or fat in a roasting tin (400°F/200°C/Gas Mark 6). When hot (3 to 5 minutes) place the onion carefully in the hot fat – it will spit, beware! Roast for 45 minutes to 1 hour. Onions are delicious roasted with a joint of meat and roast potatoes.

BAKED ONION

Allow 1 large onion per person. Spanish onions are the best. Rinse the onion, top and tail it, but do not peel it. Put it in a tin or baking dish, and bake for 45 minutes to 1 hour (400°F/200°C/Gas Mark 6). Slit and serve with butter.

BOILED ONION

Allow 1 medium onion per person. Top, tail and peel the onion. Put it in a pan of boiling water and simmer for 20 to 30 minutes, according to its size, until tender.

FRIED ONION

Allow 1 onion per person. Top, tail and peel the onion and slice into rings. Fry them gently in a saucepan with a little oil and butter, for 5 to 10 minutes, until soft and golden, stirring occasionally. Delicious with liver and bacon.

PARSNIPS

These are very tasty and can be roasted on their own, or with roast potatoes.

Allow 1 parsnip per person if small, or a large parsnip will cut into 5 or 6 pieces.

Parsnips are cooked in the same way as roast potatoes (see page 72), but do not cut them into too small pieces or they get too crispy. If you peel them before you are ready to cook them, keep them covered in a pan of cold water, as they go brown very quickly. (If this should happen, the parsnips will still be all right to cook, they will just look a bit speckled.)

PEAS

Most commonly available tinned or frozen nowadays. But fresh peas are a lovely treat in the summer, so try some.

Allow 8 oz (225g) peas in the pod per serving.

Shell the peas and remove any maggotty ones. Boil them gently in salted water, with a sprig of mint if possible, for 5 to 10 minutes. Drain them well, remove the mint and serve with a sprinkle of sugar and a knob of butter.

FROZEN PEAS

Allow 3–4 oz (75–100g) per serving. Cook as directed on the packet.

MANGETOUT PEAS OR SUGAR SNAP PEAS

Becoming widely available in supermarkets. Quite expensive but can be bought in small amounts and you eat the lot, including the pods!

Allow approximately 4 oz (100g) per serving.

Top and tail the peas with a vegetable knife or a pair of scissors. Wash them and leave them whole. Put them into a pan of boiling, salted water and boil for 2 to 3 minutes. They are slightly crumbly when cooked. Serve hot with a knob of butter.

GREEN, RED OR YELLOW PEPPERS

Use raw in a green salad, or cook, filled with rice or meat stuffing, for a lunch or supper dish (see below), or stewed in oil with tomatoes and garlic as a filling vegetable dish. *Peppers can be bought singly*. Choose crisp, firm-looking ones and store them in the fridge to keep them fresh.

Rinse them in cold water, cut off the top, scoop out the core and seeds. Cut into rings or chunks and use in salad or as a garnish.

STUFFED PEPPERS *Serves 1*

Green peppers are available in the shops all year round, but their price varies considerably, so shop around for a 'good buy'. As with avocados, peppers come from different countries and the price will vary during the year. Serve with a side salad and brown crusty bread.

Preparation and cooking time: 45 minutes.

1 small onion
1 tbsp oil (for frying)
4 oz (100g) minced beef
1 small tomato
1 tsp tomato purée (or ketchup)
½ stock cube
½ cup boiling water
Salt and pepper
Pinch of herbs
1 tbsp raw rice or 2 tbsp cooked rice if you have any left-over (optional)
1–2 green peppers

Peel and chop the onion. Heat the oil in a saucepan. Add the onion and fry gently for a few minutes, until soft. Add the minced beef to the onion, and continue to fry for 2 to 3 minutes, stirring frequently. Wash and chop the tomato. Add it to the meat in the pan, with the tomato purée (or ketchup).

Dissolve the stock cube in the boiling water. Add it to the meat, with the salt, pepper and herbs. Continue simmering over a moderate heat. Stir in the washed raw rice and leave to simmer for 15 to 20 minutes, stirring occasionally. The stock should be almost completely absorbed. Cut the tops off the peppers. Remove the seeds and wash the peppers.

Grease an oven-proof dish. Remove the meat mixture from the heat. Strain off any excess liquid (the mixture wants to be damp but not swimming in gravy). If you are using left-over cooked rice, mix it in with the meat mixture. Fill the peppers with the meat mixture and put them into the greased oven-proof dish. Bake in a hot oven (350°F/180°C/Gas Mark 4–5) for 30 minutes.

BOILED POTATOES

Try to select potatoes of the same size to cook together, or cut large potatoes into evenly-sized pieces, so that all the potatoes will be cooked at the same time. (Very big potatoes will go soggy on the outside before the inside is cooked if left whole.) Do not let the water boil too fast, or the potatoes will tend to break up.

Allow 2–4 potato pieces per person.

Peel the potatoes as thinly as you can. Dig out any eyes or any black bits with as little waste as possible. Put them in a saucepan. Cover with hot water and add a pinch of salt. Bring to the boil, then lower the heat and simmer for 15 to 20 minutes, until they feel just soft when tested with a knife. Drain and serve hot.

MASHED POTATOES

The best way of serving boiled potatoes that have broken up during cooking. Prepare the boiled potatoes as described above. (If you are in a hurry, cut the potatoes into thick slices and cook for less time, about 10 minutes.) When they are cooked, drain the potatoes well. Mash them with a fork or masher until fluffy, then heap onto a serving dish.

CREAMED POTATOES

Prepare mashed potatoes as above. When they are really fluffy beat in a knob of butter and a little top of the milk. Fork into a heap on a serving dish and top with a dab of butter.

POTATO CASTLES

Prepare creamed potatoes as above. Grease a flat baking tin or an oven-proof plate, and pile the potatoes onto it, in 2 or 3 evenly-sized heaps. Fork them into castles, top with a bit of butter and either brown under the grill for a minute or two, or put them into a hot oven (400°F/200°C/Gas Mark 6) for 5 to 10 minutes, until crisp and golden brown.

CHEESY POTATOES

Prepare creamed potatoes as above, beating 1–2 oz (25–50g) grated cheese into the potatoes with the butter. Pile the potatoes into a greased oven-proof dish, fork down evenly and top with a little grated cheese. Brown under a hot grill for a minute or two, or put into a hot oven (400°F/200°C/Gas Mark 6) for 5 to 10 minutes, until golden.

ROAST POTATOES

These can be cooked around the joint if you are cooking a roast dinner, or in a baking tin, with a little hot fat, to cook on their own. *Allow 2–4 potato pieces per person.*

Peel the potatoes and cut them into evenly-sized pieces. Put them in a saucepan of hot water, bring to the boil and simmer for 2 to 3 minutes. Put a little fat in a roasting tin. (Use lard, margarine, dripping or oil. Do not use butter on its own as it burns and goes brown.) Heat the tin in the oven (400–425°F/200–220°C/Gas Mark 6–7). Drain the potatoes and shake them in the pan over the heat for a moment to dry them. Put the potatoes into the hot roasting tin, but be careful that the hot fat does not spit and burn you. Roast for 45 to 60 minutes, according to size, until crisp and golden brown.

NEW POTATOES

Lovely and easy – no peeling! *Allow 3–6 new potatoes, according to size and appetite.*

Wash the potatoes well under running water and scrub them with a pan scrubber or a brush. If you prefer, scrape them with a vegetable knife also. Put them in a pan, cover with boiling water, add salt and a sprig of mint. Bring to the boil and simmer for 15 to 20 minutes, until tender. Drain well, tip onto a plate and top with a little butter.

SAUTÉ POTATOES

A way of using up left-over boiled or roast potatoes. Alternatively potatoes can be boiled specially, and then sautéed when they have gone cold. *Allow approximately 3–4 cold cooked potato pieces, according to appetite.*

Slice the potatoes thinly. Heat a little oil and butter in a frying pan. Add the potato slices and fry them gently for 5 minutes, until crisp and golden, turning frequently with a fish slice or spatula.

ONION SAUTÉ POTATOES

Peel and thinly slice a small onion. Fry the onion in a frying pan with a little oil and butter until it is just soft, then add the cold, sliced potatoes and fry as above until crisp and delicious. Serve at once.

JACKET SPUDS

These can be served as an accompaniment to meat or fish or made into a meal on their own, with any one of a number of fillings heaped on top of them. *Allow 1 medium – large potato per person.*

Choose potatoes that do not have any mouldy-looking patches on the skin. Remember that very large potatoes will take longer to cook, so if you're hungry it's better to cook 2 medium-sized spuds. Wash and scrub the potato. Prick it several times with a fork. For quicker cooking, spear potatoes onto a metal skewer or potato baker.

TRADITIONAL WAY

Put the potato into the oven (400°F/200°C/Gas Mark 6) for 1 to 1½ hours according to size. The skin should be crisp and the inside soft and fluffy when ready. If you prefer softer skin, or don't want to risk the potato bursting all over the oven, wrap the spud loosely in a piece of cooking foil before putting it into the oven.

QUICKER WAY

Put the potato into a saucepan, cover with hot water, bring to the boil and cook for 5 to 10 minutes according to size. Drain it carefully, lift the potato out with a cloth, and put into a hot oven (400°F/200°C/Gas Mark 6) for 30 to 60 minutes, according to size, until it feels soft.

If you are cooking a casserole in the oven at a lower temperature, put the potato in the oven with it, and allow extra cooking time.

BAKED STUFFED POTATO

Useful to serve with cold meat or with steak, as it can be prepared in advance and heated up at the last minute.

Scrub and bake a largish jacket potato as described above. When the potato is soft, remove from the oven, and cut it carefully in half lengthways. Scoop the soft potato into a bowl, and mash with a fork, adding ½ oz (12g) butter and ½ oz (12g) grated cheese. Pile the filling back into the skin again and fork down evenly. Place on a baking tin or oven-proof plate, sprinkle a little grated cheese on top, and either brown under the hot grill for a few minutes, or put into a hot oven (400°F/200°C/Gas Mark 6) for 5 to 10 minutes, until browned.

A FEW FILLINGS

Prepare and cook the jacket spuds. When soft, put them onto a plate, split open and top with your chosen filling and a knob of butter.

Cheese

1–2 oz (25–50g) grated cheese.

Cheese and Onion

1 small finely-sliced onion and 1–2 oz (25–50g) grated cheese.

Cheese and Pickle

1–2 oz (25–50g) grated cheese and 1 tsp pickle or chutney.

Cottage Cheese

2–3 tbsp cottage cheese (plain or with chives, pineapple, etc.).

Baked Beans

Heat a small tin of baked beans and pour over the potato.

Bolognese

Top with Bolognese sauce (see page 158). This is a good way of using up any extra sauce left over from Spaghetti Bolognese.

Bacon

Chop 1–2 rashers of bacon into pieces. Fry them for a few minutes, until crisp, then pour over the potato.

Egg

Top with 1–2 fried eggs, a scrambled egg or an omelette.

Curry

Top with any left-over curry sauce, heated gently in a saucepan until piping hot.

SCALLOPED POTATOES

Tasty and impressive-looking potatoes. Quick to prepare but they take an hour to cook, so they can be put in the oven and left while you are preparing the rest of the meal, or they can cook on a shelf above a casserole in the oven. (The potatoes need a higher temperature so put them on the top shelf and the casserole lower down.)

Allow 1–2 potatoes per person according to size and appetite.

Grease an oven-proof dish well. Peel the potatoes and slice them as thinly as possible. Put them in layers in the greased dish, sprinkling each layer with a little flour, salt and pepper. Almost cover them with ½–1 cup of milk (or milk and water). Dot with a large knob of butter. Put the dish, uncovered, in a hot oven (400°F/200°C/Gas Mark 6) for about an hour, until the potatoes are soft and most of the liquid has been absorbed. The top should be crispy.

Packets of scalloped potatoes are available in supermarkets. They are more expensive than making your own, but are easy to prepare following the packet instructions.

CHIPS

If you must make your own chips do take great care. There are many good 'ready-made' frozen chips which you can buy at the supermarket, which can be cooked in the oven or shallow-fried in a little fat in an ordinary frying pan. You would be well-advised to use these when you want chips, unless you are an experienced cook and have the correct equipment for deep-fat frying. Please, please don't attempt to make chips, or indeed do any deep-fat frying, unless you have the use of a 'proper' chip pan (the electric thermostatically-controlled type preferably) and have had some previous experience of deep-fat frying under supervision. *Allow 2–3 large potatoes per person.*

Only pour enough oil into the chip pan to cover as far as the marks on the pan, which will be no more than a quarter of the way up the pan, as the hot fat rises alarmingly when the chips or other foods are lowered into it. If the pan should catch alight, turn off the cooker and put the lid on the pan immediately. Do not move the pan or throw water over it. Follow the manufacturer's instructions carefully about using the pan, and heat the oil to the correct setting (probably about 380°F/190°C), so that it is hot and just hazing, not smoking, when you are ready to cook the chips.

Peel the potatoes, and cut them into slices ¼ in (0.5cm) thick, and cut these slices into chips. Dry the chips on a clean cloth or kitchen paper, and sprinkle with a little salt, if desired. When the fat is the correct temperature, put the chips into the chip basket and lower this carefully into the fat. Cook for 3 to 4 minutes, shaking the basket occasionally to ensure the chips are cooking evenly – don't let the fat splash onto you or the surroundings.

Remove the basket and rest it on the rim of the pan, letting the oil on the chips drip into the oil in the pan. Allow the oil in the pan to heat up again. Plunge the basket back into the oil for another minute to crisp the chips. Remove from the fat and drain as before for just a moment, then tip the hot chips onto the kitchen paper to drain. SWITCH OFF THE CHIP PAN. Serve the chips immediately. When the fat is cold, it should be strained through a fine sieve to get rid of any burnt bits or crumbs, and stored for future use, either in the chip pan or in a clean jar.

INSTANT MASH

Although more expensive then fresh potato, this makes a quick standby which saves you the trouble of peeling potatoes. The flavour and price of the different makes vary (the most expensive may not necessarily be the best), so try them out until you find one you prefer. Afterwards, it is usually more economical to buy the large size, as it keeps fresh in a container for ages. To make up the potato, follow the packet instructions. The amounts given are for rather small servings, and you may need to make extra if you're hungry. A big knob of butter (added just before serving) improves both the flavour and the appearance.

PUMPKIN

Generally associated with Hallowe'en, Cinderella and American Thanksgiving Day! It is available fresh in England around the end of October when it may be quite cheap. It is prepared and cooked in the same way as marrow. See page 66.

SALSIFY

A less well-known root vegetable, with soft, white flesh.

Allow 1–2 salsify roots per person.

Scrape the roots in a bowl of cold water. The roots must be kept under the cold water when being scraped, to stop discolouration. Cut them into evenly-sized rings. Cook, as soon as possible, in boiling water for 5 to 15 minutes, until tender. Drain, and serve with a knob of butter.

SPINACH

Allow 8 oz (225g) per person.

Spinach must be washed thoroughly in cold water, to get rid of all dust and grit. This will take several rinses. Remove any tough-looking leaves and stalks and cut into convenient-sized lengths (4 in/10cm). Put the spinach in a large saucepan, with no extra water, and cook over a medium heat for 7 to 10 minutes, until soft. As the spinach boils down, chop it about with a metal spoon or knife, and turn it over so that it cooks evenly, in its own juices. Drain very well, pressing the water out to get the spinach as dry as possible. Put a knob of butter in the pan with the drained spinach, and reheat for a few moments. Serve with the melted butter, seasoned well with salt and pepper.

FROZEN SPINACH

Allow 4 oz (100g) per person. Packets of frozen spinach are available all the year round in supermarkets. Cook as instructed on the packet and serve with butter as above.

SWEDE ('NEEPS' IN SCOTLAND)

Known as 'poisonous' by one member of our family, but really it is a delicious winter vegetable.

Buy a very small swede for one person, or a slightly larger one for 2 servings.

Peel thickly, so that no brown or green skin remains. Cut into ½ in (1.25cm) chunks. Cook in boiling, salted water for 15 to 20 minutes, until tender. Drain well (if you are making gravy at the same time, save the water for the gravy liquid), and mash with a fork or potato masher, adding a knob of butter and plenty of pepper.

If you wish, peel 1 or 2 carrots, cut them into rings and cook them with the swede, mashing the two vegetables together with butter as above, or just mix the two together without mashing.

SWEETCORN

Frozen corn-on-the-cob is available all the year round. Cook as directed on the packet. Fresh cobs are in the shops from August to October, although imported sweetcorn is sometimes available at other times.

Cut off the stalk, remove the leaves and silky threads – this may be a bit fiddly, but try and pull all the threads off. Put the sweetcorn into a large pan of boiling, unsalted water, and simmer for 8 to 10 minutes, until the kernels are tender. Drain and serve with plenty of butter by melting a little in the hot saucepan and pouring it over the cobs. Tooth picks, cocktail sticks or 2 forks will serve as corn-on-the-cob holders.

SWEET POTATOES

Not directly related to ordinary potatoes. Becoming more widely available in many supermarkets. Peel, boil and purée them like creamed potatoes or cook them like roast potatoes.

TOMATOES

'Love apples' add colour and flavour to many dishes. They are used raw in salads or as a garnish, can be grilled or fried, chopped up and added to casseroles or stews, or stuffed as a supper dish. Choose firm tomatoes and keep them in the fridge for freshness. Cheaper soft tomatoes are a good buy for cooking, provided that you are going to use them straightaway.

Wash and dry the tomatoes, cut them into slices or quarters to use in a salad or as a garnish. Tomatoes are easy to cut or slice thinly if you use a bread knife or a vegetable knife with a serrated edge. The skin will then cut more easily without the inside squidging out.

GRILLED

Cut them in half, dot with butter and grill for 3 to 5 minutes. Alternatively, put them in the grill pan under the grid when grilling sausages, bacon, chops or steak, as the tomatoes will then cook with the meat.

FRIED

Cut the tomatoes in half and fry them in a little oil or fat, on both sides, over a medium heat, for a few minutes until soft. Serve with bacon and sausages, or place on a slice of toast or fried bread.

BAKED

Cut a cross in the top of any small or medium-sized tomatoes and halve any large ones. Put them into a greased, oven-proof dish or tin, with a knob of butter on top. Bake for 10 to 15 minutes (350°F/180°C/Gas Mark 4), until soft.

TURNIPS

Small white root vegetables, not to be confused with swedes.

Allow ½–2 turnips per serving, according to size and appetite.

Peel the turnips thickly. Leave small ones whole but cut large turnips in half or quarters. Cook them in boiling, salted water for 10 minutes, until soft. Drain them well. Return the turnips to the pan and shake over a low heat for a few moments to dry them out. Serve with a knob of butter.

Turnips can also be served with 1 or 2 diced carrots. Just peel them and cut them into large dice, mix them with the carrots and boil them together for 5 to 10 minutes. Drain and dry as above.

PURÉE

Peel the turnips and cut them into chunks. Cook them in boiling water for 5 to 10 minutes, until soft. Drain well, and dry as above. Mash with a fork or potato masher, with a knob of butter and some pepper.

BOILED RICE

A good quick standby, which saves peeling potatoes. Long grain, or Patna type, rice is used for savoury rice; the smaller, round grain type is used for puddings. Brown rice is also used for savoury dishes, but takes longer to cook. Rice is cheaper to buy in a large packet, and keeps for ages if decanted into a jar or plastic container. You can buy prepared and 'easy cook' rice of several types in the supermarkets, which must be cooked exactly as described on the packet. This type of rice is very good and easy to cook, but is usually more expensive than plain, long grain rice.

METHOD ONE

I prefer to use this method, as I tend to let the pan boil dry with the alternative method! However, you do need a largish pan and it's a bit steamy as the rice must be cooked without the lid on, otherwise it boils over.

Preparation and cooking time: 13 minutes.

½ cup (3 oz/75g) long grain rice – white or brown
½ tsp salt

Wash the rice well to get rid of the starch (put it into a saucepan and slosh it around in several rinses of cold water). Put the rice into a largish pan. Fill the pan two-thirds full of boiling water. Add the salt. Bring back to the boil and boil gently for 10 to 12 minutes for white rice, 20 to 25 minutes for brown rice, until the rice is cooked but still firm. Do not overcook or it will go sticky and puddingy. Drain well. Fluff with a fork and serve.

METHOD TWO

Be careful that the rice doesn't boil dry.

Preparation and cooking time: 13–16 minutes.

½ cup (3 oz/75g) long grain white rice
1 tsp oil or small knob of butter
1 cup boiling water
Pinch of salt

Wash the rice as in method one. Put the oil or butter in a smallish saucepan and heat gently. Then add the rice, stirring all the time, to coat each grain. Add the boiling water and a pinch of salt, bring up to simmering point and stir. Put on the lid and leave the rice to simmer over a very gentle heat for 12 to 15 minutes. Test to see if the rice is cooked: all the liquid should be absorbed and the rice should be cooked but not soggy. Lightly fluff with a fork and serve.

FRIED RICE

Serves 1

A good way of using up left-over boiled rice.

Preparation and cooking time: 15 minutes (plus 15 minutes if you have to boil the rice first).

1 cup cooked boiled rice (use ½ cup raw rice)
½ onion or 1 spring onion
½ slice cooked, chopped ham (optional)
1 tbsp cooking oil
1 tbsp frozen peas and/or sweetcorn (optional)

Cook the rice if necessary (see page 81). Peel and chop the onion, or wash and chop the spring onion. Chop the ham. Heat the oil in a frying pan over a medium heat. Add the chopped onion and fry, turning frequently, until soft. Add the cooked rice, and fry for 4 to 5 minutes, stirring all the time. Add the frozen peas (still frozen; they will defrost in the pan), sweetcorn and ham, and cook for a further 2 to 3 minutes, stirring all the time, until it is all heated through.

You can make this more substantial by adding more vegetables and chopped cooked meat (ham, salami, garlic sausage, etc.) if you wish.

BUBBLE AND SQUEAK

Serves 1

A lovely warm way of using up cold, left-over vegetables; you can, of course, cook some fresh vegetables specially if you wish.

Preparation and cooking time: 15 minutes.

3–4 cold cooked potatoes
1 cup cold cooked cabbage (or Brussels sprouts)
Little oil and a knob of butter

Slice the potatoes and chop up the cabbage or slice the sprouts. Heat the oil and butter in a frying pan over a medium heat. Put the potatoes and cabbage (or sprouts) into the frying pan and fry gently for 5 to 10 minutes, turning frequently, until the cabbage is cooked and the potatoes are golden and crispy. Serve hot with cold meat, bacon or fried eggs.

RISOTTO

Serves 1

A cheap meal if you have any 'pickings' of chicken left over. Or use a thick slice of cooked ham, chicken or turkey. It can be served with a green salad. (You don't need all the vegetables listed here; choose those you like.)

Preparation and cooking time: 35 minutes.

1 egg
1 cup rice
1 small onion
1 tbsp oil (or large knob of butter or fat)
1 stock cube and 2 cups (½ pt/300ml) boiling water
1 slice (1–2 oz/25–50g) of cooked ham, chicken or turkey
2–3 mushrooms (sliced)
1 tomato
1 tbsp frozen or canned peas
1 tbsp frozen or canned sweetcorn
Salt, pepper, Worcester sauce
1 oz (25g) grated cheese and Parmesan cheese (optional)

Hard boil the egg for 10 minutes. Wash the rice in several rinses of cold water to get rid of the starch. Peel and chop the onion finely. Heat the oil or fat in a medium saucepan or frying pan with a lid. Fry the onion for 3 to 4 minutes, until soft. Add the rice and fry, stirring well, for a further 3 minutes. Dissolve the stock cube in the boiling water. Add this to the rice, stir and leave to simmer with the lid on, stirring occasionally, for 10 to 15 minutes, until the rice is tender, and the liquid almost absorbed.

Chop the meat. Peel and chop the hard-boiled egg. Wash the sliced mushrooms. Wash and chop the tomato. Add the peas, sweetcorn, mushrooms and tomato to the rice. Cook for 2 to 3 minutes, stirring gently. Then add the chopped meat and egg, and continue stirring gently until heated right through. Season with salt, pepper and Worcester sauce. Serve with lots of grated cheese and/or Parmesan and a dash of Worcester sauce.

VEGETABLE HOT POT

Serves 1

This can be made with or without cheese, to provide a tasty dish for lunch or supper, or it can be served as a vegetable accompaniment to meat, to make a substantial meal if you're really hungry. You can either buy fresh, raw vegetables, or use up left-over vegetables. This recipe is particularly suitable for vegetarians.

Preparation and cooking time: 50 minutes.

1 small onion
1–2 oz (25–50g) cheese (optional)
2–3 potatoes
Oil and knob of butter
1–2 cups (4–8 oz/100–225g) mixed vegetables – carrots, cauliflower, leeks, celery, swede, turnip etc. Keep raw and cooked vegetables separate at this stage.
1 cup (½ small can/¼ pt/150ml) vegetable soup
Salt and pepper

Peel and slice the onion. Grate the cheese. Peel the potatoes and cut them into thick slices (¼ in/0.5cm). Heat the oil and butter in a saucepan over a moderate heat, and fry the onion for 2 to 3 minutes, until soft. Add the raw vegetables (not the potatoes) and continue to fry gently for a few minutes. Stir in the soup. Bring to the boil, and then lower the heat and simmer gently for 5 to 10 minutes, until the vegetables are tender, adding any cooked vegetables for the last 2 to 3 minutes to heat them through.

Meanwhile partly cook the sliced potatoes separately in boiling, salted water for 4 to 5 minutes. Drain them. Arrange the mixed vegetables in a casserole or oven-proof dish. Stir in half the cheese and cover with the hot soup. Season with salt and pepper. Top with a thick layer of potato slices. Dot with some butter. Sprinkle with the rest of the cheese. Bake in a hot oven (400°F/200°C/Gas Mark 6–7) for 15 to 20 minutes, until the top is golden brown. Serve hot.

VEGETABLE CURRY

Serves 1

You can use either fresh raw vegetables, left-over cooked vegetables, frozen vegetables (sold for stews or casseroles), or a mixture of them all. Serve with boiled rice.

Preparation and cooking time: 50 minutes.

1 small onion
2 cups (8 oz/225g) mixed vegetables: carrots, cauliflower, potatoes, celery, swede, turnip, etc. Keep the raw and cooked vegetables separate at this stage if you are using both.
Little oil for frying
1–2 tsp curry powder (or to taste)
½ tsp paprika pepper
1 tsp tomato purée (or ketchup)
1 tsp apricot jam (or redcurrant jelly)
½ tsp lemon juice
1 cup (¼ pt/150ml) milk (or milk and water)
1 tbsp sultanas (or raisins)
1 egg (optional)

Peel and chop the onion. Wash and prepare the fresh vegetables and cut them into largish pieces. Heat the oil in a saucepan over a moderate heat and fry the onion for a few minutes, stirring occasionally, until soft. Add the curry powder and paprika, and cook, stirring as before, for 2 to 3 minutes. Stir in the tomato purée, apricot jam (or redcurrant jelly), lemon juice, milk and/or water and the sultanas (or raisins). Bring to the boil, then reduce the heat and leave to simmer with the lid on for 10 minutes.

Cook the raw or frozen vegetables, in boiling water, for 5 to 10 minutes. Drain them. Hard boil the egg in boiling water for 10 minutes. Then peel it and slice it thickly. Gently stir the vegetables into the curry sauce and simmer for a further 5 to 10 minutes, until the vegetables are completely cooked and the curry is hot. While the curry is simmering, cook the boiled rice. Garnish the curry with the hard-boiled egg.

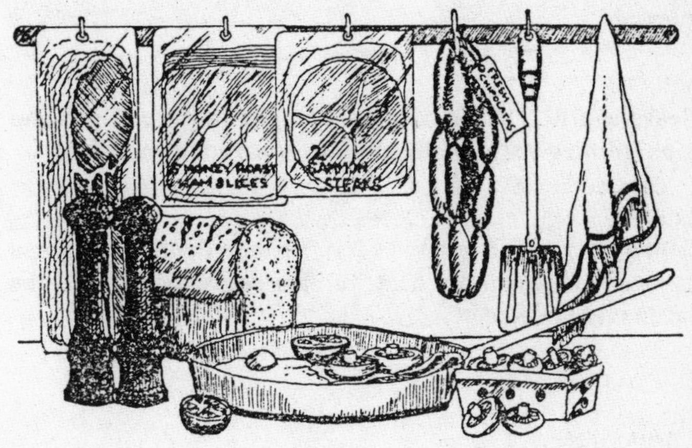

6
BACON, SAUSAGES AND HAM

Lots of quick, but substantial snacks in this chapter. Bacon and sausages don't take long to cook and are useful when you come home hungry and want a meal in a hurry.

BACON

Streaky bacon is the cheapest, then shoulder rashers, while back and gammon are the most expensive. *Serve 1 to 2 rashers of bacon per person.* How well cooked you like your bacon is a very personal thing; I know someone who likes hers cremated! As a rough guide: cook for between 1 and 5 minutes. Tomatoes and/or mushrooms can be cooked in the grill pan under the rashers of bacon; the fat from the bacon will give them a good flavour.

Cut off the bacon rinds if you wish or just snip the rinds at intervals.

GRILLED

Heat the grill. Put the bacon on the grid in the grill pan and cook, turning occasionally, until it is cooked to your taste.

FRIED

Heat a smear of oil or fat in a frying pan. Add the bacon, and fry over a medium-hot heat, turning occasionally, until the bacon is as you like it.

SAUSAGES

These come in all shapes, sizes and pieces; the thicker the sausage the longer it takes to cook. Have you tried eating sausages with marmalade? I'm told it is delicious, and a boarding school speciality.

Cook as many sausages as you can eat. Always prick the sausages (except for skinless ones) with a fork before cooking to stop the sausages bursting open.

GRILLED

Heat the grill. Put the sausages on the grid in the grill pan, and cook, turning occasionally, until brown and delicious (about 10 to 20 minutes). Thicker sausages may brown on the outside before the middle is cooked, so turn the heat down to medium for the last 5 to 10 minutes of cooking time.

FRIED

Heat a smear of oil or fat in a frying pan, over a medium heat (too hot a pan will make the sausages burst their skins), add the sausages and fry gently, turning occasionally, until they are brown and crispy (10 to 20 minutes). Cook thick sausages for the longer time, using a lower heat if the outsides start getting too brown.

ROAST

Roast chipolata (thin) sausages are traditionally served as accompaniments to roast turkey and chicken. Roasting is an easy way of cooking sausages if you're not in a hurry. Place the sausages in a lightly-greased tin and bake in a hot oven (400°F/200°C/Gas Mark 6), turning occasionally to cook all over, until crisp and brown (20 to 30 minutes). Thicker sausages take the longer time.

A PROPER BREAKFAST

Serves 1

Tastes just as good for lunch or supper.

Preparation and cooking time: 20 minutes.

Use any combination of ingredients according to taste and appetite:

1–4 sausages
1–2 rashers of bacon – streaky, back or collar
1 tomato
3–4 mushrooms
1–2 left-over cold boiled potatoes
1 tbsp oil (for frying)
1–2 eggs
1 slice of bread (for fried bread)
Knob of butter
Several slices of bread (for toast)

The breakfast, apart from the eggs, potatoes and fried bread which are better fried, can be grilled if you prefer. Get everything ready before you actually start cooking: prick the sausages, de-rind the bacon, wash and halve the tomato, wash the mushrooms and slice the potatoes. Warm a plate, put the kettle on ready for tea or coffee, get the bread ready to make the toast, and you're all set to start. In both methods, start cooking the sausages first, as they take the longest to cook, gradually adding the rest of the ingredients to the pan.

FRYING

Heat the oil in a frying pan over a moderate heat and fry the sausages gently, turning occasionally, allowing 10 to 20 minutes for them to cook according to size. When the sausages are half-cooked, put the bacon in the pan with them and fry for 1 to 5 minutes with the sausages, until they are cooked to your taste. Push the sausages and bacon to one side or remove and keep warm. Put the potato slices into the pan and fry until crispy. Fry the tomato and mushrooms at the same time, turning them occasionally until cooked (about 4 to 5 minutes).

Remove the food from the pan and keep hot. Break the eggs into a cup, and slide into the hot fat in the pan over a low heat. Fry them gently until cooked (see page 20). Remove them from the pan and put them with the bacon, sausages, etc. Cut the slice of bread in half, and fry in the fat in the pan, adding a little extra oil or butter if necessary, until golden and crispy, turning to cook both sides (1 to 2 minutes). Remove from the pan and put onto the plate with the rest of the breakfast. Make the toast, coffee or tea, and eat at once.

GRILLING

Heat the grill. Put the tomato halves and mushrooms in the base of the grill pan, arrange the sausages above on the grid, and grill until half cooked (5 to 10 minutes) turning to cook on all sides. Arrange the bacon on the grid with the sausages, and continue cooking for a further 3 to 5 minutes, turning to cook both sides. Remove everything from the pan and keep it warm. Pour the fat from the grill pan into a frying pan, add extra oil or butter if necessary, then fry the potato slices, eggs and fried bread as described above, and enjoy it all with lots of toast, marmalade, and lovely strong coffee or tea.

BANGERS AND MASH

Serves 1

Fast, filling, cheap and tasty!

Preparation and cooking time: 30 minutes.

2–3 potatoes – according to size and appetite (or instant mashed potato – use amount specified in the instructions on the packet)
2–4 sausages – according to size and appetite
Knob of butter

Gravy:
1 tsp flour or cornflour and 1 tsp gravy flavouring powder or 2 tsp gravy granules
1 cup (¼ pt/150ml) water (use the water the potatoes cooked in)
Little fat from the sausages

Peel the potatoes, cut into small, evenly-sized pieces, and cook in boiling, salted water for 10 to 20 minutes, according to size, until soft. Prick the sausages, cook under a hot grill for 10 to 15 minutes, turning frequently, or fry over a medium heat, with a smear of oil to stop them sticking, turning often, for 10 to 15 minutes, until brown. (Make the instant mash, if used, according to the instructions on the packet. Keep it warm.) Test the potatoes for softness, and drain them as soon as they are cooked. Mash them with a fork or potato masher, and beat in the knob of butter. Keep them warm.

Make the gravy, by mixing the flour or cornflour and gravy flavouring powder, or gravy granules, into a smooth paste with a little cold water, or wine, sherry, beer, etc. Add one cup of the vegetable water and any juices from the sausages. Pour the mixture into a small saucepan, and bring to the boil, stirring all the time. Cook until the mixture thickens. Add more liquid if it's too thick. Arrange the mashed potato on a hot plate, stick the sausages round it and pour the gravy over the top.

BRAISED SAUSAGES

Serves 1

These take longer to cook, but make a change from the usual fried or grilled sausages. Serve with mashed potatoes.

Preparation and cooking time: 50–60 minutes.

2–3 thick sausages (the spicy, herb sort are the best)
1–2 rashers of streaky bacon
1 small onion (or 2–3 shallots)
2–3 mushrooms
2 tsp oil
1 tsp flour
1 small cup (¼ pt/150ml approx.) wine, beer, or cider or ½ stock cube dissolved in 1 cup boiling water
Pinch of dried herbs
Pinch of garlic powder
Salt and pepper

Prick the sausages. De-rind and chop the bacon. Peel and thickly slice the onion or peel the shallots and leave whole. Wash the mushrooms and slice if large.

Heat the oil in a casserole or thick saucepan, over a moderate heat, and lightly brown the sausages. Remove them from the pan.

Add the bacon and onion, and fry for 2 to 3 minutes. Stir in the flour, and gradually add the wine, beer, cider or stock, stirring as the sauce thickens.

Return the sausages to the pan. Add the mushrooms, herbs, garlic, salt and pepper. Reheat, then put on the lid, lower the heat and leave to simmer gently for 35 to 45 minutes, removing the lid for the last 15 minutes of cooking time. Add a little more liquid if it gets too dry.

SAVOURY SAUSAGE-MEAT PIE

Serves 1

The apple gives the sausage-meat a tangy taste.

Preparation and cooking time: 50 minutes.

3–4 potato pieces (or a large serving of instant mashed potato, use amount specified in the instructions on the packet)
1 cooking apple
1 onion
2 tomatoes (tinned or fresh)
1 tsp sugar
4 oz (100g) sausage-meat (or 2–4 sausages)
Knob of butter

Prepare the mashed potato (see page 71) or make up the instant potato as instructed on the packet. Peel, core and slice the apple. Peel and chop the onion. Slice the fresh tomatoes, or drain and slice the tinned tomatoes.

Place the apple slices in the base of a greased, oven-proof dish. Sprinkle with the sugar. If using sausages, slit the sausage skins to remove the sausage-meat and dispose of the skins. Mix the chopped onion with the sausage-meat or the skinned sausages and spread the sausage mixture over the apples.

Spoon the mashed potato round the dish to make a border or 'nest' for the sausage. Cover the sausage with the tomatoes. Dot the potato with the butter, and bake in an oven (400°F/200°C/Gas Mark 6) for 30 minutes, until the sausage is cooked and the potato is crisp and golden-brown on top.

TOAD IN THE HOLE *Serves 1*

You can use either large sausages (toads) or chipolatas (frogs) for this meal, whichever you prefer! Some people believe that a better Yorkshire Pudding is made if the ingredients are mixed together first and the batter is then left to stand in the fridge while you prepare the rest of the meal. Alternatively, make the batter while the sausages are cooking.

Preparation and cooking time: 45–55 minutes.

3–6 sausages (according to appetite and size)
1 tbsp cooking oil

Yorkshire Pudding batter:
2 heaped tbsp plain flour
Pinch of salt
1 egg
1 cup (¼ pt/150ml) milk

Heat the oven (425°F/220°C/Gas Mark 7–8). Prick the sausages. Put them into a baking tin with the oil. (Any baking tin can be used, but not one with a loose base. You do not get as good a result with a pyrex-type dish.) Cook the chipolatas for 5 minutes or the larger ones for 10 minutes.

Make the batter while the sausages are cooking. Put the flour and salt in a basin, add the egg, and beat it into the flour, gradually adding the milk, to make a smooth batter. (This is easier with a hand or electric mixer, but with a bit of old-fashioned effort you can get just as good a result using a whisk, wooden spoon or even a fork.) Pour the batter into the baking tin on top of the hot sausages. Bake for a further 20 to 25 minutes, until the Yorkshire pud is golden. Try not to open the oven door for the first 10 to 15 minutes, so that the pudding will rise well. Serve at once.

HAWAIIAN SAUSAGES

Serves 1

An unusual variation on the sausage and bean theme.

Preparation and cooking time: 30 minutes.

3–6 sausages, according to size and appetite
½ small can (7¾ oz/220g size) pineapple rings
1 small onion (or 2 spring onions)
Knob of butter
1 small can (7.9 oz/225g) baked beans
1 tsp vinegar
Salt and pepper

Prick the sausages. Fry or grill them until cooked and brown (see page 88). Add 1 or 2 pineapple rings and heat through with the sausages for a minute or two. Save 2 sausages, and keep hot with the pineapple rings (for decoration). Slice the rest of the sausages.

Peel and slice the onion, or wash and chop the spring onions. Chop another 1 or 2 pineapple rings.

Heat the butter in a saucepan over a moderate heat, and fry the onion and pineapple pieces until soft (2 to 3 minutes). Add the beans, sliced sausages, vinegar, salt and pepper, and simmer for 3 to 4 minutes.

Pour into a warm serving dish. Decorate with the whole sausages and pineapple rings you are keeping hot. Serve with crispy bread rolls or hot toast.

SAUSAGE AND BACON HUBBLE BUBBLE *Serves 1*

A tasty way of using up odds and ends from the fridge.

Preparation and cooking time: 30 minutes.

2–3 cooked boiled potatoes
1 small onion
1 rasher of bacon
2–4 sausages
2 tsp oil (for frying)
1 egg
½ cup milk
Salt and pepper

Heat the oven (375°F/190°C/Gas Mark 5–6). Grease an oven-proof dish.

Slice the cooked potatoes. Peel and chop the onion. De-rind the bacon. Prick the sausages.

Heat the oil in a frying pan, and fry the sausages, bacon and onion gently for 5 minutes, turning frequently.

Place the potato slices in the dish. Arrange the onions, sausages and bacon on top. Beat the egg with the milk, salt and pepper in a small basin, using a whisk or fork. Pour the egg mixture over the top, and bake in a hot oven for about 15 minutes, until the egg mixture is set.

CHEESY SAUSAGES

Serves 1

A quick and tasty lunch or supper.

Preparation and cooking time: 25 minutes.

2 or 3 thick sausages
2 or 3 rashers of back bacon
1–2 oz (25–50g) Cheddar cheese
1 tbsp pickle (or sweet chutney)
Few wooden cocktail sticks or toothpicks
1–2 slices of bread
Little butter

Prick the sausages with a fork. Grill them under a moderate heat for about 15 minutes. Make a slit in each sausage, lengthways, and wedge a slice of cheese in each slit. Cut the rind from the bacon, and spread with the chutney.

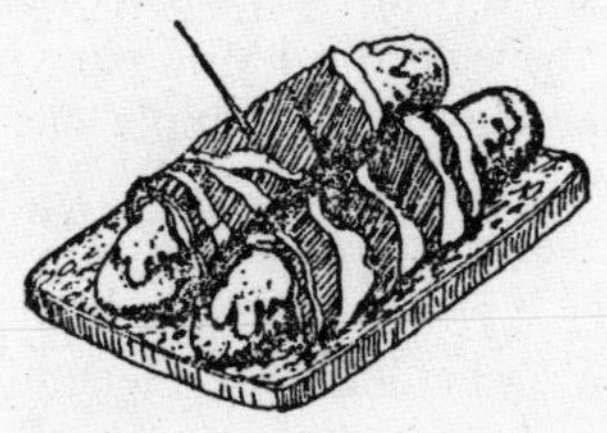

7. Cheesy sausages

Wrap the bacon round the sausages and pin securely with cocktail sticks or toothpicks (not plastic ones!). Return to the hot grill, and cook for about 5 minutes, until the bacon is crisp and the cheese is melting. Toast the bread, spread with the butter and serve with the sausages.

GAMMON STEAK WITH PINEAPPLE OR FRIED EGG

Serves 1

Buy a thick slice (½ in/1.25cm at least) of gammon, if possible, as thin slices just go crispy, like bacon. Serve with boiled new potatoes and salad in summer and sauté or jacket potatoes and peas in winter.

Preparation and cooking time: 6–10 minutes according to taste.

1 steak or slice (about 6 oz/175g) gammon
Little oil
1–2 tinned pineapple rings
or 1 egg

GRILLED

Heat the grill. Snip the gammon rind at intervals. Brush or wipe both sides of the gammon with a smear of oil. Place the gammon on the grid of the grill pan and cook each side under the hot grill for 3 to 5 minutes, until brown. Put the pineapple slices on top of the gammon and heat for a few moments or fry the egg in a frying pan, in a little hot fat. Serve the gammon with the pineapple slices or with the egg on top.

FRIED

Snip the gammon rind at intervals. Heat a smear of oil or fat in a frying pan. Add the gammon and cook each side for 3 to 5 minutes, until brown. Add the pineapple rings to the pan and heat for a few moments or fry the egg in the hot fat. Serve the gammon with the pineapple rings or with the egg on top.

ST DAVID'S DAY SUPPER

Serves 2

Leeks, of course, are the main ingredients.

Preparation and cooking time: 40 minutes.

5–6 potatoes
2 medium-sized leeks
Salt and pepper
4 oz (100g) cooked ham
1 small can (10.4 oz/295g) cream of chicken soup
1 tomato

Wash and peel the potatoes. Cut them into thick slices. Cut off the roots and leaves of the leeks and wash thoroughly (see page 65) and slice.

Put the potato and leek slices in a saucepan, cover with boiling, salted water, and cook for 8 to 10 minutes, until half cooked. Drain well.

Grease an oven-proof dish, put the vegetable mixture into the dish, and sprinkle with the salt and pepper. Chop the ham. Put the ham on top of the vegetables. Pour the chicken soup over the top, and heat through in the oven (400°F/200°C/Gas Mark 6) for about 20 minutes.

Wash and slice the tomato and place on top of the vegetables for the last 5 minutes of cooking time. Serve with hot bread rolls and butter.

LUNCHEON MEAT PATTIES

Serves 1

Cheap and tasty, and filling enough for lunch or supper if served with fried eggs.

Preparation and cooking time: 20 minutes.

3–4 potatoes
1 small onion
4 oz (100g) luncheon meat (canned or sliced)
A little beaten egg
Salt and pepper
Pinch of dried herbs
Oil (for frying)
Knob of butter (for frying)

Peel and thickly slice the potatoes. Cook them in boiling, salted water for 10 minutes, until soft. Drain them and mash well.

Peel and finely chop or grate the onion. Chop the luncheon meat.

Mix together the potato, onion, luncheon meat, and bind with the well-beaten egg, adding sufficient egg to hold it all together. Season with the salt, pepper and herbs. Form the mixture into 3 or 4 equal portions. Shape each into a ball and then flatten to form 'beefburger' shapes about ¾ in (2cm) thick.

Heat the oil and butter in a frying pan, and fry over a moderate heat for 3 to 5 minutes, turning to cook both sides, until crisp and golden brown. Serve with fresh or fried tomatoes and/or a couple of fried eggs, if you're really hungry.

BACON-STUFFED COURGETTES *Serves 1*

In the autumn, when marrows are cheap, you can make a very economical and tasty meal using marrow instead.

Preparation and cooking time: 1 hour.

1 onion
4 oz (100g/2–3 rashers) bacon – odd slices of bacon, sometimes sold cheaply as they are left-over end pieces, are suitable for this dish too
1 tomato
2 tsp cooking oil
½ tsp dried mixed herbs
Salt and pepper
2 medium courgettes

Peel and chop the onion. Cut the rind from the bacon; cut or chop it into small pieces. Chop the tomato. Heat the oil in a frying pan, add the onion and fry gently for 3 to 4 minutes, until soft. Add the bacon, and cook for a further 8 to 10 minutes, stirring well. Add the tomato and seasoning.

Wash the courgettes in cold water and cut a wedge-shaped 'lid' along the length of each courgette, to leave a hollow. Pile the filling into the hollow. Put the courgettes carefully into a greased, oven-proof dish and top with the 'lids'. Cover with a piece of foil and bake in a moderate oven (350°F/180°C/Gas Mark 4–5) for about 45 minutes. Serve with hot, brown bread rolls and butter, and a green salad.

VEGETABLE MARROW

These are often fairly large, so increase the quantity of stuffing, and make enough for several people. Remove a thick slice from the top of the marrow (to be used later). Scoop out the seeds. Fill the marrow with the prepared stuffing. Top with the 'lid' you sliced off. Brush lightly with a little cooking oil or softened butter, and carefully put the marrow on a greased baking dish. Bake in a moderate oven (350°F/180°C/Gas Mark 4–5) for about 1 hour.

FARMHOUSE SUPPER

Serves 1

A tasty way of using up cooked potato and food from the fridge to make a meal.

Preparation and cooking time: 20 minutes.

3–4 cooked, boiled potatoes (see page 71 if you don't have any cooked)
1 small onion
1–2 rashers of bacon
½ small green pepper
1 oz (25g) cheese
Little oil for frying
Knob of butter
1–2 eggs

Slice and dice the potatoes. Peel and chop the onion. De-rind and dice the bacon. Core and chop the pepper. Grate the cheese.

Heat the oil in a frying pan, add the bacon, and fry gently for 3 to 4 minutes. Remove the bacon from the pan and save on a saucer.

Put the potatoes, onion and green pepper into the hot fat in the pan, and continue to fry gently for 5 to 10 minutes, until lightly browned.

Mix the bacon with the vegetables and place in an oven-proof dish. Melt the butter in the pan and fry the eggs. Carefully put the eggs on top of the vegetables and bacon. Cover with the grated cheese, and brown for a few minutes under a hot grill, until the cheese is bubbly. Serve at once.

7

OFFAL AND COOKED MEATS

This means kidney, liver, tripe and sweetbreads etc. They are extraordinarily cheap, and besides being such good value for money, are very nourishing. Lamb's liver and kidney are more expensive than pig's liver and kidney which have a stronger taste, are very cheap, and make a tasty meal as well.

FRIED LIVER AND BACON WITH FRIED ONIONS

Serves 1

Lamb's liver is delicious fried, but if you are really counting the pennies, buy pig's liver and soak it for an hour in a little milk to give it a more delicate flavour.

Preparation and cooking time: 15 minutes (plus 30–60 minutes soaking time for the pig's liver).

4–6 oz (100–175g) lamb's or pig's liver (sliced)
Milk (for soaking)
1 rasher of bacon
1 onion
Little oil (for frying)
Knob of butter (for frying)

Gravy:
2 tsp gravy granules
or 1 tsp flour (or cornflour) and 1 tsp gravy flavouring powder
1 tsp cold water, sherry or wine (optional)
½ cup water (or water used in cooking the vegetables)

Put the pig's liver slices in a shallow dish, cover with a little milk, and leave to soak for 30 to 60 minutes. Lamb's liver does not need soaking. De-rind the bacon. Peel and slice the onion into rings. Dry the liver on kitchen paper. Heat the oil and butter in a frying pan over a moderate heat. Add the onion slices and fry for 3 to 4 minutes, stirring frequently, until soft. Push the onion to one side of the pan and stir occasionally while frying the bacon and liver.

Put the bacon and liver in the hot fat in the pan, and fry gently for 3 to 5 minutes, turning frequently, until cooked to taste – liver should be soft on the outside, not crispy. Remove the liver, bacon and onion from the pan and serve on a hot plate.

Either pour the meat juices from the pan over the liver and serve with crusty new bread; or make gravy with the juices and serve with boiled potatoes and a green vegetable. For the gravy: mix the gravy granules (or flour and gravy flavouring powder) into a smooth paste with the sherry, wine or cold water. Add the half cup of vegetable water or cold water and mix well. Pour onto the meat juices in the pan, stirring well. Bring to the boil, stirring all the time until the gravy thickens. Pour over the liver and vegetables.

SAVOURY CORNED BEEF HASH

Serves 1

Every cowboy's favourite standby!

Preparation and cooking time: 30 minutes.

3–4 potatoes
½ small onion
2–4 oz (50–100g) corned beef
Salt and pepper
1 tbsp oil (for frying)
1 egg
1 tsp tomato purée (or ketchup)
1 tbsp hot water
A dash of Worcester sauce
A dash of tabasco sauce

Peel the potatoes, cut into large dice, and cook for 5 to 6 minutes, in boiling, salted water, until half cooked. Drain well.

Peel and finely chop the onion. Dice the corned beef. Mix together the potato cubes, onion and corned beef. Season with salt and pepper. Grease well a frying pan with oil and put the meat and potato mixture into the pan.

Beat the egg. Dissolve the tomato purée or ketchup in 1 tbsp of hot water, beat this into the egg, add the Worcester and tabasco sauces then pour onto the meat mixture. Fry gently for about 15 minutes, stirring occasionally. Serve hot.

I have known people to make this gourmet dish using cooked rice instead of cooked potatoes, but it has not been particularly successful.

SAUCY LIVER SAVOURY

Serves 1

This is a real money saver, as it can be made with the cheaper pig's liver (but remember to allow the soaking time to give the liver a more delicate flavour – see method below). Serve with creamy, mashed potatoes or plain boiled rice or crusty bread rolls and butter, and a green salad.

Preparation and cooking time: 25 minutes (plus 30–60 minutes soaking time).

4–6 oz (100–175g) pig's or lamb's liver
½ cup cold milk
1 onion
Clove of garlic (or pinch of garlic powder or garlic paste)
Knob of butter (for frying)
Little oil (for frying)
1 tsp flour
1 tbsp tomato purée (or tomato ketchup)
Pinch of dried mixed herbs
Salt and pepper
½ stock cube and ½ cup hot water

Cut the liver into 1 in (2.5cm) strips, and soak the pig's liver in cold milk for 30 to 60 minutes, if possible. Lamb's liver need not be soaked. Peel and slice the onion. Peel and chop the fresh garlic. Remove the liver from the milk, but reserve the milk to use in the sauce.

Heat the butter and oil in a frying pan over a moderate heat, and fry the onion for 2 to 3 minutes, stirring occasionally, until just soft. Add the liver pieces, fry gently, turning frequently to brown on all sides (3 to 5 minutes). Stir in the flour, garlic, tomato purée, herbs, salt and pepper. Remove from the heat. Dissolve the stock cube in the hot water. Gradually mix in the stock and milk, return to the heat and stir continuously until the sauce thickens. Lower the heat, cover the pan and leave to simmer for 10 minutes until the liver is tender.

LIVER HOT POT

Serves 1

Make this with the really cheap pig's liver if you're counting the pennies, but remember to soak the slices to give it a more delicate flavour. Serve hot with a green vegetable.

Preparation and cooking time: 1 hour (plus 30–60 minutes soaking time).

4–6 oz (100–175g) lamb's or pig's liver (sliced)
Milk (for soaking)
3–4 potatoes
1 onion
1 tomato
2–3 mushrooms
Oil (for frying)
Salt and pepper
Pinch of dried herbs
½ stock cube
½ cup hot water
Knob of butter

Soak the pig's liver slices in milk for 30 to 60 minutes, if possible. Lamb's liver need not be soaked. Peel the potatoes, thickly slice them (¼ in/0.5cm) and cook for 5 minutes in boiling, salted water, until partly cooked. Drain them. Peel and slice the onion into rings. Wash and slice the tomato and mushrooms. Heat the oil in a frying pan, and fry the onion rings gently for 2 to 3 minutes, until just soft. Push them to one side of the pan. Add the liver slices and fry these, turning to cook both sides, for 1 to 2 minutes.

Grease an oven-proof dish or casserole, and arrange the slices of onion, liver, mushrooms and tomato in layers. Sprinkle with the salt, pepper and herbs. Dissolve the stock cube in the ½ cup of hot water and pour the stock into the casserole. Cover the casserole with a thick layer of the sliced potatoes. Dot the potatoes with the butter, and bake in an oven (375°F/190°C/Gas Mark 5–6) for about 35 to 45 minutes, until the potatoes are brown and crispy on the top.

KIDNEY STROGANOFF

Serves 1

A special kidney dish, but much cheaper than beef stroganoff, so treat yourself to lamb's kidneys and enjoy them. Serve with plain, boiled rice.

Preparation and cooking time: 35 minutes.

1 small onion
2–3 mushrooms
3–4 lamb's kidneys
Knob of butter (for frying)
1 tsp oil (for frying)
1 tsp flour (or cornflour)
Salt and pepper
⅔ cup milk (just under ¼ pint/150ml)
½ cup (3 oz/75g) raw, long grain rice
2 tbsp plain yoghurt

Peel and chop the onion. Wash and slice the mushrooms. Cut the kidneys in half lengthways. Remove the white fatty core and cut the kidneys into quarters

Melt the butter and oil in a saucepan over a moderate heat, and fry the onion gently for 2 to 3 minutes to soften. Add the mushrooms and stir. Add the kidneys, flour, salt and pepper, and continue to cook for another 3 to 5 minutes until the kidneys are browned on all sides.

Remove the pan from the heat and gradually stir in the milk. Return to the heat and slowly bring the sauce to the boil, stirring gently all the time as the sauce thickens. Lower the heat, cover the pan and simmer very gently for 10 to 15 minutes, until the kidneys are cooked. Cook the rice (while the kidneys are simmering) in boiling, salted water. Stir the yoghurt into the kidney sauce. Drain the rice and serve hot with the kidneys.

QUICK KIDNEY SPECIAL

Serves 1

This is delicious made with lamb's kidney, and makes a complete supper with sauté potatoes, served with a green salad.

Preparation and cooking time: 35 minutes.

3–4 small potatoes
1 small onion
2–3 lamb's kidneys
Oil (for frying)
Knob of butter (for frying)
Salt and pepper
Pinch of garlic powder (or clove of garlic)
1 tbsp sherry (or wine)
1 tbsp cream (or sour cream or plain yoghurt)

Peel the potatoes. Slice them thickly (¼ in/0.5cm) and cook gently in boiling, salted water for 5 to 10 minutes, until just soft. Drain them.

Peel the onion, slice it into thin rings. Cut the kidneys in halves, and remove the fatty white core. Then cut the kidneys into quarters.

Heat the oil and butter in a frying pan, and fry the potatoes, turning occasionally, for a few minutes, until golden and crispy. Remove from the pan, drain on kitchen paper and keep warm on a hot plate.

Add a little more butter to the frying pan if necessary, and fry the onion rings and kidneys over a gentle heat, stirring gently, for 5 to 10 minutes, until the kidneys are cooked. Season with the salt and pepper and garlic. Stir in the sherry and cream, stirring to heat thoroughly, but do not allow to boil. Make the potatoes into a 'nest'. Pour the kidneys and sauce into the middle of the potatoes and serve at once.

KIDNEY DINNER

Serves 1

This can be made with lamb's kidneys or the cheaper pig's kidney, according to how rich you are feeling – both are tasty and delicious. Serve with boiled rice or boiled new potatoes; these can be prepared in advance and kept warm while the kidneys are cooking.

Preparation and cooking time: 20 minutes.

8 oz (225g/3–4) lamb's kidneys or (1–1½) pig's kidneys
1 tsp oil (for frying)
Knob of butter (for frying)
½ small tin (10.4 oz/295g size) of kidney (or oxtail) soup
1 tsp flour (or cornflour) and ½ tsp gravy flavouring powder or 2 tsp gravy granules
1 tbsp water or sherry or wine (your choice)
1 tbsp cream (optional)

Cut the kidneys in half, lengthways, and remove the white, fatty core. Cut the kidneys into pieces.

Heat the oil and butter gently in a saucepan. Add the kidneys and fry over a moderate heat, stirring until the kidneys are browned on all sides. Gradually stir in about 1 cup of soup and leave to simmer for 10 minutes, over a very low heat, until the kidneys are tender.

Mix the flour and gravy flavouring powder (or gravy granules) into a smooth paste with the sherry, wine or water, and add to the kidney sauce, stirring as the sauce thickens. Stir in the cream, if using, and heat through, but do not let the cream boil.

KEBABS

Serves 1

This is an economical recipe, using kidney, sausages and bacon, instead of the much more expensive steak, cubed pork or lamb. The supermarkets sell packets of ready-prepared assorted kebab meats, which are good value, as it is rather expensive buying small quantities of different meats. Serve with boiled rice or bread rolls, and a green salad and barbecue sauce.

Preparation and cooking time: 20–25 minutes.

Use any mixture of the following:

1–2 rashers of bacon
1–2 chipolata sausages
1–2 lamb's kidneys
2–4 button mushrooms
1–2 tomatoes
Few pieces of green pepper
1 onion
1–2 pickled onions
Few pineapple cubes
Allow 1–2 long skewers per person
Oil for cooking

Heat the oven (400°F/200°C/Gas Mark 6–7) or the grill. Start cooking the rice, if used, in boiling salted water (see page 81). Prepare the salad and put aside.

Assemble and prepare your chosen ingredients as follows. De-rind the bacon. Cut the rashers in half to make them shorter in length, and roll them into little bacon rolls. Twist and halve the chipolata sausages. Halve the kidneys length-ways and remove the white, fatty core. Wash the mushrooms. Wash the tomatoes, cut into halves or quarters, according to size. Slice the green pepper into chunks. Peel the onion and cut into quarters. Drain the pickled onions and the pineapple cubes.

8. Kebabs

Thread the skewers with the chosen food, arranging it as you wish. Brush or wipe with oil. Either grill under a moderate grill on the grill rack, or balance the skewers across a baking tin in the hot oven, and cook for about 15 minutes, turning frequently. Drain the rice. Serve the kebabs on the skewers – be careful: they will be hot, so have a paper napkin handy.

8
FISH

Fresh or frozen fish can be used in these recipes according to availability. Fishmongers and market stalls sell wet fish, but most fish sold in the supermarkets is frozen and ready to use. The inevitable fish finger is well-known and widely available, along with other packets of frozen fish ready for frying. These need not be deep-fried, but are good cooked in a frying pan in a little butter and oil, or grilled. Eaten with bread, butter and tomato sauce these make a really quick supper. There are also many commercially-frozen fish dishes sold in the supermarkets, which are quite cheap, and quick and easy to cook, often by simply heating the packets in a saucepan of boiling water. Follow the instructions given on the packet carefully (short cuts aren't usually very successful) and serve with boiled or mashed potatoes, fresh or frozen vegetables, bread rolls or a side salad.

FRIED FISH WITH BUTTER

Serves 1

Serve with plain boiled potatoes.

Preparation and cooking time: 15–20 minutes (according to the type of fish used).

2–4 potato pieces
6–8 oz (175–225g) fillet of white fish (fresh or frozen) – cod, haddock, or plaice are the cheapest
1–2 oz (25–50g) butter
1 tsp cooking oil
Parsley (optional)
Slice of lemon (optional)

Peel and boil the potatoes (see page 71). Wash and dry the fish on kitchen paper.

Melt the butter in a frying pan with the oil (the oil stops the butter going too brown), add the fish and fry until tender (about 5 to 10 minutes), spooning the melted butter over it as it cooks. (The thicker the fish the longer it will take to cook.)

Lift the fish carefully onto a warm plate, add a little chopped parsley (if used) to the butter in the pan and heat thoroughly. Pour the buttery juice over the fish and garnish with the lemon slice. Drain the potatoes and serve.

FRIED OR GRILLED TROUT (OR MACKEREL)

Serves 1

These can be bought quite cheaply fresh from trout farms, but frozen trout are also good value, as they provide a filling meal with just bread and butter. Mackerel are cheap, delicious and are cooked in the same way.

Preparation and cooking time: 15–20 minutes.

1 trout or mackerel
1 tsp oil (for frying)
½ oz (12g) butter
Slice of lemon (optional)
Vinegar (optional)

Clean the fish by removing its head, entrails, fins and gills. (The fishmonger will usually do this for you. Frozen fish is already cleaned.)

FRIED
Heat the oil and butter in a frying pan, and fry the fish over a moderate heat, for about 5 minutes on each side.

GRILLED
Dot with the butter and grill on both sides until done (about 5 minutes each side for a medium-sized fish).

Serve with a slice of lemon, or vinegar, and brown or French bread and butter.

CHEESY COD STEAKS

Serves 1

Thick pieces of cod or haddock, or frozen fish steaks can be used. The frozen steaks are easy to cook and keep a good shape as they are individually wrapped and so can be separated easily while still frozen.

Preparation and cooking time: 20 minutes.

6–8 oz (175–225g) piece of cod (or 1–2 frozen fish steaks)
Salt and pepper
½ slice of bread
½ oz (12g) Cheddar cheese
½ oz (12g) butter

Wipe the fish and season with salt and pepper. Grate or crumble the bread, grate or finely chop the cheese, and mix together.

Put the fish in the base of a greased grill pan, dot with half the butter and grill for 5 minutes. Turn the fish over, cover with the cheese mixture, dot with the remaining butter and grill for another 5 minutes.

Serve on a warm plate.

TOMATO FISH BAKE

Serves 1

Brill is very tasty in this recipe, but cod or haddock are good too (and probably cheaper).

Preparation and cooking time: 35 minutes.

1 portion (6 oz/150g) fillet of brill, cod or haddock
2 tsp cooking oil
½ small onion
½ small can (8 oz/230g size) tomatoes (or use 1 or 2 fresh tomatoes)
Salt and pepper
¼ green pepper (optional)
1 stick of celery (optional)

Put the fish in a greased oven-proof dish.

Heat the oil in a small saucepan, chop the onion and fry it gently in the oil, until soft (2 to 3 minutes).

Add the tinned tomatoes or chopped fresh tomatoes and seasoning. Bring to the boil and cook gently until the liquid is reduced to a thin purée (3 to 5 minutes).

Chop the celery and/or pepper if used, stir into the tomato mixture, and spoon the sauce over the fish. Cover with a lid or cooking foil, and bake for about 20 minutes in an oven (375°F/190°C/Gas Mark 5). Serve hot.

TUNA BAKE

Serves 1

Serve with crispy bread rolls or toast.

Preparation and cooking time: 20 minutes.

½–1 can (200g size) tuna fish (use the rest for sandwiches or in Tuna Fiesta or Tuna Continental)
½ can (10 oz/298g size) condensed mushroom soup
1 slice of bread (crumbled into breadcrumbs)
1 oz (25g) butter
Few mushrooms (optional)

Drain the tuna fish and flake it into large flakes. Heat the soup in a saucepan, add the fish and cook for 2 to 3 minutes.

Pour the mixture into a heat-proof dish. Sprinkle with the breadcrumbs and dot with half the butter. Grill for 5 minutes or until golden brown.

Meanwhile wash the mushrooms, if used, melt the remaining butter in the pan, add the mushrooms and cook gently for 4 to 5 minutes. Place on top of the hot tuna bake and serve at once.

Do not leave the remainder of the tuna fish or the soup in the cans. Put them into covered containers or cups in the fridge and use within 24 hours.

TUNA FIESTA

Serves 1

Serve with boiled rice or mashed potatoes.

Preparation and cooking time: 25 minutes.

½ cup (3 oz/75g) long grained rice, or 2–4 potato pieces
1 small onion
½ oz (12g) margarine (or butter or 1 tsp cooking oil)
2 oz (50g) mushrooms
½ green pepper
2 oz (50g) peas
2 tbsp tinned tomato soup
Salt and pepper
Garlic powder
½ can (200g size) tuna fish (use the rest for sandwiches or in Tuna Bake or Tuna Continental)

Peel the potatoes (or wash the rice) and boil (see pages 71 and 81).

Peel and slice the onion and fry it gently in the butter or oil in a saucepan, until soft (2 to 3 minutes).

Wash and slice the mushrooms and pepper. Add them to the onion and fry gently, until soft (2 minutes). Add the peas, tomato soup, salt, pepper and garlic. Gently stir in the drained tuna and cook for a few minutes, until hot.

Strain the potatoes and mash (or drain and fork the rice). Spoon the potatoes or rice onto a plate, press into a ring and pour the tuna sauce into the middle.

Do not leave the remainder of the tuna fish or soup in the cans. Put them into covered containers or cups in the fridge and use within 24 hours.

COD IN CIDER

Serves 1

White wine can be used instead of cider for a taste of real luxury!

Preparation and cooking time: 30–35 minutes.

1 small onion
Slice of lemon (optional)
Salt and pepper
6–8 oz (175–225g) piece of cod (or 1–2 frozen fish steaks)
½ cup cider
½ slice of bread
½ oz (12g) butter

Grease an oven-proof dish.

Peel and slice the onion finely, and arrange half in the dish. Add a squeeze of lemon, salt and pepper. Put the fish on top, cover with the rest of the onion and another squeeze of lemon. Carefully pour in the cider.

Crumble the bread into crumbs and sprinkle on top of the fish. Dot with the butter.

Bake in a moderate oven (375°F/190°C/Gas Mark 5) until golden brown.

9
BEEF

Generally the most expensive meat, especially if you buy the cuts for grilling or roasting. However, stewing steak and mince are much cheaper and can be made into delicious dishes, but they do take longer to prepare and cook, as the cheaper the meat the longer the cooking time.

BEEF CASSEROLE OR STEW *Serves 1*

You can use any mixture of stewing beef and vegetables to make a casserole (cooked in the oven) or a stew (simmered in a covered pan on top of the stove), so just combine the vegetables you like. If you want the meal to go further add extra vegetables. Some supermarkets sell small packets of mixed root vegetables especially for casseroles. These are useful as you only need a small amount of each vegetable. As this dish is easier to cook in larger quantities (smaller quantities tend to dry up during cooking) why not double or triple the ingredients to make enough for 2 or 3 friends?

Preparation and cooking time: 1 hour 50 minutes – 2 hours 50 minutes.

(For one person cook 4 oz stewing steak for 1 hour 30 minutes; for 2 people cook 8 oz stewing steak for about 2 hours; for larger quantities cook for 2 hours 30 minutes.)

1 onion
Little oil or fat (for frying)
4–6 oz (100–175g) stewing steak
1 oz (25g) kidney (optional) – ox kidney is usually stewed
1 stock cube
½ glass of wine or beer (optional)

Vegetables – any mixture according to taste:
1 carrot – peeled and sliced
Piece of swede (or small turnip) – peeled thickly, cut into 1 in (2.5cm) chunks
Stick of celery – washed and cut into ½ in (1.25cm) lengths
½ green pepper – washed, with the core and seeds removed, cut into short strips
1 courgette (or small aubergine) – washed, cut into ½ in (1.25cm) pieces
1 potato – peeled, cut into 1 in (2.5cm) chunks
1 oz (25g) mushrooms – washed, sliced
Clove of garlic – peeled, finely chopped
1 cup of water
Pinch of herbs
Garlic powder
Salt and pepper

For thicker gravy:
½ tsp gravy flavouring powder and 1 tsp flour (or cornflour) or 2 tsp gravy granules
A little wine, beer or water to mix

Peel and slice the onion and fry it gently in a casserole or a saucepan, until soft (about 2 to 3 minutes).

Cut the meat into 1 in (2.5cm) pieces, (kidney in ½ in (1cm) pieces), add to the onion in the pan, and fry until brown (3 to 5 minutes) stirring so that it cooks evenly. Stir in the stock cube and add the wine or beer if used.

Prepare the vegetables but do no cut them too small. Add them to the meat. Stir in the water so that it just covers the meat and vegetables. Add the herbs, salt, pepper and garlic powder. Bring to the boil and stir well.

Then either put the covered casserole dish in the middle of a moderate oven (325°F/170°C/Gas Mark 3–4), or lower the heat and leave to simmer with the lid on the pan for 1½ hours to 2½ hours according to the amount of meat used, stirring occasionally. If it seems to be drying up, add a little more wine, beer or water.

If you like the gravy thicker, mix the gravy flavouring powder and flour (or cornflour) or gravy granules into a thin paste with a little wine, beer or water, and add to the gravy in the dish for the last half hour of cooking time.

Serve very hot, on its own, or with jacket spuds (cooked in the oven with the casserole), boiled potatoes or hot French bread and butter.

SHEPHERD'S PIE

Serves 1

Forget about school dinners, this can be made into a really delicious meal! For a change, add a little grated cheese to the potato topping, and sprinkle the top with grated cheese before grilling. The meat mixture can also be served on its own, or with boiled or mashed potatoes and vegetables.

Preparation and cooking time: 55 minutes.

1 small onion
2 tsp oil or fat (for frying)
4 oz (100g) minced beef
Little wine or beer (if you have any opened)
2 tsp tomato ketchup (optional)
Shake of Worcester sauce (optional)
½ stock cube
½ cup water
2–3 potatoes
½ oz (12g) butter or margarine
1 tomato (optional)

Peel and chop the onion. Put the oil or fat in a saucepan, and fry the onion gently for 2 to 3 minutes, until soft. Add the minced meat, and continue to fry gently, stirring all the time, until the meat is brown (about 2 to 3 minutes). Add the wine or beer, and sauces, stock cube and water. Stir well. Bring to the boil, then reduce the heat and leave to simmer for 20 to 30 minutes, until the meat is tender.

Meanwhile, peel the potatoes, cut them into evenly-sized pieces, and cook in boiling, salted water for 15 to 20 minutes, until soft. Drain and mash them with a potato masher or fork. Add the butter and beat until creamy. Pour the meat mixture into an oven-proof dish, cover with the mashed potato and fork down smoothly. Dot the top with a little butter, top with a sliced tomato if liked, and grill under a hot grill for a minute or two, until golden brown, or put on the top shelf of a hot oven (400°F/200°C/Gas Mark 6) for 5 to 10 minutes, until it is brown on top.

INSTANT SHEPHERD'S PIE

Serves 1

This really is an 'instant' meal, but is made quite tasty by adding a dash of your favourite sauces to the meat.

Preparation and cooking time: 10 minutes.

1 small tin (7 oz/198g) minced steak (or stewing steak)

Optional sauces:
Tomato ketchup
Brown sauce
Worcester sauce
Soy sauce
Few drops of tabasco sauce

Garlic powder (optional)
Pinch of dried herbs (optional)
1 small packet instant mashed potatoes – use the amount specified in the instructions on the packet
½ oz (12g) butter or margarine
Hot water
1 oz (25g) grated cheese (optional)
1 tomato (optional)

Empty the meat into a saucepan and bring it gently to the boil, stirring well. Add your chosen sauces and garlic powder and herbs. Simmer for 2 to 3 minutes until really hot.

Make up the instant mashed potato as directed on the packet using the butter and hot water and add most of the grated cheese (saving a little for the top).

Pour the meat mixture into an oven-proof dish, top with the mashed potato, and sprinkle with the remainder of the cheese and/or sliced tomato if used. Dot with a little butter or margarine. Cook under a hot grill, until golden brown (2 to 3 minutes).

POTATO BOLOGNESE

Serves 1

For those of you who don't like pasta, or want a change from spaghetti. Use either traditional or quick Bolognese sauce.

Preparation and cooking time: 45 minutes (traditional) or 25 minutes (quick).

Traditional Bolognese sauce (see page 158) or Quick Bolognese sauce (see page 159)
3–4 potatoes
Knob of butter
1 oz (25g) grated cheese (or Parmesan cheese)

TRADITIONAL METHOD

Prepare the Bolognese sauce and leave to simmer.

Peel and slice the potatoes thickly and cook in boiling, salted water for 10 minutes, until soft (see page 71).

Drain and mash the potatoes with the butter, beating them well. Pile them onto a hot dish, forming them into a border or 'nest'. Pour the Bolognese sauce into the potato nest.

Serve with grated or Parmesan cheese.

QUICK METHOD

Peel and cook the potatoes first, preparing the quick sauce while the potatoes are cooking. Then prepare the dish as above in the traditional method.

BEEF CURRY

Serves 1

A change from the Indian take-away. This is a medium-hot curry, and is easier to prepare for two or more people, as very small amounts tend to dry up during cooking. Why not try double the quantity?

Serve with plain boiled rice (see page 81), poppadums and some side dishes (see overleaf).

Preparation and cooking time: 1 hour 50 minutes – 2 hours 50 minutes.

(For one person cook 4 oz stewing beef for 1 hour 30 minutes; for 2 people cook 8 oz stewing beef for about 2 hours; for larger quantities cook for 2 hours 30 minutes.)

1 onion
4–6 oz (100–175g) stewing beef
Little cooking oil (for frying)
2 level tsp curry powder (more or less according to taste)
1 small apple (preferably a cooker)
1 tomato
½ stock cube and 1 cup (¼ pt/150ml) boiling water (or ½ a 295g can mulligatawny soup)
2 tsp sultanas
1 tsp sugar
2 tsp pickle or chutney

Peel and slice the onion. Cut the beef into 1 in (2.5cm) cubes.

Heat the oil in a medium-sized saucepan and fry the onion gently, to soften it, for 3 to 5 minutes. Add the beef and fry for a further 5 minutes, until the meat is browned. Sprinkle the curry powder over the meat, and stir for a few minutes over a medium heat.

Peel and chop the apple, wash and chop the tomato, and add both to the meat and continue frying for 3 to 4 minutes, stirring gently.

Dissolve the stock cube in 1 cup of boiling water and add the stock to the meat, or add the mulligatawny soup. Wash and drain the sultanas. Add them to the curry with the sugar and pickle or chutney. Stir well and simmer gently, with the lid on, stirring occasionally, for 1½ to 2½ hours (the longer time is needed for larger quantities) until the meat is tender.

Side Dishes for Curries
Salted nuts
Chopped green peppers
Plain yoghurt
Sliced onions
Sliced banana (sprinkle with lemon juice to keep it white)
Chopped apple (sprinkle with lemon juice to keep it white)
Chopped cucumber
Chopped, hard-boiled egg
Washed, drained sultanas
Mango chutney
Desiccated coconut

POPPADUMS

Great fun to cook. Buy a packet of Indian poppadums, on sale at large supermarkets.

Heat 3–4 tbsp cooking oil in a frying pan over a medium heat (enough to cover the base of the pan). When the oil is hot float a poppadum on top, and it will puff up immediately, only taking a few moments to cook. Remove it carefully and leave it to drain on kitchen paper while cooking the next poppadum. Do not let the fat get too hot, or it will get smoky and burn.

HOME-MADE BEEFBURGERS *Serves 1*

These are quite a change from the commercially-produced beefburgers. You can make them bun-sized or 'half pounders'. Buy a good quality mince, as finely chopped as possible.

Serve in soft bread rolls (these are traditionally lightly toasted on one side) with tomato or barbecue sauce, or with potatoes, vegetables or a salad.

Preparation and cooking time: 20–25 minutes according to size.

½ small onion
4–8 oz (125–225g) minced beef, according to appetite
Salt and pepper
Pinch of dried herbs
Worcester (or tabasco) sauce
Little beaten egg (or egg yolk)
Little oil (for frying)

Peel and finely chop the onion, and mix well in a bowl with the minced beef, using a fork. Mix in the salt, pepper, herbs and sauce and bind together with a little egg. The mixture should be wet enough so the ingredients mould together, but not soggy. Divide this into 2 portions, shape each into a ball, and then flatten into a circle, about ¾ in (2cm) thick.

Heat the oil in a frying pan over a medium heat. Put the beefburgers carefully in the pan, and fry for 10 to 15 minutes, according to size, turning occasionally to cook both sides. Do not have the heat too high, as the beefburgers need to cook right through to the middle without burning the outside.

BOEUF STROGANOFF *Serves 2*

Absolutely delicious, rather expensive and very impressive if you have a special friend to dinner. Serve with plain boiled rice, noodles or new potatoes, and a salad.

Preparation and cooking time: 25 minutes.

1 cup plain boiled rice (or 2 cups noodles or 3–6 new potatoes)
8 oz (225g) fillet (or rump) steak
1 medium onion
1 oz (25g) butter (or little cooking oil)
4 oz (100g) mushrooms
1 small green pepper
Salt and pepper
Garlic powder
3–4 tbsp soured cream (or double cream or plain yoghurt)
Chopped parsley

Cook the rice, noodles or scrubbed new potatoes in boiling salted water. Cut the steak into thin strips: 2 in (5cm) long by ½ in (1cm) wide by ¼ in (0.5cm) thick. Peel and chop the onion finely and fry in half the oil or butter in a frying pan or wok, until soft (2 to 3 minutes). Wash and slice the mushrooms. Wash the pepper, remove its core and seeds, and cut it into strips. Add the mushrooms and the pepper to the frying pan and fry gently for a further 4 to 5 minutes.

Remove all the vegetables from the pan and place onto a plate. Melt the remaining butter or oil in the pan, then add the steak strips and fry for 3 to 4 minutes, turning frequently so that they cook evenly. Return the onion, pepper and mushrooms to the pan. Add the salt, pepper and garlic powder. Gently stir in the cream or yoghurt and mix well. Heat carefully until piping hot, but try not to let the sauce boil. Sprinkle with chopped parsley if you want it to look impressive. Drain the rice, noodles or potatoes and serve at once.

CHILLI CON CARNE

Serves 1

This is another dish which is easier to make in slightly larger quantities than are given below, so if possible double the ingredients and cook for 2 people. You can use mince or stewing steak. If using raw kidney beans be very careful: they must be fast boiled in water for half an hour before using in this recipe, otherwise they could be poisonous.

Preparation and cooking time: 2 hours 55 minutes (if using stewing steak) 1 hour 25 minutes (if using mince).

1 small onion
1 clove of garlic (or little garlic powder)
Little cooking oil
½ oz (12g) butter
1 rasher of bacon (or bacon trimmings)
4 oz (100g) stewing steak (or minced beef)
1 tbsp tomato purée (or ketchup)
1 cup water
Salt and pepper
½ level tsp chilli powder
½ small (7.5 oz/213g size) can cooked red kidney beans or 4 oz (100g) pre-cooked kidney beans (boiled for half an hour in fast boiling water, then drained)
Few drops of tabasco sauce (optional)

Peel and chop the onion and garlic. Put the oil and butter into a saucepan. Add the onion and fry gently until soft (2 to 3 minutes). Cut the bacon into small pieces. Add the bacon and stewing steak (or mince) to the pan and fry until browned, stirring so that it cooks evenly. Add the tomato purée (or ketchup), water, salt, pepper and chilli powder. Bring to the boil. Cover, lower the heat and leave to simmer for 1 hour (if using mince) or for 2½ hours (if using stewing steak), stirring occasionally (adding a little extra water if it gets too dry). Add the kidney beans. Simmer for a further 10 minutes. Taste (but be careful not to burn your tongue) and add tabasco sauce if liked. Serve hot.

GRILLED (OR FRIED) STEAK

Serves 1

A very special treat! Cheaper 'tenderised' steak can be bought in the supermarket. This is often good value, as it cooks very much like the more expensive cuts. You can buy a smaller amount of steak and add sausages, lamb's kidneys or beefburgers to your meal. Grilled tomatoes and mushrooms are also tasty with steak (see below). Serve with jacket spuds, sauté potatoes, boiled potatoes, baked stuffed potatoes or bread rolls, and a salad or peas. Prepare the vegetables before cooking the meat, as steak is best eaten immediately it is ready. To cook the vegetables see Chapter 5. Grilling is the best way to cook steak, but it can be fried too.

CUTS OF BEEF TO CHOOSE

Minute

Very thin slices, good for a steak sandwich.

Rump

Good flavour, quite lean. Cut it into portions at least ¾ in (2cm) thick.

Sirloin

Very tender, with some fat. Cut as rump.

Fillet

Very tender, very expensive! Cut into even thicker portions 1–1½ in (2.5–3.75cm) thick so that it stays juicy during cooking.

Tournedos

Fillet steak tied into rounds by the butcher; very, very expensive.

Preparation time: 2–3 minutes.
Cooking time: see method.

Allow 6–8 oz (175–225g) steak per serving
A little cooking oil (or butter)

GRILLED

Heat the grill. Put the steak on the greased grid of the grill pan and brush or wipe it with the oil or butter. Cook on one side, then turn it over carefully (do not stab the meat). Brush or wipe the second side with the oil or butter and cook to suit your taste:

Minute steak: 1 minute cooking on each side.

'Rare' steak: 2–4 minutes each side, depending on thickness.

Medium steak: Cook as 'rare', then lower the heat for a further 3–4 minutes each side.

Well done steak: Cook as 'rare', then lower the heat for a further 4–5 minutes each side.

FRIED

Heat the frying pan gently. Put a little oil or fat in the pan. Add the steak, and cook over a medium-high heat, as for grilled steak above. Serve immediately with chosen vegetables.

Sausages and beefburgers can be cooked with the steak. Thick sausages may need a bit longer to cook than the steak, so put them under the grill or in the frying pan first, then add the steak. (See page 88.) Cut lamb's kidney in half lengthways, remove the fatty 'core', and grill or fry for 3 to 5 minutes, with the steak. Cut tomatoes in half and grill under the steak in the grill pan, or fry in the frying pan with the meat, for 3 to 5 minutes. Mushrooms are best cooked in the bottom of the grill pan with a little butter, with the meat juices dripping onto them, or they can be fried in the frying pan with the steak. They will take from 3 to 5 minutes, according to size.

10
CHICKEN

Fresh and frozen chicken (whole, chicken joints, boneless or fillets) are extremely good value for money. There is very little waste, as all the scraps can be eaten cold or used up in sandwiches or risotto.

Chicken must be thoroughly defrosted before you start cooking, by leaving the chicken on a plate at room temperature for several hours, according to the instructions on the packet. You can hurry the defrosting process by putting the nearly-thawed chicken in a bowl of cold (not hot) water to get rid of all the ice crystals. Chicken defrosted too quickly in hot water will be tough when cooked. If chicken is not completely thawed before cooking it may not cook right through and any bacteria present will not be destroyed and could make you ill.

Chicken must be cooked thoroughly too. The juices should run clear, not tinged with pink, when pierced with a knife at the thickest part of the joint.

There are also lots of delicious, ready-prepared chicken dishes available at supermarkets, both chilled and frozen. These must be defrosted and cooked strictly according to the instructions on the packet.

FRIED CHICKEN

Serves 1

A quick and easy dinner, served with new or sauté potatoes, peas or a green salad. It is also tasty when eaten with new bread rolls and butter.

Preparation and cooking time: 20–22 minutes plus defrosting time.

1 chicken breast or leg joint – 6–8 oz (175–225g) according to your appetite
Little oil and a knob of butter (for frying)

Defrost the chicken for several hours at room temperature according to the instructions on the packet. (See page 134.) Wash the chicken pieces and dry them on kitchen paper.

Heat the oil and butter in a frying pan over a moderate heat, add the chicken and fry it gently for 15 to 20 minutes, according to size, turning it occasionally so that it browns on both sides. If the chicken seems to be getting too brown, lower the heat, but continue cooking, as the chicken needs to cook right through. Remove from the pan, and drain on kitchen paper. Serve hot or cold.

CHICKEN WITH SWEETCORN *Serves 2*

The sweetcorn and potato sauce turns fried chicken into a complete meal. Serve with rice or potatoes.

Preparation and cooking time: 25–30 minutes plus defrosting time.

2 chicken breasts or leg joints – each joint 6–8 oz (175–225g) according to your appetite
Little oil and knob of butter (for frying)
1 onion
1 can (10 oz/284g) new potatoes
½ can (11½ oz/329g size) sweetcorn
½ oz (12g) butter
2 tsp flour
1 cup (5 fl oz/150ml) milk
Salt and pepper

Defrost the chicken for several hours at room temperature. (See page 134.)

Fry the chicken in the oil and butter, turning occasionally, for 15 to 20 minutes, until cooked and golden brown (see page 135).

Make the sauce while the chicken is frying. Peel and slice the onion. Drain the potatoes and sweetcorn. Melt the butter in a saucepan over a moderate heat, and fry the onion gently for 2 to 3 minutes. Add the potatoes and cook for a further 5 minutes, stirring gently.

Add the sweetcorn and mix well. Stir in the flour, and cook for 2 to 3 minutes. Remove from the heat, and gradually add the milk. Return to the heat and bring to the boil, stirring until the sauce thickens. Simmer for a few minutes, stirring gently, trying not to break up the potatoes. Season the sauce with the salt and pepper. Put the chicken onto a warm serving dish, cover with the sauce and serve at once.

CHICKEN IN TOMATO AND MUSHROOM SAUCE

Serves 1

Fried chicken served in a tasty sauce. This dish is good with boiled rice or potatoes which can be cooked while the chicken is frying.

Preparation and cooking time: 40 minutes plus defrosting time.

1 chicken breast or leg joint – 6–8 oz (175–225g) according to your appetite
Little oil and knob of butter (for frying)
½ small onion
2–3 mushrooms
½ stock cube
½ cup hot water
2 tsp tomato purée (or tomato ketchup)
Pinch of dried mixed herbs
Salt and pepper
Pinch of garlic powder

Defrost the chicken for several hours at room temperature. (See page 134.)

Heat the oil and butter in a frying pan over a moderate heat, and fry the chicken for 15 to 20 minutes, turning occasionally, until cooked through and golden brown (see page 135). Remove the chicken to a warm dish and keep hot.

Peel and chop the onion, put it into the oil in the frying pan and fry gently for 2 to 3 minutes, until soft. Wash and slice the mushrooms, and add to the onion. Dissolve the stock cube in the hot water, add to the onion in the pan, bring to the boil, stirring all the time, then reduce the heat and cook for a further 5 minutes. Add the tomato purée, herbs, seasoning, and garlic powder, and continue cooking for another 4 to 5 minutes – the sauce should now be thick and will coat the chicken. Pour the sauce over the chicken.

ROAST CHICKEN PIECES *Serves 1*

A quick and economical roast dinner. The chicken pieces are cooked in a roasting tin in the oven in the same way as a whole roast chicken, and can be served with thyme and parsley stuffing, sausages, bread sauce, apple sauce, roast potatoes and vegetables to make a traditional roast dinner.

Preparation and cooking time: 35–45 minutes according to size (plus defrosting time).

Quarter (6–8 oz/175–225g) of a chicken (breast or leg) or 2 chicken pieces
2 tsp oil and ½ oz (12g) butter (for cooking)
Dried herbs (optional)
Cooking foil

Defrost the chicken thoroughly for several hours at room temperature. (See page 134.)

Heat the oven at 400°F/200°C/Gas Mark 6–7. Rub the chicken with the oil and dot with the butter. Sprinkle with herbs, if liked. Place in a well-greased roasting tin and cover with cooking foil.

Roast for 30 to 40 minutes, according to the size of the chicken pieces, until the juices run clear (not pink) when tested with a fork. (If still pink, cook for a few more minutes.) Remove the foil for the last 10 minutes of cooking time to brown the chicken. Chipolata sausages, roast potatoes and parsnips can be cooked round the chicken pieces. Remove the chicken, and the sausages, potatoes and parsnips (if used) from the tin, and keep warm. Use the juices left in the roasting tin to make the gravy (see page 173).

EASY CHICKEN CASSEROLE

Serves 2

Make this for 2 people, otherwise the sauce will dry up before the chicken is cooked. It can be prepared very quickly and popped into the oven. Put a couple of jacket potatoes to cook in the oven with it, and you have a complete meal.

Preparation and cooking time: 1 hour 10 minutes plus defrosting time.

2 chicken breast or leg joints – each joint 6–8 oz (175–225g) according to your appetite
Little oil (for frying)
4 oz (100–125g) can or frozen mixed vegetables
1 small can (10.4 oz/295g) condensed chicken soup
Salt and pepper
Garlic powder or paste (optional)

Defrost the chicken for several hours at room temperature. (See page 134.) Heat the oil in a frying pan over a moderate heat, and fry the chicken for 5 minutes, turning so that it browns on all sides. Remove the chicken. Put it into a casserole with the frozen vegetables. Heat the soup in the pan with the chicken juices, adding the seasoning and garlic. Pour this sauce over the chicken. Cover with a lid, and cook for about an hour, until the chicken is tender, either in a moderate oven (350°F/180°C/Gas Mark 4) or over a very low heat on top of the stove.

CHICKEN CURRY

Serves 1

Defrost the chicken joint at room temperature. (See page 134.) Make the curry using the recipe given for beef curry (on page 127), substituting the chicken joint for the stewing beef. Chicken cooks more quickly than stewing beef, so the curry need only be simmered for about an hour. Serve with boiled rice (see page 81) and curry side dishes as suggested on page 128.

HAWAIIAN CHICKEN

Serves 1

Cook half the tin of pineapple with the chicken, then eat the rest for pudding, with ice-cream, cream or yoghurt. Serve the Hawaiian chicken with new or sauté potatoes, or potato castles, and green beans or peas.

Preparation and cooking time: 40 minutes plus defrosting time.

1 chicken joint (6–8 oz/175–225g)
1 tsp oil and knob of butter (for cooking)
½ small can (7¾ oz/220g size) pineapple pieces, chunks or slices in syrup
1 tsp flour or cornflour
1 tsp soy sauce
1 tsp Worcester sauce

Defrost the chicken for several hours at room temperature (see page 134).

Heat the oil and butter in a frying pan, and fry the chicken over a moderate heat for 10 minutes, turning occasionally so that it browns on all sides. Remove from the pan for a few minutes.

Drain the pineapple, saving the syrup. Mix the flour (or cornflour) into a smooth paste with a little of the syrup. Add the remainder of the syrup and stir this liquid into the juices in the frying pan, stirring until the sauce thickens. Return the chicken to the pan, add the pineapple pieces, and pour the soy sauce and Worcester sauce over the chicken. Stir well, then lower the heat and simmer for 15 minutes, stirring occasionally.

CHICKEN IN WINE

Serves 1

This can be made with a chicken joint on the bone, but is super made with boneless chicken breast or filleted turkey, according to your taste and pocket. Serve with new potatoes and peas.

Preparation and cooking time: 45–60 minutes plus defrosting time (chicken on the bone takes the longest time).

1 chicken joint (6–8 oz/175–225g), boneless chicken breast or slice of turkey fillet
1 small onion
1 stock cube – preferably chicken flavour
½ cup hot water
1 tsp oil and knob of butter
1 wine glass of white wine (or cider)
½ tsp herbs
Salt and pepper
1 tsp flour (or cornflour)

Defrost the chicken thoroughly for several hours at room temperature (see page 134). Peel and finely chop the onion. Dissolve the stock cube in the ½ cup of hot water. Heat the oil and butter over a moderate heat, in a casserole or thick saucepan, and fry the chicken gently for a few minutes, turning it so that it browns on all sides. Remove from the pan. Add the onion to the pan, and stir over the moderate heat for a few minutes to soften.

Pour most of the wine (or cider) onto the onion, stir well and allow to bubble for a minute. Return the chicken to the sauce. Stir in the stock, herbs, salt and pepper (according to taste). Cover the pan, and simmer very gently for 30–45 minutes, until the chicken is tender. Mix the flour with the rest of the wine (or cider) to make a smooth paste, and gradually stir this into the chicken sauce, until it has thickened a little. Serve hot.

11 LAMB

Leg and shoulder are the dearest joints of lamb, with leg costing more than shoulder. These are strictly 'special occasion' meals, and are explained under 'Sunday Lunch Dishes' in Chapter 14. Lamb chops (loin, chump and leg chops are the big ones; cutlets are the small ones) make a quickly-cooked, tasty meal, but are also quite expensive. Stewing lamb (middle and best end of lamb, scrag end and breast of lamb) is much cheaper. These cuts of lamb are stewed with the meat left on the bone (so you buy more weight of meat than you do with beef) but need long, slow cooking. They make really delicious meals fairly cheaply. Breast of lamb can be boned, stuffed, rolled and roasted, and makes a very cheap and tasty Sunday dinner.

LAMB CHOPS – GRILLED OR FRIED *Serves 1*

Choose lean chops, but remember that lamb is basically a fatty kind of meat, and the fat gives the meat a good flavour. Chump and loin chops are larger than cutlets. Very small cutlets are sold in some supermarkets as 'breakfast chops', so decide how hungry you are feeling when you choose your chop.

Sausages, lamb's kidney or beefburgers can be cooked with the chops. Grill or fry the sausages first as they take longer to cook than the lamb. Tomatoes, mushrooms, new potatoes and peas go well with it too. Traditionally mint sauce (see page 177), mint jelly, redcurrant jelly or onion sauce (see page 175) are served with lamb.

Preparation and cooking time: 12–17 minutes.

1 chump or loin chop or 1–2 lamb cutlets
Little oil

GRILLED

Heat the grill. Brush or rub both sides of the chop with a smear of the oil. Place the chop on the greased grid of the grill pan and grill for 8 to 10 minutes, according to its size and your taste, turning the meat so that it browns evenly on both sides. Lamb is traditionally served pink and underdone in the middle, and brown and crispy on the outside, but cook the chops how you like them.

FRIED

Heat a little oil in a frying pan over a medium heat. Put the chops in the pan and fry, turning several times, for 8 to 10 minutes, until the chops are brown and crispy and cooked according to taste.

OVEN CHOP

Serves 1

A tasty dinner, served with a jacket potato which can cook in the oven with the casserole. This dish is equally good made with a pork chop.

Preparation and cooking time: 50–55 minutes.

1 small onion
3–4 mushrooms
½ tbsp oil (for frying)
1 chump or loin chop
½ small (8 oz/230g size) can tomatoes
Salt and pepper
Pinch of herbs

Peel and slice the onion. Wash and slice the mushrooms. Heat the oil in a frying pan over a medium heat. Fry the onion for 3 to 4 minutes to soften it. Add the chop to the pan, and cook on both sides for a few minutes, to brown. Add the mushrooms and cook for another minute. Put the chop into a casserole or oven-proof dish and pour the onion and mushrooms on the top.

Heat the tomatoes in the frying pan with the meat juices. Add these to the casserole, with the salt, pepper and herbs. Cover with a lid or cooking foil. Bake in a hot oven (400°F/200°C/Gas Mark 6) for 45 minutes, removing the lid for the last 15 minutes, to reduce the sauce to make it thicker.

If serving with a jacket potato, scrub and prick the potato, and cook it in boiling water for 10 minutes. Drain the potato. Lift it out carefully and put it into the oven to bake with the casserole for 30 to 45 minutes, according to size.

IRISH STEW WITH DUMPLINGS

Serves 2

This should satisfy even the hungriest Irishman. It makes a substantial meal on its own but can be served with extra potatoes or bread rolls, and a green vegetable.

Preparation and cooking time: 2 hours 20 minutes – 2 hours 50 minutes.

¾–1 lb (350–450g) middle neck or scrag end of lamb
2 onions
2 carrots
1–2 potatoes
1 tbsp oil (for frying)
1 stock cube
2–3 cups boiling water
½ tsp mixed herbs
Salt and pepper

For the dumplings:
4 oz (100g/4 heaped tbsp) self-raising flour
Salt and pepper
2 oz (50g/2 tbsp) shredded suet

For thicker gravy:
1 tbsp gravy granules
or 2 tsp flour (or cornflour) and 1 tsp gravy flavouring powder
1 tbsp cold water, sherry, beer or wine

Cut the lamb into pieces suitable for serving. Trim off any large pieces of fat. Peel and slice the onions and carrots. Peel the potatoes and cut them into chunks.

Heat the oil in a large saucepan. Fry the onion and carrots over a medium heat for 3–4 minutes, stirring occasionally. Add the pieces of meat and fry for a further 2–3 minutes, trying to brown all the sides of the meat. Add the potato chunks. Dissolve the stock cube in 1 cup of boiling water, and pour it over the meat, adding enough extra water to cover the meat and vegetables. Add the herbs, salt and pepper. Stir gently and bring back to the boil, then reduce the heat and simmer over a very low heat for 1½ hours, with the lid on.

Make the dumplings by mixing together the self-raising flour, salt, pepper and suet. Add just enough cold water to make a dough – like very soft putty or plasticine. Divide this into 4 pieces and shape into dumplings. Carefully lower the dumplings into the stew and cook for a further 25–30 minutes, making sure the liquid is boiling gently all the time (keep the lid on the pan as much as possible, without letting it boil over).

If the gravy needs to be thicker, mix the gravy granules or the flour (or cornflour) and gravy flavouring powder into a smooth paste with a little cold water, sherry, wine or beer. Stir it into the stew, stirring well while the gravy thickens.

REAL LANCASHIRE HOT POT *Serves 2*

This dish may also be eaten by Yorkshiremen, and those from other lesser counties!

Preparation and cooking time: 2 hours 15 minutes.

12–16 oz (350–450g) best end or middle neck of lamb
1 lamb's kidney
2 onions
1 carrot
1 very small turnip (optional)
3 or 4 potatoes, total weight 1 lb (450g)
1 tbsp oil (for frying)
1 stock cube
2 cups (½ pt/300ml) approx. boiling water
2 tsp flour or cornflour
Salt and pepper
Pinch of dried herbs
Knob of butter

Cut the lamb into pieces suitable for serving. Skin the kidney, cut in half lengthways, cut out the white fatty core and cut the kidney into pieces. Peel and slice the onions, carrot and turnip (if used). Peel and slice the potatoes and cut into thick slices (½ in/1.25cm).

Heat the oil in a frying pan, and brown the lamb pieces, over a medium heat, turning them so that they cook on all sides. Brown the kidney, and arrange all the meat in a casserole or oven-proof dish. Fry the onion in the pan for 3 to 4 minutes, to soften it. Add the sliced carrot and turnip (if used) and continue to fry gently, stirring all the time, for a further 3 minutes.

Add the vegetables to the meat in the casserole. Dissolve the stock cube in 2 cups of boiling water. Sprinkle the flour over the remaining juices in the frying pan, and stir. Gradually stir in the stock, stirring hard to make a smooth gravy and adding the salt, pepper and herbs. Pour the gravy over the meat in the casserole, to cover the meat and vegetables.

Then cover the meat with a thick layer of potato slices, placing them so that they overlap and form a thick crust. Dot with the butter. Cover with a lid or piece of tight-fitting foil, and cook in a moderate oven (325°F/170°C/Gas Mark 3–4) for 1½–2 hours, removing the lid for the last half hour of cooking time, to brown the top. If the top does not seem to be getting crispy enough, either increase the oven heat to 400°F/200°C/Gas Mark 6–7, or pop the casserole dish under a hot grill for a few minutes.

If you have to cook the casserole on top of the stove because an oven is not available, simmer the casserole very gently for 1½ to 2 hours, then brown the potato topping under the grill as described above.

12
PORK

Pork is quite a 'good buy', being generally cheaper than beef or the better cuts of lamb. It is a rich meat, so is filling too. It is important that pork is cooked thoroughly; it is better over-cooked than underdone, and must never, ever, be served pink, as rare pork can make you ill with food poisoning. The meat must look pale-coloured, right through. Cold roast pork should not be re-heated; eat it cold if you have any left over. If you are heating cooked pork dishes in a sauce, make sure this pork is really re-cooked right through to kill any bacteria, not just warmed up. Leg, shoulder and loin of pork are the more expensive cuts, and make far too much for one person. Details of how to cook them are given under 'Sunday Lunch Dishes', Chapter 14. Chops, spare ribs and belly are more suitable and economical for small quantities, so here are some ideas!

PORK CHOP – GRILLED OR FRIED *Serves 1*

Quick and easy, and not too expensive. Tastes good with sauté potatoes, a grilled or fried tomato, pineapple rings or a spoonful of apple sauce. Pork is better grilled, as it can be a bit fatty, but frying is quite acceptable if you don't have a grill. Whichever way you choose to cook it, make sure it is cooked thoroughly, the juices must run clear, not pink, and the meat must be pale-coloured right through. Undercooked pork can make you ill, so do cook it thoroughly.

Preparation and cooking time: 14–16 minutes.

1 pork chop
Little oil or butter
½ tsp dried mixed herbs (or dried sage)
1 tomato (or 1–2 pineapple rings or 1 tbsp apple sauce)
Cooked, cold, boiled potatoes to sauté

Heat the grill or heat a frying pan over a moderate heat with a smear of oil. Rub both sides of the chop with the oil or butter, sprinkle with the herbs. Either put the chop under the hot grill, turning frequently, until brown and crispy, 12 to 15 minutes (lowering the heat if the chop starts getting too brown); or, put the chop into the hot frying pan and fry over a moderate heat for 12 to 15 minutes, turning frequently, until brown and cooked thoroughly.

ACCOMPANIMENTS

Cut the tomato in half, dot with butter and put under the grill or into the frying pan for the last 3 to 4 minutes of cooking time; or, put the pineapple slices on top of the chop under the grill or in the frying pan for 1 to 2 minutes to warm slightly; or, prepare the apple sauce in advance from the recipe on page 176 (or use apple sauce from a jar or can from the supermarket). Fry the sauté potatoes while the chop is cooking (see page 73). If you have only one frying pan you can cook them in the pan with the chop.

MUSTARD-GLAZED PORK CHOP *Serves 1*

A tangy hot grilled chop. Serve with new or sauté potatoes and a green vegetable.

Preparation and cooking time: 17–20 minutes.

1 tsp mustard
1 tsp brown sugar
Knob of butter
1 pork chop

Heat the grill.

Mix the mustard, sugar and small knob of butter together in a cup. Spread this mixture over both sides of the chop.

Cook the chop under the hot grill, turning frequently, until brown and crispy (12 to 15 minutes). Lower the heat if the chop gets too brown too quickly. The pork must be cooked right through. The juices must run clear not pink, and the meat must be pale-coloured right through. Under-cooked pork can make you ill, so do cook it thoroughly.

PORK CHOP IN CIDER

Serves 1

Absolutely delicious and the smell of the meal cooking gives you a real appetite.

Preparation and cooking time: 1 hour.

1 tsp cooking oil
½ oz (12g) butter
1 pork chop (preferably a loin chop) or 1 pork steak
1 small onion
1 small cooking apple (you can use an eating apple if necessary)
½–1 cup cider
Salt and pepper
Pinch of dried herbs
1 tbsp cream (you can use plain yoghurt or soured cream)

Heat the oil and butter in a frying pan. Fry both sides of the chop until brown (4 to 5 minutes). Place it in a casserole or an oven-proof dish.

Peel and slice the onion, peel and chop the apple, and fry them together in the frying pan, stirring frequently (4 to 5 minutes) until the onion is soft. Add to the meat in the casserole. Pour enough cider into the casserole so that it covers the meat. Add the salt, pepper and herbs.

Cover, with a lid or piece of foil, and bake in a moderate oven (350°F/180°C/Gas Mark 4–5) for approximately 45 minutes. (If you don't have an oven, this can be cooked very, very, gently in a saucepan on top of the stove for 45 minutes.) Stir in the cream and serve at once.

PORK IN A PACKET

Serves 1

An easy way of cooking pork, without much washing up!

Preparation and cooking time: 1 hour.

1–2 tbsp uncooked long grain rice (or 3 tbsp cold cooked rice)
2 tbsp canned or frozen sweetcorn
2 tbsp frozen peas
1 spring onion (or ½ small onion)
Salt and pepper
Cooking oil
Butter (for greasing the foil)
1 pork chop
1 tsp soy (or Worcester) sauce
1 tbsp cider, white wine or beer

Cook the raw rice in boiling, salted water for 8 to 10 minutes, until just soft. Add the frozen sweetcorn and peas for the last 2 minutes and cook with the rice, or cook by themselves if you are using up cooked rice. (Canned sweetcorn does not need cooking and can be used straight from the can.)

Drain well. Wash and chop the spring onion or peel and chop the onion. Add the onion to the rice mixture, mix well and season with salt and pepper.

Cut a square of cooking foil, large enough to wrap the chop loosely. Grease the foil with the butter, and put the chop in the centre of the foil. Sprinkle with soy or Worcester sauce. Top with the rice mixture and moisten with the cider, wine or beer. Wrap the foil around the chop into a parcel, and put carefully onto a baking tin or dish. Bake in a moderate oven (350°F/180°C/Gas Mark 4–5) for 40 minutes.

CRUNCHY FRIED PORK *Serves 1*

Shoulder and belly pork are cheap and tasty. Try to buy thin slices of meat for this dish and flatten them by banging them with a rolling pin. (If you don't have one, use an unopened can of beans etc., wrapped in a polythene bag, to stamp the slices flat.) A crisp green salad or a fresh tomato can accompany this dish.

Preparation and cooking time: 30 minutes.

1–2 potatoes (you can use up cooked potatoes if you have them)
4–6 oz (100–175g/1 or 2 slices) belly or shoulder pork
½ beaten egg (use the rest in scrambled egg)
1 tbsp packet sage and onion stuffing (or 1 tbsp porridge oats)
1 tbsp oil (for frying)
1 onion

Peel the potatoes, cut them in quarters and cook in boiling salted water for 15 minutes, until soft.

Flatten the pork as best you can and, if the pieces are large, cut them into portions. Beat the egg. Dip the pork pieces into the egg, and then toss them in the dry stuffing or porridge oats to coat the meat thoroughly.

Heat the oil in a frying pan. Put the pork pieces carefully into the hot fat and fry both sides of the pork over a medium heat, until brown and cooked right through (about 15 minutes). Put the pork onto a hot dish and keep warm.

Drain the potato when cooked. Cut into dice. Peel and chop the onion and cook in the fat in the frying pan. Add the diced potato and continue cooking until just turning brown and crispy, stirring occasionally. Sprinkle the onion and potatoes over the meat, and serve hot.

SPARE RIBS

Serves 1

Cheap and cheerful. Messy but fun to eat, and filling if you serve with a large jacket potato and plenty of butter. You'll need finger bowls and lots of paper napkins!

Preparation and cooking time: 1 hour 30 minutes – 1 hour 45 minutes.

12–16 oz (350–450g) Chinese-style spare ribs
1 small clove of garlic (or ¼ tsp garlic powder)
1 tbsp soy sauce
1 tsp orange marmalade
1 small onion
Salt and pepper
½ stock cube
½ cup boiling water
1 tsp vinegar

Heat the grill. Put the ribs in the grill pan and brown them under the grill, turning frequently, to seal in the juices. If you don't have a grill, brown the ribs in a frying pan, with a little oil or butter, over a medium heat, for 2 to 3 minutes, turning often. Peel and crush the garlic clove.

Mix the soy sauce, marmalade and garlic, and spread over the ribs. Peel and slice the onion. Put the onion in a casserole or oven-proof dish. Place the ribs on top and season with salt and pepper.

Dissolve the stock cube in ½ cup of boiling water, add the vinegar and pour it all over the ribs. Cover and cook in a hot oven (400°F/200°C/Gas Mark 6–7) for 1¼ to 1½ hours (the longer time for the larger amount). Remove the lid for the last 20 minutes to allow the meat to become crisp. The sauce should be sticky when cooked. The jacket potato can be cooked in the oven with the casserole (see page 73).

13
PASTA

There are numerous shapes of pasta, but they are all cooked in the same way, and most of the different shapes are interchangeable in most recipes, with the exception of the lasagne and cannelloni types.

Spaghetti
Available in various lengths and thicknesses.

Tagliatelle and other Noodle varieties
Sold in strands and bunches.

Fancy shapes
Shells, bows, etc.

Macaroni types
Thicker tubular shapes.

Lasagne
Large flat sheets.

Cannelloni
Usually filled with a tasty stuffing.

Most makes of pasta have the cooking instructions on the packet, and the best advice is to follow these carefully.

Allow approximately 1 cup (3 oz/75g) pasta per serving.

Pasta must be cooked in a large pan of boiling, salted water, with a few drops of cooking oil added to the water to help stop the pasta sticking. Long spaghetti is stood in the pan and pushed down gradually as it softens. Let the water come to the boil, then lower the heat and leave to simmer (without the lid or it will boil over) for 8 to 10 minutes until the pasta is just cooked (*al dente*). Drain well, in a colander preferably, otherwise you risk losing the pasta down the sink. Serve at once.

MACARONI CHEESE *Serves 1*

This is traditionally made with the thick, tubular macaroni pasta, but it is equally good made with spaghetti or pasta shapes, shells, bows, etc.

Preparation and cooking time: 30 minutes.

1 cup (3 oz/75g) macaroni or chosen pasta (uncooked)
Pinch of salt
½ tsp cooking oil

For the cheese sauce (or use packet sauce mix):
2 oz (50–75g) cheese
2 tsp flour or cornflour

1 cup (¼ pt/150ml) milk
½ oz (12g) butter
Salt, pepper, and mustard
Tomato (optional)

For the topping
1 oz (25g) grated cheese

Heat the oven (400°F/200°C/Gas Mark 6). Cook the macaroni or pasta in a large saucepan of boiling water, with a pinch of salt and a few drops of cooking oil, for 10 to 15 minutes, until just cooked (*al dente*).

While the macaroni is cooking, make the cheese sauce either according to the instructions on the packet or by using the following method. Grate the cheese, put the cornflour or flour in a small basin and mix it into paste with a little of the milk. Bring the rest of the milk to the boil in a small pan, then pour it into the flour mixture, stirring all the time. Pour the mixture back into the pan, return to the heat and bring back to the boil, stirring all the time until the sauce thickens. Beat in the butter, salt, pepper, pinch of mustard and the grated cheese.

Drain the macaroni well, and put it into a greased, ovenproof dish. Pour the cheese over the macaroni, and mix slightly. Sprinkle the rest of the cheese on top. Put into the hot oven for 10 minutes, until the cheese is crisp and bubbling, and the macaroni is hot.

This dish can be topped with sliced, fresh tomato and served with a salad. The top can be browned under the grill instead of in the oven, provided the sauce and macaroni are hot when mixed.

TRADITIONAL BOLOGNESE SAUCE *Serves 1*

This thick meaty sauce can be used with spaghetti, pasta shapes, lasagne or even mashed potato, for a cheap and cheerful dinner.

Preparation and cooking time: 45 minutes.

1 small onion
½ carrot (optional)
½ rasher of bacon (optional)
Clove of garlic or pinch of garlic powder (optional)
2 tsp oil or a little fat (for frying)
3–4 oz (75–100g) minced beef
½ small can (8 oz/230g size) tomatoes or 2 fresh tomatoes
2 tsp tomato purée or tomato ketchup
½ beef stock cube and ½ cup water or ½ small tin (10.4 oz/295g size) of tomato soup
Pinch of salt and pepper
Pinch of sugar
Pinch of dried herbs

Peel and chop the onion. Peel and chop or grate the carrot. Chop the bacon. Peel, chop and crush the garlic clove.

Fry the onion and bacon gently in the oil or fat in a saucepan, stirring until the onion is soft (2 to 3 minutes). Add the minced beef and continue cooking, stirring until it is lightly browned. Add the carrot, tinned tomatoes (or chopped fresh ones), tomato purée (or ketchup), stock cube and water (or the soup) stirring well. Add the salt, pepper, sugar and herbs.

Bring to the boil, then lower the heat and simmer, stirring occasionally, for 20 to 30 minutes, until the meat is tender.

QUICK BOLOGNESE SAUCE

Serves 1

Very fast and easy to prepare. Use instead of Bolognese sauce made with fresh minced beef.

Preparation and cooking time: 10 minutes.

1 small tin (7 oz/198g) minced steak
1 or 2 tomatoes (tinned or fresh)
2 tsp tomato purée (or tomato ketchup)
Pinch of garlic powder (optional)
Pinch of salt and pepper
Pinch of sugar
½ tsp dried herbs

Empty the minced steak into a saucepan. Chop the tinned or fresh tomatoes, add to the beef, with the tomato purée (or ketchup), garlic powder, salt, pepper, sugar and herbs. Bring gently to the boil, stirring well, then lower the heat and simmer for 5 minutes, stirring occasionally. Use as traditional Bolognese sauce.

SPAGHETTI BOLOGNESE

Serves 1

Grated Cheddar cheese can be used instead of Parmesan, but a drum of Parmesan keeps for ages in the fridge and goes a long way.

Preparation and cooking time: 25–55 minutes.

Traditional Bolognese Sauce (see page 158) or Quick Bolognese Sauce (see page 159)
3 oz (75g) spaghetti (or 1 cup pasta shells, bows, etc)
½ tsp cooking oil
2 tsp Parmesan cheese (or 1 oz/25g grated Cheddar cheese)

Prepare the Bolognese sauce.

Cook the spaghetti or chosen pasta in a pan of boiling, salted water with ½ tsp cooking oil for 10 to 12 minutes. (If you want to have long spaghetti, stand the bundle of spaghetti in the boiling water and, as it softens, coil it round into the water without breaking.)

Drain the spaghetti and put it onto a hot plate. Pour the sauce into the centre of the spaghetti and sprinkle the cheese on the top. Serve at once.

SPAGHETTI PORK SAVOURY *Serves 1*

Belly pork is one of the cheapest cuts of meat you can buy.

Preparation and cooking time: 30 minutes.

1 generous cup (3 oz/75g) pasta – spaghetti, shells, noodles, etc.
Little cooking oil
2 oz (50g/1–2 slices) belly pork
1 onion
2 fresh tomatoes (or 1 small tin (8 oz/230g) tomatoes)
1 oz (25g) Cheddar cheese (or a little Parmesan)

Cook the chosen pasta in a large saucepan of boiling, salted water, with a few drops of cooking oil, for 10 to 12 minutes. Drain and keep hot. Meanwhile, cut the pork into tiny strips, discarding any rind and gristly bits. Peel and chop the onion and chop the fresh tomatoes (if used).

Heat some oil in a frying pan. Add the onion and fry for a few minutes to soften it. Add the pork strips and fry, stirring well, until browned. Add the tomato pieces or tinned tomatoes (not the juice) and stir well.

Cook over a low heat for another 10 minutes, stirring to break up the tomatoes, making a thick, saucy mixture. Grate the cheese. Pour the hot sauce over the spaghetti, and serve at once, sprinkled with the grated cheese.

QUICK LASAGNE

Serves 1

For this recipe you can use the traditional Bolognese sauce (page 158), or else make it up using the first four ingredients listed here. Serve with a green salad.

Preparation and cooking time: 25–30 minutes.

Small tin minced steak (7 oz/198g)
2 tsp tomato purée or tomato ketchup
Pinch of garlic powder
Salt and pepper
3–4 sheets (2 oz/50g) instant lasagne – plain or verdi
½ can (10.4 oz/295g size) condensed chicken (or mushroom) soup mixed with milk or water (enough to fill ¼ of the soup can)
1 oz (25g) cheese – grated or thinly sliced

Put the canned meat into a small saucepan with the tomato purée, garlic, salt and pepper, or put the Bolognese sauce in a pan, and heat gently for 3 to 5 minutes, stirring well, to make a runny sauce (add a little water if needed).

Grease an oven-proof dish – the square foil dishes are excellent for one portion. Put layers of the meat sauce, lasagne sheets and the soup in the dish, ending with a layer of soup. Make sure the lasagne is completely covered with the sauce. Top with the grated or thinly-sliced cheese. Bake for 15 to 20 minutes in an oven (375°F/190°C/Gas Mark 5–6) until the cheese is golden and bubbling.

CHEESY NOODLES

Serves 1

A cheap dish for using up the contents of the cupboard or fridge. Serve with a piece of cheese, tomato or a salad.

Preparation and cooking time: 15 minutes.

1 cup (3 oz/75g) uncooked noodles
1 tsp oil
2 oz (50g) cheese
1 oz (25g) butter
Salt and pepper

Cook the noodles in a large saucepan of boiling, salted water with 1 tsp cooking oil, until just soft (about 7 to 10 minutes).

Grate the cheese, or chop it finely into very small cubes.

Drain the noodles, return to the hot, dry pan and shake for a moment in the pan over the heat, to dry them and keep them hot. Remove from the heat and stir in the cheese and the butter. Season with the salt and pepper and pile onto a hot dish. Serve at once.

14
'SUNDAY LUNCH' DISHES

This chapter shows simply and clearly how to cook the traditional Sunday lunch: how to roast beef, chicken, lamb and pork. For those who don't eat meat, I've included a recipe for a Nut Roast. At the end of the chapter, there are also recipes on how to make gravy and all the other different sauces that accompany the various meats. All the traditional 'Sunday Lunch' recipes are for several people – according to the size of joint you buy – which is useful when you have weekend visitors.

ROAST BEEF

It is best if several people can share a joint, as a very small joint is not an economical buy, for it tends to shrink up during cooking. Therefore you get better value with a larger joint which should turn out moist and delicious.

JOINTS TO CHOOSE FOR ROASTING:

Topside
Lean.

Sirloin
Delicious, but it does have a fair amount of fat around the lean meat.

Rolled Rib
May be a little cheaper than sirloin.

Choose a joint of beef that looks appetising with clear bright red lean meat and firm pale-cream fat. A good joint must have a little fat with it, or it will be too dry when roasted.

Make sure you know the weight of the joint you buy, as cooking time depends on the weight. *You should allow approximately 6 oz (175g) uncooked weight of beef per person*, so a joint weighing 2½–3 lb (1–1.5kg) should provide 6 to 8 helpings (remember you can save some cold meat for dinner next day). For underdone 'rare' beef allow 15 minutes per lb (450g) plus an extra 15 minutes. For medium-done beef allow 20 minutes per lb (450g) plus an extra 20 minutes. Remember that a small joint will cook through quicker, as it is not so thick as a big joint, so allow slightly less time.

Serve beef with Yorkshire pudding, horseradish sauce, gravy, roast potatoes and assorted vegetables or a green salad.

Place the joint in a greased roasting tin, with a little lard, dripping, margarine or oil on top. The joint, or the whole tin, may be covered with foil, to help keep the meat moist. Roast in a hot oven (400°F/200°C/Gas Mark 6–7) for the appropriate time (as explained above). Test that the meat is cooked by stabbing it with a fork or vegetable knife, and note the colour of the juices that run out: the redder the juice the more rare the meat. When the meat is cooked, lift it out carefully onto a hot plate and make the gravy (see page 173).

For the roast potatoes: calculate when the joint will be ready and allow the potatoes 45 to 60 minutes roasting time, according to size. They can be roasted around the joint, or in a separate tin in the oven. (See page 72.)

YORKSHIRE PUDDING

Individual Yorkshire puddings are baked in patty (bun) tins, but a larger pudding can be cooked in any baking tin (not one with a loose base!), but they do not cook very well in a pyrex-type dish.

Preparation and cooking time: 25 minutes (small)
40–45 minutes (large).

4 heaped tbsp PLAIN flour
Pinch of salt
1 egg
2 cups (½ pt/300ml) milk
Little oil or fat

Put the flour and salt in a basin (use a clean saucepan if you do not have a large basin). Add the egg and beat into the flour, gradually adding the milk, and beating to make a smooth batter. (The easiest way of doing this is with a hand or electric mixer, but with a bit more effort you get just as good a result using a whisk, a wooden spoon or even a fork.) Beat well.

Put the tins, with the fat in, on the top shelf of the oven (400°F/200°C/Gas Mark 6–7) for a few minutes to get hot. Give the batter a final whisk, and pour it into the tins. Bake until firm and golden brown. Try not to open the oven door for the first 10 minutes so that the puds rise well. If you want meat and puds ready together, start cooking the puds 25 minutes before the meat is ready for small puds, 40–45 minutes before for large puds.

ROAST CHICKEN

It may sound odd, but larger chickens are far more economical: you get more meat and less bone for your money, so it's worth sharing a chicken between several people, and keeping some cold for the next day (keep it in the fridge and don't keep it too long). The scrappy bits left on the carcass can be chopped up and used to make a risotto.

Before cooking a frozen chicken, make sure the chicken is completely defrosted by leaving it out at room temperature for several hours according to the instructions on the wrapper. It can be soaked in cold (not hot) water to get rid of the last bits of ice and hurry the thawing process but do not try to thaw it in hot water as the chicken will be tough when cooked. (See page 134.)

A 2–2½ lb (900–1100g) chicken will serve 2 to 3 people, while a 3–4 lb (1350–1800g) chicken will serve 4 to 6 people, according to appetite. Make sure you know the weight of the bird as cooking time depends on the weight. Allow 20 minutes per lb (450g) plus 20 minutes extra. Very small chickens (2–2½ lb/900–1100g) may only need 15 minutes per lb (450g) plus 15 minutes extra.

Chicken is traditionally served with chipolata sausages, thyme and parsley stuffing and bread sauce. We like apple sauce or cranberry sauce with it as well. Roast potatoes, parsnips, carrots and sprouts are tasty with chicken in the winter, while new potatoes and peas make a good summer dinner.

1 chicken (completely defrosted)
Small potato (optional)
Oil and butter (for roasting)
Cooking foil

Heat the oven (400°F/200°C/Gas Mark 6–7). Rinse the chicken in cold water and dry with kitchen paper. It is now thought best to roast chicken without putting stuffing inside. The stuffing sometimes causes the meat not to be thoroughly cooked. If you are making stuffing, cook it separately in a greased dish, according to the instructions on the packet (see page 177), or only put a little inside the chicken. I sometimes put a small, peeled raw potato inside the chicken as the steam from the potato keeps the chicken moist.

Spread the butter and oil liberally over the chicken (you can cover the breast and legs with butter papers if you have any) and either wrap the chicken loosely in foil and put it into a tin, or put it into a greased roasting tin and cover the tin with foil. Put the chicken in the tin into the hot oven. Calculate the cooking time so that the rest of the dinner is ready at the same time.

Sausages, roast potatoes and parsnips can be cooked round the chicken or in a separate roasting tin. Sausages will take 20 to 30 minutes; potatoes and parsnips about 45 minutes to 1 hour.

Remove or open the foil for the last 15 minutes of cooking time, to brown the chicken. Test that the chicken is cooked by prodding it with a pointed knife or fork in the thickest part, inside the thigh. The juices should run clear; if they are still pink, cook for a little longer. Remove the chicken carefully onto a hot plate, and use the juices in the tin to make the gravy. (See page 173.)

ROAST LAMB

Leg and shoulder are both expensive joints. Shoulder is cheaper than leg, but tends to be more fatty. These joints are usually sold on the bone, so you have to allow more weight of meat for each person than you do with beef. However, trying to carve a shoulder of lamb can provide quite an entertaining cabaret act! *Allow at least 8 oz (225g) per serving*; so a joint weighing 2¼–2½ lb (about 1kg) should serve 4 people adequately.

Stuffed breast of lamb is a far more economical joint and makes a cheap Sunday dinner. A large breast of lamb will serve at least 2 generous helpings. The traditional accompaniments for lamb are mint sauce, mint jelly, redcurrant jelly or onion sauce. Serve with roast potatoes, parsnips or other vegetables.

ROAST LEG OR SHOULDER OF LAMB

You don't have to buy a whole leg or shoulder; half legs and shoulders, or a piece of a very large joint can be bought. Make sure you know the weight of the meat you buy as cooking time depends on the weight. *Allow 20 minutes per lb (450g) plus an extra 20 minutes.*

Joint of leg or shoulder of lamb
Oil or dripping (for roasting)
2–3 cloves of garlic (optional)
2–3 sprigs of rosemary (optional)

Heat the oven (400°F/200°C/Gas Mark 6–7). Place the joint in a roasting tin, with a little oil or dripping. If you like the flavour of garlic, you can insert 1 or 2 peeled cloves under the skin of the meat, near the bone, to impart a garlic flavour to the meat, but lamb has a lovely flavour so this is not really necessary. Rosemary sprigs can be used in the same way.

Cover the joint, or the whole tin, with cooking foil. (This helps to stop the meat shrivelling up.) Roast it in the hot oven for the calculated time, removing the foil for the last 20 to 30 minutes of the cooking time, to brown the meat, if it is a bit pale under the foil. Roast potatoes and parsnips can be cooked with the joint for the last hour of cooking time.

Test that the lamb is cooked at the end of the cooking time by stabbing it with a fork or vegetable knife. Lamb is traditionally served pink in the middle, but many people prefer it cooked more; it is entirely a matter of personal preference. The meat juices should run slightly tinged with pink for underdone lamb, and clear when the lamb is better cooked. When the meat is cooked satisfactorily, lift it carefully onto a hot plate and make the gravy. Serve with mint sauce.

ROAST STUFFED BREAST OF LAMB

An extremely economical roast. A large breast of lamb will serve 2 people and makes a very cheap roast dinner. Try to buy boned meat or ask the butcher to bone it for you. If you purchase one with the bones in, it is fairly easy to remove them yourself with a sharp knife, but be careful not to bone your fingers at the same time!

Serve with gravy, mint sauce, roast potatoes and parsnips, or other vegetables.

Preparation and cooking time: 1 hour 40 minutes – 2 hours 10 minutes.

1 packet (3 oz/75g size) thyme and parsley stuffing
Juice of ½ lemon (optional)
1 large breast (2 lb/900g approx.) of lamb (boned if possible)
½ yard (0.5 metre) clean string or 6 wooden cocktail sticks or toothpicks
1 tbsp oil (for cooking)
Piece of cooking foil

Heat the oven (350°F/180°C/Gas Mark 4–5). Make the stuffing as directed on the packet, adding lemon juice to the hot water before mixing the stuffing to give a tangy flavour.

Spread the stuffing over the lamb, and roll it up carefully, not too tightly. Tie it up in 2 or 3 places with the string, or secure in a roll with cocktail sticks. Lightly rub the outside of the meat with the oil, and either wrap the meat in the foil and place it in a roasting tin, or put the meat in a greased roasting tin and cover the tin with the foil.

Cook in the oven for 1½ to 2 hours, according to the size of the joint (a bigger joint will take longer) unwrapping or removing the foil for the last half hour of the cooking time to brown the meat.

ROAST PORK

Most pork joints are sold with the bone in, so you have to allow more weight of meat per serving to make up for this. (It also makes it more difficult to carve.)

Joints to choose for roasting:
Leg: the leanest and most expensive.
Shoulder: cheaper and just as tasty.
Loin: chops, left in one piece, not cut up.

Allow about 8 oz (250g) per serving; a 2½–3 lb (1125–1350g) joint should serve 4 to 6 people. Make sure you know the weight of your joint, as cooking time depends on the weight. *Allow 25 minutes per lb (450g) plus 25 minutes extra.*

Pork is traditionally served with sage and onion stuffing, and apple sauce. Also serve it with roast potatoes and parsnips or other vegetables.

Heat the oven (400°F/200°C/Gas Mark 6–7) so that the joint goes into a hot oven, to make the crackling crisp. Rub the pork skin with oil, and sprinkle with salt to give the cracking a good flavour. Place the joint in the roasting tin with a little oil or fat to stop it sticking to the tin. Put the tin into the hot oven and calculate the cooking time so that the rest of the dinner can be ready at the right time.

After 20 minutes or so, when the crackling is looking crisp, the joint or the whole tin can be covered with foil to stop the meat getting too brown (smaller joints will brown more easily). Roast potatoes or parsnips can be cooked around the meat for the last hour of the cooking time, or in a separate roasting tin. Cook the stuffing in a greased dish, according to the instructions on the packet (see page 177).

Test that the meat is cooked at the end of the cooking time: the juices should run clear when prodded with a knife or fork. If they are still pink, cook for a bit longer. Pork must be cooked right through (it is better overcooked than underdone) as rare pork can cause food poisoning. The meat should be pale-coloured, not pink. When it is completely cooked, lift it onto a hot plate and make the gravy.

NUT ROAST

Serves 2

The traditional vegetarian 'Sunday Lunch' meal that everyone has heard of. This recipe makes enough for two portions since cold nut roast is tasty too. If you have a freezer, the second portion can be frozen, uncooked, for use later. Serve with tomato sauce.

Preparation and cooking time: 45 minutes (individual dishes)
60 minutes (larger dishes).

1 onion
1 stick of celery
4 oz (100g/1 very full cup) mixed nuts, roughly chopped (a processor or liquidiser is useful for this)
2 large fresh tomatoes or use the tomatoes from a small (7 oz/230g) can of tomatoes (you can use the juice as an aperitif)
1 tbsp oil and a knob of butter (for frying)
3 oz (75g/3 full cups) fresh wholemeal breadcrumbs
Salt and pepper
½ tsp mixed herbs
Pinch of chilli powder
1 egg
Piece of foil (for covering the dishes)

Grease two individual dishes or one larger tin (foil dishes are useful for this). Heat the oven to 400°F/200°C/Gas Mark 6–7.

Peel and chop the onion. Wash and chop the celery. Chop the nuts. Chop the tomatoes.

Heat the oil and butter in a large frying pan or saucepan over a moderate heat and fry the onion and celery gently for 4 to 5 minutes until softened but not browned. Remove from the heat. Add the nuts, breadcrumbs, chopped tomatoes, salt, pepper, herbs and chilli powder.

Beat the egg in a small basin or cup and stir into the mixture. Taste, and adjust the seasoning and herbs if necessary.

Spoon into the well-greased tins and cover lightly with greased cooking foil. Bake in the hot oven as follows: small tins – 20 to 30 minutes, removing the foil after 15 minutes; large tins – 45 to 60 minutes, removing the foil after 30 minutes.

GRAVY

Often the meat juices alone from grilled or fried meat make a tasty sauce poured over the meat. But if you want to make 'real' gravy remember the more flour you use the thicker the gravy. The liquid can be any mixture of water, vegetable water, wine, sherry, beer or cider.

Preparation and cooking time: 4 minutes.

1–2 tsp cornflour or flour and 1 tsp gravy flavouring powder or 2 tsp gravy granules
1 cup (¼ pt/150ml) water or vegetable water and/or wine, beer, sherry, cider
Any juices from the meat

Mix the cornflour or flour and the gravy flavouring powder (if used) into a smooth paste with a little of the cold water, wine, cider, sherry or even beer (depending on what you're drinking). Add the rest of the water and the meat juices from the roasting tin.

Pour the mixture into a small saucepan, and bring to the boil, stirring all the time. Stir gravy granules, if used, straight into the hot liquid. Add more liquid if the gravy is too thick, or more flour mixture if it is too thin.

To thicken the gravy used in stews and casseroles, make the gravy mixture as above. Stir the mixture into the stew or casserole and bring to the boil so that the gravy can thicken as it cooks.

WHITE SAUCE

This is a quick way to make a basic sauce, to which you can add other ingredients or flavourings.

Preparation and cooking time: 5 minutes.

2 tsp cornflour (or flour)
1 cup (¼ pt/150ml) milk
½ oz (12g) butter (or margarine)
Salt and pepper

Put the cornflour or flour in a large cup or small basin. Mix it into a runny paste with 1 tbsp of the milk. Boil the rest of the milk in a saucepan. Pour it onto the well-stirred flour mixture, stirring all the time. Pour the mixture back into the saucepan, return to the heat and bring to the boil, stirring all the time, until the sauce thickens. Beat in the butter or margarine. Season with the salt and pepper.

CHEESE SAUCE

Grate 1–2 oz (25–50g) cheese. Add to the white sauce with the butter, and add a dash of mustard if you have any.

PARSLEY SAUCE

Wash and drain a handful of sprigs of parsley. Chop them finely with a knife or scissors, and add to the sauce with the salt and pepper.

ONION SAUCE

A quick and easy method. Onion sauce is traditionally served with lamb, and is also tasty poured over cauliflower.

Preparation and cooking time: 25 minutes.

1 onion
1 cup (¼ pt/150ml) water
2 tsp flour or cornflour
1 cup (¼ pt/150ml) milk
Knob of butter
Salt and pepper

Peel and finely chop the onion. Put it into a small saucepan, with the cup of water. Bring to the boil, then lower the heat and cook gently for 10 to 15 minutes, until the onion is soft.

In a bowl mix the flour or cornflour into a paste with a little of the milk. Gradually add this to the onion mixture, stirring all the time as the mixture thickens. Add more milk, until the sauce is just thick enough – not runny, but not like blancmange. Beat in the knob of butter, and season with the salt and pepper. Serve hot.

'INSTANT' SAUCE MIX

Several makes of sauce mix are now widely available at supermarkets. Follow the instructions on the packet, and only make up as much sauce as is needed for the recipe. Keep the rest of the packet for later, tightly closed, in a dry cupboard or fridge.

BREAD SAUCE

Serve it with chicken. I generally use a packet of bread sauce mix, which is very easy to make, cooks quickly and tastes good, especially with the addition of a little extra butter and a spoonful of cream. Allow 1 cup (¼ pt) milk for 1 to 2 servings; 2 cups (½ pt) milk will make enough sauce for 2 to 4 people, according to your appetites.

1 packet bread sauce mix (you may only need to use part of the packet, but the rest will keep in the store cupboard)
1 cup (¼ pt/150ml) milk
Knob of butter (¼ oz/8g) – optional
2 tsp cream – optional

Make the sauce according to the instructions on the packet. Stir in the butter and cream just before serving. Left-over sauce will keep overnight in the fridge and can be used on cold chicken sandwiches.

APPLE SAUCE

You can buy jars or tins of apple purée, but it is cheaper and very easy to make your own. Apple sauce is served with roast pork or poultry.

Preparation and cooking time: 10–15 minutes.

1–2 cooking apples
2–3 tbsp water
1–2 tbsp sugar

Peel, core and slice the apples. Put them in a saucepan with the water and bring to the boil gently. Simmer for 5 to 10 minutes, until the apples are soft (do not let them boil dry). Add the sugar to taste (be careful, the apples will be *very* hot) and mash with a fork until smooth.

MINT SAUCE

You can buy jars of mint sauce at the supermarket, but I think they taste better if you re-mix the sauce with a little sugar and 1 to 2 teaspoons of fresh vinegar. Mint sauce is traditionally served with lamb.

'BOUGHT' MINT SAUCE

3–4 tsp 'bought' mint sauce
1 tsp granulated sugar
1–2 tsp vinegar

Mix all the above ingredients together in a small glass or dish.

'FRESH' MINT SAUCE

Handful of fresh mint sprigs
2–3 tbsp vinegar (wine vinegar if you have it)
1–2 tsp granulated sugar

Strip the leaves from the stems. Wash well, drain and chop the mint as finely as possible. Mix the mint, vinegar and sugar in a small glass or dish, and serve with the lamb. This sauce will keep in a small, covered jar in the fridge.

STUFFING

Traditionally, sage and onion stuffing goes with pork, while thyme and parsley goes with chicken, but any mixture of herbs is tasty.

Preparation and cooking time: 35–45 minutes.

1 packet (3 oz/75g size) stuffing
A little butter or margarine
Hot water – you can use water from the kettle or vegetable water

Make up the stuffing according to the packet. Grease an oven-proof dish, put the stuffing into the dish, dot with the butter. Bake in the oven (400°F/200°C/Gas Mark 6–7) with the joint, for 30 to 40 minutes, until crispy on top.

15
PUDDINGS AND CAKES

A few easy recipes for those with a sweet tooth.

Lots of delicious chilled and frozen desserts, gooey gateaux and sticky buns are widely available ready-made in the shops and can provide an instant treat.

Scan the packets of cake, pudding and biscuit mixes on the supermarket shelves. With the addition of butter and eggs, you can easily produce a home-made cake.

QUICK CHOCOLATE SAUCE – FOR ICE-CREAM

Serves 1

Fast, easy and most effective. It has a lovely, chocolatey flavour but is not too rich.

Preparation and cooking time: 5 minutes.

1 chocolate bar (1–2 oz/25–50g size)
1 tsp cold water

Break the chocolate into a pottery or pyrex basin or jug, with 1 tsp of water. Stand the basin in 1 in (2.5cm) hot water in a saucepan over a low heat, and simmer gently until the chocolate melts. Stir well, and pour the chocolate sauce over scoops of ice-cream.

HOT CHOCOLATE SAUCE – SERVE WITH ICE-CREAM

Serves 1

A rich fudgy sauce, delicious with vanilla, chocolate or coffee-flavoured ice-cream.

Preparation and cooking time: 10 minutes.

2 oz (50g) chocolate chips, chocolate cake covering or a chocolate bar
1 tbsp brown sugar
1 tbsp cold water
1 oz (25g) butter (unsalted is best)
2 tsp rum (optional)

Put the chocolate, sugar and water into a small saucepan, over a low heat, and stir until the chocolate melts and the mixture is smooth and creamy. Remove from the heat. Add the butter in small flakes. Beat well. Beat in the rum, if used. Serve, poured over scoops of ice-cream. If necessary, re-heat the sauce later by putting it into a pyrex or pottery basin or jug, and stand this in 1 in (2.5cm) hot water in a saucepan. Put the saucepan over a low heat and simmer gently until the sauce melts again, stirring well.

BANANA SPLIT

Serves 1

Full of calories, but absolutely delicious!

Preparation time: 5 minutes (plus the time for making the chocolate sauce).

1 large banana
2–3 tbsp ice-cream
1 tbsp chocolate sauce (bought or home-made – see page 179)
1 tbsp thick cream – spooning cream is ideal
Chopped nuts (for decoration – optional)
Chocolate sprinkles (for decoration – optional)

Split the banana in half, lengthways, then place it on a plate. Sandwich the banana halves together with spoonfuls of ice-cream. Spoon the chocolate sauce over the top. Decorate with the cream and sprinkle nuts or chocolate sprinkles on the top. Eat immediately.

FRUIT PAVLOVA

Serves 1

A super summer sweet. Make it with cream, ice-cream – or both!

Preparation time: 5 minutes.

1–2 tbsp fresh or canned fruit – raspberries, strawberries, canned peaches, mandarins, pineapples, pears
1–2 tbsp thick cream (spooning cream is good) and/or 1–2 tbsp ice-cream
1–2 meringue nests (available in packets from supermarkets)

Prepare this dish just before you are ready to eat it. Wash and drain the fresh fruit, or drain the canned fruit. Spread the ice-cream over the meringue nests. Arrange the fresh or canned fruit carefully on top of the cream or ice-cream. Decorate with a spoonful of thick cream. Serve at once.

SPONGE FRUIT FLAN

Serves 2

So easy, yet looks most impressive. Choose fruit and jelly whose flavours complement each other.

Preparation and cooking time: 10 minutes (plus setting time).

½ tin (15½ oz/439g size) fruit in natural juice or syrup (oranges, peaches, pineapples, pears, etc.)
Water if necessary
1 packet (1 pt size) jelly – any flavour
A 6 in/15cm sponge flan case or 2 individual flan cases (available from large supermarkets)

Open the tin of fruit and strain the juice or syrup into a cup. Make up ½ pint (2 cupfuls) of the fruit juice by adding water if necessary. Heat the juice and water in a saucepan, until it is just boiling. Remove from the heat and add the jelly. Stir until the jelly melts. Leave a few minutes to cool, then put into the fridge, freezer or other cold place, until the jelly is half-set. (This will take about ½ to 1 hour according to the temperature; the colder it is, the quicker the jelly will set.)

When the jelly is half-set, arrange the fruit in the sponge flan in pretty patterns. Spoon the half-set jelly on the top and leave in a cool place to set completely (15–30 minutes, depending on the temperature). Leave any spare jelly to set, then mash with a fork and serve separately with any spare fruit. (If the jelly gets too set before you remember to finish the flan, it can be thinned down by carefully adding 1 to 2 tbsp boiling water to the set jelly and stirring hard, to make it soft again.)

CRUNCHY CREAM PIE *Serves 2–3*

Easy to make, and delicious served with cream or ice-cream. You can use any flavour of instant flavoured milk dessert for the filling – chocolate or butterscotch are lovely.

Preparation time: 15 minutes.

3–4 oz (75–100g) plain digestive biscuits
2 oz (50g) butter or block margarine
2 heaped tbsp brown sugar (use white if you haven't any brown)
1 packet instant flavoured milk dessert
2 cups (½ pt/300ml) milk

Put the biscuits into a deep bowl or a clean polythene bag and crush them into crumbs with a rolling pin or wooden spoon. Melt the butter in a saucepan over a very low heat (do not let it brown or burn), then stir in the sugar and biscuit crumbs and mix well. Press this mixture into a greased deep pie plate, pie dish or baking tin (6–7 in/15–18cm in diameter), spreading it round to make a flan case (there is no cooking, so it does not have to be an oven-proof dish).

Put the flan in a cold place to cool. Make up the instant flavoured milk dessert with the milk as instructed on the packet. Whisk with a whisk, mixer or fork. Leave for a minute so that it partly sets. Pour into the biscuit crust and smooth the top. Leave it in a cool place or fridge for a few minutes to set.

PANCAKES

Makes 6–8 pancakes

These can be sweet or savoury, and are delicious any day, not just on Shrove Tuesday (Pancake Day). Sweet pancakes are traditionally served sprinkled with 1 tsp sugar and a squeeze of lemon. For sweet and savoury fillings see page 30.

Preparation time: 10 minutes (plus 1 minute per pancake cooking time).

4 heaped tbsp (4 oz/100g) plain flour
1 egg
2 cups (½ pt/300ml) milk
Oil or lard for frying – not butter

Prepare the filling if used. Put the flour into a bowl (use a medium-sized saucepan if you don't have one). Add the egg, and beat it into the flour. Gradually add the milk and beat to make a smooth batter (the easiest way of doing this is with a hand or electric mixer, but with a bit of effort you get just as good a result using a wooden spoon or even a fork).

Heat a clean frying pan over a moderate heat, and when hot, but not burning, grease the pan with a smear of oil or lard (approximately ½ tsp). Pour in a little batter, enough to cover the pan thinly. Tilt the pan to spread the batter over it. Fry briskly, until just set on top, and lightly browned underneath, shaking the pan occasionally to stop the pancake sticking – this will only take a few moments.

Toss the pancake, or flip it over with a knife, and fry for a few more moments to cook the other side. Turn it out onto a warm plate. Sprinkle with lemon and sugar, or add the filling, and roll up or fold into four.

Pancakes taste best eaten at once, straight from the pan, but they can be filled, rolled up and kept warm while you cook the rest. Wipe the pan with a pad of kitchen paper, re-heat and re-grease the pan, and cook the next pancake as before.

SYRUPY PEACHES

Serves 1

Make this lovely pudding when fresh peaches are cheap in the greengrocer's. Serve hot with cream or ice-cream. (This dish can be prepared, but not cooked, in advance, the cold fruit being left to soak in the syrup, and then put in the oven to cook while you are eating your first course.)

Preparation and cooking time: 15 minutes.

2 tbsp brown sugar
½ cup water
1–2 peaches

Make the syrup: put the brown sugar and water into a small saucepan, bring to the boil, stirring occasionally, and simmer gently for 3 to 4 minutes to dissolve the sugar. Wash the peaches (do not peel) and cut them in half, from top to bottom. Remove the stones. Put the peaches into an oven-proof dish with the cut sides face upwards, and pour the hot syrup over the fruit, spooning it into the holes left by the stones. Put into a warm oven (350°F/180°C/Gas Mark 4), for 10 to 15 minutes, until the fruit is hot and the syrup bubbling.

GRILLED PEACHES

Serves 1

Absolutely delicious with fresh peaches, but very good with tinned fruit too. Buy cheap peaches in the summer for a treat. Serve with cream or ice-cream.

Preparation and cooking time: 5 minutes.

1–2 fresh peaches or ½ a tin (15 oz/425g size) of peaches
1 oz (25g) butter
2 tbsp demerara sugar

Peel and slice the fresh peaches or drain and slice the tinned peaches. Butter an oven-proof dish, and place the peach slices in the dish. Sprinkle thickly with the brown sugar, dot with some butter. Place the dish under a hot grill for a minute or two, so that the sugar melts and the peach slices warm through. Serve at once.

LIQUEUR ORANGES

Serves 2

Delicious, simple and rather unusual, so save it for when you are entertaining a special friend.

Preparation time: 5 minutes.
Chilling time: 1–2 hours, but longer if possible; all day is best.

2 large, sweet oranges
2 tbsp sugar
1 tbsp orange liqueur – Cointreau, Grand Marnier or Curaçao (you can buy a miniature bottle of liqueur)
Thick cream (optional)

Peel the oranges and scrape away any white pith. Cut the oranges into thin rings, and arrange the slices in a shallow serving dish. Sprinkle with the sugar and liqueur. Cover the dish with a plate or cling film and leave it in the fridge or in a cold place for at least an hour, but all day if possible, to chill and let the liqueur soak in. Serve alone or with thick cream.

PEANUT CRUNCH

A crunchy cake to eat with coffee.

Preparation time: 10 minutes (plus setting time).

1 packet (7–8 oz/200–225g) plain digestive, rich tea or other plain biscuits
2 oz (50g) butter or block margarine
2 tbsp brown sugar (white will do)
4 tbsp golden syrup or honey
4 tbsp crunchy peanut butter

Grease a square or round shallow tin (approximately 7 in (17.5cm) in diameter). Put the biscuits in a deep bowl or a polythene bag and crush them not too finely with a rolling pin or wooden spoon. Melt the butter, sugar and syrup in a saucepan over a low heat, stirring well, until the butter is melted and the sugar has dissolved. Remove from the heat, and stir in the peanut butter. Mix in the biscuits, stir well. Press into the greased tin, and leave in the fridge or a cool place until set (½–1 hour according to temperature). Cut into squares or fingers.

CHOCOLATE CRUNCHIES

This has to be the easiest cake recipe there is, anywhere.

Preparation and cooking time: 5 minutes.

4 oz (100g) chocolate cake covering, cooking chocolate or chocolate bar
2 cups (2 oz/50g) cornflakes or rice crispies
12–15 paper cases

Break the chocolate into a pyrex or pottery basin. Stand this in 1 in (2.5cm) of hot water in a saucepan. Simmer this over a gentle heat until the chocolate melts. Remove the basin from the pan (use a cloth, the basin will be hot) and stir in the cornflakes or crispies, and mix until they are well-coated with the chocolate. Spoon into heaps in the paper cases, and leave to set. Store in a tin or plastic box.

CHOCOLATE KRISPIES

Almost everyone likes these, and they're cheap too. Instead of the sugar and cocoa you can use 4 tbsp drinking chocolate.

Preparation and cooking time: 15 minutes.

2 oz (50g) butter or block margarine
2 tbsp sugar
2 tbsp golden syrup
2 tbsp (level) cocoa
3 cups (3 oz/75g) cornflakes or rice crispies
12–15 paper cases

Put the butter (or margarine), sugar and syrup in a medium-sized saucepan, and heat over a gentle heat until melted. Stir in the cocoa (or drinking chocolate) and stir well to make a chocolate syrup. Stir in the cornflakes or crispies, and mix well to coat them thoroughly. Heap them into the paper cases and leave to set. Store in a tin or plastic box.

CHOCOLATE BISCUIT CAKE

This can be made in any shape of shallow baking tin or dish. It does not need baking, just leave it to cool, then cover with melted chocolate and cut into squares.

Preparation and cooking time: 20 minutes (plus setting time).

1 packet (7–8 oz/200–225g) plain digestive or rich tea biscuits
4 oz (100g) butter or block margarine
2 tsp sugar
2 tsp cocoa or 4 tsp drinking chocolate
1 tbsp golden syrup or honey
½ packet (4 oz/100g) chocolate cake covering (you can use cooking chocolate or chocolate bars)

Grease a square or round shallow sandwich cake baking tin (approximately 7–8 in/17.5–20cm in diameter). Crush the biscuits (not too finely) by putting them into a deep bowl or a clean polythene bag, and crushing them with a rolling pin or wooden spoon.

Put the butter, sugar, cocoa and syrup into a medium-sized saucepan, and melt slowly over a low heat, stirring occasionally. Remove from the heat. Add the crushed biscuits and mix well. Press into the prepared tin, spread flat and leave to cool (10 to 15 minutes).

Melt the chocolate by breaking it into a pyrex or pottery basin or jug and standing this in 1 in (2.5cm) hot water in a saucepan over a low heat. Simmer gently until the chocolate melts. Pour the chocolate over the biscuit cake, spread evenly and leave to set for 15–30 minutes in a cool place. Cut into squares or fingers and store in a tin or plastic box.

DROP SCONES OR SCOTCH PANCAKES

Fun to make for tea on a cold weekend afternoon.

Preparation and cooking time: 20 minutes.

4 heaped tbsp self-raising flour
or 4 heaped tbsp plain flour and 1 tsp cream of tartar and ½ tsp bicarbonate of soda
1 egg
1 cup (¼ pt/150ml) milk
Little oil or lard (not butter) for greasing
Clean tea-towel or napkin

Put the flour (and cream of tartar and bicarbonate of soda if using plain flour) into a bowl. (Use a medium-sized saucepan if you don't have a bowl.) Add the egg, and beat it into the flour, gradually adding the milk and beating to make a smooth batter. (Use a hand or electric mixer if you have one, but you get just as good a result using a wooden spoon or a fork.) The batter will be much thicker than pancake or Yorkshire Pudding batter.

Heat a clean frying pan, or a griddle (a flat iron pan for baking cakes), over a moderate heat. When it is quite hot, but not burning, grease it lightly with the oil or lard, and drop one tablespoon of the batter at a time onto the pan. Drop the tablespoonfuls so that they fall far enough apart from each other to allow room for each of them to spread slightly. You can probably cook 3 or 4 pancakes at a time. Cook for 1½ to 2 minutes, until there are little bubbles on the top of the pancakes and the underneath is light brown. Turn them over gently with a knife and cook the other side for a few minutes. Remove them from the pan and place them on a clean cloth, folding it over to keep the scones moist as they cool. Serve with lots of butter, jam, or clotted cream for a treat.

INDEX